Microsoft Exchange Server 2016 PowerShell Cookbook

Fourth Edition

Powerful recipes to automate time-consuming administrative tasks

Jonas Andersson
Nuno Mota
Mike Pfeiffer

BIRMINGHAM - MUMBAI

Microsoft Exchange Server 2016 PowerShell Cookbook

Fourth Edition

First published: July 2011

Second edition: May 2013

Third edition: July 2015

Fourth edition: July 2017

Production reference: 1130717

Published by Packt Publishing Ltd.
Livery Place
35 Livery Street
Birmingham
B3 2PB, UK.

ISBN 978-1-78712-693-0

www.packtpub.com

Credits

Authors
Jonas Andersson
Nuno Mota
Mike Pfeiffer

Reviewers
Florian Klaffenbach
Anderson Patricio

Commissioning Editor
Vijin Boricha

Acquisition Editor
Meeta Rajani

Content Development Editor
Sweeny Dias

Technical Editor
Mohit Hassija

Copy Editor
Safis Editing

Project Coordinator
Virginia Dias

Proofreader
Safis Editing

Indexer
Rekha Nair

Graphics
Kirk D'Penha

Production Coordinator
Aparna Bhagat

About the Authors

Jonas Andersson is devoted to constantly developing himself and his skills. He started out in the IT business in 2004 and initially worked in a support center, where he acquired a basic knowledge of the industry. In 2007, he started his career as a Microsoft Infrastructure consultant, and from 2008 onwards his focus has been on Unified Communication. At the start of 2010, he was employed at a large outsourcing company as a messaging specialist, specializing in Microsoft Exchange. His work included designing, implementing, and developing messaging solutions for enterprise customers. In 2014, he joined Microsoft Consulting Services, and from then onward his main focus has been Office 365. His role was of a deployment consultant with Microsoft's Office 365 Global Practice EMEA team. In 2016, he started to work for Sweden's largest retail companies with a known brand as a Product Specialist for Office 365, mostly focusing on Skype for Business Online but also on the other workloads. As a reward for his work in the community, he was awarded the Microsoft Most Valuable Professional for the Microsoft Exchange Server product in 2014.

This is my third book, a great experience and honor to once more get the opportunity to write a book. This time together with Nuno Mota, a great and skilled guy.

I look forward continuing these side projects, on the side of my regular work.

There are a lot of people I would like to thank, firstly of course my family, my beautiful wife, and daughter Alice, for the love and energy they keep on giving me. Besides my family I want to thank Nuno for the great team effort and also the Packt Publishing staff behind the scene with Sweeny as the lead.

I hope that you will enjoy the book and that its content will help you to develop your skills in the area.

Nuno Mota is a Senior Microsoft Messaging Consultant currently working for a large sovereign wealth fund. He has been responsible for designing and deploying Exchange and Office 365 solutions for organizations across the UK. He also shares a passion for Skype for Business, Active Directory, and PowerShell.

Besides writing his personal Exchange blog, called LetsExchange, he is also an author on the MSExchange website with dozens of published articles and product reviews as well as multiple scripts on TechNet.

He has also been awarded the Microsoft Most Valuable Professional (MVP) on Exchange five times since 2012.

I dedicate this book to my parents, Preciosa and António Mota, and my sister, Carla, who are always there for me no matter what, for all their unconditional support, and for teaching me never to give up.

To my beautiful wife, Linda, for her support, patience, and love towards me.

To all of you, a big thank you! Love you.

Also, a big thank you to the Packt Publishing team, and to Jonas for his professionalism and hard work, it was a pleasure co-authoring this book with you!

Mike Pfeiffer is a 20-year IT industry veteran, published author, and international conference speaker. He's a former architect for Amazon Web Services and engineer for Microsoft. Today, Pfeiffer serves as chief technologist for CloudSkills, a cloud computing training and consulting firm.

About the Reviewers

Florian Klaffenbach started in 2004 with his IT carrier as a 1st and 2nd Level IT Support Technician and IT Salesman Trainee for a B2B online shop. After that, he joined a small company as an IT Project Manager, planning, implementing, and integrating from industrial plants & laundries into enterprise IT. After spending some years there, he changed his path to join Dell Germany. There, he started from scratch as an Enterprise technical Support Analyst and later worked on a project to start Dell technical Communities and support over social media in Europe and outside of the U.S. Currently, he is working as a Solutions Architect & Consultant for Microsoft Infrastructure & Cloud, specializing in Microsoft Hyper-V, Fileservices, System Center Virtual Machine Manager, and Microsoft Azure IaaS.

In addition to his job engagement, he is active as a Microsoft blogger and lecturer. He blogs, for example, on his own page Datacenter-Flo.de or Brocade Germany Community. Together with a very good friend, he founded the Windows Server User Group Berlin to create a network of Microsoft ITPros in Berlin. Florian maintains a very tight network with many vendors such as Cisco, Dell, or Microsoft and Communities. That helps him expand his experience and get the best out of a solution for his customers. Since 2016, he has also been Co-Chairman of Azure Community Germany. In April 2016, Microsoft awarded and recognized Florian as Microsoft Most Valuable Professional for Cloud and Datacenter Management.

Florian worked for several companies such as Dell Germany, CGI Germany, or his first employer, TACK GmbH. Currently, he is working at msg service ag as a Sr. Consultant, Microsoft Cloud Infrastructure.

He has also contributed to these books:

- *Taking Control with System Center App Controller*
- *Microsoft Azure Storage Essentials*
- *Mastering Microsoft Azure Development*
- *Mastering Microsoft Deployment Toolkit 2013*
- *Windows Server 2016 Cookbook*

I want to thank Packt Publishing for giving me the chance to review the book.

Anderson Patricio is a Canadian Microsoft MVP and an IT Consultant based in Toronto. His areas of expertise include Microsoft Exchange, Skype for Business, Azure, System Center, and Active Directory.

Anderson is an active member of the Exchange Community, and he contributes to forums, blogs, articles, and videos. In English, he contributes regularly at ITPROCentral, MSExchange, and TechGenix websites, besides his speaking engagements at TechED in South America and MVA Academy training courses. In Portuguese, his website contains thousands of Microsoft Tutorials to help the local community. You can follow him on Twitter.

He has been a reviewer of several books such as *Windows PowerShell in Action* by *Bruce Payette*, *PowerShell in Practice* by *Richard Siddaway*, and *Microsoft Exchange 2010 PowerShell Cookbook* by *Mike Pfeiffer*.

www.PacktPub.com

For support files and downloads related to your book, please visit www.PacktPub.com. Did you know that Packt offers eBook versions of every book published, with PDF and ePub files available? You can upgrade to the eBook version at www.PacktPub.com and as a print book customer, you are entitled to a discount on the eBook copy. Get in touch with us at service@packtpub.com for more details. At www.PacktPub.com, you can also read a collection of free technical articles, sign up for a range of free newsletters and receive exclusive discounts and offers on Packt books and eBooks.

https://www.packtpub.com/mapt

Get the most in-demand software skills with Mapt. Mapt gives you full access to all Packt books and video courses, as well as industry-leading tools to help you plan your personal development and advance your career.

Why subscribe?

- Fully searchable across every book published by Packt
- Copy and paste, print, and bookmark content
- On demand and accessible via a web browser

Customer Feedback

Thanks for purchasing this Packt book. At Packt, quality is at the heart of our editorial process. To help us improve, please leave us an honest review on this book's Amazon page at http://www.amazon.in/dp/1787126935. If you'd like to join our team of regular reviewers, you can e-mail us at customerreviews@packtpub.com. We award our regular reviewers with free eBooks and videos in exchange for their valuable feedback. Help us be relentless in improving our products!

Table of Contents

Preface

The book is full of immediately usable task-based recipes for managing and maintaining your Microsoft Exchange 2016 environment with Windows PowerShell 5.0 and the Exchange Management Shell. The focus of this book is to show you how to automate routine tasks and solve common problems. While the Exchange Management Shell literally provides hundreds of cmdlets, we will not cover every single one of them individually. Instead, we'll focus on common, real-world scenarios. You'll be able to leverage these recipes right away, allowing you to get the job done quickly, and the techniques that you'll learn will allow you to write your own amazing one-liners and scripts with ease.

What this book covers

Chapter 1, *PowerShell Key Concepts*, introduces several core PowerShell concepts such as command syntax and parameters, working with the pipeline, and loops and conditional logic. The topics covered in this chapter lay the foundation for the remaining code samples in each chapter.

Chapter 2, *Exchange Management Shell Command Tasks*, covers day-to-day tasks and general techniques for managing Exchange from the command line. Topics include configuring manual remote shell connections, exporting reports to external files, sending email messages from scripts, and scheduling scripts to run with the Task Scheduler.

Chapter 3, *Managing Recipients*, demonstrates some of the most common recipient-related management tasks, such as creating mailboxes, distribution groups, and contacts. You'll also learn how to manage server-side inbox rules and Out of Office settings and import user photos.

Chapter 4, *Managing Mailboxes*, shows how to perform various mailbox management tasks including moving mailboxes, importing and exporting mailbox data, and the detection and repair of corrupt mailboxes. In addition, you'll learn how to delete and restore items from a mailbox and manage public folders.

Chapter 5, *Distribution Groups and Address Lists*, takes you deeper into distribution group management. Topics include distribution group reporting, distribution group naming policies, and allowing end users to manage distribution group membership. You'll also learn how to create Address Lists and Hierarchal Address Books.

Chapter 6, *Mailbox Database Management*, shows how to set database settings and limits. Report generation for mailbox database size, average mailbox size per database, and backup status are also covered in this chapter.

Chapter 7, *Managing Client Access*, covers the management of ActiveSync, OWA, POP, and IMAP as well as the configuration of these components in Exchange 2016. We'll also take a look at controlling connections from various clients, including ActiveSync devices.

Chapter 8, *Managing Transport Servers*, explains various methods used to control mail flow within your Exchange organization. You'll learn how to create send and receive connectors, allow application servers to relay mail, search message tracking logs, and manage transport queues.

Chapter 9, *Exchange Security*, introduces the new Role Based Access Control (RBAC) permissions model. You'll learn how to create custom RBAC roles for administrators and end users and also how to manage mailbox permissions and implement SSL certificates.

Chapter 10, *Compliance and Audit Logging*, covers the compliance and auditing features included in Exchange 2016. Topics such as Journaling, Data Loss Prevention, Archive mailboxes, and eDiscovery searches are covered here as well as administrator and mailbox audit logging.

Chapter 11, *High Availability*, covers the implementation and management tasks related to Database Availability Groups (DAGs). Topics include creating DAGs, adding mailbox database copies, and performing maintenance on DAG members. It also covers the new feature called Automatic Reseed.

Chapter 12, *Monitoring Exchange Health*, explores how to check and monitor the health of an Exchange environment using the built-in test commands, health probes, and through several purpose-built reports to monitor mail queues and database redundancy, for example.

Chapter 13, *Integration*, explains different integrations that can be established between Exchange Server and Skype for Business and Office Online Server, and to wrap this up, we have a section on how to validate the Exchange Hybrid configuration.

Chapter 14, *Scripting with the Exchange Web Services Managed API*, introduces advanced scripting topics that leverage Exchange Web Services. In this chapter, you'll learn how to write scripts and functions that go beyond the capabilities of the Exchange Management Shell cmdlets.

`Appendix A`, *Common Shell Information*, is an appendix to be used as a reference for commonly used automatic shell variables and type accelerators, along with a list of scripts that come with Exchange 2016. Additionally, common filterable properties supported by shell cmdlets that include filter parameters are outlined in detail.

`Appendix B`, *Query Syntaxes*, should be used as a reference for the Keyword Query Language (KQL). Here you will find many different examples that can be used in the real world.

What you need for this book

To complete the recipes in this book, you'll need the following:

- PowerShell v5, which is installed by default on Windows 10 and Windows Server 2016, is recommended, but v4 will work for the majority of the recipes.
- Ideally, your Exchange Servers will run on Windows Server 2016, but they can also run on Windows Server 2012 R2, if preferred.
- A fully operational lab environment with an Active Directory forest and Exchange organization is needed.
- You'll need to have at least one Microsoft Exchange 2016 server, but note that some topics such as Database Availability Groups require two servers.
- It is assumed that the account you are using is a member the Organization Management role group. The user account used to install Exchange 2016 is automatically added to this group.
- If possible, you'll want to run the commands, scripts, and functions in this book from a client machine. The 64-bit version of Windows 10 with the Exchange 2016 Management Tools installed is a good choice. You can also run the tools on Windows 8.1, for example. Each client will need some additional prerequisites in order to run the tools, so refer to Microsoft's TechNet documentation for full details.
- If you don't have a client machine, you can run the management shell from an Exchange 2016 server.
- Chapter 14, *Scripting with the Exchange Web Services Managed API* requires the Exchange Web Services Managed API version 2.2, which can be downloaded from the following URL: `http://www.microsoft.com/en-us/download/details.aspx?id=42951`

The code samples in this book should be run in a lab environment and fully tested before being deployed into production. If you don't have a lab environment set up, you can download the software from `http://technet.microsoft.com/en-us/exchange/` and then build the servers on your preferred virtualization engine.

Who this book is for

This book is for messaging professionals who want to learn how to build real-world scripts with Windows PowerShell 5.0 and the Exchange Management Shell. If you are a network or systems administrator responsible for managing and maintaining the on-premises version of Exchange Server 2016, then this book is for you.

The recipes in this cookbook touch on each of the core Exchange 2016 server roles and require a working knowledge of the supporting technologies, such as Windows Server 2012 R2 or 2016, Active Directory, and DNS.

All of the topics in the book are focused on the on-premises version of Exchange 2016, the only exception being the validation of Exchange Hybrid configuration. In this book, we will not cover Microsoft's hosted version of Exchange Online in Office 365. However, the concepts you'll learn in this book will allow you to hit the ground running with that platform since it will give you an understanding of PowerShell's command syntax and object-based nature. Additionally, many scripts and tasks presented in this book also apply to Exchange Online.

Sections

In this book, you will find several headings that appear frequently (Getting ready, How to do it…, How it works…, There's more…, and See also). To give clear instructions on how to complete a recipe, we use these sections as follows:

Getting ready

This section tells you what to expect in the recipe, and describes how to set up any software or any preliminary settings required for the recipe.

How to do it…

This section contains the steps required to follow the recipe.

How it works...

This section usually consists of a detailed explanation of what happened in the previous section.

There's more...

This section consists of additional information about the recipe in order to make the reader more knowledgeable about the recipe.

See also

This section provides helpful links to other useful information for the recipe.

Conventions

In this book, you will find a number of styles of text that distinguish between different kinds of information. Here are some examples of these styles, and an explanation of their meaning.

Code words in text are shown as follows: "We can read the content of a file into the shell using the Get-Content cmdlet"

Commands and blocks of code are set as follows:

```
Get-Mailbox -ResultSize Unlimited | Out-File C:\report.txt
```

Commands like this can be invoked interactively in the shell, or from within a script or function.

Most of the commands you'll be working with will be very long. In order for them to fit into the pages of this book, we'll need to use line continuation. For example, here is a command that creates a mailbox:

```
New-Mailbox -UserPrincipalName jsmith@contoso.com `
-FirstName John `
-LastName Smith `
-Alias jsmith `
-Database DB1 `
-Password $password
```

Notice that the last character on each line is the backtick (`) symbol, also referred to as the grave accent. This is PowerShell's line continuation character. You can run this command as is, but make sure there aren't any trailing spaces at the end of each line. You can also remove the backtick and carriage returns, and run the command on one single line. Just ensure that the spaces between the parameters and arguments are maintained.

You'll also see long pipeline commands formatted like the following example:

```
Get-Mailbox -ResultSize Unlimited |
  Select-Object DisplayName, ServerName, Database |
    Export-Csv c:\mbreport.csv -NoTypeInformation
```

PowerShell uses the pipe character (|) to send objects' output from a command down the pipeline, so it can be used as input by another command. The pipe character does not need to be escaped. You can enter the previous command as is or you can format the command so that everything is in one line.

Any command-line input or output that must be done interactively at the shell console is written as follows:

```
[PS] C:\>Get-Mailbox administrator | FT ServerName, Database -Auto
ServerName Database
---------- --------
mbx1       DB01
```

New terms and **important words** are shown in bold. Words that you see on the screen, in menus or dialog boxes for example, appear in the text like this: "Clicking the **Next** button moves you to the next screen."

Warnings or important notes appear in a box like this.

Tips and tricks appear like this.

Reader feedback

Feedback from our readers is always welcome. Let us know what you think about this book-what you liked or disliked. Reader feedback is important for us as it helps us develop titles that you will really get the most out of. To send us general feedback, simply e-mail feedback@packtpub.com, and mention the book's title in the subject of your message. If there is a topic that you have expertise in and you are interested in either writing or contributing to a book, see our author guide at www.packtpub.com/authors .

Customer support

Now that you are the proud owner of a Packt book, we have a number of things to help you to get the most from your purchase.

Downloading the example code

You can download the example code files for this book from your account at http://www.packtpub.com. If you purchased this book elsewhere, you can visit http://www.packtpub.com/support and register to have the files e-mailed directly to you. You can download the code files by following these steps:

1. Log in or register to our website using your e-mail address and password.
2. Hover the mouse pointer on the **SUPPORT** tab at the top.
3. Click on **Code Downloads & Errata**.
4. Enter the name of the book in the **Search** box.
5. Select the book for which you're looking to download the code files.
6. Choose from the drop-down menu where you purchased this book from.
7. Click on **Code Download**.

You can also download the code files by clicking on the **Code Files** button on the book's webpage at the Packt Publishing website. This page can be accessed by entering the book's name in the **Search** box. Please note that you need to be logged in to your Packt account. Once the file is downloaded, please make sure that you unzip or extract the folder using the latest version of:

- WinRAR / 7-Zip for Windows
- Zipeg / iZip / UnRarX for Mac
- 7-Zip / PeaZip for Linux

The code bundle for the book is also hosted on GitHub at
`https://github.com/PacktPublishing/Microsoft-Exchange-Server-2016-PowerShell-Co`
`okbook-Fourth-Edition`. We also have other code bundles from our rich catalog of books
and videos available at `https://github.com/PacktPublishing/`. Check them out!

Downloading the color images of this book

We also provide you with a PDF file that has color images of the screenshots/diagrams used
in this book. The color images will help you better understand the changes in the output.
You can download this file from `https://www.packtpub.com/sites/default/files/down`
`loads/MicrosoftExchangeServer2016PowerShellCookbookFourthEdition_ColorImages`
`.pdf`.

Errata

Although we have taken every care to ensure the accuracy of our content, mistakes do
happen. If you find a mistake in one of our books-maybe a mistake in the text or the code-
we would be grateful if you could report this to us. By doing so, you can save other readers
from frustration and help us improve subsequent versions of this book. If you find any
errata, please report them by visiting `http://www.packtpub.com/submit-errata`, selecting
your book, clicking on the **Errata Submission Form** link, and entering the details of your
errata. Once your errata are verified, your submission will be accepted and the errata will
be uploaded to our website or added to any list of existing errata under the Errata section of
that title. To view the previously submitted errata, go to `https://www.packtpub.com/book`
`s/content/support`and enter the name of the book in the search field. The required
information will appear under the **Errata** section.

Piracy

Piracy of copyrighted material on the Internet is an ongoing problem across all media. At Packt, we take the protection of our copyright and licenses very seriously. If you come across any illegal copies of our works in any form on the Internet, please provide us with the location address or website name immediately so that we can pursue a remedy. Please contact us at copyright@packtpub.com with a link to the suspected pirated material. We appreciate your help in protecting our authors and our ability to bring you valuable content.

Questions

If you have a problem with any aspect of this book, you can contact us at questions@packtpub.com, and we will do our best to address the problem.

1

PowerShell Key Concepts

In this chapter, we will cover the following:

- Using the help system
- Understanding command syntax and parameters
- Command aliases
- Setting up a PowerShell profile
- Understanding the pipeline
- Working with variables and objects
- Working with arrays and hash tables
- Looping through items
- Creating custom objects
- Using debugger functions
- Understanding the new execution policy
- Using the Save-Help function
- Working with script repositories

Introduction

So, your organization has decided to move to Exchange Server 2016 to take advantage of the many exciting new features such as integrated email archiving, discovery capabilities, and high availability functionality. Like it or not, you've realized that PowerShell is now an integral part of Exchange Server management and you need to learn the basics and have a point of reference for building your own scripts. That's what this book is all about. In this chapter, we'll cover some core PowerShell concepts that will provide you with a foundation of knowledge for using the remaining examples in this book. If you are already familiar with PowerShell, you may want to use this chapter as a review or as a reference for later after you've started writing scripts.

If you're completely new to PowerShell, the concept may be familiar if you've worked with UNIX command shells. Like UNIX-based shells, PowerShell allows you to string multiple commands together on one line using a technique called pipelining. This means that the output of one command becomes the input for another. But, unlike UNIX shells that pass text output from one command to another, PowerShell uses an object model based on the .NET Framework, and objects are passed between commands in a pipeline, as opposed to plain text. From an Exchange perspective, working with objects gives us the ability to access very detailed information about servers, mailboxes, databases, and more. For example, every mailbox you manage within the shell is an object with multiple properties, such as an email address, database location, or send and receive limits. The ability to access this type of information through simple commands means that we can build powerful scripts that generate reports, make configuration changes, and perform maintenance tasks with ease.

 This book is based on PowerShell version 5.1 using Windows 2016 Server, version 5.1, build 14393.

Performing some basic steps

To work with the code samples in this chapter, follow these steps to launch the Exchange Management Shell:

1. Log onto a workstation or server with the Exchange Management Tools installed.

2. You can connect using remote PowerShell if you for some reason don't have Exchange Management Tools installed. Use the following command:

```
$Session = New-PSSession -ConfigurationName Microsoft.Exchange `
-ConnectionUri http://servername/PowerShell/ `
-Authentication Kerberos
Import-PSSession $Session
```

3. Alternatively, open the Exchange Management Shell by clicking the windows button and go to **Microsoft Exchange Server 2016 | Exchange Management Shell**.

> Remember to start the Exchange Management Shell using **Run as Administrator** to avoid permission problems. In the chapter, notice that in the examples of cmdlets, I have used the back tick (`` ` ``) character for breaking up long commands into multiple lines. The purpose with this is to make it easier to read. The back ticks are not required and should only be used if needed. Notice that the Exchange variables, such as $exscripts, are not available when using the preceding method.

Using the help system

The Exchange Management Shell includes over 830 cmdlets, each with a set of multiple parameters. For instance, the New-Mailbox cmdlet accepts up to more than 60 parameters, and the Set-Mailbox cmdlet has approximately 200 available parameters. It's safe to say that even the most experienced PowerShell expert would be at a disadvantage without a good help system. In this recipe, we'll take a look at how to get help in the Exchange Management Shell.

How to do it...

To get help information for a cmdlet, type Get-Help, followed by the cmdlet name. For example, to get help information about the Get-Mailbox cmdlet, run the following command:

```
Get-Help Get-Mailbox -full
```

How it works...

When running `Get-Help` for a cmdlet, a synopsis and description for the cmdlet will be displayed in the shell. The `Get-Help` cmdlet is one of the best discovery tools to use in PowerShell. You can use it when you're not quite sure how a cmdlet works or what parameters it provides.

You can use the following switch parameters to get specific information using the `Get-Help` cmdlet:

- **Detailed**: The detailed view provides parameter descriptions and examples and uses the following syntax:

```
Get-Help <cmdletname> -Detailed
```

- **Examples**: You can view multiple examples of how to use a cmdlet by running the following syntax:

```
Get-Help <cmdletname> -Examples
```

- **Full**: Use the following syntax to view the complete contents of the help file for a cmdlet:

```
Get-Help <cmdletname> -Full
```

- **Online**: Use the following syntax to view the online version of the contents for the help file of a cmdlet:

```
Get-Help <cmdletname> -Online
```

Some parameters accept simple strings as input, while others require an actual object. When creating a mailbox using the `New-Mailbox` cmdlet, you'll need to provide a secure string object for the `-Password` parameter. You can determine the data type required for a parameter using `Get-Help`:

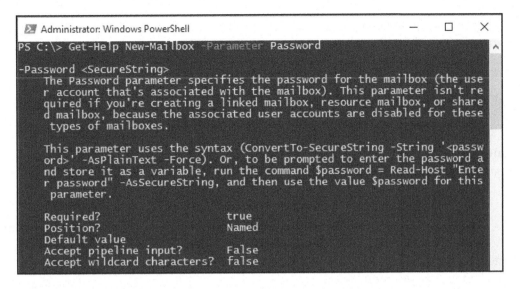

You can see from the command output that we get several pieces of key information about the -Password parameter. In addition to the required data type of <SecureString>, we can see that this is a named parameter. It is required when running the New-Mailbox cmdlet and it does not accept wildcard characters. You can use Get-Help when examining the parameters for any cmdlet to determine whether or not they support these settings.

During the writing of this book there were issues while performing Get-Help New-Mailbox from Exchange Management Shell. I've used an unsupported workaround based on Add-PSSnapin -Name Microsoft.Exchange.Management.PowerShell.E2010 from a regular Windows PowerShell and, from there, performed the Get-Help New-Mailbox cmdlet. This is a known issue and will be solved in the future.

You could run Get-Help New-Mailbox -Examples to determine the syntax required to create a secure string password object and how to use it to create a mailbox. This is also covered in detail in the recipe titled *Adding, modifying, and removing mailboxes* in Chapter 3, *Managing Recipients*.

There's more...

There will be times when you'll need to search for a cmdlet without knowing its full name. In this case, there are a couple of commands you can use to find the cmdlets you are looking for.

To find all cmdlets that contain the word "mailbox", you can use a wildcard, as shown in the following command:

```
Get-Command *Mailbox*
```

You can use the `-Verb` parameter to find all cmdlets starting with a particular verb:

```
Get-Command -Verb Set
```

To search for commands that use a particular noun, specify the name with the `-Noun` parameter:

```
Get-Command -Noun Mailbox
```

The `Get-Command` cmdlet is a built-in PowerShell core cmdlet, and it will return commands from both Windows PowerShell as well as the Exchange Management Shell. The Exchange Management Shell also adds a special function called `Get-Ex` command that will return only Exchange specific commands.

In addition to getting cmdlet help for cmdlets, you can use `Get-Help` to view supplemental help files that explain general PowerShell concepts that focus primarily on scripting. To display the help file for a particular concept, type `Get-Help about_` followed by the concept name. For example, to view the help for the core PowerShell commands type the following:

```
Get-Help about_Core_Commands
```

You can view the entire list of conceptual help files using the following command:

```
Get-Help about_*
```

Don't worry about trying to memorize all the Exchange or PowerShell cmdlet names. As long as you can remember `Get-Command` and `Get-Help`, you can search for commands and figure out the syntax to do just about anything.

Getting help with cmdlets and functions

One of the things that can be confusing at first is the distinction between cmdlets and functions. When you launch the Exchange Management Shell, a remote PowerShell session is initiated to an Exchange server and specific commands, called proxy functions, are imported into your shell session. These proxy functions are essentially just blocks of code that have a name, such as `Get-Mailbox`, and that correspond to the compiled cmdlets installed on the server. This is true even if you have a single server and when you are running the shell locally on a server.

When you run the `Get-Mailbox` function from the shell, data is passed between your machine and the Exchange server through a remote PowerShell session. The `Get-Mailbox` cmdlet is actually executing on the remote Exchange server, and the results are being passed back to your machine. One of the benefits of this is that it allows you to run the cmdlets remotely regardless of whether your servers are on-premises or in the cloud.

We'll get into the details of all this throughout the remaining chapters in the book. The bottom line is that, for now, you need to understand that, when you are working with the help system, the Exchange 2016 cmdlets will show up as functions and not as cmdlets.

Consider the following command and output:

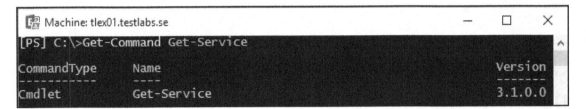

Here we are running `Get-Command` against a PowerShell v5 core cmdlet. Notice that the `CommandType` shows that this is a `Cmdlet`.

Now try the same thing for the `Get-Mailbox` cmdlet:

And as you can see, the `CommandType` for the `Get-Mailbox` cmdlet shows that it is actually a `Function`. So, there are a couple of key points to take away from this. First, throughout the course of this book, we will refer to the Exchange 2016 cmdlets as cmdlets, even though they will show up as functions when running `Get-Command`. Second, keep in mind that you can run `Get-Help` against any function name, such as `Get-Mailbox`, and you'll still get the help file for that cmdlet. But if you are unsure of the exact name of a cmdlet, use `Get-Command` to perform a wildcard search as an aid in the discovery process. Once you've determined the name of the cmdlet you are looking for, you can run `Get-Help` against that cmdlet for complete details on how to use it.

Try using the help system before going to the internet to find answers. You'll find that the answers to most of your questions are already documented within the built-in cmdlet help.

See also

- The *Understanding command syntax and parameters* recipe in this chapter
- The *Manually configuring remote PowerShell connections* recipe from `Chapter 2`, *Exchange Management Shell Common Tasks*
- The *Working with Role Based Access Control* recipe from `Chapter 10`, *Exchange Security*

Understanding command syntax and parameters

Windows PowerShell provides a large number of built-in cmdlets (pronounced *command-lets*) that perform specific operations. The Exchange Management Shell adds an additional set of PowerShell cmdlets used specifically for managing Exchange. We can also run these cmdlets interactively in the shell, or through automated scripts. When executing a cmdlet, parameters can be used to provide information, such as which mailbox or server to work with, or which attribute of those objects should be modified. In this recipe, we'll take a look at basic PowerShell command syntax and how parameters are used with cmdlets.

How to do it...

When running a PowerShell command, you type the cmdlet name, followed by any parameters required. Parameter names are preceded by a hyphen (–) followed by the value of the parameter. Let's start with a basic example. To get mailbox information for a user named `testuser`, use the following command syntax:

```
Get-Mailbox -Identity testuser
```

Alternatively, the following syntax also works and provides the same output, because the `–Identity` parameter is a positional parameter:

```
Get-Mailbox testuser
```

Most cmdlets support a number of parameters that can be used within a single command.

We can use the following command to modify two separate settings on the `testuser` mailbox:

```
Set-Mailbox testuser -MaxSendSize 50Mb -MaxReceiveSize 50Mb
```

How it works...

All cmdlets follow a standard verb-noun naming convention. For example, to get a list of mailboxes you use the `Get-Mailbox` cmdlet. You can change the configuration of a mailbox using the `Set-Mailbox` cmdlet. In both examples, the verb (`Get` or `Set`) is the action you want to take on the noun (`Mailbox`). The verb is always separated from the noun using the hyphen (–) character. With the exception of a few Exchange Management Shell cmdlets, the noun is always singular.

Cmdlet names and parameters are not case sensitive. You can use a combination of upper and lowercase letters to improve the readability of your scripts, but it is not required.

Parameter input is either optional or required, depending on the parameter and cmdlet you are working with. You don't have to assign a value to the `-Identity` parameter since it is not required when running the `Get-Mailbox` cmdlet. If you simply run `Get-Mailbox` without any arguments, the first 1,000 mailboxes in the organization will be returned.

If you are working in a large environment with more than 1,000 mailboxes, you can run the `Get-Mailbox` cmdlet, setting the –`ResultSize` parameter to `Unlimited` to retrieve all of the mailboxes in your organization.

Notice that in the first two examples, we ran `Get-Mailbox` for a single user. In the first example, we used the `-Identity` parameter, but in the second example we did not. The reason we don't need to explicitly use the `-Identity` parameter in the second example is because it is a positional parameter. In this case, `-Identity` is in position 1, so the first argument received by the cmdlet is automatically bound to this parameter. There can be a number of positional parameters supported by a cmdlet, and they are numbered starting from 1. Other parameters that are not positional are known as named parameters, meaning we need to use the parameter name to provide input for the value.

The `-Identity` parameter is included with most of the Exchange Management Shell cmdlets, and it allows you to classify the object you want to take an action on.

The `-Identity` parameter used with the Exchange Management Shell cmdlets can accept different value types. In addition to the alias, the following values can be used: ADObjectID, Distinguished name, Domain\Username, GUID, LegacyExchangeDN, SmtpAddress and UserPrincipalName (UPN).

When you run a cmdlet without providing input for a required parameter, you will be prompted to enter the information before execution. This is because the cmdlet needs to know which mailbox it should modify when the command is executed.

In order to determine whether a parameter is required, named or positional, supports wildcards, or accepts input from the pipeline, you can use the `Get-Help` cmdlet which is covered in the next recipe in this chapter. Multiple data types are used for input depending on the parameter you are working with. Some parameters accept string values, while others accept integers or Boolean values. Boolean parameters are used when you need to set a parameter value to either true or false. PowerShell provides built-in shell variables for each of these values using the `$true` and `$false` automatic variables. For a complete list of PowerShell v5 automatic variables, run `Get-Helpabout_automatic_variables`. Also see *Appendix A* for a list of automatic variables added by the Exchange Management Shell.

For example, you can enable or disable a send connector using the `Set-SendConnector` cmdlet with the `-Enabled` parameter:

```
Set-SendConnector Internet -Enabled $false
```

Switch parameters don't require a value. Instead they are used to turn something on or off, or to either enable or disable a feature or setting. One common example of when you might use a switch parameter is when creating an archive mailbox for a user:

```
Enable-Mailbox testuser -Archive
```

PowerShell also provides a set of common parameters that can be used with every cmdlet. Some of the common parameters, such as the risk mitigation parameters (`-Confirm` and `-Whatif`), only work with cmdlets that make changes.

For a complete list of common parameters, run `Get-Help about_CommonParameters`.

Risk mitigation parameters allow you to preview a change or confirm a change that may be destructive. If you want to see what will happen when executing a command without actually executing it, use the -WhatIf parameter:

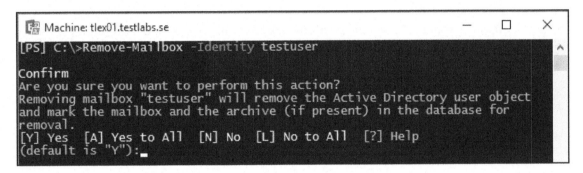

When making a change, such as removing a mailbox, you'll be prompted for confirmation, as shown in the following screenshot:

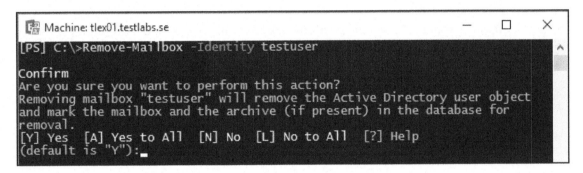

To suppress this confirmation, set the -Confirm parameter to false:

```
Remove-Mailbox testuser -Confirm:$false
```

Notice here, that when assigning the $false variable to the -Confirm parameter, we had to use a colon immediately after the parameter name and then the Boolean value. This is different to how we assigned this value earlier with the -Enabled parameter when using the Set-SendConnector cmdlet. Remember that the -Confirm parameter always requires this special syntax, and while most parameters that accept a Boolean value generally do not require this, it depends on the cmdlet with which you are working. Fortunately, PowerShell has a great built-in help system that we can use when we run into these inconsistencies.

Cmdlets and parameters support tab completion. You can start typing the first few characters of a cmdlet or a parameter name and hit the tab key to automatically complete the name or tab through a list of available names. This is very helpful in terms of discovery and can serve as a bit of a time saver.

In addition, you only need to type enough characters of a parameter name to differentiate it from another parameter name. The following command using a partial parameter name is completely valid:

```
Set-User -id testuser -Office Sales
```

Here we've used `id` as a shortcut for the `-Identity` parameter. The cmdlet does not provide any other parameters that start with `id`, so it automatically assumes you want to use the `-Identity` parameter.

Another helpful feature that some parameters support is the use of wildcards. When running the `Get-Mailbox` cmdlet, the `-Identity` parameter can be used with wildcards to return multiple mailboxes that match a certain pattern:

```
Get-Mailbox -id t*
```

In this example, all mailboxes starting with the letter `t` will be returned. Although this is fairly straightforward, you can reference the help system for details on using wildcard characters in PowerShell by running `Get-Helpabout_Wildcards`.

> Shortcuts for cmdlets might be great when doing interactive administrational tasks, but for future proofing the scripts it's recommended to use the full syntax of the cmdlets.

There's more...

Parameter values containing a space need to be enclosed in either single or double quotation marks. The following command would retrieve all of the mailboxes in the `Sales Users` OU in Active Directory. Notice that since the OU name contains a space, it is enclosed in single quotes:

```
Get-Mailbox -OrganizationalUnit 'testlabs.se/Sales Users/Seattle'
```

Use double quotes when you need to expand a variable within a string:

```
$City = 'Seattle'
Get-Mailbox -OrganizationalUnit "testlabs.se/Sales Users/$City"
```

You can see here that we first create a variable containing the name of the city, which represents a sub-OU under `Sales Users`. Next, we include the variable inside the string used for the organizational unit when running the `Get-Mailbox` cmdlet. PowerShell automatically expands the variable name inside the double quoted string where the value should appear and all mailboxes inside the `Seattle` OU are returned by the command.

> Quoting rules are documented in detail in the PowerShell help system. Run `Get-Help about_Quoting_Rules` for more information.

See also

- The *Using the help system* recipe in this chapter
- The *Working with variables and objects* recipe in this chapter

Command aliases

Throughout this book and previous books, we have referred to command aliases or cmdlet aliases: for example, the short name of the full cmdlet.

These aliases can be very handy when writing scripts where you might want to optimize and keep them as small and as short as possible.

Let us take a look at some examples of the built-in aliases. For example, we have the cmdlet `Where-Object`, which is commonly used. We have two aliases for it, which are ? or where. Another example on a regularly used cmdlet would be `ForEach-Object`; there are two aliases for it and those are % or `foreach`. The last example of a built-in alias is for the cmdlet `Select-Object`, where the alias is `select`.

How to do it...

When running a PowerShell command, instead of using the full cmdlet, we can create aliases for them. Let's have a look at a few examples of how to utilize the aliases:

```
    Get-Alias
New-Alias -Name wh -Value Write-Host
wh "Testing alias"
New-Alias -Name list -Value Get-ChildItem
list -Path "C:\Scripts"
New-Alias -Name npp -Value "C:\Program Files `
(x86)\Notepad++\notepad++.exe"
npp
```

How it works...

We start off with using the Get-Alias cmdlet. With the cmdlet, we will list all current aliases. If you haven't created any custom aliases only the built-in aliases are listed.

In the preceding examples, we have three different aliases created. Aliases could be created for cmdlets that you are using frequently or if you want to be able to launch an application using an alias directly from the PowerShell prompt.

The first example is set to wh, which is an alias for Write-Host. We can use this by type in wh "Testing alias", and the Write-Host cmdlet should be utilized in the background and show us the text on screen.

In our second example, we have to create an alias for Get-ChildItem; the alias we create for it is list. We can then get started to use list -Path "C:\Scripts" to retrieve all the files and folders from the folder C:\Scripts.

The third and final example is to create an alias for launching the Notepad++ application. This is simply done by setting the value of the alias to the full path to the .exe file of the application. Once it's done, you can from the PowerShell prompt, you can simply type in npp for launching Notepad++.

See also

- The *Setting up a PowerShell profile* recipe in this chapter
- The *Working with variables and objects* recipe in this chapter
- The *Looping through items* recipe in this chapter

Setting up a PowerShell profile

You can use a PowerShell profile to customize your shell environment and to load functions, modules, aliases, and variables into the environment when you start your Exchange Management Shell session. In this recipe, we'll take a look at how you can create a profile.

How to do it...

Profiles are not created by default, but you may want to verify one has not already been created.

1. Start off by running the `Test-Path` cmdlet:

```
Test-Path $profile
```

2. If the `Test-Path` cmdlet returns `$true`, then a profile has already been created for the current user. You can open an existing profile by invoking `notepad.exe` from the shell:

```
notepad $profile
```

3. If the `Test-Path` cmdlet returns `$false`, you can create a new profile for the current user by running the following command:

```
New-Item -type file -path $profile -force
```

How it works...

A PowerShell profile is a just a script with a `.ps1` extension that is run every time you start the shell. You can think of a profile as a logon script for your PowerShell or Exchange Management Shell session. Inside your profile you can add custom aliases, define variables, load modules, or add your own functions so that they will be available every time you start the shell. In the previous example, we used the automatic shell `$profile` variable to create a profile script for the current user, which, in this case, would create the profile in the `$env:UserProfile\Documents\WindowsPowerShell\`directory.

Since PowerShell is simply executing a `.ps1` script to load your profile, your execution policy must allow the execution of scripts on your machine. If it does not, your profile will not be loaded when starting the shell and you'll receive an error.

There are four types of profiles that can be used with PowerShell:

- `$Profile.AllUsersAllHosts`: This profile applies to all users and all shells and is located in
  `$env:Windir\system32\WindowsPowerShell\v1.0\profile.ps1`
- `$Profile.AllUsersCurrentHost`: This profile applies to all users but only the PowerShell.exe host and is located in
  `$env:Windir\system32\WindowsPowerShell\v1.0\Microsoft.PowerShell_profile.ps1`
- `$Profile.CurrentUserAllHosts`: This profile applies to the current user and all shells and is located in
  `$env:UserProfile\Documents\WindowsPowerShell\profile.ps1`
- `$Profile.CurrentUserCurrentHost`: This profile applies to the current user and only to the PowerShell.exe host and is located in
  `$env:UserProfile\Documents\WindowsPowerShell\Microsoft.PowerShell_profile.ps1`

Using the `$profile` variable alone to create the profile will default to the `CurrentUserCurrentHost` location and is probably the most commonly-used profile type. If you need to create a profile for all the users on a machine, use one of the *AllUsers* profile types.

You may be wondering at this point what the difference is between the `Current Host` and `All Hosts` profile types. The PowerShell runtime can be hosted within third-party applications, so the `All Hosts` profile types apply to those instances of PowerShell. The `Current Host` profile types can be used with `PowerShell.exe` and when you are running the Exchange Management Shell.

In addition to defining custom aliases or functions in a profile, you may want to consider loading any other modules that may be useful. For example, you may want to load the Active Directory module for PowerShell so that those cmdlets are also available to you whenever you start the shell.

When you're done making changes to your profile, save and close the file. In order for the changes to take effect, you can either restart the shell, or you can dot-source the script to reload the profile:

```
. $profile
```

You can create multiple .ps1 scripts that include aliases, functions, and variables and then dot-source these scripts within your profile to have them loaded every time you start your PowerShell session.

To give an applicable example would be to use Import-Module inside the profile script to import PowerShell modules immediately when launching Windows PowerShell or Exchange Management Shell. Functions, modules, and other PS1 script files can also be loaded into the profile script.

You can reference the help system on this topic by running Get-Helpabout_profiles.

There's more...

Trying to remember all of the profile types and their associated script paths can be a little tough. There's actually a pretty neat trick that you can use with the $profile variable to view all of the profile types and file paths in the shell. To do this, access the psextended property of the $profile object:

```
$profile.psextended | Format-List
```

This will give you a list of each profile type and the path of the .ps1 script that should be used to create the profile.

See also

- The *Command aliases* recipe in this chapter
- The *Working with variables and objects* recipe in this chapter

Understanding the pipeline

The single most important concept in PowerShell is the use of its flexible, object-based pipeline. You may have used pipelines in UNIX-based shells, or when working with the `cmd.exe` command prompt. The concept of pipelines is similar in that you are sending the output from one command to another. But, instead of passing plain text, PowerShell works with objects, and we can accomplish some very complex tasks in just a single line of code. In this recipe, you'll learn how to use pipelines to string together multiple commands and build powerful one-liners.

How to do it...

The following pipeline command would set the office location for every mailbox in the DB2 database:

```
Get-Mailbox -Database DB2 | Set-User -Office "Headquarters"
```

How it works...

In a pipeline, you separate a series of commands using the pipe (|) character. In the previous example, the `Get-Mailbox` cmdlet returns a collection of mailbox objects. Each mailbox object contains several properties that contain information such as the name of the mailbox, the location of the associated user account in Active Directory, and more. The `Set-User` cmdlet is designed to accept input from the `Get-Mailbox` cmdlet in a pipeline, and with one simple command, we can pass along an entire collection of mailboxes that can be modified in one operation.

You can also pipe output to filtering commands, such as the `Where-Object` cmdlet. In this example, the command retrieves only the mailboxes with a MaxSendSize equal to 50 megabytes:

```
Get-Mailbox | Where-Object{$_.MaxSendSize -eq 50mb}
```

The code that the `Where-Object` cmdlet uses to perform the filtering is enclosed in curly braces (`{ }`). This is called a script block, and the code within this script block is evaluated for each object that comes across the pipeline. If the result of the expression is evaluated as true, the object is returned; otherwise, it is ignored. In this example, we access the `MaxSendSize` property of each mailbox using the `$_` object, which is an automatic variable that refers to the current object in the pipeline. We use the equals (`-eq`) comparison operator to check that the `MaxSendSize` property of each mailbox is equal to 50 megabytes. If so, only those mailboxes are returned by the command.

Comparison operators allow you to compare results and find values that match a pattern. For a complete list of comparison operators, run `Get-Help about_Comparison_Operators`.

When running this command, which can also be referred to as a one-liner, each mailbox object is processed one at a time using stream processing. This means that as soon as a match is found, the mailbox information is displayed on the screen. Without this behavior, you would have to wait for every mailbox to be found before seeing any results. This may not matter if you are working in a very small environment, but without this functionality in a large organization with tens of thousands of mailboxes, you would have to wait a long time for the entire result set to be collected and returned.

One other interesting thing to note about the comparison being done inside our `Where-Object` filter is the use of the `mb` multiplier suffix. PowerShell natively supports these multipliers and they make it a lot easier for us to work with large numbers. In this example, we've used `50mb`, which is the equivalent of entering the value in bytes because behind the scenes, PowerShell is doing the math for us by replacing this value with `1024*1024*50`. PowerShell provides support for the following multipliers: `kb`, `mb`, `gb`, `tb`, and `pb`.

There's more...

You can use advanced pipelining techniques to send objects across the pipeline to other cmdlets that do not support direct pipeline input. For example, the following one-liner adds a list of users to a group:

```
Get-User |
  Where-Object{$_.title -eq "Exchange Admin"} | Foreach-Object{
      Add-RoleGroupMember -Identity "Organization Management" `
      -Member $_.name
  }
```

This pipeline command starts off with a simple filter that returns only the users that have their Title set to Exchange Admin. The output from that command is then piped to the ForEach-Object cmdlet that processes each object in the collection. Similar to the Where-Object cmdlet, the ForEach-Object cmdlet processes each item from the pipeline using a script block. Instead of filtering, this time we are running a command for each user object returned in the collection and adding them to the Organization Management role group.

Using aliases in pipelines can be helpful because it reduces the number of characters you need to type. Take a look at the previous command, modified to use aliases:

```
Get-User |
  ?{$_.title -eq "Exchange Admin"} | %{
    Add-RoleGroupMember -Identity "Organization Management" `
    -Member $_.name
  }
```

Notice the use of the question mark (?) and the percent sign (%) characters. The ? character is an alias for the Where-Object cmdlet, and the % character is an alias for the ForEach-Object cmdlet. These cmdlets are used heavily, and you'll often see them used with these aliases because it makes the commands easier to type.

You can use the Get-Alias cmdlet to find all of the aliases currently defined in your shell session and the New-Alias cmdlet to create custom aliases.

The Where-Object and ForEach-Object cmdlets have additional aliases. Here's another way you could run the previous command:

```
Get-User |
  where{$_.title -eq "Exchange Admin"} | foreach{
    Add-RoleGroupMember -Identity "Organization Management" `
    -Member $_.name
  }
```

Use aliases when you're working interactively in the shell to speed up your work and keep your commands concise. You may want to consider using the full cmdlet names in production scripts to avoid confusing others who may read your code.

See also

- The *Looping through items* recipe in this chapter
- The *Creating custom objects* recipe from in this chapter

Working with variables and objects

Every scripting language makes use of variables as placeholders for data, and PowerShell is no exception. You'll need to work with variables often to save temporary data to an object so you can work with it later. PowerShell is very different from other command shells in that everything you touch is, in fact, a rich object with properties and methods. In PowerShell, a variable is simply an instance of an object just like everything else. The properties of an object contain various bits of information depending on the type of object you're working with. In this recipe, we'll learn to create user-defined variables and work with objects in the Exchange Management Shell.

How to do it...

To create a variable that stores an instance of the `testuser` mailbox, use the following command:

```
$mailbox = Get-Mailbox testuser
```

How it works...

To create a variable, or an instance of an object, you prefix the variable name with the dollar sign ($). To the right of the variable name, use the equals (=) assignment operator, followed by the value or object that should be assigned to the variable. Keep in mind that the variables you create are only available during your current shell session and will be destroyed when you close the shell.

Let's look at another example. To create a string variable that contains an email address, use the following command:

```
$email = "testuser@contoso.com"
```

 In addition to user-defined variables, PowerShell also includes automatic and preference variables. To learn more, run Get-Help about_Automatic_Variables and Get-Help about_Preference_Variables.

Even a simple string variable is an object with properties and methods. For instance, every string has a Length property that will return the number of characters that are in the string:

```
[PS] C:\>$email.length
20
```

When accessing the properties of an object, you can use dot notation to reference the property with which you want to work. This is done by typing the object name, then a period, followed by the property name, as shown in the previous example. You access methods in the same way, except that method names always end with parentheses ().

The string data type supports several methods, such as Substring, Replace, and Split. The following example shows how the Split method can be used to split a string:

```
[PS] C:\>$email.Split("@")
testuser
contoso.com
```

You can see here that the Split method uses the @ portion of the string as a delimiter and returns two substrings as a result.

 PowerShell also provides a -Split operator that can split a string into one or more substrings. Run Get-Help about_Split for details.

There's more...

At this point, you know how to access the properties and methods of an object, but you need to be able to discover and work with these members. To determine which properties and methods are accessible on a given object, you can use the Get-Member cmdlet, which is one of the key discovery tools in PowerShell along with Get-Help and Get-Command.

To retrieve the members of an object, pipe the object to the Get-Member cmdlet. The following command will retrieve all of the instance members of the $mailbox object we created earlier:

```
$mailbox | Get-Member
```

> To filter the results returned by Get-Member, use the –MemberType parameter to specify whether the type should be a Property or a Method.

Let's take a look at a practical example of how we could use Get-Member to discover the methods of an object. Imagine that each mailbox in our environment has had a custom MaxSendSize restriction set and we need to record the value for reporting purposes. When accessing the MaxSendSize property, the following information is returned:

```
[PS] C:\>$mailbox.MaxSendSize
IsUnlimited Value
----------- -----
False       50 MB (52,428,800 bytes)
```

We can see here that the MaxSendSize property actually contains an object with two properties: IsUnlimited and Value. Based on what we've learned, we should be able to access the information for the Value property using a dot notation:

```
[PS] C:\>$mailbox.MaxSendSize.Value
50 MB (52,428,800 bytes)
```

That works, but the information returned contains not only the value in megabytes, but also the total bytes for the `MaxSendSize` value. For the purpose of what we are trying to accomplish, we only need the total megabytes. Let's see if this object provides any methods that can help us out with this using `Get-Member`:

```
Machine: tlex01.testlabs.se                                    —    □    ×
[PS] C:\>$mailbox.MaxSendSize.Value | Get-Member -MemberType Method


    TypeName: Microsoft.Exchange.Data.ByteQuantifiedSize

Name           MemberType Definition
----           ---------- ----------
CompareTo      Method     int CompareTo(Microsoft.Exchange.Data.ByteQuan...
Equals         Method     bool Equals(System.Object obj), bool Equals(Mi...
GetHashCode    Method     int GetHashCode()
GetType        Method     type GetType()
RoundUpToUnit  Method     uint64 RoundUpToUnit(Microsoft.Exchange.Data.B...
ToBytes        Method     uint64 ToBytes()
ToGB           Method     uint64 ToGB()
ToKB           Method     uint64 ToKB()
ToMB           Method     uint64 ToMB()
ToString       Method     string ToString(), string ToString(string form...
ToTB           Method     uint64 ToTB()


[PS] C:\>
```

From the output shown in the previous screenshot, we can see this object supports several methods that can be used to convert the value. To obtain the `MaxSendSize` value in megabytes, we can call the `ToMB` method:

```
[PS] C:\>$mailbox.MaxSendSize.Value.ToMB()
50
```

In a traditional shell for Exchange on-premises, you would have to perform complex string parsing to extract this type of information, but PowerShell and the .NET Framework make this much easier. As you'll see over time, this is one of the reasons why PowerShell's object-based nature really outshines a typical text-based command shell.

An important thing to point out about this last example is that it would not work if the mailbox had not had a custom `MaxSendSize` limitation configured, which would be the case for newly created mailboxes in Exchange 2016, if not specified.

Nevertheless, this provides a good illustration of the process you'll want to use when you're trying to learn about an object's properties or methods.

Variable expansion in strings

As mentioned in the first recipe in this chapter, PowerShell uses quoting rules to determine how variables should be handled inside a quoted string. When enclosing a simple variable inside a double-quoted string, PowerShell will expand that variable and replace the variable with the value of the string. Let's take a look at how this works by starting off with a simple example:

```
[PS] C:\>$name = "Bob"
[PS] C:\> "The user name is $name"
The user name is Bob
```

This is pretty straightforward. We stored the string value of Bob inside the $name variable. We then include the $name variable inside a double-quoted string that contains a message. When we hit return, the $name variable is expanded and we get back the message we expect to see on the screen.

Now let's try this with a more complex object. Let's say that we want to store an instance of a mailbox object in a variable and access the PrimarySmtpAddress property inside the quoted string:

```
[PS] C:\>$mailbox = Get-Mailbox testuser
[PS] C:\>"The email address is $mailbox.PrimarySmtpAddress"
The email address is test user.PrimarySmtpAddress
```

Notice here that when we try to access the PrimarySmtpAddress property of our mailbox object inside the double-quoted string, we're not getting back the information that we'd expect. This is a very common stumbling block when it comes to working with objects and properties inside strings. We can get around this using a sub-expression notation. This requires that you enclose the entire object within $() characters inside the string:

```
[PS] C:\>"The email address is $($mailbox.PrimarySmtpAddress)"
The email address is testuser@testlabs.se
```

Using this syntax, the PrimarySmtpAddress property of the $mailbox object is properly expanded and the correct information is returned. This technique will be useful later when extracting data from objects and generating reports or log files.

Strongly typed variables

PowerShell will automatically try to select the correct data type for a variable based on the value being assigned to it. You don't have to worry about doing this yourself, but we do have the ability to explicitly assign a type to a variable if needed. This is done by specifying the data type in square brackets before the variable name:

[string]$var2 = 32

Here we've assigned the value of 32 to the $var2 variable. Had we not strongly typed the variable using the [string] type shortcut, $var2 would have been created using the Int32 data type, since the value we assigned was a number that was not enclosed in single or double quotes. Take a look at the following screenshot:

As you can see here, the $var1 variable is initially created without any explicit typing. We use the GetType() method, which can be used on any object in the shell, to determine the data type of $var1. Since the value assigned was a number not enclosed in quotes, it was created using the Int32 data type. When using the [string] type shortcut to create $var2 with the same value, you can see that it has now been created as a string.

It is good to have an understanding of data types because when building scripts that return objects, you may need to have some control over this. For example, you may want to report on the amount of free disk space on an Exchange server. If we store this value in the property of a custom object as a string, we lose the ability to sort on that value. There are several examples throughout the book that use this technique.

See the Appendix A and B for commonly-used type shortcuts.

Working with arrays and hash tables

Like many other scripting and programming languages, Windows PowerShell allows you to work with arrays and hash tables. An array is a collection of values that can be stored in a single object. A hash table is also known as an associative array, and is a dictionary that stores a set of key-value pairs. You'll need to have a good grasp of arrays so that you can effectively manage objects in bulk and gain maximum efficiency in the shell. In this recipe, we'll take a look at how we can use both types of arrays to store and retrieve data.

How to do it...

You can initialize an array that stores a set of items by assigning multiple values to a variable. All you need to do is separate each value with a comma. The following command would create an array of server names:

```
$servers = "EX1","EX2","EX3"
```

To create an empty hash table, use the following syntax:

```
$hashtable = @{}
```

Now that we have an empty hash table, we can add key-value pairs:

```
$hashtable["server1"] = 1
$hashtable["server2"] = 2
$hashtable["server3"] = 3
```

Notice in this example that we can assign a value based on a key name, not using an index number as we saw with a regular array. Alternatively, we can create this same object using a single command using the following syntax:

```
$hashtable = @{server1 = 1; server2 = 2; server3 = 3}
```

You can see here that we used a semicolon (;) to separate each key-value pair. This is only required if the entire hash table is created in one line.

You can break this up into multiple lines to make it easier to read:

```
$hashtable = @{
    server1 = 1
    server2 = 2
    server3 = 3
}
```

To create an empty array, use the following syntax:

```
$servers = @()
```

How it works...

Let's start off by looking at how arrays work in PowerShell. When working with arrays, you can access specific items and add or remove elements. In our first example, we assigned a list of server names to the $servers array. To view all of the items in the array, simply type the variable name and hit return:

```
[PS] C:\>$servers
EX1
EX2
EX3
```

Array indexing allows you to access a specific element of an array using its index number inside square brackets ([]). PowerShell arrays are zero-based, meaning that the first item in the array starts at index zero. For example, use the second index to access the third element of the array, as shown next:

```
[PS] C:\>$servers[2]
EX3
```

To assign a value to a specific element of the array, use the equals (=) assignment operator. We can change the value from the last example using following syntax:

```
[PS] C:\>$servers[2] = "EX4"
[PS] C:\>$servers[2]
EX4
```

Let's add another server to this array. To append a value, use the plus equals (+=) assignment operator as shown here:

```
[PS] C:\>$servers += "EX5"
[PS] C:\>$servers
EX1
EX2
EX4
EX5
```

To determine how many items are in an array, we can access the Count property to retrieve the total number of array elements:

```
[PS] C:\>$servers.Count
4
```

We can loop through each element in the array with the ForEach-Object cmdlet and display the value in a string:

```
$servers | ForEach-Object {"Server Name: $_"}
```

We can also check for a value in an array using the –Contains or –NotContains conditional operators:

```
[PS] C:\>$servers –contains "EX1"
True
```

In this example, we are working with a one-dimensional array, which is what you'll commonly be dealing with in the Exchange Management Shell. PowerShell supports more complex array types such as jagged and multidimensional arrays, but these are beyond the scope of what you'll need to know for the examples in this book.

Now that we've figured out how arrays work, let's take a closer look at hash tables. When viewing the output for a hash table, the items are returned in no particular order. You'll notice this when viewing the hash-table we created earlier:

```
[PS] C:\>$hashtable
Name                          Value
----                          -----
server2                       2
server3                       3
server1                       1
```

If you want to sort the hash table, you can call the GetEnumerator method and sort by the Value property:

```
[PS] C:\>$hashtable.GetEnumerator() | sort value
Name                          Value
----                          -----
server1                       1
server2                       2
server3                       3
```

Hash tables can be used when creating custom objects, or to provide a set of parameter names and values using parameter splitting. Instead of specifying parameter names one by one with a cmdlet, you can use a hash table with keys that match the parameter's names and their associated values will automatically be used for input:

```
$parameters = @{
  Title = "Manager"
  Department = "Sales"
  Office = "Headquarters"
}
Set-User testuser @parameters
```

This command automatically populates the parameter values for Title, Department, and Office when running the Set-User cmdlet for the testuser mailbox.

For more details and examples for working with hash tables, run Get-Help about_Hash_Tables.

There's more...

You can think of a collection as an array created from the output of a command. For example, the Get-Mailbox cmdlet can be used to create an object that stores a collection of mailboxes, and we can work with this object just as we would with any other array. You'll notice that, when working with collections, such as a set of mailboxes, you can access each mailbox instance as an array element. Consider the following example:

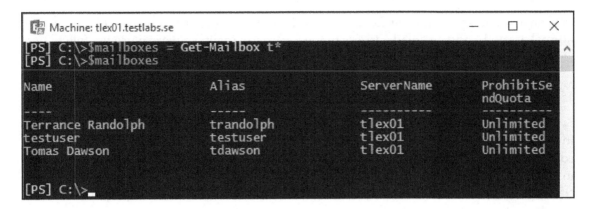

First, we retrieve a list of mailboxes that start with the letter t and assign that to the $mailboxes variable. From looking at the items in the $mailboxes object, we can see that the testuser mailbox is the second mailbox in the collection.

Since arrays are zero-based, we can access that item using the first index, as shown next:

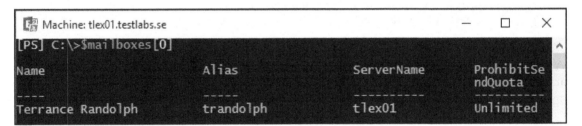

In previous version(s) of Exchange Server, we had an issue when the command only returned one item; the output could not be accessed using array notation. If you, for some reason face this, it can be solved by using the following syntax:

```
$mailboxes = @(Get-Mailbox testuser)
```

You can see here that we've wrapped the command inside the @() characters to ensure that PowerShell will always interpret the $mailboxes object as an array. This can be useful when you're building a script that always needs to work with an object as an array, regardless of the number of items returned from the command that created the object. Since the $mailboxes object has been initialized as an array, you can add and remove elements as needed.

We can also add and remove items to multi-valued properties, just as we would with a normal array. To add an email address to the `testuser` mailbox, we can use the following commands:

```
$mailbox = Get-Mailbox testuser
$mailbox.EmailAddresses += "testuser2@testlabs.se"
Set-Mailbox testuser -EmailAddresses $mailbox.EmailAddresses
```

In this example, we created an instance of the `testuser` mailbox by assigning the command to the `$mailbox` object. We can then work with the `EmailAddresses` property to view, add, and remove email addresses from this mailbox. You can see here that the plus equals (+=) operator was used to append a value to the `EmailAddresses` property.

We can also remove that value using the minus equals (−=) operator:

```
$mailbox.EmailAddresses -= "testuser2@testlabs.se"
Set-Mailbox testuser -EmailAddresses $mailbox.EmailAddresses
```

There is actually an easier way to add and remove email addresses on recipient objects. See *Adding and removing recipient email addresses* recipe in Chapter 3 for details.

We've covered the core concepts in this section that you'll need to know when working with arrays. For more details, run `Get-Help about_arrays`.

See also

- The *Working with variables and objects* recipe in this chapter
- The *Creating custom objects* recipe in this chapter

Looping through items

Loop processing is a concept that you will need to master in order to write scripts and one-liners with efficiency. You'll need to use loops to iterate over each item in an array or a collection of items, and then run one or more commands within a script block against each of those objects. In this recipe, we'll take a look at how you can use foreach loops and the `ForEach-Object` cmdlet to process items in a collection.

How to do it...

The `foreach` statement is a language construct used to iterate through values in a collection of items. The following example shows the syntax used to loop through a collection of mailboxes, returning only the name of each mailbox:

```
foreach ($mailbox in Get-Mailbox) {$mailbox.Name}
```

In addition, you can take advantage of the PowerShell pipeline and perform loop processing using the `ForEach-Object` cmdlet. This example produces the same result as the one shown previously:

```
Get-Mailbox | ForEach-Object {$_.Name}
```

You will often see the given command written using an alias of the `ForEach-Object` cmdlet, such as the percent sign (`%`):

```
Get-Mailbox | %{$_.Name}
```

How it works...

The first part of a `foreach` statement is enclosed in parentheses and represents a variable and a collection. In the previous example, the collection is the list of mailboxes returned from the `Get-Mailbox` cmdlet. The script block contains the commands that will be run for every item in the collection of mailboxes. Inside the script block, the `$mailbox` object is assigned the value of the current item being processed in the loop. This allows you to access each mailbox one at a time using the `$mailbox` variable.

When you need to perform loop processing within a pipeline, you can use the `ForEach-Object` cmdlet. The concept is similar, but the syntax is different because objects in the collection are coming across the pipeline.

The `ForEach-Object` cmdlet allows you to process each item in a collection using the `$_` automatic variable, which represents the current object in the pipeline. The `ForEach-Object` cmdlet is probably one of the most commonly-used cmdlets in PowerShell, and we'll rely on it heavily in many examples throughout the book.

The code inside the script block used with both looping methods can be more complex than just a simple expression. The script block can contain a series of commands or an entire script. Consider the following code:

```
Get-MailboxDatabase -Status | %{
    $DBName = $_.Name
    $whiteSpace = $_.AvailableNewMailboxSpace.ToMb()
    "The $DBName database has $whiteSpace MB of total white space"
}
```

In this example, we're looping through each mailbox database in the organization using the `ForEach-Object` cmdlet. Inside the script block, we've created multiple variables, calculated the total megabytes of whitespace in each database, and returned a custom message that includes the database name and corresponding whitespace value. This is a simple example, but keep in mind that inside the script block, you can run other cmdlets, work with variables, create custom objects, and more.

PowerShell also supports other language constructs for processing items such as `for`, `while`, and `do` loops. Although these can be useful in some cases, in the next recipe we will use `while` and `do` loops as examples. You can read more about them and view examples using the `get-helpabout_for`, `get-helpabout_while`, and `get-help about_do` commands in the shell.

There's more...

There are some key differences about the `foreach` statement and the `ForEach-Object` cmdlet that you'll want to be aware of when you need to work with loops. First, the `ForEach-Object` cmdlet can process one object at a time as it comes across the pipeline. When you process a collection using the `foreach` statement, this is the exact opposite. The `foreach` statement requires that all of the objects that need to be processed within a loop are collected and stored in memory before processing begins. We'll want to take advantage of the PowerShell pipeline and its streaming behavior whenever possible since it is much more efficient.

The other thing to make note of is that in PowerShell, `foreach` is not only a keyword, but also an alias. This can be a little counterintuitive, especially when you are new to PowerShell and you run into a code sample that uses the following syntax:

```
Get-Mailbox | foreach {$_.Name}
```

At first glance, this might seem like we're using the `foreach` keyword, but we're actually using an alias for the `ForEach-Object` cmdlet. The easiest way to remember this distinction is that the `foreach` language construct is always used before a pipeline. If you use `foreach` after a pipeline, PowerShell will use the `foreach` alias which corresponds to the `ForEach-Object` cmdlet.

Another common loop is the `for` loop; its ideal where the same sequence of statements need to be repeated a specific number of times. Explaining the `for` loop is probably most easily done by illustrating an example:

```
for (initialize; condition; increment) {
code block
}
```

Initialize section - You set a variable with a starting value. In the initialize segment, you can set one or more variables by separating them with commas.

Condition section - The condition is tested each time by PowerShell before it executes the code. If the condition is found to be true, your body of code will be executed. If the condition is found to be false, PowerShell stops executing the code.

Increment section - In this section, you specify how you want the variable to be updated after each run of the loop. This can be an increment or a decrement or any other change you need. After the code has been executed once, PowerShell will update your variable.

The for loop keeps on looping until your conditional turns false, just like the following example:

```
for ($i = 1; $i -le 10; $i++) {
Write-Host $i
}
```

In this example, initially $i is set to a value of 1. The loop will run until $i is less or equal to 10. Our example will write the value for $i on the screen.

Another common loop is the `do while` and `while` loop, this loop executes until the condition value is `True`. This kind of loop can be helpful when moving mailboxes. The loop can then be used for verifying that the move is proceeding as expected and has finished successfully. In that case, the move status would be the condition that the loop is using:

```
do { code block }
  while (condition)
```

The two different sections are shown in the preceding code and they are almost self-explanatory. Under the do section, the code is written; as our following example shows, we are using Write-Host.

Under the while section, the condition is set; in our example, the condition is that $i is less 10:

```
$i = 1
do {  Write-Host $i
  $i++
}
while ($i -le 10)
```

See also

- The *Working with arrays and hash tables* recipe in this chapter
- The *Understanding the pipeline* recipe in this chapter
- The *Creating custom objects* recipe in this chapter

Creating custom objects

The fact that PowerShell is an object-based shell gives us a great deal of flexibility when it comes to writing one-liners, scripts, and functions. When generating detailed reports, we need to be able to customize the data output from our code so it can be formatted or piped to other commands that can export the data in a clean, structured format. We also need to be able to control and customize the output from our code so that we can merge data from multiple sources into a single object. In this recipe, you'll learn a few techniques used to build custom objects.

How to do it...

The first thing we'll do is create a collection of mailbox objects that will be used as the data source for a new set of custom objects:

```
$mailboxes = Get-Mailbox
```

You can add custom properties to any object coming across the pipeline using calculated properties. This can be done using either the Select-Object or Format-Table together with the -AutoSize parameter:

```
$mailboxes |
  Format-Table Name,
    Database,
    @{name="Title";expression={(Get-User $_.Name).Title}},
    @{name="Dept";expression={(Get-User $_.Name).Department}} -AutoSize
```

Another easy way to do this is by assigning a hash table to the -Property parameter of the New-Object cmdlet:

```
$mailboxes | %{
  New-Object PSObject -Property @{
    Name = $_.Name
    Database = $_.Database
    Title = (Get-User $_.Name).Title
    Dept = (Get-User $_.Name).Department
  }
}
```

You can also use the New-Object cmdlet to create an empty custom object, and then use the Add-Member cmdlet to tack on any custom properties that are required:

```
$mailboxes | %{
  $obj = New-Object PSObject
  $obj | Add-Member NoteProperty Name $_.Name
  $obj | Add-Member NoteProperty Database $_.Database
  $obj | Add-Member NoteProperty Title (Get-User $_.Name).Title
  $obj | Add-Member NoteProperty Dept (Get-User $_.Name).Department
  Write-Output $obj
}
```

Each of these three code samples will output the same custom objects that combine data retrieved from both the `Get-Mailbox` and `Get-User` cmdlets. Assuming that the `Title` and `Department` fields have been defined for each user, the output would look similar to the following:

```
Machine: tlex01.testlabs.se                          —    □    ×
[PS] C:\Scripts>$mailboxes |
>>     Format-Table Name,
>>        Database,
>>        @{name="Title";expression={(Get-User $_.Name).Title}},
>>        @{name="Dept";expression={(Get-User $_.Name).Department}} -AutoSize

Name                 Database Title    Dept
----                 -------- -----    ----
Pete Dickson         DB1
Emanuel Moss         DB1
Lee Sanders          DB1
Arlene Finley        DB1
Ruben Mcleod         DB1
testuser             DB2      Manager  Sales
Terrance Randolph    DB1
Tomas Dawson         DB2
Alice Andersson      DB1
Indie Andersson      DB1
Ann Andersson        DB2
Klas Andersson       DB1
Sofie Andersson      DB2
```

How it works...

The reason we're building a custom object here is because we want to merge data from multiple sources into a single object. The `Get-Mailbox` cmdlet does not return the `Title` or `Department` properties that are tied to a user account: the `Get-User` cmdlet needs to be used to retrieve that information. Since we may want to generate a report that includes information from both the `Get-Mailbox` and `Get-User` cmdlets for each individual user, it makes sense to build a custom object that contains all of the required information. We can then pipe these objects to other cmdlets that can be used to export this information to a file.

We can modify one of our previous code samples and pipe the output to a CSV file used to document this information for the current user population:

```
$mailboxes |
  Select-Object Name,
    Database,
    @{n="Title";e={(Get-User $_.Name).Title}},
    @{n="Dept";e={(Get-User $_.Name).Department}} |
      Export-CSV -Path C:\Scripts\report.csv -NoTypeInformation
```

Keep in mind that even though you can also create calculated properties using the Format-Table cmdlet, you'll want to use Select-Object, as shown previously, when converting these objects to CSV or HTML reports. These conversion cmdlets do not understand the formatting information returned by the Format-Table cmdlet, and you'll end up with a lot of useless data if you try to do this.

When building custom objects with the Select-Object cmdlet, we can select existing properties from objects coming across the pipeline and also add one or more calculated properties. This is done using a hash table that defines a custom property name in the hash table key and a script block within the hash table value. The script block is an expression where you can run one or more commands to define the custom property value. In our previous example, you can see that we've called the Get-User cmdlet to retrieve both the Title and Department properties for a user that will be assigned to calculated properties on a new object.

The syntax for creating a calculated property looks a little strange at first glance since it uses name and expression keywords to create a hash table that defines the calculated property. You can abbreviate these keywords as shown next:

```
$mailboxes |
  Select-Object Name,
    Database,
    @{n="Title";e={(Get-User $_.Name).Title}},
    @{n="Dept";e={(Get-User $_.Name).Department}}
```

The property name uses the string value assigned to n, and the property value is assigned to e using a script block. Abbreviating these keywords with n and e just makes it easier to type. You can also use label or l to provide the calculated property name.

Using the New-Object cmdlet and assigning a hash table to the –Property parameter is a quick and easy way to create a custom object. The only issue with this technique is that the properties can be returned in a random order. This is due to how the .NET Framework assigns random numeric values to hash table keys behind the scenes, and the properties are sorted based on those values, not in the order that you've defined them. The only way to get the properties back in the order you want is to continue to pipe the command to Select-Object and select the property names in order, or use one of the other techniques shown in this recipe.

Creating an empty custom object and manually adding note properties with the Add-Member cmdlet can require a lot of extra typing, so generally this syntax is not widely used. This technique becomes useful when you want to add script methods or script properties to a custom object, but this is an advanced technique that we won't need to utilize for the recipes in the remainder of this book.

There's more...

There is another useful technique for creating custom objects which utilizes the `Select-Object` cmdlet. Take a look at the following code:

```
$mailboxes | %{
  $obj = "" | Select-Object Name,Database,Title,Dept
  $obj.Name = $_.Name
  $obj.Database = $_.Database
  $obj.Title = (Get-User $_.Name).Title
  $obj.Dept = (Get-User $_.Name).Department
  Write-Output $obj
}
```

You can create a custom object by piping an empty string variable to the `Select-Object` cmdlet, specifying the property names that should be included. The next step is to simply assign values to the properties of the object using the property names that you've defined. This code loops through the items in our `$mailboxes` object and returns a custom object for each one. The output from this code returns the same exact objects as all of the previous examples.

See also

- The *Looping through items* recipe in this chapter
- The *Working with variables and objects* recipe in this chapter
- The *Exporting reports to text and CSV files* from `Chapter 2`, *Exchange Management Shell Common Tasks*

Using debugger functions

With PowerShell version 5, great functions such as debugging scripts and code in PowerShell were added. This was introduced in Windows Management Framework (WMF) 5.0. In this recipe, we will take a look at it in more depth. This recipe is more a general PowerShell function but can of course be applied to Exchange scripts.

Let us take a look at two of these functions in detail and start with the basics and then advance from there. Both these examples can be used in the PowerShell console and in Windows PowerShell ISE.

The first method we are going to take a look at is called Break All, introduced in PowerShell v5. This method gives us the option to debug the PowerShell workflow and supports command and tab completion. We can debug nested workflow functions both in local and remote sessions.

The second function in this recipe will be to use the Debug-Job cmdlet inside more complex and advanced scripts. It uses the same basis as the Break All function.

How to do it...

First we create a variable named $i with a value of 1 and then create a loop using the Do While operator. The loop will run until $i is less or equal to 20. Within the loop a text string is written to the console with a text Value: and the value of $i.

```
$i = 1
Do {
Write-Host "Value: $i"
    $i++
    Start-Sleep -Milliseconds 200
}
While ($i -le 20)
```

As this is a basic example on how the debugger can be used, this method would be helpful for production when executing scripts. The debugger mode can be used when the script is running by pressing Ctrl + Break or Ctrl + B. When breaking the script, it will look like the following screenshot:

We can see that the script called loop.ps1 is stopped and has entered debug mode. When pressing h or ?, the help information will show up.

In debug mode, we can see the full source code (using l) in the current script; we can also step through every row in the script (using s), step to the next statement (using v), and, of course, continue running the script (using c) or stop the operation and exit debug mode (using q).

How it works...

By initializing the debugging mode, the script is stopped until using either the Continue or Quit commands. The debugging can be very helpful; for example, you can step through the code, view source code, verify variables, view the environment state, and execute commands.

As an example, from the preceding screenshot, let us take a look at what the value in the variable $i is by typing the following:

```
[PS] C:\Scripts>$i
4
```

Here we see that the value was 4 as the loop was stopped at that stage.

 One thing to mention is that the script debugging method will only debug the executed script itself and cannot collect any information from external native commands or scripts and send back the result into the debugging mode. For more advanced debugging, use managed code together with Visual Studio, Visual Studio Code, or WinDbg.

There's more...

Together with the code debugger function, we can use the Debug-Job cmdlet that was introduced in version 5 of PowerShell.

The Debug-Job cmdlet lets you break into the script debugger while running a job in a similar way as the Break All function lets us break into running script from the console or ISE.

A typical scenario where we could use Debug-Job is when we are running a long, complex script as a job and, for one reason or another, we suspect the script is not executing correctly. It may be taking longer than expected or some of the output data doesn't seem right. Now we can drop the job into the debugger by using the Debug-Job which allows us to verify that the code is being executed the way it's expected to do. It's a great and helpful function.

As you probably are aware of, or will face in the future, is that while debugging scripts, interactively they work as expected, but when they are running as jobs in production they fail. However, this can now be debugged with this new feature by setting breakpoints or using the `Wait-Debugger` cmdlet.

In the following example, we are setting a breakpoint at line 4 to debug the script and run it as a job and use the `Debug-Job` cmdlet:

```
$job = Start-Job -ScriptBlock { Set-PSBreakpoint `
C:\Scripts\MyJob.ps1-Line 4; C:\Scripts\MyJob.ps1 `
}
$job
Debug-Job $job
```

By doing this, we will enter debugging mode and can reach variables, execute commands, view the environment state, view source code, and step through the code.

```
Machine: tlex01.testlabs.se                                          —    □    ✕

[PS] C:\Scripts>$job = Start-Job -ScriptBlock { Set-PSBreakpoint C:\Scripts
\MyJob.ps1 -Line 4; C:\Scripts\MyJob.ps1 }
[PS] C:\Scripts>$job

Id     Name           PSJobTypeName    State      HasMoreData    Locat
                                                                 ion
--     ----           -------------    -----      -----------    -----
3      Job3           BackgroundJob    Running    True           lo...


[PS] C:\Scripts>Debug-Job $job
Hit Line breakpoint on 'C:\Scripts\MyJob.ps1:4'

At C:\Scripts\MyJob.ps1:4 char:3
+    $i++
+    ~~~~~
[DBG]: [Job4]: PS C:\Users\administrator.TESTLABS\Documents>> _
```

The preceding screenshot shows that the job state is `AtBreakpoint`, which means that it is waiting to be debugged. The method works similarly to the `Break All method`; it will only debug the script itself and cannot debug any external commands.

To continue the process and leave debugging mode, use the `detach` command.

See also

- The *Understanding the new execution Policy* recipe in this chapter
- The *Creating custom objects* recipe in this chapter
- The *Using the Save-Help function* recipe in this chapter

Understanding the new execution policy

Windows PowerShell implements script security to keep unwanted scripts from running in your environment. You have the option of signing your scripts with a digital signature to ensure that scripts that run are from a trusted source.

The policy has five (Unrestricted, RemoteSigned, AllSigned, Restricted, Default, Bypass, and Undefined) different states to be set in five different scopes (MachinePolicy, UserPolicy, Process, CurrentUser, and LocalMachine).

A short description of the different states and what they can or can't do follows:

- Undefined - There is no execution policy set for the current scope
- Restricted - No script, be it local, remote, or downloaded can be executed
- AllSigned - All script that is run required to be digitally signed
- RemoteSigned - All remote (UNC) or downloaded scripts required to be digitally signed
- Bypass - Nothing is blocked and there are no warnings or prompts
- Unrestricted - All scripts are allowed to be executed

And the following is a description of the different scopes:

- MachinePolicy - The execution policy set by a Group Policy applies to all users
- UserPolicy - The execution policy set by a Group Policy applies to the current user
- Process - The execution policy applies to the current Windows PowerShell process
- CurrentUser - The execution policy applies to the current user
- LocalMachine - The execution policy applies to all users of the computer

Windows PowerShell implements script security to keep unwanted scripts from running in your environment. You have the option of signing your scripts with a digital signature to ensure that scripts that are run are from a trusted source.

It is possible to manage Exchange 2016 through PowerShell remoting on a workstation or server without Exchange Tools installed. In this case, you'll need to make sure your script execution policy is set to either `RemoteSigned` or `Unrestricted`. To set the execution policy, use the following command:

```
Set-ExecutionPolicy RemoteSigned
```

Make sure you do not change the execution policy to `AllSigned` on machines where you'll be using the Exchange cmdlets. This will interfere with importing the commands through a remote PowerShell connection, which is required for the Exchange Management Shell cmdlets to run properly.

How to do it...

The following are some examples of cmdlets that can be used for configuring the execution policy:

```
Get-ExecutionPolicy -List | Format-Table -AutoSize
Set-ExecutionPolicy AllSigned
Set-ExecutionPolicy -Scope CurrentUser -ExecutionPolicy ` RemoteSigned
```

How it works...

The default scope is set to `LocalMachine` if nothing is specified, which means it will apply to everyone on this machine. If the execution policy is set to `Undefined` in all scopes, the effective execution policy is `Restricted`.

We started with listing the current policy settings and then continued with configuring the `LocalMachine` policy to require scripts to be digitally signed or else they will be prohibited from being executed.

The last cmdlet which was used configured the `CurrentUser` to `RemoteSigned` instead of `AllSigned`, which was configured to the `LocalMachine` policy.

Once this change is done, the configuration would look like the following screenshot:

```
Machine: tlex01.testlabs.se                                    —    □    ×
[PS] C:\>Get-ExecutionPolicy -List | Format-Table -AutoSize

        Scope ExecutionPolicy
        ----- ---------------
MachinePolicy       Undefined
   UserPolicy       Undefined
      Process       Undefined
  CurrentUser    RemoteSigned
 LocalMachine    RemoteSigned


[PS] C:\>
```

This makes it possible to have the execution policy configured to require digital signatures for scripts that are being executed by everyone, except the current logged in user.

If you are uncertain as to which user that is logged on, use the whoami command.

There's more...

Since the default execution policy is configured to RemoteSigned, the effect is that all remote (UNC) or downloaded scripts required to be digitally signed.

It is very common that when a script is downloaded, we need to unblock this file before it can be executed when the policy is set to default settings.

Of course, the recommendation before unblocking any downloaded file is to test it in a test environment so it doesn't harm any production environment or it doesn't contain any malicious code in some way:

```
Unblock-File -Path C:\Scripts\HarmlessScript.ps1
Get-ChildItem C:\DownloadFolder | Unblock-File
```

The first line unblocks the specified downloaded file, while the second line retrieves all files from a folder called DownloadFolder and then unblocks them. This, in the end, makes it possible to execute these files with the default configuration.

Unblock-File performs the same operation as the **Unblock** button on the **Properties** dialog box in File Explorer.

For more detailed information, use the Get-Help about_Execution_Policies cmdlet.

See also

- The *Working with the desired state configuration* recipe in this chapter
- The *Working with script repositories* recipe in this chapter
- The *Using the Save-Help function* recipe in this chapter

Using the Save-Help function

The useful help cmdlet, `Get-Help`, can provide useful information and examples. By default, PowerShell retrieves the help files from the internet if they are not available locally.

In PowerShell version 4 of Windows Management Framework (WMF), the function was introduced that made it possible to save the help files and import them into another server or client, which is great when a server or client is prohibited for having internet access.

This can be done with a few commands that will be described in the section *How it works....*

How to do it...

Let's take a look at the following example for updating the help files for the modules that have anything to do with Microsoft.PowerShell:

```
Get-Module -Name Microsoft.PowerShell*
Save-Help -Module Microsoft.PowerShell* -DestinationPath `
"C:\HelpFiles"
Update-Help-SourcePath "C:\Help" -Force
Update-Help -SourcePath "\\fileserver\HelpFilesShare" -Force
```

How it works...

Once the help files are downloaded, each module contains an XML and CAB file. These can be updated per module or all of them at one time. This is a basic task to perform.

In the preceding example, we are first retrieving the modules that are available that have a name of Microsoft.PowerShell followed by something. Then the help files are downloaded for these modules and saved into a local folder called `Help`.

If not specifying any modules, all help files for PowerShell will be downloaded into the specified folder.

Finally, these help files are then imported on another server or client, simply where they are needed by using the Update-Help cmdlet.

As shown in the preceding example, the Update-Help can either be pointing at a local folder or a UNC path or share.

Be aware that when running the Update-Help cmdlet, you may require using the Run as Admin or else it might not have the access needed for importing the files into the system.

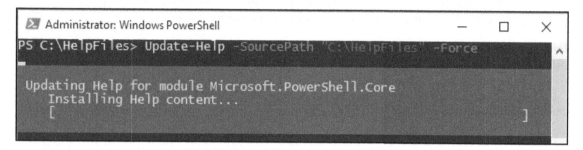

Note that -DestinationPath and -SourcePath should be pointed to a folder and not to a file. The help files contain a pair of XML and CAB files per module.

A good idea would be to always keep these help files up to date and update them in the PowerShell profile to make sure that it's the current version.

See also

- The *Using the help system* recipe in this chapter
- The *Using debugger functions* recipe in this chapter
- The *Creating custom objects* recipe in this chapter

Working with script repositories

Windows Management Framework (WMF) version 5.1 includes a package manager called PowerShellGet, which enabled functionality such as find, get, install, and uninstall packages from internal and public sources. However, this recipe is not specific to Exchange. See this recipe as a tips and tricks recipe, since it's more PowerShell general than Exchange specific.

PowerShellGet is a package manager for Windows PowerShell. Basically, it is a wrapper around the Package Manager component which simplifies the package management for PowerShell modules. PowerShellGet is built on top of the well-known package management solution, NuGet.

Package Manager is a unified package management component which allows you to search for software install, uninstall, and inventory of any type of software that it supports through the provider interface.

Package Manager works with the community based software repository called PowerShell Gallery. Currently PowerShell Gallery has more than 1,500 unique packages to download and use for free.

Chocolatey is also still available; it's also a community based software repository. Some examples of how to use these can be found in the There's more section.

There are a bunch of galleries (also referred to as providers) to use and select between, such as Chocolatey, PowerShell Resource Gallery (Microsoft supported), MyGet, Inedo ProGet, JFrog Artifactory, and many more.

For a better understanding, let's take a look at the first example.

How to do it...

In this example, we will use PowerShellGet to install two example modules from PowerShell Gallery:

```
Import-Module -Name PackageManagement
Get-Command -Module PackageManagement
Find-Package | Out-GridView
Find-Package -Name "AzureAD"
Find-Package -Name "GetUptime"
Install-Package -Name "AzureAD"
Install-Package -Name "GetUptime"
Get-Package -ProviderName PowerShellGet
```

How it works...

For illustrating how the Package Manager works, see the preceding example.

First we imported the module of Package Management, for using the cmdlets for the Package Manager. We then used the `Get-Command` cmdlet to see what commands are available with this module.

With the `Find-Package` cmdlet, we searched for the available packages. First we piped the results to a `GridView`, since this can be user friendly to watch instead of text. Once we found the packages we were looking for (in this example Notepad++ and 7zip), we were using the `Install-Package` cmdlet to install these packages. The following screenshot shows when the installation had taken place, the packages were now available for use and could be found from the start button.

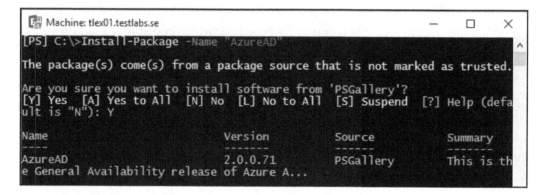

Once the packages/modules have been successfully installed they can be imported and utilized by using the following cmdlets:

```
Import-Module GetUptime
Get-Command -Module GetUptime
Get-Uptime
```

The following screenshot shows an example of the `GetUptime` module, where the module shows the server uptime:

Once the packages are in place and it has been verified that everything is working as expected, let's finalize this by uninstalling them. Some examples of cmdlets for uninstalling packages are shown here:

```
Uninstall-Package -Name "AzureAD"
Uninstall-Package -Name "GetUptime"
```

There's more...

We have now been using the built-in package manager based on PowerShellGet. In the previous book called "Microsoft Exchange Server PowerShell Cookbook - Third Edition", we also used Chocolatey, where we can install third-party rich applications.

We'll take a look at how we can utilize chocolatey with Windows 2016 Server and Exchange 2016:

```
iwr https://chocolatey.org/install.ps1 -UseBasicParsing | iex
choco upgrade chocolatey
choco install notepadplusplus.install
choco upgrade notepadplusplus.install
choco uninstall notepadplusplus.install
choco install 7zip.install
choco upgrade 7zip.install
choco uninstall 7zip.install
```

In the preceding examples, we start by installing chocolatey. The second cmdlet is used for upgrading the existing installation of chocolatey. This is followed by two examples of how to install, upgrade, and uninstall two third-party application packages (Notepad++ and 7zip).

Chocolatey is great in many ways, but probably most companies, or at least enterprise companies, want to have their own "internal", more trusted and reliable repository, but still hosted on the internet.

Let's take a look at how this can be established. First let's sign up for an account at an optional provider.

In my case, I've used http://www.myget.org as the provider and created a feed when the account was created.

Now, let's see how the feed can be used as a repository. The feed that was created had an URL of: https://www.myget.org/F/t1powershell/. Once it's created, we have to register it as a repository in PowerShell using the Register-PSRepository cmdlet:

```
Register-PSRepository -Name MyGet -SourceLocation `
https://www.myget.org/F/t1powershell/api/v1 `
-PublishLocation https://www.myget.org/F/t1powershell/ `
-InstallationPolicy Trusted
Find-Package -Source MyGet
```

Since the MyGet repository is brand new, there are currently no packages. So the next action is to upload a package to MyGet. For being able to upload a module, the module itself should have a file extension of .psm1 together with the module manifest using an extension of .psd1. In the manifest, it's necessary to include the values of Author and Description, but I want to recommend that the value of RootModule, ModuleVersion, and CompanyName, are also included. The following examples show how the manifest was created and also how the modules were published to MyGet.

```
New-ModuleManifest -Path `
C:\Windows\System32\WindowsPowerShell\v1.0\Modules\mailboxes.psd1` -Author
"Jonas Andersson" -CompanyName "Testlabs, Inc." `
 -RootModule "mailboxes" -Description `
"Module that lists mailboxes" -ModuleVersion "1.0"
    Import-Module PowerShellGet

$PSGalleryPublishUri = `
'https://www.myget.org/F/t1powershell/api/v2/package'
$PSGallerySourceUri = ` 'https://www.myget.org/F/t1powershell/api/v2'


    Publish-Module -Name mailboxes -NuGetApiKey `
a2d5b281-c862-4125-9523-be42ef21f55a -Repository MyGet
    Find-Package -Source MyGet
    Install-Package -Name "mailboxes" -Source MyGet
```

Before ending this recipe, we might want to remove the repository for some reason. This is done simply by running the following cmdlet:

```
Unregister-PSRepository -Name MyGet
```

See also

- The *Understanding the new execution policy* recipe in this chapter
- The *Creating custom objects* recipe in this chapter

2
Exchange Management Shell Common Tasks

In this chapter, we will cover:

- Manually configuring remote PowerShell connections
- Using explicit credentials with PowerShell cmdlets
- Transferring files through remote shell connections
- Managing domains or an entire forest using a recipient scope
- Exporting reports to text and CSV files
- Sending SMTP emails through PowerShell
- Scheduling scripts to run at a later time
- Logging shell sessions to a transcript
- Automating tasks with the scripting agent
- Scripting an Exchange Server installation

Introduction

Microsoft introduced some radical architectural changes in Exchange 2007, including a brand-new set of management tools. PowerShell, along with an additional set of Exchange Server specific cmdlets, finally gave administrators an interface that could be used to manage the entire product from a command line shell. This was an interesting move, and at that time the entire graphical management console was built on top of this technology.

The same architecture still existed with Exchange 2010, and PowerShell was even more tightly integrated with this product. Exchange 2010 used PowerShell v2, which relied heavily on its new remoting infrastructure. This provides seamless administrative capabilities from a single seat with the Exchange Management Tools, whether your servers are on-premises or in the cloud.

Initially when Exchange 2013 was released, it was using version 4 of PowerShell, and, during the life cycle, it could be updated to version 5 of PowerShell with a lot of new cmdlets, core functionality changes, and even more integrations with the cloud services.

Now with Exchange 2016, we have even more cmdlets and even more integrations with cloud-related integration and services. During the initial work on this book, we had 839 cmdlets with Cumulative Update 4 which was released in December 2016. This can be compared with the previous book, where at that stage we had 806 cmdlets based on Service Pack 1 and Cumulative Update 7.

It gives us an impression that Microsoft is working heavily on the integrations and that the development of the on-premises product is still ongoing. This demonstrates that more features and functionality have been added over time. It will most likely continue like this in the future as well.

In this chapter, we'll cover some of the most common topics, as well as common tasks, that will allow you to effectively write scripts with this latest release. We'll also take a look at some general tasks such as scheduling scripts, sending emails, generating reports, and more.

Performing some basic steps

To work with the code samples in this chapter, follow these steps to launch the Exchange Management Shell:

1. Log onto a workstation or server with the Exchange Management Tools installed.
2. You can connect using remote PowerShell if, for some reason, you don't have Exchange Management Tools installed. Use the following command:

```
$Session = New-PSSession -ConfigurationName Microsoft.Exchange `
-ConnectionUri http://servername/PowerShell/ `
-Authentication Kerberos
Import-PSSession $Session
```

3. Alternatively, open the Exchange Management Shell by clicking the Windows button and go to **Microsoft Exchange Server 2016 | Exchange Management Shell**.

Remember to start the Exchange Management Shell using **Run as Administrator** to avoid permission problems. In the chapter, notice that in the examples of cmdlets, I have used the back tick (`) character for breaking up long commands into multiple lines. The purpose of this is to make it easier to read. The back ticks are not required and should only be used if needed. Notice that the Exchange variables, such as $exscripts, are not available when using the preceding method.

Manually configuring remote PowerShell connections

Just like Exchange 2013, Exchange 2016 is very reliant on remote PowerShell for both on-premises and cloud services. When you double-click the Exchange Management Shell shortcut on a server or workstation with the Exchange Management Tools installed, you are connected to an Exchange server using a remote PowerShell session.

PowerShell remoting also allows you to remotely manage your Exchange servers from a workstation or a server even when the Exchange Management Tools are not installed. In this recipe, we'll create a manual remote shell connection to an Exchange server using a standard PowerShell console.

Getting ready

To complete the steps in this recipe, you'll need to log on to a workstation or a server and launch Windows PowerShell.

How to do it...

1. First, create a credential object using the `Get-Credential` cmdlet. When running this command, you'll be prompted with a Windows authentication dialog box. Enter a username and password for an account that has administrative access to your Exchange organization. Make sure you enter your user name in DOMAIN\USERNAME or UPN format (username@domain.com):

```
$credential = Get-Credential
```

2. Next, create a new session object and store it in a variable. In this example, the Exchange server we are connecting to is specified using the `-ConnectionUri` parameter. Replace the server FQDN in the following example with one of your own Exchange servers:

```
$session = New-PSSession -ConfigurationName Microsoft.Exchange `
-ConnectionUri http://tlex01.testlabs.se/PowerShell/ `
-Credential $credential
```

3. Finally, import the session object:

```
Import-PSSession $session -AllowClobber
```

4. After you execute the preceding command, the Exchange Management Shell cmdlets will be imported into your current Windows PowerShell session, as shown in the following screenshot:

How it works...

Each server runs IIS and supports remote PowerShell sessions through HTTP. Exchange servers host a PowerShell virtual directory in IIS. This contains several modules that perform authentication checks and determine which cmdlets and parameters are assigned to the user making the connection. This happens both when running the Exchange Management Shell with the tools installed, and when creating a manual remote connection. The IIS virtual directory that is being used for connecting is shown in the following screenshot:

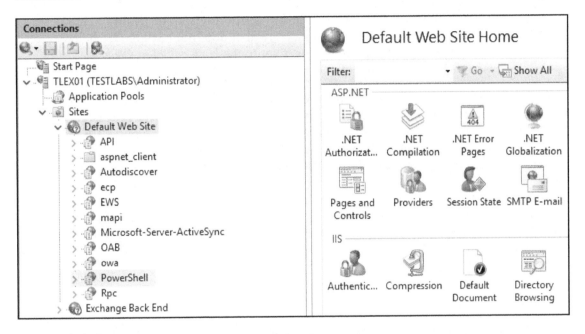

The IIS virtual directories can also be retrieved by using PowerShell with the cmdlet Get-WebVirtualDirectory. For getting the information about the web applications, use the cmdlet Get-WebApplication.

Remote PowerShell connections to Exchange 2016 servers connect almost the same way as Exchange 2013 did. This is called implicit remoting that allows us to import remote commands into the local shell session. With this feature, we can use the Exchange PowerShell cmdlets installed on the Exchange server and load the cmdlets into our local PowerShell session without installing any management tools.

However, the detailed behavior for establishing a remote PowerShell session was changed in Exchange 2013 CU11. What happens right now when a user or admin is trying to establish the PowerShell session is that it first tries to connect to the user's or admin's mailbox (anchor mailbox), if there are any. If the user doesn't have an existing mailbox, the PowerShell request will be redirected to the organization arbitration mailbox named `SystemMailbox{bb558c35-97f1-4cb9-8ff7-d53741dc928c}`. More information about this behavior change can be found on the Microsoft Exchange Team Blog at: `https://blogs.technet.microsoft.com/exchange/2016/03/01/remote-powershell-proxying-behavior-in-exchange-2013-cu12-and-exchange-2016/`.

> You'll need to allow the execution of scripts in order to create a manual remote shell connection on a machine that does not have the Exchange tools installed. For more details, refer to the *Understanding the new execution policy* recipe in `Chapter 1`, *PowerShell Key Concepts*.

You may be curious as to why Exchange uses remote PowerShell even when the tools are installed and when running the shell from the server. There are a couple of reasons for this, but some of the main factors are permissions. The Exchange 2010, 2013, and 2016 permissions model has been completely transformed in these latest versions and uses a feature called **Role Based Access Control** (**RBAC**), which defines what administrators can and cannot do. When you make a remote PowerShell connection to an Exchange 2016 server, the RBAC authorization module in IIS determines which cmdlets and parameters you have access to. Once this information is obtained, only the cmdlets and parameters that have been assigned to your account through an RBAC role are loaded into your PowerShell session using implicit remoting.

There's more...

In the previous example, we explicitly set the credentials used to create the remote shell connection. This is optional and not required if the account you are currently logged on with has the appropriate Exchange permissions assigned. To create a remote shell session using your currently logged on credentials, use the following syntax to create the session object:

```
$session = New-PSSession -ConfigurationName Microsoft.Exchange `
-ConnectionUri http://tlex01.testlabs.se/PowerShell/
```

Once again, import the session:

```
Import-PSSession $session
```

When the tasks have been completed, remove the session:

```
Remove-PSSession $session
```

You can see here that the commands are almost identical to the previous example, except this time we've removed the -Credential parameter and used the assigned credential object. After this is done, you can simply import the session and the commands will be imported into your current session using implicit remoting.

In addition to implicit remoting, Exchange 2016 servers running PowerShell v5 or above can also be managed using fan-out remoting. This is accomplished using the Invoke-Command cmdlet and it allows you to execute a script block on multiple computers in parallel. For more details, run Get-Help Invoke-Command and Get-Help about_remoting.

Since Exchange Online is commonly used by Microsoft customers nowadays, let's take a look at an example on how to connect as well. It's very similar to connecting to remote PowerShell on-premises. The following prerequisites are required: .NET Framework 4.5 or 4.5.1 and then either Windows Management Framework 3.0 or 4.0.

Create a variable of the credentials:

```
$UserCredential = Get-Credential
```

Create a session variable:

```
$session = New-PSSession -ConfigurationName Microsoft.Exchange `
-ConnectionUri https://outlook.office365.com/powershell-liveid/ `
-Credential $UserCredential -Authentication Basic `
-AllowRedirection
```

Finally, import the session:

```
Import-PSSession $session -AllowClobber
```

Perform the tasks you want to do:

```
Get-Mailbox
```

Exchange Online mailboxes are shown in the following screenshot:

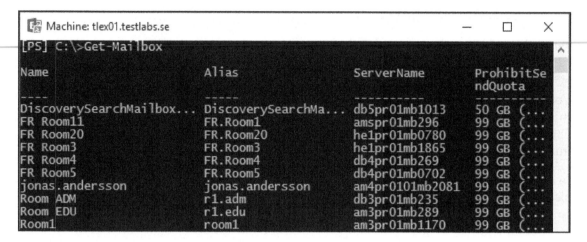

When the tasks have been completed, remove the session:

```
Remove-PSSession $session
```

See also

- The *Using explicit credentials with PowerShell cmdlets* recipe in this chapter

Using explicit credentials with PowerShell cmdlets

There are several PowerShell and Exchange Management Shell cmdlets that provide a credential parameter that allows you to use an alternate set of credentials when running a command. You may need to use alternate credentials when making manual remote shell connections, sending email messages, working in cross-forest scenarios, and more. In this recipe, we'll take a look at how you can create a credential object that can be used with commands that support the -Credential parameter.

How to do it...

To create a credential object, we can use the `Get-Credential` cmdlet. In this example, we store the credential object in a variable that can be used by the `Get-Mailbox` cmdlet:

```
$credential = Get-Credential
Get-Mailbox -Credential $credential
```

How it works...

When you run the `Get-Credential` cmdlet, you are presented with a Windows authentication dialog box requesting your username and password. In the previous example, we assigned the `Get-Credential` cmdlet to the `$credential` variable. After typing your username and password into the authentication dialog box, the credentials are saved as an object that can then be assigned to the `-Credential` parameter of a cmdlet. The cmdlet that utilizes the credential object will then run using the credentials of the specified user.

Supplying credentials to a command doesn't have to be an interactive process. You can programmatically create a credential object within your script without using the `Get-Credential` cmdlet:

```
$user = "testlabs\administrator"
$pass = ConvertTo-SecureString -AsPlainText P@ssw0rd01 -Force
$credential = New-Object ` System.Management.Automation.PSCredential `
-ArgumentList $user,$pass
```

You can see here that we've created a credential object from scratch without using the `Get-Credential` cmdlet. In order to create a credential object, we need to supply the password as a secure string type. The `ConvertTo-SecureString` cmdlet can be used to create a secure string object. We then use the `New-Object` cmdlet to create a credential object specifying the desired username and password as arguments.

If you need to prompt a user for their credentials but you do not want to invoke the Windows authentication dialog box, you can use this alternative syntax to prompt the user in the shell for their credentials:

```
$user = Read-Host "Please enter your username"
$pass = Read-Host "Please enter your password" -AsSecureString
$credential = New-Object ` System.Management.Automation.PSCredential-
ArgumentList ` $user,$pass
```

This syntax uses the `Read-Host` cmdlet to prompt the user for both their username and password. Notice that when creating the `$pass` object, we use `Read-Host` with the `-AsSecureString` parameter to ensure that the object is stored as a secure string.

There's more...

After you've created a credential object, you may need to access the properties of that object to retrieve the username and password. We can access the username and password properties of the `$credential` object created previously using the following commands:

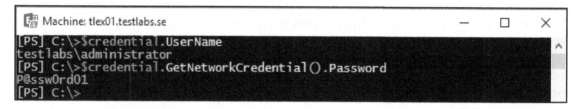

```
[PS] C:\>$credential.UserName
testlabs\administrator
[PS] C:\>$credential.GetNetworkCredential().Password
P@ssw0rd01
[PS] C:\>
```

You can see here that we can simply grab the username stored in the object by accessing the `UserName property` of the credential object. Since the `Password` property is stored as a secure string, we need to use the `GetNetworkCredential` method to convert the credential to a `NetworkCredential` object that exposes the `Password` property as a simple string.

Another powerful method for managing passwords for scripts is to encrypt them and store them into a text file. This can be easily done using the following example.

The password is stored into a variable:

```
$secureString = Read-Host -AsSecureString "Enter a secret password"
```

The variable gets converted from `SecureString` and saved to a text file:

```
$secureString | ConvertFrom-SecureString | Out-File
.\storedPassword.txt
```

The content in the text file is retrieved and converted into a `SecureString` value:

```
$secureString = Get-Content .\storedPassword.txt | ConvertTo-
SecureString
```

See also

- The *Transferring files through remote shell connections* recipe in this chapter
- The *Manually configuring remote PowerShell connections* recipe in this chapter

Transferring files through remote shell connections

Since the Exchange 2016 Management Shell commands are executed through a remote PowerShell session, importing and exporting files requires a new special syntax. There are a handful of shell cmdlets that require this, and, in this recipe, we'll take a look at the syntax that needs to be used to transfer files through a remote shell connection.

How to do it...

Let's say that we are about to import a certificate to the Exchange server, more specifically the client access services. We can import the file using the Get-Content cmdlet, using syntax similar to the following:

```
[byte[]]$data = Get-Content -Path ".\ExportedCert.pfx" `
-Encoding Byte `
-ReadCount 0
$password = Get-Credential
Import-ExchangeCertificate -FileData $data -Password $password.Password
```

In this example, the file data is first read into a variable called $data. The certificate import is done by using the Import-ExchangeCertificate cmdlet by signing the $data variable as a value to the -FileData parameter.

How it works...

When you launch the Exchange 2016 Management Shell, special commands called proxy functions are imported into your local shell session. These proxy functions represent the compiled cmdlets that are actually installed on your Exchange server. When you run these commands, any data required for input through parameters are transferred through a remote connection from your machine to the server and the command is then executed. Since the commands are actually running on the server and not on your machine, we cannot use a local path for files that need to be imported.

In the previous example, you can see that we first stored the file data in a variable. What we are doing here is reading the file content into the variable using the Get-Content cmdlet in order to create a byte-encoded object. This variable is then assigned to the cmdlet's -FileData parameter, which requires a byte-encoded value.

There are a number of Exchange Management Shell cmdlets that include a -FileData parameter used to provide external files as input:

- Import-DlpPolicyCollection: Used for importing DLP policy collections into the organization
- Import-DlpPolicyTemplate: Used for importing DLP policy template into the organization
- Import-ExchangeCertificate: Used for importing certificates
- Import-JournalRuleCollection: Imports a collection of journal rules
- Import-RecipientDataProperty: Used for importing photos or audio into Active Directory
- Import-TransportRuleCollection: Allows you to import a collection of transport rules
- Import-UMPrompt: Imports custom audio files to UM feature

This is a good example of how remote PowerShell sessions have changed behavior since back in Exchange 2010. For example, if you have worked with the shell in Exchange 2007, you may remember the Import-ExchangeCertificate cmdlet. This cmdlet used to accept a local file path when importing a certificate into a server, but due to the new remoting functionality, the commands used to perform this task have changed, even though the cmdlet name is still the same.

There's more...

We also have to take remote shell connections into consideration when exporting data. For example, let's say that we need to export the user photo associated with a mailbox from Active Directory. The command would look something like this:

```
Export-RecipientDataProperty -Identity tdawson-Picture | %{
   $_.FileData | Add-Content C:\pics\tdawson.jpg -Encoding Byte
}
```

When using the `Export-RecipientDataProperty` cmdlet with the `-Picture` switch parameter, the photo can be retrieved from the `FileData` property of the object returned. The photo data is stored in this property as a byte array. In order to export the data, we need to loop through each element stored in this property and use the `Add-Content` cmdlet to re-construct the image to an external file.

When dealing with cmdlets that import or export data, make sure you utilize the help system. Remember, you can run `Get-Help <cmdlet name> -Examples` with any of these cmdlets to determine the correct syntax.

See also

- The *Using the help system* recipe from Chapter 1, *PowerShell Key Concepts*
- The *Manually configuring remote PowerShell connections* recipe in this chapter
- The *Importing user photos into Active Directory* recipe from Chapter 3, *Managing Recipients*

Managing domains or an entire forest using a recipient scope

The Exchange Management Tools can be configured to use specific portions of your Active Directory hierarchy using a specific recipient scope. When you set the recipient scope to a location in Active Directory, such as a domain or an organizational unit, the Exchange Management Shell will only allow you to view the recipients that are stored in that location and any containers beneath it. In this recipe, we'll look at how to set the recipient scope when working with the Exchange Management Shell.

How to do it...

1. We can set the recipient scope in the Exchange Management Shell using the `Set-AdServerSettings` cmdlet. For example, to set the recipient scope to the *Sales* OU in the `testlabs.se` domain, use the following command:

    ```
    Set-AdServerSettings -RecipientViewRoot testlabs.se/sales
    ```

2. We can also specify the value using the distinguished name of the OU:

    ```
    Set-AdServerSettings -RecipientViewRoot `
    "OU=sales,DC=testlabs,DC=se"
    ```

How it works...

When you first start the Exchange Management Shell, the default recipient scope is set to the domain of the computer that is running the shell. If you change the recipient scope, the setting will not be retained when you restart the shell. The default domain scope will always be used when you launch the shell. You can override this by adding these commands to your PowerShell profile to ensure that the setting is always initially configured as needed.

In the previous example, we set the recipient scope to a specific OU in the domain. If you are working in a multi-domain forest, you can use the `-ViewEntireForest` parameter so that all recipient objects in the forest can be managed from your shell session. Use the following command to view the entire forest:

```
Set-AdServerSettings -ViewEntireForest $true
```

To change the recipient scope to a specific domain, set the `-RecipientViewRoot` to the full qualified domain name of the Active Directory domain:

```
Set-AdServerSettings -RecipientViewRoot corp.testlabs.se
```

There's more...

If you're working in a large environment with multiple domains and OUs, setting the recipient scope can improve the speed of the Exchange Management Shell, since it will limit the total number of recipients returned by your commands.

If you have Exchange recipients in multiple Active Directory domains or sites, you may have to take replication latency into account when working with a broad recipient scope. To handle this, you can use the `Set-AdServerSettings` cmdlet to specify domain controllers and global catalog servers that you want to work with.

To set the preferred domain controllers and global catalog that should be used with your recipient scope, use the `-SetPreferredDomainControllers` and `-PreferredGlobalCatalog` parameters to specify the FQDN of the servers:

```
Set-AdServerSettings -ViewEntireForest $true `
-SetPreferredDomainControllers dc1.testlabs.se `
-PreferredGlobalCatalog dc1.testlabs.se
```

Setting the preferred domain controller can be useful to ensure your commands will read the latest list of recipients in Active Directory. If you have a provisioning process that uses a specific domain controller when creating recipients, it may take some time to replicate this information throughout the forest. Setting the preferred domain controllers can be used to ensure that you are working with the latest set of recipients available, even if they haven't been replicated throughout the forest.

Exporting reports to text and CSV files

One of the added benefits of the Exchange Management Shell is the ability to run very detailed and customizable reports. With the hundreds of `Get-*` cmdlets provided between Windows PowerShell and the Exchange Management Shell, the reporting capabilities are almost endless. In this recipe, we'll cover exporting command output to plain text and CSV files that can be used to report on various resources throughout your Exchange environment.

How to do it...

1. To export command output to a text file, use the `Out-File` cmdlet.
2. To generate a report of mailboxes in a specific mailbox database that can be stored in a text file, use the following command:

```
Get-Mailbox | Select-Object Name,Alias | Out-File c:\report.txt
```

3. You can also save the output of the previous command as a CSV file that can then be opened and formatted in Microsoft Excel:

```
Get-Mailbox | Select-Object Name,Alias | `
    Export-CSV c:\report.csv -NoType
```

How it works...

The `Out-File` cmdlet is simply a redirection command that will export the output of your command to a plain text file. Perhaps one of the most useful features of this cmdlet is the ability to add data to the end of an existing file using the `-Append` parameter. This allows you to continuously update a text file when processing multiple objects or creating persistent log files or reports.

You can also use the `Add-Content`, `Set-Content`, and `Clear-Content` cmdlets to add, replace, or remove data from files.

The `Export-CSV` cmdlet converts the object's output, by your command, into a collection of comma-separated values and stores them in a CSV file. When we ran the `Get-Mailbox` cmdlet in the previous example, we filtered the output, selecting only the `Name` and `Alias` properties. When exporting, this output using `Export-CSV`, these property names are used for the column headers. Each object returned by the command will be represented in the CSV file as an individual row, therefore populating the `Name` and `Alias` columns with the associated data.

You may have noticed in the `Export-CSV` example that we used the `-NoType` switch parameter. This is commonly-used and is a shorthand notation for the full parameter name `-NoTypeInformation`. If you do not specify this switch parameter, the first line of the CSV file will contain a header specifying the .NET Framework type of the object that was exported. This is rarely useful. If you end up with a strange-looking header in one of your reports, remember to run the command again using the `-NoTypeInformation` switch parameter.

There's more...

One of the most common problems that Exchange administrators run into with `Export-CSV` is when exporting objects with multi-valued properties. Let's say we need to run a report that lists each mailbox and its associated email addresses. The command would look something like the following:

```
Get-Mailbox | `
  Select-Object Name,EmailAddresses | `
    Export-CSV c:\report.csv -NoType
```

The problem here is that each mailbox can contain multiple email addresses. When we select the `EmailAddresses` property, a multi-valued object is returned. The `Export-CSV` cmdlet does not understand how to handle this, and when you import the CSV file in PowerShell, you'll end up with a CSV file that looks like the following:

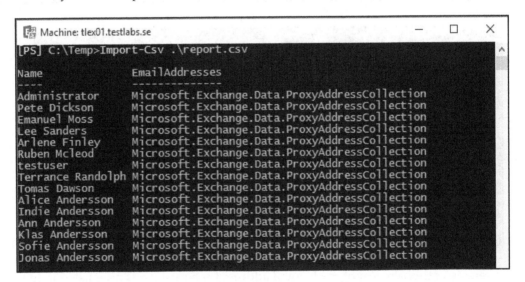

Looking at this screenshot, you can see that on the first line, we have our header names that match the properties selected during the export. In the first column, the `Name` property for each mailbox has been recorded correctly, but, as you can see, the values listed in the `EmailAddresses` column have a problem. Instead of the email addresses, we get the .NET Framework type name of the multi-valued property. To get around this, we need to help the `Export-CSV` cmdlet understand what we are trying to do and specifically reference the data that needs to be exported.

One of the best ways to handle this is to use a calculated property and join each value of the multi-valued property as a single string:

```
Get-Mailbox | `
Select-Object Name,@{n="Email";e={$_.EmailAddresses -Join ";"}}` |
Export-CSV c:\report1.csv -NoType
```

In this example, we've modified the previous command by creating a calculated property that will contain each email address for the associated mailbox. Since we need to consolidate the `EmailAddresses` property data into a single item that can be exported, we use the `-Join` operator to create a string containing a list, separated by semi-colons, of every email address associated with each mailbox. The command is then piped to the `Export-CSV` cmdlet, and the report is generated in a readable format that can be viewed using the `Import-CSV` cmdlet:

```
Machine: tlex01.testlabs.se                              —    □    ×

[PS] C:\Temp>Import-Csv .\report1.csv

Name                    Email
----                    -----
Administrator           SMTP:Administrator@testlabs.se
Pete Dickson            SMTP:pdickson@testlabs.se
Emanuel Moss            SMTP:emoss@testlabs.se
Lee Sanders             SMTP:lsanders@testlabs.se
Arlene Finley           SMTP:afinley@testlabs.se
Ruben Mcleod            SMTP:rmcleod@testlabs.se
testuser                SMTP:testuser@testlabs.se
Terrance Randolph       SMTP:trandolph@testlabs.se
Tomas Dawson            SMTP:tdawson@testlabs.se
Alice Andersson         SMTP:alice@testlabs.se
Indie Andersson         SMTP:indie@testlabs.se
Ann Andersson           SMTP:ann@testlabs.se
Klas Andersson          SMTP:klas@testlabs.se
Sofie Andersson         SMTP:sofie@testlabs.se
Jonas Andersson         smtp:jonas.andersson@testlabs.se;SMTP:jonas@testlabs.se
```

As you can see in this screenshot, each email address for a mailbox is now listed in the `Email` column and is separated using a semi-colon. Each address has an SMTP prefix associated with it. An SMTP prefix in all capital letters indicates that the address is the primary SMTP address for the mailbox. Any remaining secondary addresses use an SMTP prefix in lowercase characters. If you do not want to export the prefixes, we can modify our code even further:

```
Get-Mailbox | `
  select-Object Name, `
    @{n="Email"; `
      e={($_.EmailAddresses | %{$_.SmtpAddress}) -Join ";"} `
    } | Export-CSV c:\report2.csv -NoType
```

Here you can see that within the expression of the calculated property, we're looping through the EmailAddresses collection and retrieving only the SmtpAddress, which does not include the SMTP prefix and returns only the email addresses. Once the data is exported to a CSV file, we can review it using the Import-CSV cmdlet:

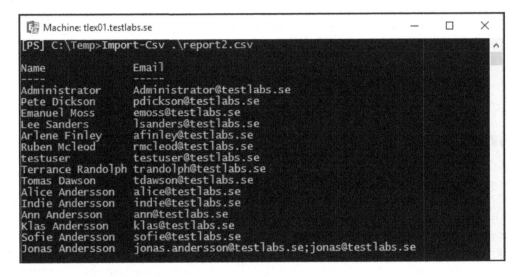

As you can see here, we now get each email address associated with each mailbox without the SMTP prefix within the Email column of our CSV file.

See also

- The *Working with arrays and hash tables* recipe from Chapter 1, *PowerShell Key Concepts*
- The *Creating custom objects* recipe from Chapter 1, *PowerShell Key Concepts*

Sending SMTP emails through PowerShell

As an Exchange administrator, you will probably need an automated solution for sending emails from your PowerShell scripts. Whether it's for sending notifications to users in a specific database or emailing the output of your scripts to a reporting mailbox, the transmission of messages like these will prove very useful in performing common day-to-day administrative scripting tasks. In this recipe, we'll take a look at how you can send SMTP email messages from PowerShell to the recipients in your Exchange organization.

How to do it...

PowerShell v2 and later includes a core cmdlet that can be used to send email messages through SMTP to one or more recipients. Use the following syntax to send an email message:

```
Send-MailMessage -To user1@testlabs.se `
-From administrator@testlabs.se `
-Subject "Test E-mail" `
-Body "This is just a test" `
-SmtpServer tlex01.testlabs.se
```

How it works...

In PowerShell v1, the `Send-MailMessage` cmdlet didn't exist. In the early days before Exchange 2007 SP2 and PowerShell v2 support, we had to use the classes in the `System.Net.Mail` namespace in the .NET Framework to send SMTP email messages. This was difficult for some administrators because working with .NET classes can be confusing without prior programming experience. The good news is that the `Send-MailMessage` cmdlet utilizes these same .NET classes that allow you to create rich email messages that can contain one or more attachments, using an HTML formatted message body, support message priority, and more. Here are some of the more useful parameters that can be used with the `Send-MailMessage` cmdlet:

- `Attachments`: This specifies the path to the file that should be attached. It separates multiple attachments with a comma.
- `Bcc`: This allows you to specify a blind-copy recipient. It separates multiple recipients using a comma.
- `Body`: This specifies the content of a message.
- `BodyAsHtml`: This is a switch parameter that ensures the message will use an HTML-formatted message body.
- `Cc`: This allows you to specify a carbon-copy recipient. It separates multiple recipients using a comma.
- `Credential`: You can provide a `PSCredential` object created by the `Get-Credential` cmdlet to send the message using the credentials of another user.
- `DeliveryNotificationOption`: This specifies the delivery notification options for the message. The default value is **None**, but other valid options are **OnSuccess**, **OnFailure**, **Delay**, and **Never**.
- `Encoding`: This specifies the encoding of the email, such as S/MIME and non-MIME character sets.

- `From`: This is the email address of the sender. You can define a display name using the following format: `Dave <dave@contoso.com>`.
- `Priority`: This specifies the importance of the message. The default value is **Normal**. The remaining valid values are **High** and **Low**.
- `SmtpServer`: This needs to be the name or IP address of your SMTP server. When working in an Exchange environment, this will be set to one of your Hub Transport servers.
- `Subject`: This is the subject of the email message.
- `To`: This allows you to specify an email recipient. It separates multiple recipients with a comma.
- `UseSsl`: This allows you to specify that the connection should be established using SSL.
- `Port`: This allows you to specify an alternate port for the SMTP server.

There's more...

When using this cmdlet, you'll need to specify an SMTP server in order to submit the message. Unless you are already using some type of mail relay system within your environment, you'll want to use a Mailbox server in your Exchange organization. Out of the box, Exchange servers will not allow workstations or untrusted servers to relay email messages. Depending on where you are sending the message from, you may need to allow the machine running your scripts to relay the email.

PowerShell v2 and later includes a preference variable called `$PSEmailServer` that can be assigned the name or IP address of an SMTP server. When this variable is defined, you can omit the `-SmtpServer` parameter when using the `Send-MailMessage` cmdlet. You can add this variable assignment to your PowerShell profile so that the setting will persist across all of your shell sessions.

Sending messages with attachments

You may want to write a script that generates a report to a text or CSV file and then email that data to an administrator mailbox. The `-Attachment` parameter can be used with the `Send-MailMessage` cmdlet to do this. For example, let's say you've generated a CSV report file for the top 10 largest mailboxes in your environment and it needs to be emailed to your staff. The following command syntax could be used in this scenario:

```
Send-MailMessage -To support@testlabs.se `
-From powershell@testlabs.se `
```

```
-Subject "Mailbox Report for $((Get-Date).ToShortDateString())" `
-Body "Please review the attached mailbox report." `
-Attachments c:\report.csv `
-SmtpServer tlex01.testlabs.se
```

Notice that all we need to do here is provide the path and filename to the -Attachment parameter. You can send multiple message attachments this way by providing a comma-separated list of files.

Sending command output in the body of a message

Instead of exporting command data to an external file and sending it as an attachment, you may want to add this information to the body of an email. In this example, we'll send a message that displays the top 10 largest mailboxes in the organization in the body of an HTML-formatted message:

```
[string]$report = Get-MailboxDatabase |
Get-MailboxStatistics| ?{(!$_.DisconnectDate) -and ` ($_.DisplayName -
notlike "*HealthMailbox*")} |
      Sort-Object TotalItemSize -Desc |
        Select-Object DisplayName,Database,TotalItemSize -First 10 |
        ConvertTo-Html
Send-MailMessage -To support@testlabs.se `
-From powershell@testlabs.se `
-Subject "Mailbox Report for $((Get-Date).ToShortDateString())" `
-Body $report `
-BodyAsHtml `
-SmtpServer tlex01.testlabs.se
```

Here you can see that the report data is generated with a fairly sophisticated one-liner and the output is saved in a string variable called $report. We need to strongly type the $report variable as a string because that is the data type required by the -Body parameter of the Send-MailMessage cmdlet. Notice that we're using the ConvertTo-Html cmdlet at the end of the one-liner to convert the objects to an HTML document. Since the $report variable will simply contain raw HTML, we can assign this value to the -Body parameter and use the -BodyAsHtml switch parameter to send the report data in the body of an HTML-formatted message.

See also

- The *Allowing application servers to relay mail* recipe from `Chapter 8`, *Managing Transport Servers*
- The *Sending email messages with EWS* recipe from `Chapter 14`, *Scripting with the Exchange Web Services Managed API*
- The *Reporting on mailbox size* recipe from `Chapter 4`, *Managing Mailboxes*

Scheduling scripts to run at a later time

One of the most common tasks that Exchange administrators perform is scheduling scripts to run at a later time. This can be useful when performing maintenance after hours or running monitoring scripts on a regular basis. In this recipe, you'll learn how to schedule your PowerShell scripts to run with the Windows Task Scheduler. In PowerShell version 4, we got some powerful new cmdlets for managing the Windows Task Scheduler.

Open the Exchange Management Shell by clicking the Windows button and go to **Microsoft Exchange Server 2016** and choose **Exchange Management Shell**.

How to do it...

To create a scheduled task that runs from one of your Exchange servers perform the following steps:

1. Open the Task Scheduler by clicking the Windows button and on **Windows Administrative Tools | Task Scheduler**.
2. From the **Task Scheduler Library | Action** menu, click **Create Basic Task**.
3. Give your task a name and description, and click **Next**.
4. On the Trigger screen, select the how often you'd like the script to run (Daily, Weekly, Monthly, and so on).
5. When asked what action you want the task to perform, select **Start a Program**.

6. Use the following syntax in the Program/Script field and click on **Next**:

- C:\Windows\System32\WindowsPowerShell\v1.0\powershel
  l.exe -command ". 'C:\Program
  Files\Microsoft\Exchange
  Server\V15\bin\RemoteExchange.ps1'; Connect-
  ExchangeServer -auto; c:\Scripts\MoveMailboxes.ps1".

- You will receive a prompt that says **It appears as though arguments have been included in the program text box. Do you want to run the following program?**

- Click **Yes**.

- This will bring you to a summary screen where you can click **Finish**.

How it works...

The syntax used in this example may look a little strange at first. What we are actually doing here is scheduling PowerShell.exe and using the -Command parameter to execute multiple statements. This allows us to pass the contents of a PowerShell script to PowerShell.exe. In this case, our script has multiple lines and each statement is separated by a semi-colon.

The first thing we do is dot-source the RemoteExchange.ps1 script located in the Exchange Server bin directory. This file initializes some Exchange shell variables and imports several Exchange specific functions.

The next line in the task calls the Connect-ExchangeServer function using the -Auto parameter, allowing the Exchange Management Shell environment to load automatically from the best Exchange server in the local AD site.

Finally, we provide the path to our .ps1 script that utilizes any required Exchange Management Shell cmdlets and the script is executed, carrying out whatever it is that we need to be done.

It's worth mentioning here that you do not have to use a .ps1 script file with this syntax. You can replace the call to the MoveMailboxes.ps1 file with any valid PowerShell commands. If you have a script that contains multiple lines, you can continue to separate each line using a semi-colon.

When using this method, make sure that you configure the scheduled task to run as a user that has administrative access to your Exchange organization. In addition, RBAC should be considered for minimizing and using the least required privileges when dealing with accounts that are used for running actions within the Task Scheduler.

Also, if you have **User Account Control (UAC)** enabled, you may need to enable the option to **Run with highest privileges** in the properties of the scheduled task, for using elevated privileges. Additionally, you will probably want to enable the option to **Run whether user is logged on or not** in the properties of the scheduled task.

There's more...

The previous example demonstrated scheduling a task from an Exchange server using the installed Exchange Management Shell tools. Since all of the Exchange Management Shell connections utilize PowerShell remoting, it is possible to schedule a script to run from a workstation or server without the Exchange tools installed.

To schedule a task from a machine without the Exchange tools installed, use the steps from the previous example, but use the following syntax for the program action:

```
C:\Windows\System32\WindowsPowerShell\v1.0\powershell.exe -command "$s
= New-PSSession -ConfigurationNameMicrosoft.Exchange -ConnectionUri
http://tlex01.contoso.com/PowerShell/; Import-PSSession $s ;
c:\Scripts\MoveMailboxes.ps1"
```

You can see, here again, we are scheduling the `PowerShell.exe` program and specifying the script using the `-Command` parameter. The difference is that this time we are not using the locally installed Exchange tools. Instead we are creating a manual implicit remoting connection to a particular Exchange server. The length of the command line wrapping makes it difficult to read, but keep in mind that this is all done on one line.

When using this method, you can configure the scheduled task to run as a user that has administrative access to your Exchange organization, or you can provide explicit credentials to create the session object and run the script as another user.

Scheduled tasks can, since version 4 of PowerShell, also be added using the cmdlets.

An example of that would look like the following:

```
    $TaskCommand = `
"c:\windows\system32\WindowsPowerShell\v1.0\powershell.exe"
    $TaskArg = '-command "$s = New-PSSession -ConfigurationName `
Microsoft.Exchange -ConnectionUri ` http://tlex01.testlabs.se/PowerShell/;
Import-PSSession $s; ` c:\Scripts\MoveMailboxes.ps1"'
    $TaskStartTime = [datetime]::Now.AddMinutes(15)
    $TaskAction = New-ScheduledTaskAction -Execute "$TaskCommand" `
 -Argument "$TaskArg"
    $TaskTrigger = New-ScheduledTaskTrigger -At $TaskStartTime -Once
    Register-ScheduledTask -Action $TaskAction -Trigger $Tasktrigger ` -
TaskName "Scheduled task - Move Mailboxes" -User ` "testlabs\administrator"
-RunLevel Highest
```

We have created a variable named `TaskCommand`, which refers to `powershell.exe`, including the full path. In the second row, we are creating the variable `TaskArg`. This is to see what arguments to `powershell.exe` should be used. `TaskStartTime` is using the current time, plus 15 minutes ahead. Finally, we are using these variables and registering the scheduled task.

See also

- The *Manually configuring remote PowerShell connections* recipe in this chapter
- The *Using explicit credentials with PowerShell cmdlets* recipe in this chapter

Logging shell sessions to a transcript

You may find it useful at times to record the output of your shell sessions in a log file. This can help you save the history of all the commands you've executed and determine the success or failure of automated scripts. In this recipe, you'll learn how to create a PowerShell transcript. An example of when this could be useful is if we are developing a script and about to implement it in a production environment. It would be neat to use transcript logging during the first run(s).

How to do it...

1. To create a transcript, execute the `Start-Transcript` cmdlet:

```
Start-Transcript c:\logfile.txt
```

2. You can stop recording the session using the `Stop-Transcript` cmdlet:

```
Stop-Transcript
```

How it works...

When starting a PowerShell transcript, you can specify a path and a file name that will be used to record your commands and their output. The use of the `-Path` parameter is optional; if you do not provide a file path, the cmdlet will create a transcript file with a random name in the default documents folder in your profile path, as shown in the following screenshot:

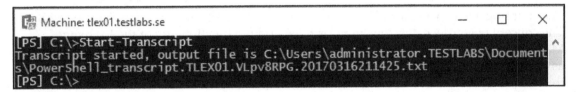

When you are done, you can run the `Stop-Transcript` cmdlet or simply exit the shell. You can use the `-Append` parameter with the `Start-Transcript` cmdlet to add a new transcript to an existing log file. When doing so, you'll need to specify the name of the file you want to append to using the `-Path` parameter.

You can record your entire session every time you start the Exchange Management Shell by adding the `Start-Transcript` cmdlet to your user profile. If you choose to do this, make sure you specify the same log file to use every time the shell starts and use the `-Append` parameter so that each session is added to the log file every time. Note that the transcript file could be huge over time when logging everything.

There's more...

By default, only the output from PowerShell cmdlets will be recorded in your transcript. If you execute an external program, such as the Exchange `eseutil.exe` utility, the output from this command will not be saved in your transcript file, even though it was run within the current shell session. You can pipe external programs to the `Out-Default` cmdlet and this will force the output to be stored in your transcript.

See also

- The *Exporting reports to text and CSV files* recipe in this chapter

- The *Automating tasks with the scripting agent* recipe in this chapter

Automating tasks with the scripting agent

The scripting agents were introduced in Exchange 2010 and still remain in Exchange 2016. The concept of cmdlet extension agents is to extend the functionality of the Exchange Management Tools. The scripting extension agent can be used to trigger custom commands as changes are being made by administrators from the management console or the shell. In this recipe, we'll take a look at how to use the scripting agent to automate a task in the Exchange Management Shell.

Getting ready

To complete the steps in the recipe, you'll need to create an XML file. You can simply use Notepad or any XML editor of your choice.

How to do it...

1. Let's say that you need to enable single item recovery for every mailbox that gets created in your organization. By default, single item recovery is disabled when you create a mailbox. To automatically enable single item recovery for each mailbox as it is created, add the following code to a new file:

```
<?xml version="1.0" encoding="utf-8" ?>
<Configuration version="1.0">
<Feature Name="MailboxProvisioning" Cmdlets="New-Mailbox">
<ApiCall Name="OnComplete">
     if($succeeded) {
       $mailbox =
          $provisioningHandler.UserSpecifiedParameters["Name"]
       Set-Mailbox $mailbox -SingleItemRecoveryEnabled $true
     }
</ApiCall>
</Feature>
</Configuration>
```

2. Next, make sure to save the file as `ScriptingAgentConfig.xml` on all Exchange servers in the `<install path>\V15\Bin\CmdletExtensionAgents` directory.
3. Finally, you need to enable the scripting agent using the following command:

```
Enable-CmdletExtensionAgent "Scripting Agent"
```

 If you have multiple Exchange servers in your environment, make sure that you copy the `ScriptingAgentConfig.xml` file to each server into the `CmdletExtentionAgents` directory as described previously.

How it works...

When the scripting agent is enabled, it is called every time a cmdlet is run in your Exchange environment. This includes cmdlets run from within the shell or any of the graphical management tools.

You can see from the code that, in this example, we're using the `OnComplete` API, which runs immediately after the cmdlet has been completed. Using the `Feature` tag, we've specified that this block of code should only be executed upon completion of the New-Mailbox cmdlet.

After the `New-Mailbox` cmdlet has completed, we check the built-in `$succeeded` variable to ensure the command was successful. If so, we retrieve the value that was used with the `-Name` parameter and store the result in the `$mailbox` variable. This value is then used to specify the identity when running the `Set-Mailbox` cmdlet to enable single item recovery.

There's more...

You can add multiple scripts to the XML file if needed by defining multiple `Feature` tags under the configuration tag. Each block of code within the `Feature` tag should have an `ApiCall` tag, as shown in the previous example.

The state of the scripting agent is an organization-wide setting. If you enable the scripting agent, it is important that the `ScriptingAgentConfig.xml` is copied to every Exchange server in your organization.

Using multiple cmdlets with the OnComplete API

Let's take a look at another example. Imagine that, in addition to enabling single-item recovery for all newly-created mailboxes, we also want to disable the ActiveSync protocol for each mailbox. This means that, in addition to calling the `Set-Mailbox` cmdlet to enable single item recovery, we'll also need to call the `Set-CASMailbox` cmdlet to disable ActiveSync. Also, mailboxes can be created using both the `New-Mailbox` and `Enable-Mailbox` cmdlets. Since we'd like our custom settings to be applied regardless of how the mailbox is created, we can use the following code in our XML file:

```
<?xml version="1.0" encoding="utf-8" ?>
<Configuration version="1.0">
<Feature Name="Mailboxes" Cmdlets="new-mailbox,enable-mailbox">
<ApiCall Name="OnComplete">
      if($succeeded) {
        $id = $provisioningHandler.UserSpecifiedParameters["Name"]
        Set-Mailbox $id -SingleItemRecoveryEnabled $true
        Set-CASMailbox $id -ActiveSyncEnabled $false
      }
</ApiCall>
</Feature>
</Configuration>
```

This code is similar to our previous example, except in this version we've specified that our custom code will be called when both the `New-Mailbox` and `Enable-Mailbox` cmdlets are used. The code in the `ApiCall` tag captures the `Alias` of the mailbox and then uses the `Set-Mailbox` and `Set-CASMailbox` to modify the settings as required.

There are multiple scripting agent APIs that can be used to extend the Exchange Management Shell functionality even further. For examples on how to use these APIs, reference the `ScriptingAgentConfig.xml.sample` file in the `<installpath>\V15\Bin\CmdletExtensionAgents` folder.

See also

- The *Adding, modifying, and removing mailboxes* recipe from `Chapter 3`, *Managing Recipients*
- The *Managing ActiveSync, OWA, POP3, and IMAP4 mailbox settings* recipe from `Chapter 7`, *Managing Client Access*

Scripting an Exchange server installation

If you are performing mass deployment of Exchange servers in a large environment, automating the installation process can minimize administrator errors and speed up the overall process. The `setup.exe` utility can be used to perform an unattended installation of Exchange, and, when combined with PowerShell and just a little bit of scripting logic, create a fairly sophisticated installation script. This recipe will provide a couple of examples that can be used to script the installation of an Exchange server.

Getting ready

You can use a standard PowerShell console from the server to run the scripts in this recipe.

How to do it...

1. In this example, we'll create an automated installation script that installs Exchange based on the hostname of the server. Using Notepad or your favorite scripting editor, add the following code to a new file:

```
Param($Path)
if(Test-Path $Path) {
  switch -wildcard ($env:computername) {
    "*-MB-*" {$role = "MB" ; break}
    "*-MG-*" {$role = "MT" ; break}
    "*-ED-*" {$role = "ET" ; break}
}
  $setup = Join-Path $Path "setup.exe"
  Invoke-Expression "$setup /mode:install `
 /r:$role /IAcceptExchangeServerLicenseTerms ` /InstallWindowsComponents"
}
else {
  Write-Host "Invalid Media Path!"
}
```

2. Save the file as `InstallExchange.ps1`.
3. Execute the script from a server where you want to install Exchange using the following syntax:

```
InstallExchange.ps1 -Path D:
```

The value provided for the `-Path` parameter should reference the Exchange 2016 media, either on DVD or extracted to a folder.

How it works...

One of the most common methods for automating an Exchange installation is determining the required roles based on the hostname of the server. In the previous example, we assume that your organization uses a standard server naming convention. When executing the script, the switch statement will evaluate the hostname of the server and determine the required roles. For example, if your mailbox servers use a server name such as `TL-MB-01`, the mailbox server role(s) will be installed. If your management server(s) use a server name such as `TL-MG-01`, the management role will be installed, and so on.

It's important to note that Exchange 2016 requires several Windows operating system roles and features, such as .NET Framework 4.6. This of course depends on which role we are installing. The required roles and features will be installed by using the switch `/InstallWindowsComponents`.

When calling the `Setup.exe` installation program within the script, we use the `/InstallWindowsComponents` and `/IAcceptExchangeServerLicenseTerms` switch, which are new `Setup.exe` features in Exchange Server 2016. This will allow the setup program to load any prerequisite Windows roles and features, such as IIS, and so on, before starting the Exchange installation. The accept agreement switch is required when using the unattended installation method.

There's more...

Scripting the installation of Exchange based on the server names may not be an option for you. Fortunately, PowerShell gives us plenty of flexibility. The following script uses similar logic, but performs the installation based on different criteria.

Let's say that your core Exchange infrastructure has already been deployed. Your corporate headquarters already has the required mailbox server infrastructure in place and therefore you only need to deploy mailbox servers in the Active Directory branch sites. All remaining remote sites will also be installing the mailbox role for the Exchange servers. Replace the code in the `InstallExchange.ps1` script with the following:

```
param($Path)
$site = [DirectoryServices.ActiveDirectory.ActiveDirectorySite]

if(Test-Path $Path) {
  switch ($site::GetComputerSite().Name) {
    "EX-Deploy" {$role = "MB"}
    Default {$role = "MT"}
  }
  $setup = Join-Path $Path "setup.exe"
  Invoke-Expression "$setup /mode:install /r:$role
/IAcceptExchangeServerLicenseTerms /InstallWindowsComponents"
}
else {
  Write-Host "Invalid Media Path!"
}
```

This preceding example determines the current Active Directory site of the computer executing the script. If the computer is in the EX-Deploy site, meaning that the server is placed in the deployment AD site, by having the server in this site, the mailbox role will be installed. If it is located at any of the other remaining Active Directory sites, the management server role is installed.

As you can see, combining the Setup.exe utility with a PowerShell script can give you many more options when performing an automated installation.

See also

- The *Looping through items* recipe from Chapter 1, *PowerShell Key Concepts*
- The *Creating custom objects* recipe from Chapter 1, *PowerShell Key Concepts*

3
Managing Recipients

In this chapter, we will cover the following:

- Creating, modifying, and removing mailboxes
- Working with contacts
- Managing distribution groups
- Managing resource mailboxes
- Creating recipients in bulk using a CSV file
- Configuring MailTips
- Working with recipient filters
- Adding and removing recipient email addresses
- Hiding recipients from address lists
- Configuring recipient moderation
- Configuring message delivery restrictions
- Managing automatic replies and out-of-office settings for a user
- Adding, modifying, and removing server-side inbox rules
- Managing mailbox folder permissions
- Importing user photos into Active Directory

Introduction

If you are like many other administrators, you probably spend the majority of your time performing recipient-related management tasks when dealing with Exchange. If you work in a large environment with thousands of recipients, creating, updating, and deleting recipients is probably a cumbersome and time-consuming process.

Of course, the obvious solution to this is to use the Exchange Management Shell. Utilizing the Exchange Management Shell, you can automate all of your recipient management tasks and drastically speed up your work.

The concept of an Exchange recipient is more than just a user with a mailbox. An Exchange recipient is any Active Directory object that has been mail enabled and can receive messages within the Exchange organization. This can be a distribution group, a contact, a mail-enabled public folder, and more. These object types include individual sets of cmdlets that can be used to completely automate the administration of the Exchange recipients in your environment.

The goal of this chapter is to show you some common solutions that can be used when performing day-to-day recipient management from the shell. Quite often, Exchange recipients are provisioned or updated in bulk through an automated process driven by a PowerShell script. The recipes in this chapter will provide solutions for these types of scripts that you can use right away. You can also use these concepts as a guide to build your own scripts from scratch to automate recipient-related tasks in your environment.

Performing some basic steps

To work with the code samples in this chapter, we'll need to launch the Exchange Management Shell using the following steps:

1. Log onto a workstation or server with the Exchange Management Tools installed.
2. You can connect using a remote PowerShell if, for some reason, you don't have Exchange Management Tools installed. Use the following command:

```
$Session = New-PSSession -ConfigurationName Microsoft.Exchange `
-ConnectionUri http://servername/PowerShell/ `
-Authentication Kerberos
Import-PSSession $Session
```

3. Alternatively, open the Exchange Management Shell by clicking the Windows button and go to **Microsoft Exchange Server 2016 | Exchange Management Shell**.

If any additional steps are required, they will be listed at the beginning of the recipe in the *Getting ready* section.

> Remember to start the Exchange Management Shell using **Run as Administrator** to avoid permission problems.

> In this chapter, note that in the examples of cmdlets, I have used the back tick (`) character for breaking up long commands into multiple lines. The purpose of this is to make it easier to read. The back ticks are not required and should only be used if needed.
> Note that the Exchange variables, like `$exscripts`, are not available when using the preceding method.

Creating, modifying, and removing mailboxes

One of the most common tasks performed within the Exchange Management Shell is mailbox management. In this recipe, we'll take a look at the command syntax required to create, update, and remove mailboxes from your Exchange organization. The concepts outlined in this recipe can be used to perform basic day-to-day tasks, and will be useful for more advanced scenarios, such as creating mailboxes in bulk.

How to do it...

1. Let's start off by creating a mailbox-enabled Active Directory user account. To do this, we can use the `New-Mailbox` cmdlet, as shown in the following example:

```
$password = ConvertTo-SecureString -AsPlainText P@ssw0rd `
-Force
New-Mailbox -UserPrincipalName dave@testlabs.se `
-Alias dave `
-Database DB1 `
-Name 'Dave Jones' `
-OrganizationalUnit Sales `
-Password $password `
-FirstName Dave `
-LastName Jones `
-DisplayName 'Dave Jones'
```

2. Once the mailbox has been created, we can modify it using the `Set-Mailbox` cmdlet:

```
Set-Mailbox -Identity dave `
-UseDatabaseQuotaDefaults $false `
-ProhibitSendReceiveQuota 5GB `
-IssueWarningQuota 4GB
```

3. To remove the Exchange attributes from the Active Directory user account and mark the mailbox in the database for removal, use the `Disablemailbox` cmdlet:

```
Disablemailbox -Identity dave -Confirm:$false
```

How it works...

When running the `New-Mailbox` cmdlet, the `-Password` parameter is required, and you need to provide a value for it using a secure string object. As you can see from the code, we've used the `ConvertTo-SecureString` cmdlet to create a `$password` variable that stores a specified value as an encrypted string. This `$password` variable is then assigned to the `-Password` parameter when running the cmdlet. There's no requirement to first store this object in a variable; we could have done it inline, as shown here:

```
New-Mailbox -UserPrincipalName dave@testlabs.se `
-Alias dave `
-Database DB1 `
-Name 'Dave Jones' `
-OrganizationalUnit Sales `
-Password (ConvertTo-SecureString -AsPlainText P@ssw0rd -Force) `
-FirstName Dave `
-LastName Jones `
-DisplayName 'Dave Jones'
```

Keep in mind that the password used here needs to comply with your Active Directory password policies, which may enforce a minimum password length and have requirements for complexity.

Only a few parameters are actually required when running `New-Mailbox`, but the cmdlet itself supports several useful parameters that can be used to set certain properties when creating the mailbox. You can run `Get-Help New-Mailbox -Detailed` to determine which additional parameters are supported.

The New-Mailbox cmdlet creates a new Active Directory user and then mailbox-enables that account. We can also create mailboxes for existing users with the Enablemailbox cmdlet, using syntax similar to the following:

```
Enablemailbox steve -Database DB1
```

The only requirement when running the Enablemailbox cmdlet is that you provide the identity of the Active Directory user that should be mailbox enabled. In the previous example, we've specified the database in which the mailbox should be created, but this is optional. The Enablemailbox cmdlet supports a number of other parameters that you can use to control the initial settings for the mailbox.

You can use a simple one-liner to create mailboxes in bulk for existing Active Directory users:

```
Get-User -RecipientTypeDetails User |
    Enablemailbox -Database DB1
```

Note that we've run the Get-User cmdlet specifying User as the value for the -RecipientTypeDetails parameter. This will retrieve only those accounts in Active Directory that have not been mailbox enabled. We then pipe those objects down to the Enablemailbox cmdlet and mailboxes are created for each of those users in one simple operation.

Once mailboxes have been created, they can be modified with the Set-Mailbox cmdlet. As you may recall from our original example, we used the Set-Mailbox cmdlet to configure custom storage quota settings after creating a mailbox for Dave Jones. Keep in mind that the Set-Mailbox cmdlet supports almost 200 parameters, so anything that can be done to modify a mailbox can be scripted.

Bulk modifications to mailboxes can be done easily by taking advantage of the pipeline and the Set-Mailbox cmdlet. Instead of configuring storage quotas on a single mailbox, we can do it for multiple users at once:

```
Get-Mailbox -OrganizationalUnit testlabs.se/sales |
    Set-Mailbox -UseDatabaseQuotaDefaults $false `
    -ProhibitSendReceiveQuota 5GB `
    -IssueWarningQuota 4GB
```

Here, we are simply retrieving every mailbox in the Sales OU using the Get-Mailbox cmdlet. The objects returned from that command are piped down to Set-Mailbox, which modifies the quota settings for each mailbox in one shot.

The `Disablemailbox` cmdlet will strip the Exchange attributes from an Active Directory user and will disconnect the associated mailbox. By default, disconnected mailboxes are retained for 30 days. You can modify this setting on the database that holds the mailbox. In addition to this, you can also use the `Removemailbox` cmdlet to delete both the Active Directory account and the mailbox at the same time:

```
Removemailbox -Identity dave -Confirm:$false
```

After running this command, the mailbox will be purged once it exceeds the deleted mailbox retention setting of the database. One common mistake is when administrators use the `Removemailbox` cmdlet when the `Disablemailbox` cmdlet should have been used. It's important to remember that the `Removemailbox` cmdlet will delete the Active Directory user account and mailbox, while the `Disablemailbox` cmdlet only removes the mailbox, but the Active Directory user account will still remain.

There's more...

When we ran the `New-Mailbox` cmdlet in the previous examples, we assigned a secure string object to the `-Password` parameter using the `ConvertTo-SecureString` cmdlet. This is a great technique to use when your scripts need complete automation, but you can also allow an operator to enter this information interactively. For example, you might build a script that prompts an operator for a password when creating one or more mailboxes. There are a couple of ways you can do this. First, you can use the `Read-Host` cmdlet to prompt the user running the script to enter a password:

```
$pass = Read-Host "Enter Password" -AsSecureString
```

Once a value has been entered into the shell, your script can assign the `$pass` variable to the `-Password` parameter of the `New-Mailbox` cmdlet.

Alternatively, you can supply a value for the `-Password` parameter using the `Get-Credential` cmdlet:

```
New-Mailbox -Name Dave -UserPrincipalName dave@contoso.com `
-Password (Get-Credential).password
```

You can see that the value we are assigning to the `-Password` parameter in this example is actually the `password` property of the object returned by the `Get-Credential` cmdlet. Executing this command will first launch a Windows authentication dialog box where the caller can enter a username and password. Once the credential object has been created, the `New-Mailbox` cmdlet will run. Even though a username and password must be entered into the authentication dialog box, only the password value will be used when the command executes.

A commonly used mailbox type is the shared mailbox, which is pretty much what the name says-a mailbox shared between different individuals. The difference between this mailbox type and the regular user mailbox is that the shared mailbox is a typical disabled active directory object. Therefore, no one can use this username to log on interactively with. These mailboxes are simply created by using the following cmdlet and parameters:

```
New-Mailbox -Name "UC Project Mailbox" -Shared
```

The preceding example shows you how to create the shared mailbox. The only difference between the shared mailbox and a regular mailbox is the addition of the parameter `-Shared` into the cmdlet.

Setting Active Directory attributes

Some of the Active Directory attributes that you may want to set when creating a mailbox might not be available using the `New-Mailbox` cmdlet. Good examples of this are a user's city, state, company, and department attributes. In order to set these attributes, you'll need to call the `Set-User` cmdlet after the mailbox has been created:

```
Set-User -Identity dave -Office IT -City Seattle -State Washington
```

You can run `Get-Help Set-User -Detailed` to view all of the available parameters supported by this cmdlet.

Note that the cmdlet `Set-User` is an Active Directory cmdlet and not an Exchange cmdlet.
In the examples using the `New-Mailbox` cmdlet for creating new mailboxes, it is not required that you use all the parameters from the example. The only required parameters are `UserPrincipalName`, `Name`, and `Password`.

See also

- *Using the help system* recipe from `Chapter 1`, *PowerShell Key Concepts*
- *Creating recipients in bulk using a CSV file* recipe in this chapter
- *Managing distribution groups* recipe from `Chapter 3`, *Managing Recipients*
- *Managing resource mailboxes* recipe from `Chapter 3`, *Managing Recipients*

Working with contacts

Once you start managing mailboxes using the Exchange Management Shell, you'll probably notice that the concepts and command syntax used to manage contacts are very similar. The difference, of course, is that we need to use a different set of cmdlets. In addition, we also have two types of contacts to deal with in Exchange. We'll take a look at how you can manage both of them in the following recipe.

How to do it...

1. To create a mail-enabled contact, use the `New-MailContact` cmdlet:

```
New-MailContact -Alias rjones `
-Name "Rob Jones" `
-ExternalEmailAddress rob@fabrikam.com `
-OrganizationalUnit sales
```

2. Mail-enabled users can be created with the `New-MailUser` cmdlet:

```
New-MailUser -Name 'John Davis' `
-Alias jdavis `
-UserPrincipalName jdavis@contoso.com `
-FirstName John `
-LastName Davis `
-Password (ConvertTo-SecureString -AsPlainText P@ssw0rd `
-Force) `
-ResetPasswordOnNextLogon $false `
-ExternalEmailAddress jdavis@fabrikam.com
```

How it works...

Mail contacts are useful when you have external email recipients that need to show up in your global address list. When you use the `New-MailContact` cmdlet, an Active Directory contact object is created and mail-enabled with the external email address assigned. You can mail-enable an existing Active Directory contact using the `EnablemailContact` cmdlet.

Mail users are similar to mail contacts in that they have an associated external email address. The difference is that these objects are mail-enabled Active Directory users, and that explains why we needed to assign a password when creating the object.

You might use a mail user for a contractor who works onsite in your organization and needs to be able to log on to your domain. When users in your organization need to email this person, they can select them from the global address list, and messages sent to these recipients will be delivered to the external address configured for the account.

Just as when dealing with mailboxes, there are a couple of things that should be taken into consideration when it comes to removing contacts and mail users. You can remove the Exchange attributes from a contact using the `DisablemailContact` cmdlet. The `RemovemailContact` cmdlet will remove the contact object from Active Directory and Exchange. Similarly, the `DisablemailUser` and `RemovemailUser` cmdlets work in the same fashion.

There's more...

Like mailboxes, mail contacts and mail-enabled user accounts have several Active Directory attributes that can be set, such as job title, company, department, and more. To update these attributes, you can use the `Set-*` cmdlets available for each respective type. For example, to update our mail contact, we could use the `Set-Contact` cmdlet with the following syntax:

```
Set-Contact -Identity rjones `
-Title 'Sales Contractor' `
-Company Fabrikam `
-Department Sales
```

To modify the same settings for a mail-enabled user, use the `Set-User` cmdlet:

```
Set-User -Identity jdavis `
-Title 'Sales Contractor' `
-Company Fabrikam `
-Department Sales
```

Both cmdlets can be used to modify a number of different settings. Use the help system to view all of the available parameters.

See also

- *Using the help system* recipe from Chapter 1, *PowerShell Key Concepts*
- *Adding, modifying, and removing mailboxes* recipe in this chapter

Managing distribution groups

In many Exchange environments, distribution groups are relied upon heavily and require frequent changes. This recipe will cover the creation of distribution groups and how to add members to groups, which might be useful when performing these tasks interactively in the shell or through automated scripts.

How to do it...

1. To create a distribution group, use the New-DistributionGroup cmdlet:

```
New-DistributionGroup -Name Sales
```

2. Once the group has been created, adding multiple members can be done easily using a one-liner:

```
Get-Mailbox -OrganizationalUnit Sales |
    Add-DistributionGroupMember -Identity Sales
```

3. We can also create distribution groups whose memberships are set dynamically:

```
New-DynamicDistributionGroup -Name Accounting `
    -Alias Accounting `
    -IncludedRecipients MailboxUsers,MailContacts `
    -OrganizationalUnit Accounting `
    -ConditionalDepartment accounting,finance `
    -RecipientContainer testlabs.se
```

How it works...

There are two types of distribution groups that can be created with Exchange. First, there are regular distribution groups, which contain a distinct list of users. Secondly, there are dynamic distribution groups, whose members are determined at the time a message is sent based on a number of conditions or filters that have been defined. Both types have a set of cmdlets that can be used to add, remove, update, enable, or disable these groups.

By default, when creating a standard distribution group, the group scope will be set to Universal. You can create a mail-enabled security group using the New-DistributionGroup cmdlet by setting the -Type parameter to Security. If you do not provide a value for the -Type parameter, the group will be created using the Distribution group type.

You can mail-enable an existing Active Directory universal distribution group using the Enable-DistributionGroup cmdlet.

After creating the Sales distribution group in our previous example, we added all of the mailboxes in the Sales OU to the group using the Add-DistributionGroupMember cmdlet. You can do this in bulk or for one user at a time using the -Member parameter:

```
Add-DistributionGroupMember -Identity Sales -Member administrator
```

Distribution groups are a large topic, and we're merely covering the basics here. See Chapter 5, *Distribution Groups and Address Lists* for in-depth coverage of distribution groups.

Dynamic distribution groups determine their membership based on a defined set of filters and conditions. When we created the Accounting distribution group, we used the -IncludedRecipients parameter to specify that only the MailboxUsers and MailContacts object types would be included in the group. This eliminates resource mailboxes, groups, or mail users from being included as members. The group will be created in the Accounting OU based on the value used with the -OrganizationalUnit parameter. Using the -ConditionalDepartment parameter, the group will only include users that have a department setting of either Accounting or Finance. Finally, since the -RecipientContainer parameter is set to the FQDN of the domain, any user located in the Active Directory could potentially be included in the group. You can create more complex filters for dynamic distribution groups using a recipient filter; see the recipe titled *Working with recipient filters* later in this chapter for an example.

You can modify both group types using the `Set-DistributionGroup` and `Set-DynamicDistributionGroup` cmdlets.

There's more...

Just as when we deal with other recipient types, there are a couple of things that should be taken into consideration when it comes to removing distribution groups. You can remove the Exchange attributes from a group using the `Disable-DistributionGroup` cmdlet. The `Remove-DistributionGroup` cmdlet will remove the group object from the Active Directory and Exchange.

See also

- *Working with recipient filters* recipe in this chapter
- *Reporting on distribution group membership* recipe in this chapter
- *Adding members to a distribution group from an external file* recipe from `Chapter 5`, *Distribution Groups and Address Lists*
- *Previewing dynamic distribution group membership* recipe from `Chapter 5`, *Distribution Groups and Address Lists*

Managing resource mailboxes

In addition to mailboxes, groups, and external contacts, recipients can also include specific rooms or pieces of equipment. Locations such as a conference room or a classroom can be given a mailbox so they can be reserved for meetings. Equipment mailboxes can be assigned to physical, non-location specific resources, such as laptops or projectors, and can then be checked out to individual users or groups by booking time with the mailbox. In this recipe, we'll take a look at how you can manage resource mailboxes using the Exchange Management Shell.

How to do it...

When creating a resource mailbox from within the shell, the syntax is similar to creating a mailbox for a regular user. For example, you still use the `New-Mailbox` cmdlet when creating a resource mailbox:

```
New-Mailbox -Name "CR7" -DisplayName "Conference Room 7" `
-UserPrincipalName CR7@contoso.com -Room
```

How it works...

There are two main differences when it comes to creating a resource mailbox as opposed to a standard user mailbox. First, you need to use either the `-Room` switch parameter or the `-Equipment` switch parameter to define the type of resource mailbox that will be created. Second, you do not need to provide a password value for the user account. When using either of these resource mailbox switch parameters to create a mailbox, the `New-Mailbox` cmdlet will create a disabled Active Directory user account that will be associated with the mailbox.

The entire concept of room and equipment mailboxes revolves around the calendars used by these resources. If you want to reserve a room or a piece of equipment, you book time with these resources through Outlook or OWA for the duration that you'll need them. The requests sent to these resources need to be accepted, either by a delegate or automatically using the Resource Booking Attendant.

To configure the room mailbox created in the previous example to automatically accept new meeting requests, we can use the `Set-CalendarProcessing` cmdlet to set the Resource Booking Attendant for that mailbox to `AutoAccept`:

```
Set-CalendarProcessing CR7 -AutomateProcessing AutoAccept
```

When the Resource Booking Attendant is set to `AutoAccept`, the request will be immediately accepted, as long as there is not a conflict with another meeting. If there is a conflict, an email message will be returned to the requestor explaining that the request was declined due to scheduling conflicts. You can allow conflicts by adding the `-AllowConflicts` switch parameter to the previous command.

When working with resource mailboxes with `AutomateProcessing` set to `AutoAccept`, you'll get an automated email response from the resource after booking time. This email message will explain whether the request was accepted or declined, depending on your settings.

You can add additional text to the response message that the meeting organizer will receive using the following syntax:

```
Set-CalendarProcessing -Identity CR7 `
-AddAdditionalResponse $true `
-AdditionalResponse 'For Assistance Contact Support at Ext. #3376'
```

This example uses the Set-CalendarProcessing cmdlet to customize the response messages sent from the CR7 room mailbox. You can see here that we've added a message that tells the user the help desk number to call if assistance is required. Keep in mind that you can only add additional response text when the AutomateProcessing property is set to AutoAccept.

If you do not want to automate the calendar processing for a resource mailbox then you'll need to add delegates that can accept or deny meetings for that resource. Again, we can turn to the Set-CalendarProcessing cmdlet to accomplish this:

```
Set-CalendarProcessing -Identity CR7 `
-ResourceDelegates "rmcleod@testlabs.se","trandolph@testlabs.se" `
-AutomateProcessing None
```

In this example, we've added two delegates to the resource mailbox and have turned off automated processing. When a request comes into the CR7 mailbox, both Ruben and Terrance will be notified, and can accept or deny the request on behalf of the resource mailbox.

There's more...

When it comes to working with resource mailboxes, another useful feature is the ability to assign custom resource properties to rooms and equipment resources. For example, you may have a total of 5, 10, or 15 conference rooms, but maybe only 4 of those have whiteboards. It might be useful for your users to know this information when booking a resource for a meeting where they will be conducting a training session.

Using the shell, we can add custom resource properties to the Exchange organization by modifying the resource schema. Once these custom resource properties have been added, they can then be assigned to specific resource mailboxes.

You can use the following code to add a whiteboard resource property to the Exchange organization's resource schema:

```
Set-ResourceConfig -ResourcePropertySchema 'Room/Whiteboard'
```

Now that the whiteboard resource property is available within the Exchange organization, we can add this to our Conference Room 7 mailbox using the following command:

```
Set-Mailbox -Identity CR7 -ResourceCustom Whiteboard
```

When users access the **Select Rooms** or **Add Rooms** dialog box in Outlook 2010, Outlook 2013, or Outlook 2016, they will see that Conference Room 7 has a whiteboard available.

Converting mailboxes

If you've moved from an old version, you may have a number of mailboxes that were being used as resource mailboxes. Once these mailboxes have been moved over, they will be identified as `Shared` mailboxes. You can convert them to other types using the `Set-Mailbox` cmdlet so that they'll have all of the properties of a resource mailbox:

```
Get-Mailbox conf* | Set-Mailbox -Type Room
```

You can run the `Set-Mailbox` cmdlet against each mailbox, one at a time, and convert them to `Room` mailboxes using the `-Type` parameter. Or, if you use a common naming convention, you may be able to do them in bulk by retrieving a list of mailboxes using a wildcard and piping them to `Set-Mailbox`, as shown previously.

See also

- *Adding, modifying, and removing mailboxes* recipe in this chapter
- *Creating recipients in bulk using a CSV file* recipe in this chapter

Creating recipients in bulk using a CSV file

One of the most common bulk-provisioning techniques used in the Exchange Management Shell makes use of comma-separated value (CSV) files. These files act in a similar way to a database table. Each record in this table is represented by one line in the file, and each field value is separated by a comma, which is used as a delimiter. In this recipe, you'll learn how to set up a CSV file and create recipients in bulk using the Exchange Management Shell.

Getting ready

In addition to the Exchange Management Shell, you'll need to use Microsoft Excel to create a CSV file.

How to do it...

1. In this example, we are going to create some mailboxes in bulk. We'll enter some data into Excel that will include the settings for five new mailboxes:

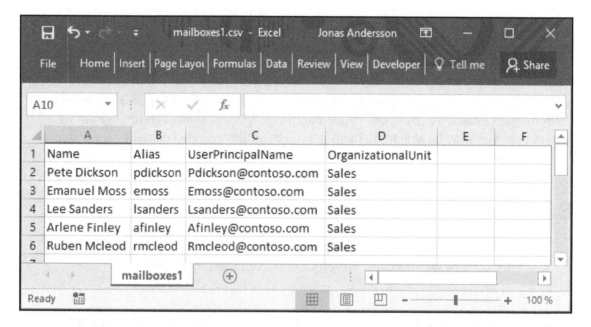

	A	B	C	D	E	F
1	Name	Alias	UserPrincipalName	OrganizationalUnit		
2	Pete Dickson	pdickson	Pdickson@contoso.com	Sales		
3	Emanuel Moss	emoss	Emoss@contoso.com	Sales		
4	Lee Sanders	lsanders	Lsanders@contoso.com	Sales		
5	Arlene Finley	afinley	Afinley@contoso.com	Sales		
6	Ruben Mcleod	rmcleod	Rmcleod@contoso.com	Sales		

2. Go to **File | Save As** and select **CSV (Comma delimited) (*.csv)** for the file type. Save the file as C:\Scripts\mailboxes1.csv.

3. Within the Exchange Management Shell, create a secure password object to be used as an initial password for each mailbox:

```
$pass = ConvertTo-SecureString –AsPlainText P@ssw0rd01 `
 -Force
```

4. Import the CSV file and create the mailboxes:

```
Import-CSV C:\Scripts\mailboxes1.csv | % {
    New-Mailbox -Name $_.Name `
    -Alias $_.Alias `
    -UserPrincipalName $_.UserPrincipalName `
    -OrganizationalUnit $_.OrganizationalUnit `
    -Password $pass `
    -ResetPasswordOnNextLogon $true
}
```

How it works...

In this example, we're importing the CSV file into the shell and piping that information to the `ForEach-Object` cmdlet (using the `%` alias). For each record in the CSV file, we're running the `New-Mailbox` cmdlet, providing values for the `-Name`, `-Alias`, `-UserPrincipalName`, and `-OrganizationalUnit` parameters. The properties for each record can be accessed inside the loop using the `$_` variable, which is the automatic variable that references the current object in the pipeline. The property names for each record match the header names used in the CSV file. As we create each mailbox, the password is set to the `$pass` variable. The `-ResetPasswordOnNextLogon` parameter is set to `$true`, which will require each user to reset their password after their first logon.

Using this technique, you can literally create thousands of mailboxes in a matter of minutes. This concept can also be applied to other recipient types, such as distribution groups and contacts. You just need to specify the appropriate parameter values in the CSV file and use the corresponding cmdlet for the recipient type. For example, if you want to bulk-provision contacts from a CSV file, use the code from the previous example as a guide, and, instead of using the `New-Mailbox` cmdlet, use the `New-MailContact` cmdlet and whatever parameters are required, based on your settings.

There's more...

Let's take a look at an alternative approach to the previous example. Let's say that you don't want to set an initial password for each user, and, instead, you want to include this information in the CSV file so that each new mailbox gets a unique password. Again, you'll need to set up a CSV file with the required values.

For this example, your CSV file would look something like this:

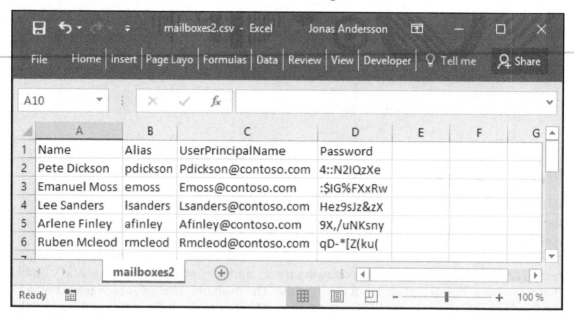

Note that in the previous screenshot, we are using different column names for this new file. We've removed the `OrganizationalUnit` column and now have a `Password` column that will be used to create each mailbox with a unique password. After you're done creating the file, save it again as `C:\Scripts\mailboxes2.csv`.

Next, you can use the following code to create the mailboxes, setting the path and filename to the CSV file created in the previous step:

```
Import-CSV C:\Scripts\Mailboxes2.CSV | % {
  $pass = ConvertTo-SecureString -AsPlainText $_.Password -Force
  New-Mailbox -Name $_.Name `
  -Alias $_.Alias `
  -UserPrincipalName $_.UserPrincipalName `
  -Password $pass
}
```

As we loop through each record in the CSV file, we create a secure password object that can be used with the `-Password` parameter. The main difference in this case compared to the previous example is that each user gets a unique password and they do not need to reset their password the first time they log on.

Taking it a step further

When provisioning recipients, you'll probably need to do multiple things, such as set Active Directory attributes and configure distribution group membership. Let's take our previous example a step further:

```
Import-CSV C:\Scripts\NewMailboxes.csv | % {
  New-Mailbox -Name $_.Name `
   -FirstName $_.FirstName `
   -LastName $_.LastName `
   -Alias $_.Alias `
   -UserPrincipalName $_.UserPrincipalName `
   -Password (ConvertTo-SecureString -AsPlainText P@ssw0rd `
    -Force) `
   -OrganizationalUnit $_.OrganizationalUnit `
   -Database DB1

  Set-User -Identity $_.Name `
   -City $_.City `
   -StateOrProvince $_.State `
   -Title $_.Title `
   -Department $_.Department

  Add-DistributionGroupMember -Identity DL_Sales `
   -Member $_.Name

  Add-DistributionGroupMember -Identity DL_Marketing `
   -Member $_.Name
}
```

Here, we're still using a CSV file, but as we loop through each record, we're calling multiple cmdlets to first create the mailbox, set some of the Active Directory attributes, and then add the mailbox to two separate distribution groups. In order to use this code, we would just need to create a CSV file that has columns for all of the values we're setting.

Now that we have this framework in place, we can add as many columns as we need to the CSV file and we can call any number of cmdlets for each record in the CSV.

See also

- *Looping through items* recipe from Chapter 1, *PowerShell Key Concepts*
- *Adding, modifying, and removing mailboxes* recipe in this chapter
- *Managing distribution groups* recipe in this chapter

Configuring MailTips

MailTips was introduced in Exchange 2010, so it has been around for quite some time, and is commonly used since it's enabled by default. It was introduced to easily illustrate and show short information to end users in a user-friendly way. It works with both Outlook and Outlook Web App. An example of when this would be a great functionality would be when a recipient has configured their Out-of-office settings. If we were about to send an email to this user's mailbox with the out of office settings configured, an infobar would show up in the mail client. Another example of this function would be if we were writing an email and wanted to send it to a distribution group that has more than 25 members (this is the default value).

In this recipe, we will take a look at how we can disable the functionality and configure it for distribution groups, but we will also look at how to customize MailTips messages.

How to do it...

1. We can easily disable or enable the MailTips functionality on an organizational level if we want to change this setting:

```
Set-OrganizationConfig -MailTipsAllTipsEnabled $false
Set-OrganizationConfig -MailTipsAllTipsEnabled $true
```

2. To retrieve the current configuration for the distribution group MailTips, we can use the following cmdlet:

```
Get-OrganizationConfig | select MailTipsLargeAudienceThreshold
[PS] C:\>Get-OrganizationConfig | fl MailTipsLargeAudienceThreshold
MailTipsLargeAudienceThreshold : 100
```

3. Let's assume that we want to adjust the default value from 25 and change it to 100, since we are a large enterprise company. This is done by running the following:

```
Set-OrganizationConfig -MailTipsLargeAudienceThreshold 100
```

How it works...

Our first example is simply to enable or disable the functionality for the entire organization. If MailTips is disabled, it means that mail tips aren't going to show up for distribution groups, single mailboxes, and so on.

In our second example, we adjusted the threshold of when the mail tip will show up and give us the infobar in Outlook Web App or Outlook when we are about to send an email to a large distribution list. This value/number can be adjusted so it applies for your organization. The value itself is a System.Int32 (integer), so it can hold a really high number if needed.

There's more...

MailTips can also be configured per mailbox simply by using the Set-Mailbox cmdlet. Let's start with validating whether we have any current value configured by using the cmdlet:

```
Get-Mailbox "HelpDesk" | fl MailTip
```

The output from this cmdlet will look similar to the following value:

```
[PS] C:\>Get-Mailbox "HelpDesk" | fl MailTip
MailTip :
```

Now we have validated that there is no existing customized value configured for the HelpDesk mailbox. We want to customize the mail tips for the HelpDesk mailbox and make sure that when someone is about to send an email to the mailbox they will get an infobar showing the value we are about to configure. The configuration is simple, and is done by running the following cmdlet:

```
Set-Mailbox "HelpDesk" -MailTip "A Help Desk representative will `
contact you within 2 hours."
```

Once this has been completed, you can validate it by using either Outlook or the OWA, and the result will be similar to the following screenshot:

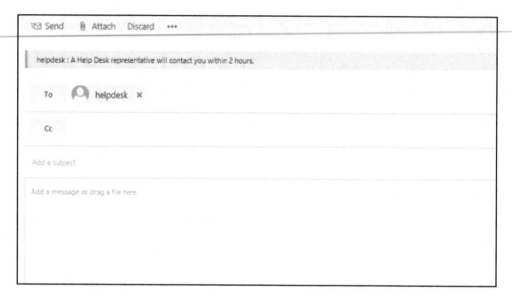

Mail tips can be customized for the following recipient types: `Mailbox`, `MailUser`, `MailContact`, `DistributionGroup`, or `DynamicDistributionGroup`.

See also

- *Working with recipient filters* recipe in this chapter
- *Managing distribution groups* recipe in this chapter

Working with recipient filters

Starting with Exchange 2007 and continuing with through the subsequent Exchange versions, address lists, dynamic distribution groups, email address policies, and global address lists can be customized with recipient filters that use the OPATH filtering syntax. This replaces the legacy LDAP filtering syntax that was used in earlier versions of Exchange. We can also perform server-side searches using filters, which can greatly speed up our work. In this recipe, you'll learn how to work with these filters in the Exchange Management Shell.

How to do it...

1. We can filter the results from the recipient `Get-*` cmdlets using the `-Filter` parameter:

```
Get-Mailbox -Filter {Office -eq 'Sales'}
```

2. In addition, we can use attribute filters to create distribution groups, email address policies, and address lists using the `-RecipientFilter` parameter:

```
New-DynamicDistributionGroup -Name DL_Accounting `
-RecipientFilter {
  (Department -eq 'Accounting') -and
  (RecipientType -eq 'UserMailbox')
}
```

How it works...

In our first example, you can see that we've used the `Get-Mailbox` cmdlet to retrieve only the users that have the `Office` property set to the value `Sales`. This is more efficient than performing the following command, which would return the same results:

```
Get-Mailbox | ?{$_.Office -eq 'Sales'}
```

This command uses the `Where-Object` cmdlet (using the `?` alias) to retrieve only the mailboxes with their `Office` property set to `Sales`. We get back the same results, but it is less efficient than our original example. When filtering with `Where-Object`, every mailbox in the organization must be retrieved and evaluated before any results are returned. The benefit of using the `-Filter` parameter with the `Get-Mailbox` cmdlet is that the filtering is done on the server and not our client machines. The `-Filter` method is preferred when working in large environments.

There are a number of cmdlets that support this parameter. You can get an entire list with a simple one-liner:

```
get-excommand | ?{$_.parameters.keys -eq 'filter'}
```

This uses the shell function `get-excommand` to retrieve a list of Exchange Management Shell cmdlets that support the `-Filter` parameter. If you are writing scripts or functions that need to query a large number of recipients, you'll want to try to use server-side filtering whenever possible.

Unfortunately, there are only a certain set of properties that can be filtered. For instance, we were able to filter using the `Office` property when using the `Get-Mailbox` cmdlet. Based on that, you may assume, since `OrganizationalUnit` is a property of a mailbox object, that you can filter that as well, but that is not the case. The `Get-Mailbox` cmdlet provides an `-OrganizationalUnit` parameter that can be used to accomplish that task, so it's not always safe to assume that a particular property can be used within a filter. To view a list of common filterable properties that can be used with the `-Filter` parameter, see Appendix A at the end of this book.

In our second example, we used the `New-DynamicDistributionGroup` cmdlet to create a query-based group. The membership of this group is determined using the OPATH filter defined with the `-RecipientFilter` parameter. The syntax is similar and the same PowerShell operators can be used. Based on the settings used with our filter when we created the `DL_Accounting` group, only mailboxes with their `Department` attribute set to `Accounting` will be included. Other recipient types, such as mail contacts and mail users, will not be included in the group, even though they may be in the `Accounting` department.

Dynamic distribution groups, address lists, and email address policies can be configured with these filters. Again, to get the list of cmdlets that support this functionality, use the `get-excommand` shell variable:

```
get-excommand | ?{$_.parameters.keys -eq 'recipientfilter'}
```

These cmdlets also have a limited number of filterable properties that can be used. To view a list of the most common properties used with the `-RecipientFilter` parameter, see *Appendix A* at the end of this book.

There's more...

Instead of using the `-RecipientFilter` parameter, you have the option of using precanned filters. In some cases, this may be easier as it allows you to simply use a set of parameters and values as opposed to an OPATH filter. The following command would create our `DL_Accounting` distribution group with the same members using the precanned filter parameters:

```
New-DynamicDistributionGroup -Name DL_Accounting `
-IncludedRecipients MailboxUsers `
-ConditionalDepartment Accounting
```

As you can see, this is a little easier to read and probably easier to type into the shell. However, there are only a few precanned parameters available, and they may not always be useful depending on what you are trying to do, but it helps to be aware of this functionality. You can use `Get-Help` to view the entire list of available parameters for each cmdlet that supports recipient filters.

Understanding variables in filters

One of the issues you may run into when working in the shell is the expansion of variables used within a filter. For example, this syntax is completely valid, but will not currently work correctly in the Exchange Management Shell:

```
$office = "sales"
Get-Mailbox -Filter {Office -eq $office}
```

You might get some results from this command, but they will probably not be what you are expecting. This is because, when running the `Get-Mailbox` cmdlet, the value of the `$office` variable will not be expanded prior to the command being executed through the remote shell. What you end up with instead is a filter checking for a `$null` value. In order to fix this, you'll need to use syntax similar to the following:

```
$office = "sales"
Get-Mailbox -Filter "Office -eq '$office'"
```

This syntax will force any variables assigned within the `-Filter` parameter to be expanded before sending the command through the remote session, and you should get back the correct results.

See also

- *Managing distribution groups* recipe in this chapter
- *Using the help system* recipe from `Chapter 1`, *PowerShell Key Concepts*
- *Previewing dynamic distribution group membership* recipe from `Chapter 5`, *Distribution Groups and Address Lists*

Adding and removing recipient email addresses

There are several recipient types in Exchange 2016, and each one of them can support multiple email addresses. Of course, the typical user mailbox recipient type is probably the first that comes to mind, but we also have distribution groups, contacts, and public folders, each of which can have one or more email addresses. The syntax used for adding and removing email addresses to each of these recipient types is essentially identical; the only thing that changes is the cmdlet that is used to set the address. In this recipe, you'll learn how to add or remove an email address from an Exchange recipient.

How to do it...

1. To add a secondary email address to a mailbox, use the following command syntax:

```
Set-Mailbox dave -EmailAddresses @{add='dave@west.contoso.com'}
```

2. Multiple addresses can also be added using this technique:

```
Set-Mailbox dave -EmailAddresses @{
  add='dave@east.contoso.com',
  'dave@west.contoso.com',
  'dave@corp.contoso.com'
}
```

3. Email addresses can also be removed using the following syntax:

```
Set-Mailbox dave -EmailAddresses @{remove='dave@west.contoso.com'}
```

4. Just as we are able to add multiple email addresses at once, we can do the same when removing an address:

```
Set-Mailbox dave -EmailAddresses @{
  remove='dave@east.contoso.com',
  'dave@corp.contoso.com'
}
```

How it works...

Adding and removing email addresses was more challenging back in the days of the Exchange 2007 management shell because it required that you work directly with the `EmailAddresses` collection, which is a multivalued property. In order to modify the collection, you first had to save the object to a variable, modify it, and then write it back to the `EmailAddresses` object on the recipient. This made it impossible to update the email addresses for a recipient with one command.

The `Set-*` cmdlets used to manage recipients in Exchange 2016 now support a new syntax that allows us to use a hash table to modify the `EmailAddresses` property. As you can see from the code samples, we can simply use the `Add` and `Remove` keys within the hash table, and the assigned email address values will either be added or removed as required. This is a nice change that makes it easier to do this in scripts, and especially when working interactively in the shell.

The `Add` and `Remove` keywords are interchangeable with the plus (+) and minus (–) characters that serve as aliases:

```
Set-Mailbox dave -EmailAddresses @{
   '+'='dave@east.contoso.com'
   '-'='dave@west.contoso.com'
}
```

In the previous example, we've added and removed email addresses from the mailbox. Note that the + and – keywords need to be enclosed in quotes so that PowerShell does not try to interpret them as the += and -= operators.

This syntax works with all of the `Set-*` cmdlets that support the `-EmailAddresses` parameter:

- `Set-CASMailbox`
- `Set-DistributionGroup`
- `Set-DynamicDistributionGroup`
- `Set-Mailbox`
- `Set-MailContact`
- `Set-MailPublicFolder`
- `Set-MailUser`
- `Set-RemoteMailbox`

Keep in mind that in most cases the best way to add an email address to a recipient is through the use of an email address policy. This may not always be an option, but should be used first if you find yourself in a situation where addresses need to be added to a large number of recipients. With that said, it is possible to do this in bulk using a simple `foreach` loop:

```
foreach($i in Get-Mailbox -OrganizationalUnit Sales) {
  Set-Mailbox $i -EmailAddresses @{
    add="$($i.alias)@west.contoso.com"
  }
}
```

This code simply iterates over each mailbox in the `Sales` OU and adds a secondary email address using the existing alias at `west.contoso.com`. You can use this technique and modify the syntax as needed to perform bulk operations.

There's more...

Imagine a situation where you need to remove all email addresses under a certain domain from all of your mailboxes. These could be secondary addresses that were added manually to each mailbox, or that used to be applied as part of an email address policy that no longer applies. The following code can be used to remove all email addresses from mailboxes under a specific domain:

```
foreach($i in Get-Mailbox -ResultSize Unlimited) {
  $i.EmailAddresses |
    ?{$_.SmtpAddress -like '*@corp.contoso.com'} | %{
      Set-Mailbox $i -EmailAddresses @{remove=$_}
    }
}
```

This code iterates through each mailbox in the organization and simply uses a filter to discover any email addresses at `corp.contoso.com`. If any exist, the `Set-Mailbox` cmdlet will attempt to remove each of them from the mailbox.

See also

- *Adding, modifying, and removing mailboxes* recipe in this chapter
- *Working with contacts* recipe in this chapter
- *Managing distribution groups* recipe in this chapter

Hiding recipients from address lists

There may be times when you'll need to hide a particular mailbox, contact, or distribution group from your Exchange address lists. This is a common task that is required when you have mailboxes, contacts, or public folders used by applications or staff in your IT department that should not be seen by end-users. In this recipe, we'll take a look at how you can disable these recipient types from the address lists using the Exchange Management Shell.

How to do it...

To hide a mailbox from the Exchange address lists, use the Set-Mailbox command:

```
Set-Mailbox dave -HiddenFromAddressListsEnabled $true
```

How it works...

As you can see, hiding a mailbox from address lists is pretty straightforward, as it requires only a simple PowerShell one-liner. The -HiddenFromAddressListsEnabled parameter accepts a Boolean value, either $true or $false. To enable this setting, set the value to $true, and to disable it, set the value to $false.

There are multiple recipient types that can be hidden from address lists. Each of the following Set-* cmdlets supports the -HiddenFromAddressListsEnabled parameter:

- Set-DistributionGroup
- Set-DynamicDistributionGroup
- Set-Mailbox
- Set-MailContact
- Set-MailPublicFolder
- Set-MailUser
- Set-RemoteMailbox

There's more...

Once you've hidden your recipients from the address lists, you may need to generate a report to list the objects that currently have the `HiddenFromAddressListsEnabled` setting enabled. Use the following command syntax to obtain this information:

```
Get-Mailbox -Filter {HiddenFromAddressListsEnabled -eq $true}
```

This searches for all mailboxes that have been hidden from the address lists. It makes use of the `-Filter` parameter, which keeps you from having to perform the filtering on the client side with the `Where-Object` cmdlet.

See also

- *Working with recipient filters* recipe in this chapter

Configuring recipient moderation

Recipient moderation allows you to require approval for all email messages sent to a particular recipient by a designated moderator. In this recipe, you'll learn how to configure the moderation settings on recipients using the Exchange Management Shell.

How to do it...

1. To enable moderation for a distribution group, use the `Set-DistributionGroup` cmdlet:

   ```
   Set-DistributionGroup -Identity Executives `
   -ModerationEnabled $true `
   -ModeratedBy administrator `
   -SendModerationNotifications Internal
   ```

2. These same parameters can be used to configure moderation for a mailbox when using the `Set-Mailbox` cmdlet:

   ```
   Set-Mailbox -Identity dave `
   -ModerationEnabled $true `
   -ModeratedBy administrator `
   -SendModerationNotifications Internal
   ```

How it works...

When you enable moderation for a recipient, any email message sent to that recipient must be reviewed by a moderator. When a message is sent to a moderated recipient, the moderator will receive the message and determine whether or not it should be accepted. This is done by the moderator through Outlook or OWA by clicking on an **Approve** or **Reject** button in the email message. If the moderator accepts the message, it is delivered to the group. If it is rejected, the message is deleted, and, depending on the SendModerationNotifications setting, the sender may receive an email informing them that the message has been rejected.

Moderation can be enabled for any recipient, whether it's a mailbox, mail contact, mail user, distribution group, or mail-enabled public folder. The cmdlets for each of these recipient types can be used to configure moderation when a recipient is being created with the New-* cmdlets, or after the fact using the Set-* cmdlets. To view the list of cmdlets that can be used to enable moderation, run the following command:

```
get-excommand | ?{$_.parameters.keys -eq 'ModerationEnabled'}
```

In our first example, we enabled moderation for the Executives distribution group, specifying that the administrator account will be used as the moderator for the group. As you can see in the example, we've used multiple parameters when running the command, but only the -ModerationEnabled parameter is required to change the moderation setting for the group. If no value is specified for the -ModeratedBy parameter, the group owner will review and approve the messages sent to the group. You can specify one or more owners when running the Set-DistributionGroup cmdlet with the -ManagedBy parameter.

The -SendModerationNotifications parameter allows you to control the status messages sent to the originator of a message that was sent to a moderated recipient. We have the option of using the following values for this parameter:

- **Always**: Notifications are sent to all internal and external senders
- **Internal**: Notifications are only sent to users within the organization
- **Never**: Notifications are not sent at all

If no value is provided for the -SendModerationNotifications parameter when you enable moderation for a group, the setting will default to Always.

There's more...

There is an exception to every rule, and, of course, there may be times when we need to bypass moderation for certain recipients. Let's say that we need to bypass specific users from moderation on the Executives distribution group. The group moderator or group owners are already exempt from moderation. To exclude others, we can specify a list of one or more recipients using the `-BypassModerationFromSendersOrMembers` parameter when running the `Set-DistributionGroup` cmdlet.

For example, to exclude a recipient named Bob from moderation on the *Executives* distribution group, run the following command:

```
Set-DistributionGroup -Identity Executives `
-BypassModerationFromSendersOrMembers bob@contoso.com
```

If you want the members of the moderated group, or any other distribution group, to be excluded from moderation, simply use the previous syntax and assign the identity of the group to the `-BypassModerationFromSendersOrMembers` parameter. You can assign multiple users or distribution groups at once by separating each value with a comma.

Keep in mind that running the previous command will overwrite the existing list of bypassed members if any have been defined. For an example of how to add a new item to a multivalued property, see the *Working with arrays and hash tables* recipe from Chapter 1, *PowerShell Key Concepts*.

Additionally, you may need to bypass moderation for a group of several individual recipients. While you could add them one by one, this could be very time consuming if you are dealing with a large number of recipients. Let's say that you want to exclude all the users in the San Diego office from moderation:

```
$exclude = Get-Mailbox -Filter {Office -eq 'Seattle'} |
   Select-Object -ExpandProperty alias

Set-DistributionGroup -Identity Executives `
-BypassModerationFromSendersOrMembers $exclude
```

In this example, we create a collection that contains the alias for each mailbox in the Seattle Office. Next, we use the `Set-DistributionGroup` cmdlet to exclude all of those recipients from moderation using a single command. While this might be useful in certain situations, it's easier to bypass moderation based on groups. If a group has been bypassed for moderation, you can simply manage the membership of the group and you don't need to worry about continuously updating individual recipients that are on the bypass list.

See also

- *Managing distribution groups* recipe in this chapter

Configuring message delivery restrictions

Since distribution groups contain multiple members, you may want to place restrictions on who can send messages to these recipients. Exchange allows you to tightly control these settings, and provides several options when it comes to placing message delivery restrictions on groups. We can also place restrictions on other recipient types in the organization. This recipe will show you how to configure these options from the Exchange Management Shell.

How to do it...

To restrict who can send messages to a group, use the `Set-DistributionGroup` cmdlet:

```
Set-DistributionGroup -Identity Sales `
-AcceptMessagesOnlyFrom 'Bob Smith','John Jones'
```

After running this command, only the users Bob Smith and John Jones can send messages to the `Sales` distribution group.

How it works...

The `-AcceptMessagesOnlyFrom` parameter allows you to specify one or more recipients who are allowed to send messages to a distribution group. These recipients can be regular users with mailboxes or contacts.

You can add individual recipients and distribution groups to the accepted senders list using the following syntax:

```
Set-DistributionGroup -Identity Sales `
-AcceptMessagesOnlyFromSendersOrMembers Marketing,bob@contoso.com
```

In this example, we're allowing both the `Marketing` distribution group and Bob, an individual recipient, to the accepted senders list for the `Sales` distribution group. Doing so will allow Bob and any members of the `Marketing` distribution group to send messages to the `Sales` group.

Keep in mind that, when using these parameters, any existing accepted recipients that have been configured will be overwritten. For an example of how to add a new item to a multivalued property, see the section in Chapter 1 titled *Working with arrays and hash tables*.

Delivery restrictions can be placed on any recipient, whether it's a mailbox, mail contact, mail user, distribution group, or mail-enabled public folder. The Set-* cmdlets for each of these recipient types can be used to configure delivery restrictions. To view the list of cmdlets that can be used to do this, run the following command:

```
get-excommand | ?{$_.parameters.keys -eq 'AcceptMessagesOnlyFrom'}
```

If you need to add a large list of users to the accepted senders list, you can create a collection and assign it to the -AcceptMessagesOnlyFrom parameter:

```
$finance = Get-Mailbox -Filter {Office -eq 'Finance'}
Set-DistributionGroup -Identity Sales `
-AcceptMessagesOnlyFrom $finance
```

You can wipe out these settings and allow messages from all senders by setting the value to $null:

```
Set-DistributionGroup -Identity Sales `
-AcceptMessagesOnlyFromSendersOrMembers $null
```

Similar to the previous examples, we can reject messages from a specific user or member of a distribution list using the -RejectMessagesFromSendersOrMembers parameter:

```
Set-DistributionGroup -Identity Executives `
-RejectMessagesFromSendersOrMembers HourlyEmployees
```

In this example, Exchange will reject any message sent from a member of the HourlyEmployees distribution group to the Executives group.

There's more...

When you create a distribution group, the default configuration is to reject messages from senders who are not authenticated. This means that users outside of your organization will not be able to send messages to your distribution groups. Generally, this is the desired configuration, but if needed, you can modify this setting on a distribution group to accept messages from external users using the following syntax:

```
Set-DistributionGroup -Identity HelpDesk `
-RequireSenderAuthenticationEnabled $false
```

You can see here that we've disabled sender authentication for the `HelpDesk` distribution group. You can re-enable it at any time by setting the previous parameter value to `$true`.

See also

- *Managing distribution groups* recipe in this chapter

Managing automatic replies and out-of-office settings for a user

Since Exchange 2010, we've got a valuable set of cmdlets that can be used to manage and automate the configuration of a user's Out of Office settings. In this recipe, we'll take a look at how to use these cmdlets from the Exchange Management Shell for Exchange 2016.

How to do it...

1. To view the Out of Office settings for a mailbox, use the following syntax:

    ```
    Get-MailboxAutoReplyConfiguration dave
    ```

2. You can change the Out of Office settings for a mailbox using the following syntax as shown:

    ```
    Set-MailboxAutoReplyConfiguration dave `
    -AutoReplyState Disabled
    ```

How it works...

Retrieving the settings for a mailbox simply requires that you run the `Get-MailboxAutoReplyConfiguration` cmdlet and specify the identity of the mailbox, as shown in the previous example. The `Set-MailboxAutoReplyConfiguration` cmdlet supports multiple parameters that can be used to customize the settings for the mailbox autoreply configuration:

```
Set-MailboxAutoReplyConfiguration dave `
-AutoReplyState Scheduled `
```

```
-StartTime 3/25/2017 `
-EndTime 4/3/2017 `
-ExternalMessage "I will be out of the office this week"
```

In this command, we set the `AutoReplyState`, specify a `StartTime` and `EndTime`, and set the `ExternalMessage`. When the `StartTime` date is reached, the mailbox will proceed to automatically reply to messages using the specified `ExternalMessage` until the `EndTime` date is reached. If you want automatic replies to be enabled indefinitely, set the `AutoReplyState` to `Enabled`.

To view the settings configured in the previous command, we can use the `Get-MailboxAutoReplyConfiguration` cmdlet, as shown in the following screenshot:

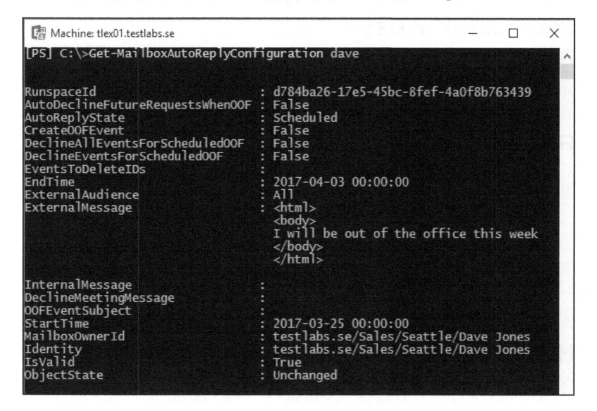

You can see from viewing the mailbox autoreply settings for this mailbox that only external replies are enabled. To enable internal out-of-office messages, you could run the previous set command and specify a message using the -InternalMessage parameter. Or you can use them both using a single command.

The -InternalMessage and -ExternalMessage parameters support HTML-formatted messages. If you want to set custom HTML code when configuring the autoreply configuration from the shell, you can use the following command syntax:

```
Set-MailboxAutoReplyConfiguration dave `
-ExternalMessage (Get-Content C:\Scripts\oof.html)
```

This command will read in a custom HTML-formatted message from an external file and use that data when setting the internal or external message. This will allow you to work on the file from the HTML editor of your choice and import the code using a simple command from the shell.

By default, the -ExternalAudience parameter will be set to All if no value is specified. The remaining options are Known and None. Setting the external audience to Known will only send automatic replies to external users who are listed as contacts in the users mailbox.

There's more...

These cmdlets can be useful when making mass updates and when running reports. For example, to determine all of the users that currently have out of office enabled, you can run the following command:

```
Get-Mailbox -ResultSize Unlimited |
  Get-MailboxAutoReplyConfiguration |
    ?{$_.AutoReplyState -ne "Disabled"} |
      Select Identity,AutoReplyState,StartTime,EndTime
```

This one-liner will check every mailbox in the organization and return only the mailboxes with the autoreply state set to either Enabled or Scheduled.

Note that the out-of-office configuration set by administrators will override any configuration done by the end user.

Adding, modifying, and removing server-side inbox rules

This set of cmdlets was introduced back in Exchange 2010, so they have been around for some time, but are still worth bringing up. They can be used to manage server-side inbox rules for mailboxes in your organization. We now have the ability to add, remove, update, enable, and disable the inbox rules for mailboxes from within the Exchange Management Shell. This new functionality allows administrators to quickly resolve mailbox issues related to inbox rules, and allows them to easily deploy and manage inbox rules in bulk using just a few simple commands. In this recipe, you'll learn how to work with the inbox rule cmdlets in Exchange 2016.

How to do it...

1. To create an inbox rule, use the New-InboxRule cmdlet:

```
New-InboxRule -Name Sales -Mailbox dave `
-From sales@contoso.com `
-MarkImportance High
```

2. You can change the configuration of an inbox rule using the Set-InboxRule cmdlet:

```
Set-InboxRule -Identity Sales -Mailbox dave `
-MarkImportance Low
```

3. Use the Enable-InboxRule and Disable-InboxRule cmdlets to turn a rule on or off:

```
Disable-InboxRule -Identity Sales -Mailbox dave
```

4. The Get-InboxRule cmdlet will return all of the server-side rules that have been created for a specified mailbox. The output from the command is shown in the following screenshot:

```
Machine: tlex01.testlabs.se                         —    □    ×

[PS] C:\>Get-InboxRule -Mailbox dave

Name   Enabled  Priority  RuleIdentity
----   -------  --------  ------------
Sales  True     1         5838072491955716097
```

5. To remove an inbox rule, use the `Remove-InboxRule` cmdlet:

```
Remove-InboxRule -Identity Sales -Mailbox dave `
-Confirm:$false
```

How it works...

Inbox rules are used to process messages sent to a mailbox based on a certain set of criteria, and to then take an action on that message if the condition is met. In the previous example, we created an inbox rule for the mailbox that would mark messages from the sales@contoso.com address with high importance. The `New-InboxRule` cmdlet provides a number of rule predicate parameters that allow you to define the conditions used for the rules you create.

Let's take a look at another example. Say that we want to create a rule that will check the subject or body of all incoming messages for a certain keyword. If there is a match, we'll send the message to the deleted items folder:

```
New-InboxRule -Name "Delete Rule" `
-Mailbox dave `
-SubjectOrBodyContainsWords "Delete Me" `
-DeleteMessage $true
```

In addition to conditions and actions, we can also add exceptions to these rules. Consider the following example:

```
New-InboxRule -Name "Redirect to Andrew" `
-Mailbox dave `
-MyNameInToOrCcBox $true `
-RedirectTo "Andrew Castaneda" `
-ExceptIfFrom "Alfonso Mcgowan" `
-StopProcessingRules $true
```

In this example, once again we're creating an inbox rule in Dave's mailbox. The condition MyNameInToOrCcBox is set to $true so that any message with the mailbox name in the To or CC fields will be processed by this rule. The action is the RedirectTo setting, and that will redirect the message to Andrews's mailbox, except if the message was sent from Alfonso's mailbox. Finally, the -StopProcessingRules parameter is set to $true, meaning that, once this rule is processed, Exchange will not process any other rules in this mailbox. The -StopProcessingRules parameter is an optional setting and is provided to give you another level of flexibility when it comes to controlling the way the rules are applied.

It's important to note that when you add, remove, update, enable, or disable server-side rules using the *-InboxRule cmdlets, any client-side rules created by Outlook will be removed.

In all of these examples, we've specified the mailbox identity and have been configuring the rules of a single mailbox. If you do not provide a value for the -Mailbox parameter, the *-InboxRule cmdlets will execute against the mailbox belonging to the user that is running the command.

There's more...

Now let's take a look at a practical example of how you might create inbox rules in bulk. The following code will create an inbox rule for every mailbox in the Sales OU:

```
$sales = Get-Mailbox -OrganizationalUnit contoso.com/sales
$sales | %{
  New-InboxRule -Name Junk `
  -Mailbox $_.alias `
  -SubjectContainsWords "[Spam]" `
  -MoveToFolder "$($_.alias):\Junk Email"
}
```

What we are doing here is using the -SubjectContainsWords parameter to check for a subject line that starts with [Spam]. If there is a match, we move the message to the Junk Email folder within that user's mailbox. As you can see, we are looping through each mailbox using the ForEach-Object cmdlet (using the % alias), and, within the loop, we specify the identity of the user when creating the inbox rule and when specifying the folder ID, using the $_.alias property.

Even if you are logged in using an account in the Organization Management group, you may receive errors when trying to use the `-MoveToFolder` parameter when creating an inbox rule in another user's mailbox. Assigning `FullAccess` permissions to the mailbox in question should resolve this issue. For more details, see *Granting administrators full access to mailboxes* in Chapter 10, *Exchange Security*.

Make sure to verify the folder names; these vary depending on the selected language, and are set per mailbox.

See also

- *Granting users full access permissions to mailboxes* recipe from Chapter 10, *Compliance and Audit Logging*

Managing mailbox folder permissions

These cmdlets where introduced back in Exchange 2010. They can be used to manage the permissions on the folders inside a mailbox. When it comes to managing recipients, one of the most common tasks that administrators and support personnel perform on a regular basis is updating the permissions on the calendar of a mailbox. In most corporate environments, calendars are shared amongst employees, and often special rights need to be delegated to other users, allowing them to add, remove, update, or change the items on a calendar. In this recipe, we'll cover the basics of managing mailbox folder permissions from within the shell, but we will focus specifically on calendar permissions since that is a common scenario. Keep in mind that the cmdlets used in this recipe can be used with any folder within a mailbox.

How to do it...

To allow users to view the calendar for a specific mailbox, use the following command:

```
Set-MailboxFolderPermission -Identity dave:\Calendar `
-User Default `
-AccessRights Reviewer
```

How it works...

In this example, we're giving the `Default` user the ability to read all items in the calendar of the specified mailbox by assigning the `Reviewer` access right. This would give every user in the organization the ability to view the calendar items for this mailbox. There are four cmdlets in total that can be used to manage the mailbox folder permissions:

- `Add-MailboxFolderPermission`
- `Get-MailboxFolderPermission`
- `RemovemailboxFolderPermission`
- `Set-MailboxFolderPermission`

The `Add` and `Set-MailboxFolderPermission` cmdlets both provide an `-AccessRights` parameter that is used to set the appropriate permissions on the folder specified in the command. In the previous example, instead of assigning the `Reviewer` role, we could have assigned the `Editor` role to the **Default** user, giving all users the ability to completely manage the items in the calendar. The possible values that can be used with the `-AccessRights` parameter are as follows:

- `ReadItems`: The user that is assigned this right can read items within the designated folder.
- `CreateItems`: The user that is assigned this right can create items within the designated folder.
- `EditOwnedItems`: The user that is assigned this right can edit the items that the user owns in the designated folder.
- `DeleteOwnedItems`: The user that is assigned this right can delete items that the user owns in the designated folder.
- `EditAllItems`: The user that is assigned this right can edit all items in the designated folder.
- `DeleteAllItems`: The user that is assigned this right can delete all items in the designated folder.
- `CreateSubfolders`: The user that is assigned this right can create subfolders in the designated folder.
- `FolderOwner`: The user that is assigned this right has the right to view and move the folder and create subfolders. The user cannot read items, edit items, delete items, or create items.

- FolderContact: The user that is assigned this right is the contact for the designated folder.
- FolderVisible: The user that is assigned this right can view the specified folder, but can't read or edit items within it.

The following roles are made up by one or more of the permissions specified in the previous list and can also be used with the -AccessRights parameter:

- **None**: FolderVisible
- **Owner**: CreateItems, ReadItems, CreateSubfolders, FolderOwner, FolderContact, FolderVisible, EditOwnedItems, EditAllItems, DeleteOwnedItems, DeleteAllItems
- **PublishingEditor**: CreateItems, ReadItems, CreateSubfolders, FolderVisible, EditOwnedItems, EditAllItems, DeleteOwnedItems, DeleteAllItems
- **Editor**: CreateItems, ReadItems, FolderVisible, EditOwnedItems, EditAllItems, DeleteOwnedItems, DeleteAllItems
- **PublishingAuthor**: CreateItems, ReadItems, CreateSubfolders, FolderVisible, EditOwnedItems, DeleteOwnedItems
- **Author**: CreateItems, ReadItems, FolderVisible, EditOwnedItems, DeleteOwnedItems
- **NonEditingAuthor**: CreateItems, ReadItems, FolderVisible
- **Reviewer**: ReadItems, FolderVisible
- **Contributor**: CreateItems, FolderVisible

There's more...

Using the *-MailboxFolderPermission cmdlets makes it easier to perform bulk operations on many mailboxes at once. For example, let's say that you need to assign Reviewer permissions to all employees on every mailbox calendar in the organization. You can use the following code to accomplish this task:

```
$mailboxes = Get-Mailbox -ResultSize Unlimited
$mailboxes | %{
$calendar = Get-MailboxFolderPermission `
 "$($_.alias):\Calendar" -User Default
  if(!($calendar.AccessRights)) {
    Add-MailboxFolderPermission "$($_.alias):\Calendar" `
    -User Default -AccessRights Reviewer
```

```
  }
  if($calendar.AccessRights -ne "Reviewer") {
    Set-MailboxFolderPermission "$($_.alias):\Calendar" `
    -User Default -AccessRights Reviewer
  }
}
```

First, we use the Get-Mailbox cmdlet to retrieve all mailboxes in the organization and store that result in the $mailboxes variable. We then loop through each mailbox in the $mailboxes collection. Within the loop, we retrieve the current calendar settings for the Default user, using the Get-MailboxFolderPermission cmdlet, and store the output in the $calendar variable. If the Default user has not been assigned any rights to the calendar, we use the Add-MailboxFolderPermission cmdlet to add the Reviewer access right.

If the Default user has been assigned calendar permissions, we check to see if the access rights are set to Reviewer. If not, we modify the existing setting for the Default user to the Reviewer access right.

 Note that if these aforementioned users have never logged into their mailbox, the cmdlet will fail on that particular mailbox.

See also

- *Granting users full access permissions to mailboxes* recipe from Chapter 10, *Compliance and Audit Logging*

Importing user photos into Active Directory

One of the most popular features back when it was introduced in Exchange 2010 was the ability to view user photos. Even though newer Outlook versions have a built-in social connector, this may be applicable to Outlook 2013/2016 as well for organizations. This feature is based on the ability to import an image into the thumbnailPhoto attribute for a given user account in Active Directory. This image can then be displayed when viewing a message or browsing the Global Address List within Outlook 2010 or newer.

This was a highly requested enhancement, and the addition of this new feature makes it easier, especially in large organizations, to identify co-workers and get to know the people you are working with. In this recipe, we'll look at how you can import user photographs into Active Directory.

Getting ready

In addition to the Exchange Management Shell, you will need access to the Active Directory administration tools for this recipe. The Remote Server Administration Tools pack (RSAT-ADDS) is a prerequisite required by the Exchange 2016 setup, so it will already be installed on an Exchange 2016 server, and you can use the tools from there, if needed.

How to do it...

First, you need to update the Active Directory Schema to ensure that the `thumbnailPhoto` attribute will be replicated to the Global Catalog. Your account will need to be a member of the schema admins group in Active Directory. On a machine with the Active Directory administration tools installed, do the following:

1. In the Exchange Management Shell or a `cmd` console, run the following command to register the Active Directory Schema extension:

```
Regsvr32 schmmgmt.dll
```

2. Start the MMC console by clicking on **Windows button** | **Run**, type `MMC,` and click **OK**.
3. Go to **File** and click on **Add/Remove Snap-In**.
4. Add the Active Directory Schema Snap-In and click **OK**.
5. Under Active Directory Schema, highlight the **Attributes** node, and locate the **thumbnailPhoto** attribute.
6. Right-click on the **thumbnailPhoto** attribute and click on **Properties**.
7. On the Properties page, select **Replicate this attribute to the Global Catalog** and click **OK**.

At this point, the required Active Directory steps have been validated and you can now import a photo into Active Directory using the new cmdlet `Set-UserPhoto`:

```
Set-UserPhoto -Identity dave -PictureData `
([System.IO.File]::ReadAllBytes("C:\Scripts\dave.jpg"))
```

How it works...

Each user account or contact object in Active Directory has a `thumbnailPhoto` attribute that can be used to store binary data. The `Set-UserPhoto` cmdlet is used for reading a `.jpg` file into a byte array and importing it into the `thumbnailPhoto` attribute of the user account or contact in Active Directory, using the parameter `PictureData` followed by the .NET class `[System.IO.File]::ReadAllBytes`. Once the data has been imported into Active Directory, Outlook will query the `thumbnailPhoto` attribute of each user and display their photo when you receive an email message from them, or when you are viewing their information in the Global Address List.

> If you need to remove a photo for a user or a contact, use the `Remove-UserPhoto` cmdlet followed by the parameter `Identity` and a unique identifier of the user/contact object.

There are a few things to keep in mind when you decide to load photos into Active Directory for your users. The recommended thumbnail photo size in pixels is 96 x 96 pixels. Finally, be conscious about the size of your NTDS database in Active Directory. If you only have a small number of users, then this will probably not be a huge issue. If you have hundreds of thousands of users there will be some serious replication traffic if you suddenly import photos for each of those users. Make sure to plan accordingly.

There's more...

Outlook clients operating in cached mode will use the `thumbnailPhoto` attribute configuration of the **offline address book (OAB)** to determine how to access photos. By default, the `thumbnailPhoto` attribute is an indicator attribute, meaning that it points Outlook to Active Directory to retrieve the image.

If you want to disable thumbnail photos for cached-mode clients, remove the attribute using the `Remove` method of the `ConfiguredAttrbutes` collection:

```
$oab = Get-OfflineAddressBook 'Default Offline Address Book'
$oab.ConfiguredAttributes.Remove('thumbnailphoto,indicator')
Set-OfflineAddressBook 'Default Offline Address Book' `
-ConfiguredAttributes $oab.ConfiguredAttributes
```

If you want offline clients to be able to view thumbnail photos, you can add the `thumbnailPhoto` attribute as a value attribute using the `Add` method:

```
$oab = Get-OfflineAddressBook 'Default Offline Address Book'
$oab.ConfiguredAttributes.Add('thumbnailphoto,value')
Set-OfflineAddressBook 'Default Offline Address Book' `
-ConfiguredAttributes $oab.ConfiguredAttributes
```

If you work in a medium or large organization, this could make for an extremely large OAB. Again, make sure to plan accordingly. Use the following command to update the OAB after these configuration changes have been made:

```
Update-OfflineAddressBook 'Default Offline Address Book'
```

Taking it a step further

If you are going to take advantage of this function, you are likely going to do this in bulk for existing employees, or as new employees are hired, and this may require some automation. Let's say that your company issues a security badge with a photo for each employee. You have each of these photos stored on a file server in JPEG format. The filenames of the photos use the Exchange alias for the associated mailbox. The following script can be used in this scenario to import the photos in bulk:

```
$photos = Get-ChildItem \\server01\employeephotos -Filter *.jpg

foreach($i in $photos) {
  [Byte[]]$data = gc -Path $i.fullname -Encoding Byte `
  -ReadCount 0  Set-UserPhoto -Identity $i.basename -PictureData $data `
  -Confirm:$false
}
```

First, this code creates a collection of jpeg files in the \\server01\employeephotos share and stores the results in the $photos object. We're using the -Filter parameter with the Get-ChildItem cmdlet so that the command only returns files with a .jpg extension. The items returned from the Get-ChildItem cmdlet are FileInfo objects that contain several properties that include detailed information about each file, such as the filename and the full path to the file.

As we loop through each photo in the collection, you can see that inside the loop we're casting the output from Get-Content (using the gc alias) to [Byte[]] and storing the result in the $data variable. We can determine the path to the file using the FullName property of the FileInfo object that represents the current JPEG file being processed in the loop. We then use the Set-UserPhoto cmdlet to import the data for the current user in the loop. The BaseName property of a FileInfo object returns the filename without the extension; therefore, we use this property value to identify which user we're importing the photo for when executing the Set-UserPhoto cmdlet.

See also

- *Transferring files through remote PowerShell* recipe from Chapter 2, *Exchange Management Shell Common Tasks*

4
Managing Mailboxes

In this chapter, we will cover the following topics:

- Reporting on mailbox sizes
- Reporting on the mailbox creation time
- Working with move requests and performing mailbox moves
- Email notification on mailbox moves
- Importing and exporting mailboxes
- Deleting messages from mailboxes using Search-Mailbox
- Deleting messages from mailboxes using Compliance Search
- Managing disconnected mailboxes
- Setting storage quotas for mailboxes
- Finding email addresses with numbers
- Finding mailboxes with different SIP and primary SMTP addresses
- Finding inactive mailboxes
- Detecting and fixing corrupt mailboxes
- Restoring deleted items from mailboxes
- Managing public folder mailboxes
- Reporting on public folder statistics
- Managing user access to public folders

Introduction

The concept of the mailbox is the core feature of any Exchange solution, and it's likely that almost everything you do as an Exchange administrator will revolve around this component. Now in Exchange 2016, the architecture has changed once more, and lots of new cmdlets and features have been introduced that make life much easier for any Exchange administrator, allowing you to do just about anything you can think of when it comes to managing mailboxes through scripts and one-liners. This includes tasks such as moving, importing, exporting, removing, searching, and reconnecting mailboxes, just to name a few. In this chapter, you will learn how to generate reports, perform bulk mailbox changes, repair corrupt mailboxes, search and delete emails, and much more.

Performing some basic steps

To work with the code samples in this chapter, follow these steps to launch the Exchange Management Shell:

1. Log on to a workstation or server with the Exchange Management Tools installed.
2. Alternatively, open the Exchange Management Shell by navigating to **Start | All Programs | Exchange Server 2016**.
3. Click on the **Exchange Management Shell** shortcut.

Remember to start the Exchange Management Shell using **Run as Administrator** to avoid permission problems.

In this chapter, in some cmdlet examples, you might notice the use of a back tick (`` ` ``) character to break up long commands into multiple lines. The purpose of this is to make it easier to read. The back ticks are not required and should be used only if needed.

Reporting on mailbox sizes

Using cmdlets from both the Exchange Management Shell and Windows PowerShell gives us the ability to generate detailed reports. In this recipe, we will use these cmdlets to report on all of the mailboxes within an organization and their total size.

How to do it...

Let's look at how to generate and export the report of a mailbox using the following steps:

1. Use the following command to generate a report of each mailbox in the organization and the total mailbox size:

```
Get-MailboxDatabase | Get-MailboxStatistics | `
? {!$_.DisconnectDate} | Select-Object DisplayName, TotalItemSize
```

2. Pipe the command even further to export the report to a CSV file that can be opened and formatted in Excel:

```
Get-MailboxDatabase | Get-MailboxStatistics | `
? {!$_.DisconnectDate} | Select-Object DisplayName,  TotalItemSize |

Export-CSV C:MBreport.csv -NoType
```

How it works...

In both the commands, we're using the Get-MailboxDatabase cmdlet to pipe each database in the organization to the Get-MailboxStatistics cmdlet. Note that in the next stage of the pipeline, we are filtering on the DisconnectDate property. Inside the filter, we are using the exclamation (!) character, which is a shortcut for the -not operator in PowerShell. So we are basically asking to get all the mailboxes in the organization that are not in a disconnected state. These can be standard mailboxes as well as archive mailboxes. We then select the DisplayName and TotalItemSize properties that give us the name and total mailbox size of each mailbox.

There's more...

When using the first example to view the mailboxes and their total size, you will see that the output in the Shell is similar to what is shown in the following screenshot:

```
Machine: tlex01.testlabs.se                          _  □  x

[PS] C:\Scripts>Get-MailboxDatabase | Get-MailboxStatistics | ?{!$_.Disconn
ectDate} | Select-Object DisplayName,TotalItemSize

DisplayName                    TotalItemSize
-----------                    -------------
admins                         13.34 MB (13,993,029 bytes)
Klas Andersson                 10.9 MB (11,425,207 bytes)
Jonas Andersson                12.18 MB (12,770,516 bytes)
Sofie Andersson                11.91 MB (12,488,421 bytes)
Ann Andersson                  9.449 MB (9,908,020 bytes)
Indie Andersson                11.4 MB (11,955,851 bytes)
```

Here, you can see that we get the total size in megabytes as well as in bytes. If you find that this additional information is not useful, you can extend the previous one-liner using a calculated property:

```
Get-MailboxDatabase | Get-MailboxStatistics | ? {!$_.DisconnectDate} | `
Select-Object DisplayName, @{n="SizeMB";e={$_.TotalItemSize.value.ToMb()}}
| `
Sort-Object SizeMB –Descending
```

Running the preceding one-liner will provide output similar to the following:

```
Machine: tlex01.testlabs.se                          _  □  x

ectDate} | Select-Object DisplayName,@{n="SizeMB";e={$_.TotalItemSize.value
.ToMb()}} | Sort-Object SizeMB -Descending

DisplayName                                              SizeMB
-----------                                              ------
HealthMailbox-tlex01-DB1                                    153
HealthMailbox-tlex01-DB2                                    153
HealthMailbox-tlex01-001                                     40
admins                                                      13
Jonas Andersson                                             12
Sofie Andersson                                             11
testuser                                                    11
Indie Andersson                                             11
Klas Andersson                                             10
Ann Andersson                                                9
```

Note that we now have a custom property called `SizeMB` that reports only the mailbox size in megabytes. We have also sorted this property in the `Descending` order and the mailboxes are now listed from largest to smallest based on their size. You can continue to pipe this command down to `Export-CSV` cmdlet to generate a report that can be viewed outside the Shell.

See also

- *Creating, modifying, and removing mailboxes* recipe from Chapter 3, *Managing Recipients*
- *Working with move requests and performing mailbox moves* recipe in this chapter
- *Reporting on the mailbox database size* recipe from Chapter 6, *Mailbox Database Management*
- *Finding the total number of mailboxes in a database* recipe from Chapter 6, *Mailbox Database Management*
- *Determining the average mailbox size per database* recipe from Chapter 6, *Mailbox Database Management*

Reporting on the mailbox creation time

If you work in an environment where new employees are frequently hired, you may have a process in place to provision your mailboxes in bulk. You may have already used this book to help you do this. Now you might like to generate reports or retrieve a list of mailboxes that were created during a specific time frame or after a specific date. In this recipe, you will learn a couple of ways to do this using the Exchange Management Shell.

How to do it...

Let's start off with a simple example. To generate a report of mailboxes created in the previous week, execute the following command:

```
Get-Mailbox -ResultSize Unlimited | `
? {$_.WhenMailboxCreated -ge (Get-Date).AddDays(-7)} | `
Select DisplayName, WhenMailboxCreated, Database | `
Export-CSV C:\mb_report.CSV -NoType
```

How it works...

This one-liner searches through every mailbox in the organization by checking the WhenMailboxCreated property. If the date is within the last 7 days, we select a few useful properties for each mailbox and export the list to a CSV file.

Mailboxes also have a property called `WhenCreated`, so why don't we just check this property instead? The is because the `WhenCreated` property is an Active Directory attribute that stores the creation date of the user account and not the mailbox. It is quite possible that your user accounts are created in Active Directory long before they are mail-enabled, so using this property may not be reliable in your environment.

There's more...

The `WhenMailboxCreated` property returns a `DateTime` object that can be compared to other `DateTime` objects. In the previous example, we used the following filter with the `Where-Object` cmdlet:

```
$_.WhenMailboxCreated -ge (Get-Date).AddDays(-7)
```

When running the `Get-Date` cmdlet without any parameters, a `DateTime` object for the current date and time is returned. Every `DateTime` object provides an `AddDays` method that can be used to create a new `DateTime` object. So, to get the `DateTime` object from 7 days ago, we simply provide a negative value when calling this method, and the result is the date and time from a week ago. We compare the `WhenMailboxCreated` date to this value and if it is greater than or equal to the date 7 days ago, the command retrieves the mailbox.

You can use other `DateTime` properties when performing a comparison. For example, let's say that the last month was October, the tenth month of the year. We can use the following command to retrieve all the mailboxes created in October of any past year:

```
Get-Mailbox | ? {$_.WhenMailboxCreated.Month -eq 10}
```

This gives us the ability to generate very customizable reports, such as reporting only on mailboxes that were created on Mondays in October:

```
Get-Mailbox | ?{
  ($_.WhenMailboxCreated.DayOfWeek -eq "Monday") -and `
  ($_.WhenMailboxCreated.Month -eq 10)
}
```

As you can see, there is a lot of flexibility here that you can use to customize the output in order to meet your needs. This is a good example of how we can extend the Exchange Management Shell by tapping into the capabilities of the .NET Framework.

See also

- *Working with variables and objects* recipe from `Chapter 1`, *PowerShell Key Concepts*
- *Exporting reports to text and CSV files* recipe from `Chapter 2`, *Exchange Management Shell Common Tasks*

Working with move requests and performing mailbox moves

Even if you performed mailbox moves with PowerShell in Exchange 2007 or 2010, it's important that you understand that the process has evolved in Exchange 2013 and 2016 with new features, such as the ability to move reports together with batch move requests. There is a new set of cmdlets available for performing and managing mailbox moves. The architecture used by Exchange to perform mailbox moves uses a new concept known as move requests, which have been implemented in Exchange 2010 and have been further developed in Exchange 2013. In this recipe, you will learn how to manage move requests from the Exchange Management Shell.

How to do it...

To create a move request and move a mailbox to another database within the Exchange organization, use the `New-MoveRequest` cmdlet, as shown in the following command:

```
New-MoveRequest -Identity testuser -TargetDatabase DB2
```

How it works...

Mailbox moves are performed asynchronously with this method; the `New-MoveRequest` cmdlet does not perform the actual mailbox move. Mailbox moves are handled by the **Microsoft Exchange Mailbox Replication Service** (MRS). This is a major improvement because the mailbox data does not move through an administrative workstation when performing a move; instead, the service is responsible for transferring the data from one database to another. Not only does this make the mailbox move faster, but it also allows you to kick off one or more mailbox moves from any machine in the organization. You can later check on the status of these move requests from any other machine with PowerShell or the Exchange Admin Center.

When you create a new move request with the `New-MoveRequest` cmdlet, the command places a special message in the target mailbox database's system mailbox. The MRS scans the system mailboxes on a regular basis, looking for queued mailbox move requests, and if any is found, it starts the move process. Once the move has been completed, a record of the mailbox move is saved and can be viewed using the `Get-MoveRequest` cmdlet.

> This recipe covers only local move requests that are performed within an Exchange organization. It is also possible to use the `New-MoveRequest` and `New-MigrationBatch` cmdlets to perform a mailbox move across Active Directory forest boundaries.

If you automate mailbox moves using the Exchange Management Shell, it is likely that you will be doing that in bulk. The following example shows how you can move all of the mailboxes from one database to another:

```
Get-Mailbox -Database DB1 | New-MoveRequest -TargetDatabase DB2
```

In this example, we are retrieving all of the mailboxes in the `DB1` database and creating a new move request for each one, which will then move them to the target database `DB2`. The `-TargetDatabase` parameter is actually an optional parameter. If you have multiple mailbox databases in your organization, you can omit the `-TargetDatabase` parameter in the previous command and the mailboxes will be moved evenly across the available mailbox databases as long as those databases have not been suspended or excluded from provisioning and as long as the **Mailbox Resources Management** agent is enabled, which is the default setting.

There's more...

In order to view the detailed information about move requests, you can use the `Get-MoveRequestStatistics` cmdlet. This will return a great deal of useful information for a given move request, such as the move status, percentage complete, the total bytes transferred, and more. You can also use the `-IncludeReport` switch parameter when running the cmdlet to provide debug level details of mailbox move. This can be very beneficial when troubleshooting an issue.

One of the greatest uses of this cmdlet is to report on the current status of mailbox moves in progress, especially during large migrations. The following command can be used to gather the statistics of the currently running mailbox moves and can be run periodically throughout the migration to check the status:

```
Get-MoveRequest | ? {$_.Status -ne 'Completed'} | Get-MoveRequestStatistics
| `
Select DisplayName, PercentComplete, BytesTransferred
```

The preceding command will produce an output for each mailbox, which is similar to the following screenshot:

In this example, we're selecting just a few of the properties from the output of the command. Alternatively, it may be useful to export this information to a CSV file or email the results to an administrator. Either way, it gives you a method to monitor the status of your mailbox moves interactively in the Shell or through an automated script.

If you just want to do some basic interactive monitoring from the Shell to determine when all the moves are complete, you can use the following code:

```
While ($True) {
  Get-MoveRequest | ? {$_.Status -ne 'Completed'}
  Start-Sleep 5
  Clear-Host
}
```

The output from this command will give you a view of all the incomplete move requests and will refresh every 5 seconds. This is done using an endless while loop that runs Get-MoveRequest, waits for 5 seconds, clears the screen, and starts over again. Once all the moves are completed, just press Ctrl + C to break out of the loop.

Removing move requests

You cannot perform a move request for a mailbox if there is already an existing move request associated with that mailbox. This is true regardless of the move request status, whether it is complete, pending, canceled, or failed. You can use the Remove-MoveRequest cmdlet to delete an existing move request for a single mailbox using the following syntax:

```
Remove-MoveRequest testuser -Confirm:$False
```

If you perform frequent moves, you may find it necessary to regularly delete all the existing move requests in the organization. To do this, use the following command:

```
Get-MoveRequest -ResultSize Unlimited | Remove-MoveRequest -Confirm:$False
```

Keep in mind that stored move requests can provide detailed information, which can be used to monitor or generate reports for mailbox moves. Make sure you no longer need this information before removing these move requests.

Moving archive mailboxes

Consider that the testuser account has a mailbox in the DB1 database and also a personal archive mailbox in the DB1 database. We can use the following command to move testuser to DB2:

```
New-MoveRequest testuser -TargetDatabase DB2
```

In this case, both the primary mailbox and the archive mailbox will be moved to DB2. We can customize this behavior using some additional parameters that are made available by the New-MoveRequest cmdlet. For example, if we want to move only this user's primary mailbox and leave the archive mailbox in its current location, we can use the following command:

```
New-MoveRequest testuser -TargetDatabase DB2 -PrimaryOnly
```

This command adds the -PrimaryOnly switch parameter, which will indicate to the New-MoveRequest cmdlet that we do not want to move the archive mailbox, and we do want to move the primary mailbox to the DB2 database. Use the following command to move only the archive mailbox:

```
New-MoveRequest testuser -ArchiveOnly -ArchiveTargetDatabase DB3
```

This time, we have added the $-$ArchiveOnly switch parameter so that only the archive mailbox is moved. The $-$ArchiveTargetDatabase parameter is also used to specify that we want to move the archive mailbox to the DB3 database.

Moving mailboxes in batches

When performing migrations or moving multiple mailboxes in bulk, it can be useful to move them in batches. The New-MoveRequest cmdlet provides a $-$BatchName parameter to group multiple mailbox moves into a single, logical collection. Let's say that we are migrating multiple mailboxes to several different databases and we want to easily track the mailbox moves based on a certain criterion. We can do this using the following command:

```
$mailboxes = Get-Mailbox -RecipientTypeDetails UserMailbox `
 -Database DB1 | Get-MailboxStatistics | `
 ? {$_.TotalItemSize -gt 2gb}

$mailboxes | % { `
 New-MoveRequest $_.Alias `
 -BatchName 'Large Mailboxes' `
 -TargetDatabase DB2 `
 }
```

Here, we are retrieving all the mailboxes in the DB1 database that are larger than 2 gigabytes and storing the results in the $mailboxes variable. We then pipe the $mailboxes object to the ForEach-Object cmdlet (using the % alias) and loop through each item. As each mailbox in the collection is processed within the loop, we create a new move request for that mailbox, indicating that it should be included in the Large Mailboxes batch and moved to the DB2 database. At this point, we can easily track the moves in the batch using a simple command:

```
Get-MoveRequest -BatchName 'Large Mailboxes'
```

The preceding command will return each move request included in the Large Mailboxes batch and will provide several details, including the display name, move status, and the target database.

Moving mailboxes with corrupt items

When migrating from a previous version of Exchange or when migrating large mailboxes, it's not uncommon to run into problems with users that have corrupted items in their mailbox. You can use the `-BadItemLimit` parameter to specify the acceptable number of corrupt, or bad, items to skip when performing a mailbox move. Keep in mind that if you set the `-BadItemLimit` parameter to a value higher than 50, then you need to also use the `-AcceptLargeDataLoss` switch parameter, as shown in the following example:

```
New-MoveRequest testuser `
 -BadItemLimit 100 `
 -AcceptLargeDataLoss `
 -TargetDatabase DB2
```

When executing this command, a move request will be created for the `testuser` mailbox. Up to 100 corrupt items in the source mailbox will be allowed to perform a successful move to the new database. You will see a warning in the Shell when using these parameters, and any corrupt items found in the source mailbox will be skipped when the mailbox is moved. If more than 100 corrupt items are found during the move, then the move request will fail.

See also

- *Email notification on mailbox moves* recipe in this chapter
- *Importing and exporting mailboxes* recipe in this chapter
- *Reporting on mailbox sizes* recipe in this chapter
- *Managing archive mailboxes* recipe from Chapter 10, *Compliance and Audit Logging*
- *Creating, modifying, and removing mailboxes* recipe from Chapter 3, *Managing Recipients*

Email notification on mailbox moves

Exchange 2013 introduced the new `New-MigrationBatch` cmdlet, which includes a built-in automatic reporting feature to move mailboxes, together with a more flexible way of moving collections of mailboxes. In this recipe, we will take a look at how to move mailboxes with these features and check out the report.

How to do it...

To create a migration batch (move request) to move a collection of mailboxes to another database within the Exchange organization, use the `New-MigrationBatch` cmdlet, as shown in the following command:

```
New-MigrationBatch -Name "Move Batch #1" -CSVData `
 ([System.IO.File]::ReadAllBytes("C:localmove.csv")) `
 -Local -TargetDatabase DB2 -NotificationEmails `
 nuno@testlabs.se, jonas@testlabs.se -AutoStart

Get-MigrationUser | Get-MigrationUserStatistics | FT -Autosize

Complete-MigrationBatch -Identity "Move Batch #1"
```

The following is a screenshot with the migration statistics:

```
Machine: TLEX1.testlabs.se                                    —    □    ✕
[PS] C:\>Get-MigrationUser | Get-MigrationUserStatistics | FT -Autosize

Identity              Batch          Status   Items Synced Items Skipped
--------              -----          ------   ------------ -------------
admin@testlabs.se     Move Batch #1 Syncing 15            0
jonas@testlabs.se     Move Batch #1 Syncing 3             0
nuno@testlabs.se      Move Batch #1 Syncing 19            0
testuser@testlabs.se  Move Batch #1 Syncing 3             0


[PS] C:\>_
```

The following screenshot shows an example from a notification report that was sent after a migration batch was completed:

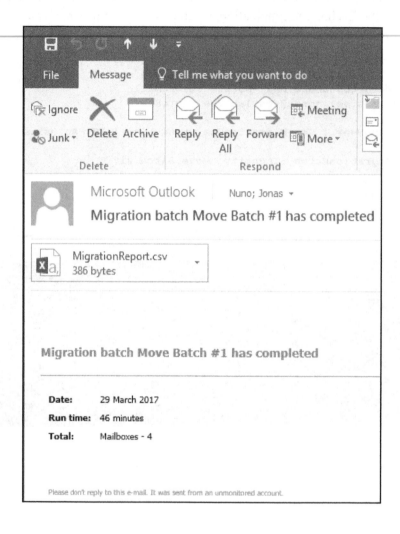

How it works...

Using the `New-MigrationBatch` cmdlet, we create a collection of mailboxes that are going to be moved to another mailbox database. What's important to know is that the full file path to the CSV needs to be specified. The `-Local` parameter means that it's a local move; the `-NotificationEmails` parameter needs to be used if a move report is required. The cmdlet to create the migration batch, by default, won't start the move, which is good in some cases, for example, when creating a couple of migration batches and then manually starting each of them. In the preceding example, using the `-AutoStart` parameter, the mailbox data synchronization will start right away when the batch is created successfully.

You need to be aware that the move will be paused right before the finalization of the move. The completion of the move needs to be done using the `Complete-MigrationBatch` cmdlet. A parameter for the completion can be used; it's called `-AutoComplete` and can be added at the end of the initial cmdlet.

There's more...

As was described in the previous section, I would like to give you an example of how to create, start, and complete the migration batch using the following command:

```
New-MigrationBatch -Name "Move Batch #2" -CSVData `
  ([System.IO.File]::ReadAllBytes("C:\localmove.csv")) -Local `
  -TargetDatabase DB2 -NotificationEmails `
  'administrator@contoso.com','dave@contoso.com' -AutoStart `
  -AutoComplete
```

This command will create a migration batch called `Move Batch #2`. It will read the `localmove` CSV file located under `C:` to determine which mailboxes to move to `DB2` and the notification email will be sent to the `administrator` and `dave` mailboxes. With this command, the migration batch will start moving the mail data immediately, and when everything is done, it will finalize the move and update the Active Directory attributes.

Be aware that even if the mailbox move has been completed, it can take a while for the Active Directory to replicate the information. In such cases, the clients may get interrupted. Read more about Active Directory replication at `http://technet.microsoft.com/en-us/library/cc 755994.aspx`.

See also

- *Working with move requests and performing mailbox moves* recipe in this chapter
- *Importing and exporting mailboxes* recipe in this chapter
- *Managing archive mailboxes* recipe from `Chapter 10`, *Compliance and Audit Logging*
- *Creating, modifying, and removing mailboxes* recipe from `Chapter 3`, *Managing Recipients*

Importing and exporting mailboxes

If you have worked with Exchange for a long time, you have probably used utilities such as ExMerge or the Exchange 2007 Management Shell to import and export data between mailboxes and PST files. While these tools were useful for their time, they had some limitations. For example, ExMerge was the main import and export utility, starting with Exchange 5.5 and continuing on to Exchange 2003, but it was difficult to automate. Exchange 2007 included the `Import-Mailbox` and `Export-Mailbox` cmdlets that made it easier to automate these tasks through PowerShell scripts. Unfortunately, the `Export-Mailbox` cmdlet required both a 32-bit workstation running the 32-bit version of the Exchange 2007 Management tools and Microsoft Outlook 2003 Service Pack 2 or higher.

With the release of Exchange 2010, administrators were given a new set of cmdlets that can be used to manage the import and export operations for Exchange mailboxes. These new cmdlets have no dependencies on a management workstation and there is no requirement to install Outlook to perform these tasks. Exchange 2010 introduced a new concept called mailbox import and export requests that implement this functionality as a server-side process. In this recipe, you will learn how to configure your environment and use these cmdlets to automate mailbox import and export requests.

How to do it...

Let's look at how to import and export a mailbox using the following steps:

1. Let's start off by exporting a mailbox to a PST file. First, you need to assign the `Mailbox Import Export` RBAC role to your account using the following command. You will need to restart the Shell after running this command for the assigned cmdlets to be visible:

   ```
   New-ManagementRoleAssignment -Role "Mailbox Import Export" `
   ```

```
-User administrator
```

2. Next, you will need to create a network share that can be used to store the PST file. When you create the share, make sure that the `Exchange Trusted Subsystem` group in Active Directory has at least read and write NTFS permissions to the folder and also has modify share permissions.

3. The last step is to use the `New-MailboxExportRequest` cmdlet to export the data for a mailbox:

```
New-MailboxExportRequest -Mailbox testuser `
  -Filepath contoso-ex01exporttestuser.pst
```

How it works...

By default, the built-in `Mailbox Import Export` role is not assigned to anyone, including administrators. This means that out of the box, you will not be able to run the `*-MailboxExportRequest` cmdlets even if you are a member of the `Organization Management` role group. Therefore, the first step in the process is to assign your account to this role using the `New-ManagementRoleAssignment` cmdlet. In the previous example, you can see that we created a direct assignment in the user account of administrator. This can be your administrative account or an actual role group that you are already a member of. If needed, you can specify that the role be assigned to a role group or an Active Directory security group using the `-SecurityGroup` parameter.

The location used for imported and exported PSTs must be a valid UNC path that the `Exchange Trusted Subsystem` group has access to. This is because the cmdlets that you execute are actually running under the security context of the Exchange servers in this group. This is required to implement the new RBAC security model and, therefore, the share and NTFS permissions must be assigned to this group and not to your user account specifically.

The syntax for the import and export commands is fairly straightforward. If you take a look at the command used in the previous example, you can see that we were able to easily create an export request for a specified mailbox using a specific file share on the network.

Using additional parameters, we can do other interesting things, such as only exporting specific folders of a mailbox to a PST:

```
New-MailboxExportRequest -Mailbox testuser `
 -IncludeFolders "#SentItems#" `
 -FilePath contoso-ex01exporttestuser_sent.pst `
 -ExcludeDumpster
```

As you can see from the preceding command, we are only exporting the Sent Items well-known folder from the testuser mailbox, and we are excluding the items in the dumpster. By surrounding the name of the well-known folder with #, Exchange will export that folder regardless if the folder's name is in another language.

Here is another example that exports data from an archive mailbox:

```
New-MailboxExportRequest -Mailbox testuser `
 -ContentFilter {Received -lt "01/01/2014"} `
 -FilePath contoso-ex01exporttestuser_archive.pst `
 -ExcludeDumpster -IsArchive
```

Here, we are specifying that we want to only export data from the archive mailbox using the -IsArchive switch parameter. In addition, we are limiting the amount of data exported from the mailbox using the -ContentFilter parameter. We are including only those items that were received before 01/01/2014. In addition to the Received property, the -ContentFilter parameter allows you to highly customize the data that is exported.

 You can create up to 10 mailbox export requests per mailbox without manually specifying a name for the export request. Once you have reached this limit, you need to either specify a unique name for the export request or delete some of the previous export requests using the Remove-MailboxExportRequest cmdlet.

Using the -ContentFilter parameter, you can filter the recipient, types of attachments that were included in a message, text in the body, and more. For a complete list of available property names, check out the filterable properties for the -ContentFilter parameter on TechNet. This can be found at http://technet.microsoft.com/en-us/library/ff 601762.aspx.

There's more...

You can use the `Get-MailboxImportRequest` and `Get-MailboxExportRequest` cmdlets to view the status of your import and export tasks. To view all requests, simply run the appropriate `Get-*` cmdlet. If you want to narrow your search, you can use the `-Mailbox` and `-Status` parameters:

```
Get-MailboxExportRequest -Mailbox testuser -Status Failed
```

This command will return all of the export requests made for the `testuser` mailbox that have a failed status. You can use the same syntax with the import version of this cmdlet to review similar information.

When it comes to advanced reporting of import or export requests, there are two cmdlets available that you can use. `Get-MailboxExportRequestStatistics` and `Get-MailboxImportRequestStatistics` can be used to provide detailed information about the tasks associated with a particular operation. For example, let's take a look at the following script:

```
ForEach ($export in Get-MailboxExportRequest) { `
  Get-MailboxExportRequestStatistics $export | `
  Select-Object SourceAlias, Status, PercentComplete
}
```

This will provide a brief report of each export request. This can be useful when you are performing multiple import or export operations and need to check the status of each one.

Importing data into mailboxes

The `New-MailboxImportRequest` cmdlet works similar to the `New-MailboxExportRequest` cmdlet. Most of the parameters shown in the previous examples are available with both cmdlets. For example, we can import data into a specific folder in an inbox with the following command:

```
New-MailboxImportRequest -Mailbox sysadmin `
  -TargetRootFolder "Recover" `
  -FilePath contoso-ex01exporttestuser_sent.pst
```

This command imports the `testuser` PST into the `Recover` folder of the `sysadmin` mailbox. In addition to exporting data from archive mailboxes, we can also import data into archive mailboxes with the `-IsArchive` switch parameter.

Taking it a step further

Let's create a script that will export all of the mailboxes in your organization to individual PST files stored in a central location. Create a new file called `Export.ps1` and save it in the `C:` drive. Using a text editor, open the file and add the following code, and then save the file:

```
param($Path, $BatchName)
ForEach ($mbx in Get-Mailbox -ResultSize Unlimited) {
    $filepath = Join-Path -Path $Path -ChildPath "$($mbx.alias).pst"
    New-MailboxExportRequest -Mailbox $mbx -FilePath $filepath `
    -BatchName $BatchName
}
```

This script provides a couple of parameters used to control the behavior of the mailbox export requests. First, the −Path parameter will allow us to specify a UNC share for our exported mailboxes. Secondly, the −BatchName parameter is used to logically group the export requests using a friendly common name.

As we loop through each mailbox, we are doing a few things. We are using the value of the −Path parameter as the root directory of the PST file, and we are using the alias property of the mailbox for the base filename. This will ensure that each PST file is stored centrally in the required location using a unique filename that matches the mailbox alias.

To execute the preceding script, the command might look something like the following:

```
$batch = "Export for (Get-Date).ToShortDateString()"
.Export.ps1 -Path contosoex01export -BatchName $batch
```

This will create each mailbox export request using a batch name, such as Export for 3/1/2017. Then, you can easily check the status of all the mailbox export requests that are grouped into that batch name using the following command:

```
Get-MailboxExportRequestStatistics | `
 ? {$_.BatchName -eq "Export for 3/1/2017"} | `
 Select SourceAlias, Status, PercentComplete
```

This one-liner will give you a brief report on each of the export requests performed in the batch created on 3/1/2017 the report can be reviewed in the Shell, exported to a text or CSV file, or e-mailed to another user.

See also

- *Exporting reports to text and CSV files* recipe from `Chapter 2`, *Exchange Management Shell Common Tasks*
- *Sending SMTP emails through PowerShell* recipe from `Chapter 2`, *Exchange Management Shell Common Tasks*

Deleting messages from mailboxes using Search-Mailbox

At some point, you are bound to find yourself in a situation where you need to remove an email message from one or more mailboxes. This may be due to a message being sent to one of your distribution lists or as a part of some kind of spam or virus-related outbreak.

If you have worked with Exchange 2007, you may be familiar with the `Export-Mailbox` cmdlet that could previously be used to perform this task. With Exchange 2010 SP1, the cmdlet `Search-Mailbox` was introduced. This cmdlet, which received further improvements in Exchange 2013, can be used to clean up mailboxes. In this recipe, we will take a look at how to do that.

How to do it...

Let's look at how to delete messages from mailboxes using the following steps:

1. If you have not already done so, you will need to use the following command to assign your account the `Mailbox Import Export` and `Mailbox Search` RBAC roles. You will need to restart the Shell after running these commands for the `Search-Mailbox` cmdlet to be visible:

```
    New-ManagementRoleAssignment -Role `
"Mailbox Import Export" -User administrator
    New-ManagementRoleAssignment -Role `
"Mailbox Search" -User administrator
```

2. Next, use the `Search-Mailbox` cmdlet to delete items from a mailbox. In this example, we use a search query to delete items with the word `suppress` in the subject line:

```
Search-Mailbox -Identity testuser `
 -SearchQuery "Subject:'suppress'" `
 -DeleteContent -Force
```

How it works...

The key to deleting items from a mailbox is the `-DeleteContent` switch parameter used in the `Search-Mailbox` cmdlet. When executing the command in the previous example, any message matching the subject specified in the search query will be deleted without any confirmation, and an output similar to the following will be displayed:

As you can see, there is a lot of useful information returned that indicates whether or not the delete operation was successful, how many items were deleted, the total item size of the deleted messages, and so on.

Keep in mind that the `Search-Mailbox` cmdlet will include messages in a user's archive mailbox and the dumpster within the primary mailbox as part of the search. To exclude these, use the following syntax:

```
Search-Mailbox -Identity testuser `
 -SearchQuery "Subject:'free ipad'" `
 -DoNotIncludeArchive `
 -SearchDumpster:$false `
 -DeleteContent -Force
```

There's more...

The -SearchQuery parameter is used to specify the criteria of your search using **Keyword Query Language** (KQL), which is the same query syntax used in SharePoint. When composing a command, you need to use the property name, followed by a colon and then the text you want to query. There are several KQL properties that can be used; some of the most common properties are Subject, Body, Sent, To, From, and Attachment. Refer to Appendix B, Query Syntaxes at the end of this book for a list of KQL properties and common search queries.

Running reports before deleting data

Of course, permanently deleting data from someone's mailbox is not something that should be done without total confidence. If you are unsure of the results or if you just want to cover your bases, you can use the following syntax to generate a report of the items that will be deleted:

```
Get-Mailbox | `
  Search-Mailbox -SearchQuery "from:spammer@contoso.com" `
  -EstimateResultOnly | Export-CSV C:report.csv -NoType
```

This example uses the -EstimateResultOnly parameter when executing the Search-Mailbox cmdlet. You can see here that we are executing a one-liner that will search each mailbox for messages sent from spammer@contoso.com. The estimate of the result is exported to a CSV file that you can use to determine how much data will be cleaned up out of each individual mailbox.

If you need a more detailed report, we can use the logging capabilities of the Search-Mailbox cmdlet. The following command performs a search on the testuser mailbox and generates some reports that we can be used to determine exactly what will be deleted:

```
Search-Mailbox -Identity testuser `
  -SearchQuery "Subject:'Accounting Reports'" `
  -TargetMailbox sysadmin `
  -TargetFolder "Delete Log" `
  -LogOnly -LogLevel Full
```

This is made possible by the -LogOnly switch parameter. This will generate a message in a target mailbox folder that you specify. In this example, you can see that the target folder of the report is the Delete Log folder in the sysadmin mailbox. This report will provide you with a summary of the items that will be deleted in the search if you were to run this command with the -DeleteContent parameter. When setting the -LogLevel parameter value to Full, a ZIP file containing a CSV report that lists each of the items returned by the search will be attached to this message.

Deleting messages in bulk

Most likely, you will need to delete items from several mailboxes in a bulk operation. The following one-liner can be used to delete messages from every mailbox in the organization:

```
Get-Mailbox -ResultSize Unlimited | `
  Search-Mailbox -SearchQuery 'from:spammer@contoso.com' `
  -DeleteContent -Force
```

In this example, we are piping all the mailboxes in the organization to the Search-Mailbox cmdlet. Any messages sent from the spammer@contoso.com email address will be deleted.

See also

- *Deleting messages from mailboxes using Compliance Search* recipe in this chapter
- *Restoring deleted items from mailboxes* recipe in this chapter
- *Performing eDiscovery and Compliance searches* recipe from Chapter 10, *Compliance and Audit Logging*
- *Deleting email items from a mailbox with EWS* recipe from Chapter 14, *Scripting with the Exchange Web Services Managed API*

Deleting messages from mailboxes using Compliance Search

In the previous recipe, we looked at how we can use the Search-Mailbox cmdlet together with the -DeleteContent parameter to search for and delete e-mail messages from mailboxes in our environment. Although we can still use this method in Exchange 2016, the new New-ComplianceSearch and New-ComplianceSearchAction cmdlets can be used instead of Search-Mailbox to delete messages.

Why use these new cmdlets instead of using `Search-Mailbox`? With this cmdlet, we are limited to searching a maximum of 10,000 mailboxes per single search. On the other hand, `New-ComplianceSearch` has no such limitations, allowing large organizations to easily perform organization-wide searches and delete operations.

However, a maximum of **10** items per mailbox can be deleted in one go using the new cmdlets. This is because `New-ComplianceSearch` was designed as an incident-response tool to quickly delete items from mailboxes, thus this limitation was introduced.

In this recipe, we will look at how to search for and delete e-mails from mailboxes using these two new cmdlets.

How to do it...

The first step to use these cmdlets to create and run a Compliance Search is to assign the `Mailbox Search` management role:

```
New-ManagementRoleAssignment -Role `
"Mailbox Search" -User administrator
```

Now we can use the new cmdlets to search and delete particular emails from one or more mailboxes:

```
New-ComplianceSearch -Name "Delete Spam" -ExchangeLocation testuser `
-ContentMatchQuery 'subject:"New HR Form"'

Start-ComplianceSearch "Delete Spam"

New-ComplianceSearchAction -SearchName "Delete Spam" -Purge -PurgeType
SoftDelete
```

How it works...

In this example, we started with using `New-ComplianceSearch` to create a **Compliance Search** to find the emails we want to remove from the `testuser`'s mailbox. We used the `-ExchangeLocation` to specify a single mailbox, but we could have used `All` to search all mailboxes in the organization. Similar to the `SearchQuery` parameter in `Search-Mailbox`, we can be more specific in our search using `ContentMatchQuery` and specify a `From` or `Received` search parameters for example. In this example, we are only searching for e-mails with the subject `New HR Form` no matter who the sender is.

Next, we start our search using the Start-ComplianceSearch cmdlet since this does not happen when we run New-ComplianceSearch. Once the search is complete, we can use Get-ComplianceSearch to retrieve the Status of our search as well as to find out how many items matched our search. If we run a search against multiple mailboxes, we can look into the SuccessResults field to find out how many items were found in each mailbox:

```
Machine: TLEX1.testlabs.se                                      —    □    ×
[PS] C:\>Get-ComplianceSearch "Delete Spam" | Select Status, Items, SuccessResults, Num
FailedSources, NumBindings, ExchangeLocation


Status            : Completed
Items             : 7
SuccessResults    : {Location: nuno@testlabs.se, Item count: 4, Total size: 29436,
                    Location: testuser@testlabs.se, Item count: 1, Total size: 10142,
                    Location: admin@testlabs.se, Item count: 1, Total size: 10131,
                    Location: jonas@testlabs.se, Item count: 1, Total size: 10121,
                    Location: IT@testlabs.se, Item count: 0, Total size: 0}
NumFailedSources  : 0
NumBindings       : 5
ExchangeLocation  : {All}


[PS] C:\>
```

Once we are happy with our search and its results, we run the New-ComplianceSearchAction cmdlet together with the -Purge and -PurgeType parameters to delete the emails that matched our search. As already mentioned, this cmdlet will delete a maximum of 10 emails per mailbox.

Deleted messages are moved to the Deletions folder in the user's Recoverable Items folder. This means the user is able to recover these messages for the duration of the deleted item retention period configured for the mailbox.

See also

- *Deleting messages from mailboxes using Search-Mailbox* recipe from this chapter
- *Restoring deleted items from mailboxes* recipe in this chapter

- *Performing eDiscovery and Compliance searches* recipe from `Chapter 10`, *Compliance and Audit Logging*
- *Deleting email items from a mailbox with EWS* recipe from `Chapter 14`, *Scripting with the Exchange Web Services Managed API*

Managing disconnected mailboxes

Exchange allows us to disassociate a mailbox from an Active Directory user account and later reconnect that mailbox to the same or a different account. For some organizations, a mailbox database has a low deleted mailbox retention setting, and once a mailbox has been disconnected for a user, it is forgotten about and purged from the database once the retention period elapses (which is 30 days by default). However, if you maintain your deleted mailboxes for any amount of time, having the ability to retrieve these mailboxes after they have been removed from a user can, at times, be very helpful. In this recipe, we will take a look at how to manage disconnected mailboxes using the Exchange Management Shell.

How to do it...

To reconnect a disconnected mailbox to a user account, use the `Connect-Mailbox` cmdlet. The following command reconnects a disconnected mailbox to the `tuser1009` account on the Active Directory:

```
Connect-Mailbox -Identity 'Test User' `
-Database DB1 `
-User 'contosotuser1009' `
-Alias tuser1009
```

How it works...

When you use the `Remove-Mailbox` or `Disable-Mailbox` cmdlets to delete a mailbox for a user, that mailbox can actually be retained in its source database for a period of time. This is determined by the deleted mailbox retention setting of the database the mailbox resides in. For example, let's say that the deleted mailbox retention for the database hosting the `testuser` mailbox is set to 30 days. After the `testuser` mailbox has been deleted, this gives us 30 days to reconnect that mailbox to an Active Directory user account before the retention period is met and the mailbox is permanently purged.

The `-Identity` parameter, used with the `Connect-Mailbox` cmdlet, specifies the mailbox that should be connected to an Active Directory account and that can accept the `MailboxGuid`, `DisplayName`, or `LegacyExchangeDN` values as input. Finding this information requires a little digging, as there is no `Get` cmdlet when it comes to searching for disconnected mailboxes. You can find this information with the `Get-MailboxStatistics` cmdlet:

```
Get-MailboxDatabase | `
Get-MailboxStatistics | ? {$_.DisconnectDate} | `
FL DisplayName, MailboxGuid, LegacyExchangeDN, DisconnectDate
```

This command will search each database for mailboxes that have a `DisconnectDate` variable defined. The values that can be used to identify a disconnected mailbox when running the `Connect-Mailbox` cmdlet will be displayed in the list format.
It is possible that there could be multiple disconnected mailboxes with the same `DisplayName` property. In this case, you can use the `MailboxGuid` value to identify the disconnected mailbox that should be reconnected.

The previous command will return both disconnected mailboxes and also disconnected archive mailboxes, so you may need to filter them out if you have implemented personal archives in your environment, as follows:

```
Get-MailboxDatabase | `
Get-MailboxStatistics | `
? {$_.DisconnectDate -and $_.IsArchiveMailbox -eq $False} | `
FL DisplayName, MailboxGuid, LegacyExchangeDN, DisconnectDate
```

This one-liner will search for disconnected mailboxes in all the databases that do not have their `IsArchiveMailbox` property set to `$True`.

All of these commands can be a little cumbersome to type, and if you use them often, it might make sense to write custom code to make it easier. Let's take a look at the following function that has been written to automate the process:

```
Function Get-DisconnectedMailbox {
 param(
   [String] $Name = '*',
   [Switch] $Archive
 )

 $databases = Get-MailboxDatabase
 $databases | % {
   $db = Get-Mailboxstatistics -Database $_ | `
   ? {$_.DisconnectDate -and $_.IsArchiveMailbox -eq $Archive}
   $db | ? {$_.displayname -like $Name} | Select DisplayName, `
```

```
      MailboxGuid, Database, DisconnectReason
   }
}
```

This function can be added to your PowerShell profile, and it will then be available every time you start the Exchange Management Shell. This way, you can run the function just like a regular cmdlet. By default, if you run the cmdlet without parameters, all of the disconnected mailboxes in your environment will be returned. You can also narrow your search using wildcards, as shown in the following screenshot:

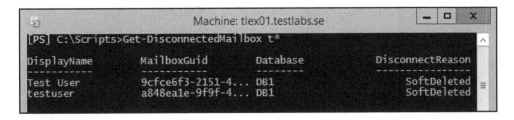

Here, you can see that we have used a wildcard with the function to find all the disconnected mailboxes starting with the letter t. To use the function and to find disconnected archive mailboxes, simply use the −Archive switch parameter.

There's more...

Following are some of the functionalities used for managing disconnected mailboxes.

Purging mailboxes

When the move request was introduced in Exchange 2010 SP1, some new functionality was added that you will need to be aware of when managing disconnected mailboxes. When you use the New-MoveRequest cmdlet to move a mailbox from one database to another, the mailbox in the source database is not deleted but is disconnected and marked as SoftDeleted instead. You can check the value of the DisconnectReason property when working with a disconnected mailbox using the Get-MailboxStatistics cmdlet. The Get-DisconnectedMailbox function included earlier in this recipe will also return the value of this property for each disconnected mailbox.

If you move or remove mailboxes frequently, you may end up with hundreds or even thousands of disconnected mailboxes at any given time. Disconnected mailboxes can be purged using the `Remove-StoreMailbox` cmdlet by specifying the identity of the mailbox, the database it is located in, and the disconnect state that it is in, as shown in the following example:

```
Remove-StoreMailbox -Identity `
 1c097bde-edec-47df-aa4e-535cbfaa13b4 `
 -Database DB1 `
 -MailboxState SoftDeleted `
 -Confirm:$false
```

Keep in mind that if you want to delete every single disconnected mailbox in your environment, you will need to run the `Remove-StoreMailbox` cmdlet for mailboxes in both the `Disabled` and `SoftDeleted` state. If you want to purge every disconnected mailbox from the organization, regardless of the location or the reason of disconnection, you can use the following code:

```
$mb = Get-MailboxDatabase | Get-MailboxStatistics | `
 ? {$_.DisconnectDate}

ForEach ($i in $mb) { `
 Remove-StoreMailbox -Identity $i.MailboxGuid `
 -Database $i.Database `
 -MailboxState $i.DisconnectReason.ToString() `
 -Confirm:$false
}
```

Mailboxes within a recovery database will be reported by the `Get-MailboxStatistics` cmdlet as disconnected and disabled. You cannot purge them with the `Remove-StoreMailbox` cmdlet; if you try to do that, you will get an error.

Cleaning databases

In Exchange 2007 and 2010, we had the `Clean-MailboxDatabase` cmdlet to get disconnected mailboxes visible in the GUI without having to wait for the maintenance schedule.

However, in Exchange 2013 and 2016, this cmdlet no longer exists, but the same problem persists: disconnected mailboxes are not immediately visible in the Exchange Admin Center after being removed or disabled. `Clean-MailboxDatabase` has been replaced by `Update-StoreMailboxState`, which forces the mailbox store state in the Exchange store to be synchronized with the corresponding Active Directory user account. Its syntax is as follows:

```
Update-StoreMailboxState -Database "DatabaseIdParameter" -Identity
"StoreMailboxIdParameter" [-Confirm [SwitchParameter]] [-WhatIf
[SwitchParameter]]
```

Both the `-Database` and `-Identity` parameters are required, which means we need to know the identity of the mailbox (mailbox GUID) that we want to update the store state for. To do that, we can run the following cmdlet we already looked at:

```
Get-MailboxDatabase | Get-MailboxStatistics | `
? {$_.DisconnectDate} | FT DisplayName, MailboxGuid, `
Database, DisconnectReason, DisconnectDate -Auto
```

Once we know the mailbox's GUID and the database in which it was located in, we can update its state by running the following:

```
Update-StoreMailboxState "mailbox_guid" -Database "db_name"
```

If we want to update the mailbox state for all mailboxes on a particular database, we can update the cmdlet to this:

```
Get-MailboxStatistics -Database "db_name" | ForEach { `
Update-StoreMailboxState -Database $_.Database `
-Identity $_.MailboxGuid -Confirm:$False}
```

Finally, if we want to just update the mailbox state for all disconnected mailboxes on a particular database, we can run this:

```
Get-MailboxStatistics -Database "db_name" | `
? {$_.DisconnectReason -ne $null } | `
ForEach {Update-StoreMailboxState $_.MailboxGuid `
-Database $_.Database -Confirm:$False}
```

See also

- *Managing archive mailboxes* recipe from Chapter 10, *Compliance and Audit Logging*
- *Restoring data from a recovery database* recipe from Chapter 6, *Mailbox Database Management*

Setting storage quotas for mailboxes

One thing that has been around for several versions of Exchange is the concept of storage quotas. Using quotas, we can control the size of each mailbox to ensure that our mailbox databases don't grow out of control. In addition to setting storage quotas at the database level, we can also configure storage quotas on a per-mailbox basis. In this recipe, we will take a look at how to configure mailbox storage quotas from the Exchange Management Shell.

How to do it...

Use the following command syntax to set custom limits on mailboxes:

```
Set-Mailbox testuser `
-IssueWarningQuota 1024mb `
-ProhibitSendQuota 1536mb `
-ProhibitSendReceiveQuota 2048mb `
-UseDatabaseQuotaDefaults $False
```

How it works...

The `Set-Mailbox` cmdlet is used to configure the quota warning and the send and receive limits for each mailbox. In this example, we are setting the `-IssueWarningQuota` parameter to 1 gigabyte. When the user's mailbox exceeds this size, they will receive a warning message from the system that they are approaching their quota limit. In this example, we could have used `-IssueWarningQuota 1GB` instead of `1024mb`.

The `-ProhibitSendQuota` parameter is set to 1.5 gigabytes, and when the total mailbox size exceeds this limit, the user will no longer be able to send messages, although new incoming e-mail messages will still be received.

We've set the `-ProhibitSendReceiveQuota` parameter value to 2 gigabytes. Once the mailbox reaches this size, the user will no longer be able to send or receive emails.

It's important to point out here that we have disabled the option to inherit the storage quota limits from the database by setting the `-UseDatabaseQuotaDefaults` parameter to `$False`. If this setting was set to `$True`, the custom mailbox quota settings would not be used.

There's more...

By default, mailboxes are configured to inherit their storage quota limits from their database. In most cases, this is ideal, since you can centrally control the settings of each mailbox in a particular database. However, it is unlikely that having a single quota limit for the entire organization will be sufficient. For example, you will probably have a group of managers, VIP users, or executives that require a larger amount of space for their mailboxes.

Even though you could create a separate database for these users with higher quota values, this might not make sense in your environment. Instead, you may want to override the database quota defaults with a custom setting on an individual basis. Let's say that all the users with their `Title` property set to `Manager` should have a custom quota setting. We can use the following commands to make this change in bulk:

```
Get-User -RecipientTypeDetails UserMailbox `
 -Filter {Title -eq 'Manager'} | `
 Set-Mailbox -IssueWarningQuota 2048mb ` -ProhibitSendQuota 2560mb `
 -ProhibitSendReceiveQuota 3072mb `
 -UseDatabaseQuotaDefaults $False
```

What we are doing here is searching Active Directory with the `Get-User` cmdlet and filtering the results so that only mailbox-enabled users with their `Title` property set to `Manager` are returned. This command is piped further to the `Set-Mailbox` cmdlet, which configures the mailbox quota values and disables the option to use the database quotas.

See also

- *Restoring deleted items from mailboxes* recipe in this chapter
- *Managing public folder mailboxes* recipe in this chapter
- *Managing archive mailboxes* recipe from `Chapter 10`, *Compliance and Audit Logging*

Finding email addresses with numbers

In certain countries, or in large organizations, it is common to have two or more users with the same display name, especially when these are simply based on first and last names. When the Exchange email address policy tries to assign an email address to a new user that is already assigned to an existing user, it adds a number to it. For example, if there is a John Smith with an email address of john.smith@contoso.com, when a new John Smith joins the organization, it will be assigned the email address john.smith2@contoso.com. This depending on the current organizations' email address policy of course.

What some organizations do is, for example, add an initial to the e-mail address such as john.k.smith@contoso.com to make it more professional and easier to distinguish between the two users.

In this recipe, we will look into how we can get a list of all e-mail addresses that contain a number so we can avoid the previous scenario and correct the e-mail address.

How to do it...

Use the following command to list all email addresses that contain a digit:

```
Get-Mailbox -ResultSize Unlimited | `
? {$_.PrimarySmtpAddress -match "[0-9]"} | `
FT DisplayName, SamAccountName, PrimarySmtpAddress -Auto
```

How it works...

We start by getting a list of all mailboxes in the organization using the Get-Mailbox cmdlet. For each one of them, we retrieve their PrimarySmtpAddress property and check whether any part of it is made up of a digit between 0 and 9 using a regular expression. Here, we could have used -match "d" instead and the result would have been the same.

If a match is found, we then print the mailbox's display name, username, and email address.

There's more...

Alternatively, we could check Active Directory instead of using the Exchange cmdlet, which is typically faster. To achieve the same result as the previous example, we would run the following command:

```
Get-ADUser -Filter {mail -like "*"} `
-Properties mail, SamAccountName, DisplayName | `
? {$_.mail -match "d"} | `
FT DisplayName, SamAccountName, mail -Auto
```

In this example, instead of using `Get-Mailbox`, we use the `Get-ADUser` cmdlet to retrieve any Active Directory account that has something on its `mail` attribute. Then, we check whether the content of this property has a digit in it and, if yes, we print the same user details as before. The reason why we check `mail` twice is because `-Filter` does not support the `-match` operator.

We could be more specific and specify that we are only interested in e-mail addresses that contain one or more digits right before the @ sign. To do this, we would update the `-match` comparison to `{$_.mail -match "d@contoso.com"}`.

The only downside of using `Get-ADUser` instead of `Get-Mailbox` is that it might return unwanted recipients, such as contacts, for example, that we are not interested in. This can be easily prevented by adding a filter.

See also

- *Finding mailboxes with different SIP and Primary SMTP addresses* recipe in this chapter
- *Reporting on mailbox sizes* recipe in this chapter
- *Reporting on mailbox creation time* recipe in this chapter
- *Finding inactive mailboxes* recipe in this chapter

Finding mailboxes with different SIP and Primary SMTP addresses

In environments with Lync or Skype for Business server, it is important that a user's email address is the same as their SIP address for the best user experience. In this recipe, we will look at how we can find users where their SIP address is different than their primary email address.

How to do it...

To list all users whose e-mail address (`mail`) does not match their SIP address (`msRTCSIP-PrimaryUserAddress`), run the following command:

```
Get-ADUser -Filter {mail -like "*" `
-and msRTCSIP-PrimaryUserAddress -like "*" `
-and msExchMailboxGuid -like "*"} `
-Properties msRTCSIP-PrimaryUserAddress, mail, DisplayName, SamAccountName
| `
Where {$_."msRTCSIP-PrimaryUserAddress" -notmatch $_.mail} | `
Sort DisplayName | FT DisplayName, SamAccountName, `
mail, msRTCSIP-PrimaryUserAddress -AutoSize
```

How it works...

In this recipe, we start by using the `Get-ADUser` cmdlet to list Active Directory users that have their `mail` attribute populated as well as an SIP address (`msRTCSIP-PrimaryUserAddress`). We also make sure `msExchMailboxGuid` is not empty just as a way to ensure any users found are indeed Exchange users. Here, we could have used another Exchange attribute, such as `homeMDB` .

Once we have our list of users, we simply compare `msRTCSIP-PrimaryUserAddress` with `mail` , and if they do not match, we list some of the user's details.

There's more...

Alternatively, we could have used the `Get-Mailbox` cmdlet instead, but it wouldn't be as straightforward or as fast. For each mailbox, we would have to get its `PrimarySmtpAddress` and then look into the `EmailAddresses` property and retrieve the entry with a `PrefixString` equal to `sip` in order to get the user's SIP address. Once we have these two values, we can compare them to see whether they match or not.

The end result would be the following script:

```
[String] $strPrimaryAddress = $strSIP = $null
[Array] $mbxCol = @()

Get-Mailbox -ResultSize Unlimited | ForEach {
  $strSIP = $NULL
  $strPrimaryAddress = $_.PrimarySmtpAddress

  $_.EmailAddresses | ForEach {If ($_.PrefixString -eq "sip") {$strSIP =
$_.AddressString}}

  If ($strSIP -and ($strPrimaryAddress -ne $strSIP)) {
    $mbxObj = New-Object PSObject -Property @{
    "Display Name" = $_.DisplayName
    "Primary SMTP Address" = $strPrimaryAddress
    SIP = $strSIP
    Username = $_.SamAccountName
  }

  $mbxCol += $mbxObj
  }
}
$mbxCol | Sort "Display Name" | FT "Display Name", Username, SIP, "Primary
SMTP Address" -AutoSize
```

See also

- *Reporting on mailbox sizes* recipe in this chapter
- *Reporting on mailbox creation* time recipe in this chapter
- *Finding inactive mailboxes* recipe in this chapter

Finding inactive mailboxes

If you support a large Exchange environment, it's likely that users come and go frequently. In this case, it's quite possible that over time, you will end up with multiple unused mailboxes. In this recipe, you will learn a couple of techniques used when searching for inactive mailboxes with the Exchange Management Shell.

How to do it...

The following command will retrieve a list of mailboxes that have not been logged on to in over 90 days:

```
Get-Mailbox -ResultSize Unlimited | ? { `
(Get-MailboxStatistics $_).LastLogonTime -and `
(Get-MailboxStatistics $_).LastLogonTime -le `
(Get-Date).AddDays(-90)
}
```

How it works...

Here, you can see that we're retrieving all of the mailboxes in the organization using the Get-Mailbox cmdlet. We then pipe this collection to the Where-Object cmdlet (using the ? alias) and use the Get-MailboxStatistics cmdlet to build a filter. This first part of this filter indicates that we only want to retrieve mailboxes that have a value set for the LastLogonTime property. If this value is $null, it indicates that these mailboxes have never been used and have probably been recently created, which means that they will probably soon become active mailboxes. We could also include the WhenMailboxCreated property to check when they were created.

The second part of the filter compares the value for the LastLogonTime property. If this value is less than or equal to the date 90 days ago, then we have a match and the mailbox will be returned.

There's more...

Finding unused mailboxes in your environment might be as simple as searching for disabled user accounts in Active Directory that are mailbox-enabled. If that is the case, you can use the following one-liner to discover these mailboxes:

```
Get-ADUser -Filter {Enabled -eq $False -and mail -like "*"} | `
ForEach {Get-Mailbox $_.SamAccountName -ErrorAction SilentlyContinue | `
? {$_.RecipientTypeDetails -eq "UserMailbox"}} | `
Select DisplayName, SamAccountName, PrimarySmtpAddress
```

This command uses the `Get-ADUser` cmdlet to search through all disabled Active Directory accounts. We include only those that have a mailbox by ensuring the `mail` attribute is populated. This is not strictly necessary, but it will save us time by not passing unnecessary accounts down the pipe. We then process all accounts found using `Get-Mailbox` and list only those that are of `UserMailbox` type. This is because Exchange Shared Mailboxes have their Active Directory accounts disabled by default and we don't want to include these in our report.

In some cases, the first cmdlet might return recipients that do not have a mailbox but do have the `mail` attribute populated and their Active Directory account disabled. This is why we include `-ErrorAction SilentlyContinue` as the `Get-Mailbox` cmdlet will fail for these users but we can ignore them because we are not interested in them.

See also

- *Working with variables and objects* recipe from `Chapter 1`, *PowerShell Key Concepts*
- *Looping through items* recipe from `Chapter 1`, *PowerShell Key Concepts*

Detecting and fixing corrupt mailboxes

For years, Exchange administrators have used `Information Store Integrity Checker`, more commonly known as the **ISInteg** utility, to detect and repair mailbox database corruption. You may have used ISInteg in previous versions of Exchange to correct a corruption issue, preventing a user from opening their mailbox or from opening a particular message.

Unfortunately, in order to repair a mailbox with ISInteg, you have to dismount the database hosting the mailbox, taking it offline for everyone else that has a mailbox stored on that database. Obviously, taking an entire mailbox database down for maintenance when it is only affecting one user is less than ideal. In Exchange 2010 SP1, a new cmdlet called `New-MailboxRepairRequest` was introduced, which replaced the ISInteg tool and that allows you to detect and repair mailbox corruption while the database is online and mounted. In this recipe, we will take a look at how to use this cmdlet and automate the detection and repair of corrupt mailboxes.

How to do it...

Let's look at how to detect and fix corrupt mailboxes using the following steps:

1. To detect corruption for a single mailbox, use the `New-MailboxRepairRequest` cmdlet with the following syntax:

   ```
   New-MailboxRepairRequest -Mailbox testuser `
   -CorruptionType SearchFolder, ProvisionedFolder, FolderView, AggregateCounts `
   -DetectOnly
   ```

2. The `-DetectOnly` switch parameter indicates that we do not want to perform a repair and that we only want to check for corruption within this mailbox. To perform a repair, simply remove the `-DetectOnly` switch parameter from the previous command:

   ```
   New-MailboxRepairRequest -Mailbox testuser `
   -CorruptionType SearchFolder, ProvisionedFolder, FolderView, AggregateCounts
   ```

How it works...

The `New-MailboxRepairRequest` cmdlet can be run against a single mailbox or an entire mailbox database. In the previous example, we specified the `testuser` mailbox using the `-Mailbox` parameter. If needed, we can use the `-Database` parameter instead and provide the name of a database that we want to check or repair.

The -CorruptionType parameter accepts one or more of the outlined values in the following list:

- SearchFolder: This is used to detect and repair links to folders that no longer exist
- AggregateCounts: This specifies the aggregate counts on folders that do not indicate the correct values that should be repaired or detected
- FolderView: This is used to detect and repair views with incorrect content
- ProvisionedFolder: This specifies the links between provisioned and unprovisioned folders that should be detected and repaired

As always, we can take advantage of the PowerShell pipeline to perform operations in bulk. Perhaps you want to perform detection on a group of mailboxes but not on every mailbox in a database. Just pipe the results of the Get-Mailbox cmdlet to the New-MailboxRepairRequest cmdlet:

```
Get-Mailbox -OrganizationalUnit "OU=Sales,DC=contoso,DC=com" | `
New-MailboxRepairRequest -CorruptionType SearchFolder `
-DetectOnly
```

In this example, we're only performing detection on mailboxes in the Sales OU. This is just one example of how you can do this. Use the -Filter parameter in combination with the Get-Mailbox or the Where-Object cmdlet to limit which mailboxes are sent to the pipeline.

The New-MailboxRepairRequest cmdlet can also be used against archive mailboxes when using the -Archive switch parameter.

There's more...

Similar to many other cmdlets, we can use Get-MailboxRepairRequest to retrieve information about current mailbox repair requests.

Continuing with our original example, we can get its current state by running the following cmdlet:

```
Get-MailboxRepairRequest -Mailbox testuser
```

Once completed, we can get more information regarding the repair request by listing further details:

```
Get-MailboxRepairRequest -Mailbox testuser | Select DetectOnly, JobState,
Progress, Tasks, CorruptionsDetected, ErrorCode, CorruptionsFixed,
Corruptions
```

If we run the `New-MailboxRepairRequest` against an entire database, for example, we can retrieve all the repair requests for that particular database:

```
Get-MailboxRepairRequest -Database DB1
```

Restoring deleted items from mailboxes

One of the most common requests that Exchange administrators are asked to perform is to restore deleted items from a user's mailbox. In previous versions of Exchange, there were usually a couple of ways to handle this. First, you can use your traditional brick-level backup solution to restore individual items in a mailbox. Of course, there is also the more time-consuming process of exporting data from a mailbox located in a recovery database. Exchange 2010 reduced the complexity of restoring deleted items by implementing a feature called **Single Item Recovery**. When this feature is enabled, administrators can recover the purged data from an end user's mailbox using the `Search-Mailbox` cmdlet. In this recipe, we will take a look at how this restore process works from within the Exchange Management Shell.

How to do it...

Let's look at how to restore deleted items from mailboxes using the following steps:

1. If you have not already done so, you will need to use the following command syntax to assign the `Mailbox Import Export` and `Mailbox Search` RBAC roles to your account. You will need to restart the Shell after running these commands for the assigned cmdlet to be visible:

```
    New-ManagementRoleAssignment -Role `
"Mailbox Import Export" -User administrator
    New-ManagementRoleAssignment -Role `
"Mailbox Search" -User administrator
```

2. To restore deleted data from an end user's mailbox, use the `Search-Mailbox` cmdlet:

```
Search-Mailbox testuser `
 -SearchQuery "subject:'Expense Report'" `
 -TargetMailbox restoremailbox `
 -TargetFolder "Test Restore" `
 -SearchDumpsterOnly
```

How it works...

The `Search-Mailbox` cmdlet provides the capability to search only the dumpster containing the deleted items for a given mailbox using the `-SearchDumpsterOnly` switch parameter. In this example, we used the `-SearchQuery` parameter to limit the search results to items that contain the term `Expense Report` within the subject line. After this command has been run, an administrator can access the target mailbox to retrieve the restored data. The items that matched the search query will be restored to a subfolder of the target folder in the target mailbox specified.

The `-SearchQuery` parameter uses **Keyword Query Language** (KQL) to define the conditions for your search. Refer to `Appendix B, Query Syntaxes` at the end of this book for more information on KQL.

There's more...

You can perform very granular searches with KQL and the `-SearchQuery` parameter. Let's say we want to restore all the deleted items from the mailbox that were received after a certain date. We can use the following command to accomplish this:

```
Search-Mailbox testuser `
 -SearchQuery "received:>2/5/2017" `
 -TargetMailbox administrator `
 -TargetFolder "Test Restore" `
 -SearchDumpsterOnly
```

Similar to the previous example, we are restoring data from the `testuser` mailbox to the same target folder in the `administrator` mailbox. The difference is that this time, the search query is only going to look for messages that have been received after `February 5, 2017`. Here, you can see that we are using the greater than (>) symbol to indicate that any message older than `2/5/2017` should be restored.

You can open the target mailbox in Outlook to retrieve the restored messages or export them using the `New-MailboxExportRequest` cmdlet.

Keep in mind that the `-SearchQuery` parameter is optional. If you want to restore all of the end user's deleted items, you can simply omit this parameter for the commands in the previous examples. Also, you can restore messages when performing a discovery search with the `New-MailboxSearch` cmdlet.

See also

- *Performing eDiscovery and Compliance searches* recipe from `Chapter 10`, *Compliance and Audit Logging*
- *Restoring data from a recovery database* recipe from `Chapter 6`, *Mailbox Database Management*
- *Importing and exporting mailboxes* recipe in this chapter

Managing public folder mailboxes

For how many years has Microsoft said that public folders were going to be removed in future releases of Exchange? I don't know for sure. What I know is that the public folders are here to stay; at least they remain in Exchange 2016. Microsoft got rid of the public folder database and, therefore, the public folder replication as well. The legacy public folder architecture has now been replaced, and starting in Exchange 2013, the public folder mailbox was introduced.

This also means that we now have the availability to use a **Database Availability Group (DAG)** to replicate the public folder mailboxes between servers, just like normal mailboxes.

In this recipe, we are going to create a structure of public folders and finally, mail-enable one of them.

How to do it...

To create the initial public folder hierarchy and a structure, use the following commands:

```
New-Mailbox -Name PF_Master_Hierarchy -Alias PF_Master_Hierarchy `
-Database DB1 -OrganizationalUnit "CN=Users,DC=contoso,DC=com" `
-PublicFolder
New-PublicFolder "EURO"
New-PublicFolder "AMER"
New-PublicFolder "USA" -Path "AMER"
New-PublicFolder "Projects" -Path "AMERUSA"
Enable-MailPublicFolder "AMERUSAProjects"
```

How it works...

In this example, we are creating an initial public folder hierarchy mailbox that handles the public folder contents; it's created in the DB1 database. We are also creating a few folders and subfolders.

Finally, the Projects folder is mail-enabled, which means that it shows up in the global Address List by default and, therefore, can be used to send mails.

Let's take a look at the example in the following screenshot:

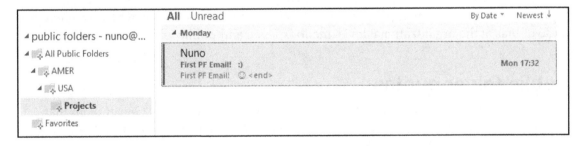

The public folder hierarchy contains the folder properties and organizational information, including the hierarchy structure. When the first public folder mailbox is created, it becomes the **primary hierarchy mailbox**, the only writable copy of the Public Folder Hierarchy. Any public folder mailboxes created later will be **secondary hierarchy mailboxes** and contain a read-only copy of the hierarchy. Any changes in the hierarchy are redirected to the primary hierarchy mailbox and then replicated to all other public folder mailboxes in order to avoid any conflicts.

By default, all public folder mailboxes deployed in the environment can serve hierarchy connections to the clients.

Outlook on the web is supported but with certain limitations. We can add and remove public folders from our `Favorites` and perform item-level operations, such as creating, editing, deleting, and replying to posts. However, it is not possible to create or delete public folders from OWA. Also, only `Mail`, `Post`, `Calendar`, and `Contact` public folders can be added to `Favorites`.

There's more...

Just like normal mailboxes, Public Folders have their own quotas, which have changed slightly from a configuration perspective with their new architecture. We can now configure these quotas at the organizational level, mailbox level, and public folder level.

Public folder quotas

Since public folders have been totally rebuilt, there are lots of changes. One of them that needs to be pointed out is that the global quota and retention settings are now configured using the `Set-OrganizationConfig` cmdlet.

For example, if you want to configure `DefaultPublicFolderIssueWarningQuota` to 5 GB, this can be done using the following command:

```
Set-OrganizationConfig -DefaultPublicFolderIssueWarningQuota 5GB
```

Using the `Set-OrganizationConfig` cmdlet, we can configure further settings at a global level that affect all public folders in the organization:

- `DefaultPublicFolderAgeLimit`
- `DefaultPublicFolderDeletedItemRetention`
- `DefaultPublicFolderMaxItemSize`
- `DefaultPublicFolderMovedItemRetention`
- `DefaultPublicFolderProhibitPostQuota`

Back into quotas, and similarly to normal mailboxes, global public folder quotas can be overwritten by setting individual quotas, such as the following:

```
Set-PublicFolder "AMERUSAProjects" -IssueWarningQuota 3GB -
ProhibitPostQuota 4GB
```

However, because public folders are now part of a mailbox, quotas can also be set at the mailbox level:

```
Set-Mailbox PF_Master_Hierarchy -PublicFolder `
-IssueWarningQuota 2.5GB `
-ProhibitSendReceiveQuota 3GB `
-UseDatabaseQuotaDefaults $False
```

See also

- *Reporting on public folder statistics* recipe in this chapter
- *Managing user access to public folders* recipe in this chapter
- *Setting storage quotas for mailboxes* recipe in this chapter

Reporting on public folder statistics

Since the public folder structure got created in the earlier recipe, it's now time to gather some public folder statistics and information about their contents.

This is basically done using the `Get-Mailbox` and `Get-PublicFolderStatistics` cmdlets.

In this recipe, we will also take a look at exporting the statistics to a CSV file, and finally, we will check out the quota settings.

How to do it...

The following commands will retrieve statistics about the public folder structure:

```
Get-Mailbox -PublicFolder | Get-MailboxStatistics | `
FT DisplayName, TotalItemSize -AutoSize
Get-PublicFolderStatistics | FT Name, `
ItemCount, TotalItemSize, TotalDeletedItemSize, `
FolderPath, MailboxOwnerId -AutoSize
Get-Mailbox -PublicFolder | Get-MailboxStatistics | `
Select DisplayName, TotalItemSize | `
Export-CSV C:PF_Hierarchy.csv -Notype
Get-PublicFolderStatistics | Select Name, `
ItemCount, TotalItemSize, TotalDeletedItemSize, FolderPath, `
MailboxOwnerId | Export-CSV C:PFs.csv -Notype
```

How it works...

In the first of these examples, we are querying all the public folder mailboxes and choosing to view their `DisplayName` and `TotalItemSize` values. So far, we have created only one, but you can have multiple public folder mailboxes, each containing their own set of public folders. This is useful to geographically distribute public folders closer to where users are located, for example.

The second command is used to retrieve the statistics information about the public folder contents: the number of items, the size, the public folder the contents are placed in, and the path.

In the previous two examples, we select the information we want and export it to a CSV file.

See also

- *Managing public folder mailboxes* recipe in this chapter
- *Managing user access to public folders* recipe in this chapter

Managing user access to public folders

Now that we have a public folder structure, we realize that the default permissions aren't appropriate. So we want to change them a little bit.

First, we don't want end users to create items in folders they shouldn't have access to. The Default user is given author permissions, which means that they can read and create items in that folder. A full permission list can be found in this section.

In this recipe, we will start by changing the permissions for the Default user, and later on, we will configure some security groups with public folder permissions.

How to do it...

The following commands remove the permissions for the Default user and add new permissions:

```
Get-PublicFolder -Recurse | Get-PublicFolderClientPermission
Get-PublicFolder -Recurse | % { `
Remove-PublicFolderClientPermission $_ -User Default}
Get-PublicFolder -Recurse | % { `
Add-PublicFolderClientPermission $_ -User testuser -AccessRights Reviewer}
```

How it works...

Our mission with this recipe was to change the permissions for the Default user. We start off by checking the default permissions for the public folders.

The second command removes the Default permissions from all public folders.

Finally, we give testuser Reviewer permissions to all public folders. The difference now is that the Reviewer isn't able to create items in the folder, which was our objective.

You might wonder which permissions can be used and what kind of access they provide. The possible values that can be used with the -AccessRights parameter are as follows:

- **Read Items**: The user assigned with this permission can read items within the designated folder.
- **Create Items**: The user assigned with this permission can create items within the designated folder.

- **Edit Owned Items**: The user assigned with this permission can edit the items that the user owns in the designated folder.
- **Delete Owned tems**: The user assigned with this permission can delete items that the user owns in the designated folder.
- **Edit All Items**: The user assigned with this permission can edit all items in the designated folder.
- **Delete All Items**: The user assigned with this permission can delete all items in the designated folder.
- **Create Subfolders**: The user assigned with this permission can create subfolders in the designated folder.
- **Folder Owner**: The user assigned with this permission has the right to view and move the folder and create subfolders. The user cannot read items, edit items, delete items, or create items.
- **Folder Contact**: The user assigned this permission is the contact for the designated folder.
- **Folder Visible**: The user assigned this permission can view the specified folder but can't read or edit items within it.

The following roles are made up of one or more of the permissions specified in the previous list and can also be used with the `-AccessRights` parameter:

- **None**: This role has the FolderVisible permission
- **Owner**: This role has CreateItems, ReadItems, CreateSubfolders, FolderOwner, FolderContact, FolderVisible, EditOwnedItems, EditAllItems, DeleteOwnedItems, and DeleteAllItems permissions
- **Publishing Editor**: This role has CreateItems, ReadItems, CreateSubfolders, FolderVisible, EditOwnedItems, EditAllItems, DeleteOwnedItems, and DeleteAllItems permissions
- **Editor**: This role has CreateItems, ReadItems, FolderVisible, EditOwnedItems, EditAllItems, DeleteOwnedItems, and DeleteAllItems permissions
- **Publishing Author**: This role has CreateItems, ReadItems, CreateSubfolders, FolderVisible, EditOwnedItems, and DeleteOwnedItems permissions
- **Author**: This role has CreateItems, ReadItems, FolderVisible, EditOwnedItems, and DeleteOwnedItems permissions
- **Non Editing Author**: This role has CreateItems, ReadItems, and FolderVisible permissions
- **Reviewer**: This role has ReadItems and FolderVisible permissions
- **Contributor**: This role has CreateItems and FolderVisible permissions

There's more...

Dealing with permissions in large environments isn't always easy, and it's recommended that you use security groups as it makes it much easier to manage; this also applies to public folders.

I've created a universal mail-enabled security group and added members to it. In my example, it is called PF_AMER_USA_Projects_Owners. Let's add this group as Owner to the Projects public folder. To do that, we use the following commands:

```
Add-PublicFolderClientPermission "" -User PF_AMER_USA_Projects_Owners
-AccessRights FolderVisible

Add-PublicFolderClientPermission "AMER" -User PF_AMER_USA_Projects_Owners
-AccessRights FolderVisible

Add-PublicFolderClientPermission "AMERUSA" -User
PF_AMER_USA_Projects_Owners -AccessRights FolderVisible

Add-PublicFolderClientPermission "AMERUSAProjects" -User
PF_AMER_USA_Projects_Owners -AccessRights Owner
```

 Because we removed the default permissions, in this example, we have to make the top-level public folder as well as all public folders up to AMERUSAProjects, visible so users can at least navigate to the Projects public folder.

Using groups instead of specific user permissions makes it at least a little bit easier to administrate the permissions. In a large infrastructure, make sure that you plan the structure well before you start making changes.

See also

- *Managing public folder mailboxes* recipe in this chapter
- *Managing user access to public folders* recipe in this chapter

5
Distribution Groups and Address Lists

In this chapter, we will cover the following:

- Reporting on distribution group membership
- Adding members to a distribution group from an external file
- Previewing dynamic distribution group membership
- Backing up distribution groups membership
- Excluding hidden recipients from a dynamic distribution group
- Converting and upgrading distribution groups
- Allowing managers to modify group permissions
- Removing disabled users from distribution groups
- Working with distribution group naming policies
- Working with distribution group membership approval
- Creating address lists
- Exporting address list membership to a CSV file
- Configuring hierarchical address books

Introduction

In Chapter 3, *Managing Recipients* we looked at managing recipients, which covered the process of creating and modifying the membership of both regular and dynamic distribution groups. In this chapter, we are going to dive deeper into distribution group management within the Exchange Management Shell. The recipes in this chapter provide solutions to some of the most common distribution group management tasks that can, and sometimes must, be handled from the command-line. Some of the topics we'll cover include the implementation of group naming policies, allowing group managers to modify the memberships of distribution groups, and more. We'll also go over the process of some basic address list management that can be automated through the shell.

Performing some basic steps

To work with the code samples in this chapter, follow these steps to launch the Exchange Management Shell:

1. Log onto a workstation or server with the Exchange Management Tools installed.
2. You can connect using remote PowerShell if for some reason you don't have Exchange Management Tools installed. Use the following command:

```
$Session = New-PSSession -ConfigurationName Microsoft.Exchange `
-ConnectionUri http://servername/PowerShell/ `
-Authentication Kerberos
Import-PSSession $Session
```

3. Alternatively, open the Exchange Management Shell by clicking the Windows button and go to **Microsoft Exchange Server 2016 | Exchange Management Shell**.

If any additional steps are required they will be listed at the beginning of the recipe in the *Getting ready* section.

 Remember to start the Exchange Management Shell using **Run as Administrator** to avoid permission problems. In the chapter, notice that in the examples of cmdlets, I have used the back tick (`) character for breaking up long commands into multiple lines. The purpose of this is to make it easier to read. The back ticks are not required and should only be used if needed.

Notice that the Exchange variables, like $exscripts, are not available when using the preceding method.

Reporting on distribution group membership

One of the common requests you are likely to receive as an Exchange administrator is to generate a report detailing which recipients are members of one or more distribution groups. In this recipe, we'll take a look at how to retrieve this information from the Exchange Management Shell.

How to do it...

To view a list of each distribution group member interactively, use the following code:

```
foreach($i in Get-DistributionGroup -ResultSize Unlimited) {
  Get-DistributionGroupMember $i -ResultSize Unlimited |
    Select-Object @{n="Member";e={$_.Name}},
      RecipientType,
      @{n="Group";e={$i.Name}}
}
```

This will generate a list of Exchange recipients and their associated distribution group membership.

How it works...

This code loops through each item returned from the `Get-DistributionGroup` cmdlet. As we process each group, we run the `Get-DistributionGroupMember` cmdlet to determine the member list for each group and then use `Select-Object` to construct a custom object that provides `Member`, `RecipientType`, and `Group` properties. Notice that, when running both Exchange cmdlets, we're setting the `-ResultSize` parameter to Unlimited to ensure that the details will be retrieved in the event that there are more than 1,000 groups or group members. The result of the preceding cmdlets will look similar to the following screenshot:

```
Machine: tlex01.testlabs.se                                      —  □  ×

[PS] C:\>foreach($i in Get-DistributionGroup -ResultSize Unlimited) {
>>     Get-DistributionGroupMember $i -ResultSize Unlimited |
>>       Select-Object @{n="Member";e={$_.Name}},
>>         RecipientType,
>>         @{n="Group";e={$i.Name}}
>> }

Member            RecipientType  Group
------            -------------  -----
Pete Dickson      UserMailbox    DL_Marketing
Emanuel Moss      UserMailbox    DL_Marketing
Lee Sanders       UserMailbox    DL_Marketing
Arlene Finley     UserMailbox    DL_Marketing
Ruben Mcleod      UserMailbox    DL_Marketing
Pete Dickson      UserMailbox    DL_Sales
Emanuel Moss      UserMailbox    DL_Sales
Lee Sanders       UserMailbox    DL_Sales
```

There's more...

The previous code sample will allow you to view the output in the shell. If you want to export this information to a CSV file, use the following code:

```
$report=foreach($i in Get-DistributionGroup -ResultSize Unlimited) {
  Get-DistributionGroupMember $i -ResultSize Unlimited |
    Select-Object @{n="Member";e={$_.Name}},
      RecipientType,
      @{n="Group";e={$i.Name}}
}

$report | Export-CSV c:\GroupMembers.csv -NoType
```

The difference this time is that the output from our code is being saved in the $report variable. Once the report has been generated, the $report object is then exported to a CSV file that can be opened in Excel.

See also

- The *Previewing dynamic distribution group membership* recipe in this chapter
- The *Adding members to a distribution group from an external file* recipe in this chapter

Adding members to a distribution group from an external file

When working in large or complex environments, performing bulk operations is the key to efficiency. Using PowerShell core cmdlets such as Get-Content and Import-CSV, we can easily import external data into the shell and use this information to perform bulk operations on hundreds or thousands of objects in a matter of seconds. Obviously, this can vastly speed up the time we spend on routine tasks and greatly increase our efficiency. In this recipe, we'll use these concepts to add members to distribution groups in bulk from a text or CSV file using the Exchange Management Shell.

How to do it...

1. Create a text file called c:\Scripts\users.txt that lists the recipients in your organization that you want to add to a group. Make sure you enter them one line at a time, as shown in the following screenshot:

```
users.txt - Notepad                                    —    □    ×
File   Edit   Format   View   Help
afinley@testlabs.se
rmcleod@testlabs.se
emoss@testlabs.se
pdickson@testlabs.se
```

2. Next, execute the following code to add the list of recipients to a distribution group:

```
Get-Content c:\Scripts\users.txt | % {
    Add-DistributionGroupMember -Identity Sales -Member $_
}
```

When the code runs, each user listed in the c:\Scripts\users.txt file will be added to the Sales distribution group.

How it works...

When importing data from a plain text file, we use the Get-Content cmdlet, which will read the content of the file into the shell one line at a time. In this example, we pipe the content of the file to the ForEach-Object cmdlet, and, as each line is processed, we execute the Add-DistributionGroupMember cmdlet.

Inside the ForEach-Object script block we use the Add-DistributionGroupMember cmdlet and assign the $_ object, which is the current recipient item in the pipeline, to the -Member parameter.

> To remove recipients from a distribution group, you can use the Remove-DistributionGroupMember cmdlet

Keep in mind that this text file does not have to contain the SMTP address of the recipient. You can also use the Active Directory account name, User Principal Name, Distinguished Name, GUID, or LegacyExchangeDN values. The important thing is that the file contains a valid and unique value for each recipient. If the identity of the recipient cannot be determined, the Add-DistributionGroupMember command will fail.

There's more...

In addition to using plain text files, we can also import recipients from a CSV file and add them to a distribution group. Let's say that you have a CSV file set up with multiple columns, such as FirstName, LastName, and EmailAddress. When you import the CSV file, the data can be accessed using the column headers as the property names for each object. Take a look at the following screenshot:

```
[PS] C:\>Import-Csv C:\Scripts\users.csv

FirstName LastName EmailAddress
--------- -------- ------------
Alexander Lucas    alucas@testlabs.se
Alejandro Jones    ajones@testlabs.se
Charlene  Munoz    cmunoz@testlabs.se
Alex      Knowles  aknowles@testlabs.se
Cassandra Peck     cpeck@testlabs.se
```

Here you can see that each item in this collection has an EmailAddress property. As long as this information corresponds to the recipient data in the Exchange organization, we can simply loop through each record in the CSV file and add these recipients to a distribution group:

```
Import-Csv C:\Scripts\users.csv | % {
    Add-DistributionGroupMember Sales -Member $_.EmailAddress
}
```

The given code uses the Import-Csv cmdlet to loop through each item in the collection. As we process each record, we add the recipient to the Sales distribution group using the $_.EmailAddress object.

See also

- *Managing distribution groups* recipe from Chapter 3, *Managing Recipients*

Previewing dynamic distribution group membership

The concept of the dynamic distribution group was introduced with the initial release of Exchange 2007 and included a new way to create and manage distribution groups. Unlike regular distribution groups whose members are statically defined, a dynamic distribution group determines its members based on a recipient filter. These recipient filters can be very complex, or they can be based on simple conditions, such as including all the users with a common value set for their `Company` or `Department` attributes in Active Directory. Since these dynamic groups are based on a query, they do not actually contain group members and, if you want to preview the results of the groups query in the shell you need to use a series of commands. In this recipe, we'll take a look at how to view the membership of dynamic distribution groups in the Exchange Management Shell.

How to do it...

Imagine that we have a dynamic distribution group named `Legal` that includes all of the users in Active Directory with a `Department` attribute set to the word `Legal`. We can use the following commands to retrieve the current list of recipients for this group:

```
$legal= Get-DynamicDistributionGroup -Identity legal
Get-Recipient -RecipientPreviewFilter $legal.RecipientFilter
```

How it works...

Recipient filters for dynamic distribution groups use OPATH filters that are accessible through the `RecipientFilter` property of a dynamic distribution group object. As you can see here, we have specified the `Legal` groups OPATH filter when running the `Get-Recipient` cmdlet with the `-RecipientPreviewFilter` parameter. Conceptually, this would be similar to running the following command:

```
Get-Recipient -RecipientPreviewFilter "Department -eq 'Legal'"
```

Technically, there is a little bit more to it than that. If we were to actually look at the value for the `RecipientFilter` property of this dynamic distribution group, we would see much more information in addition to the filter defined for the `Legal` department. This is because Exchange automatically adds several additional filters when it creates a dynamic distribution group that excludes system mailboxes, discovery mailboxes, arbitration mailboxes, and more. This ends up being quite a bit of information, and creating an object instance of the dynamic distribution group gives us easy access to the existing OPATH filter that can be previewed with the `Get-Recipient` cmdlet.

There's more...

When working with regular distribution groups, you may notice that there is a cmdlet called `Get-DistributionGroupMember`. This allows you to retrieve a list of every user that is a member of a distribution group. Unfortunately, there is no equivalent cmdlet for dynamic distribution groups, and we need to use the method outlined previously that uses the `Get-Recipient` cmdlet to determine the list of recipients in a dynamic distribution group.

If you find yourself doing this frequently, it probably makes sense to wrap these commands up into a function that can be added to your PowerShell profile. This will allow you to determine the members of a dynamic distribution group using a single command that will be available to you every time you start the shell. Here is the code for a function called `Get-DynamicDistributionGroupMember`, which can be used to determine the list of recipients included in a dynamic distribution group:

```
function Get-DynamicDistributionGroupMember {
  param(
  [Parameter(Mandatory=$true)]
  $Identity
  )

  $group = Get-DynamicDistributionGroup -Identity $Identity
  Get-Recipient -RecipientPreviewFilter $group.RecipientFilter
}
```

Once this function is loaded into your shell session, you can run it just like a cmdlet:

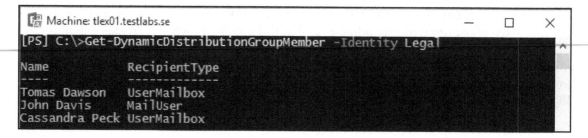

You can see that the command returns the recipients that match the OPATH filter for the Legal distribution group and is much easier to type than the original example.

See also

- The *Reporting on distribution group membership* recipe in this chapter
- The *Working with recipient filters* recipe in this chapter

Backing up distribution groups membership

Now we've worked with distribution groups in the earlier recipe, we know the basics of them. Now we want to utilize PowerShell for backing up the distribution groups and the membership. There could be a lot of reasons for this, but a migration is the most likely one I can think of; examples include a cross-forest migration or, from Exchange on-premises to Exchange Online without having the full Exchange Hybrid with synchronizing all objects, and so on.

In this recipe, we will find all distribution groups and their members to extract that information; we will also be able to restore this information.

How to do it...

In this section, we will see the full script for extracting the information. This can be copied into a PowerShell PS1 file, name it Backup-DistributionGroups.ps1. When done, it can be executed using the Exchange Management Shell.

The full script can be found in the following:

```
$groups = Get-DistributionGroup -ResultSize Unlimited
$totalcount = $groups.Count
 $count = 0
 [array]$array = @()

 $groups | foreach {
 $count++
    $GroupName = $_.DisplayName
    $GroupMail = $_.PrimarySmtpAddress.Address
    $GroupProxies = ($_.EmailAddresses | %{$_.SmtpAddress}) `
-Join ";"
    $GroupType = $_.RecipientTypeDetails
    $GroupLegDN = $_.LegacyExchangeDN

    $Manager = (($_.ManagedBy.DistinguishedName) | `
Get-Recipient).PrimarySmtpAddress

 [string]$Members = ""

 $GroupMembers = $_.Identity | Get-DistributionGroupMember
    $GroupMembers | foreach {
        $Members += $_.PrimarySmtpAddress.Address.ToString() + ";"
    }

 $Object = New-Object PSObject -Property @{
        GroupName = $GroupName
        GroupMail = $GroupMail
        GroupProxies = $GroupProxies
        GroupType = $GroupType
        GroupLegDN = $GroupLegDN
        Manager = $Manager
       Members = $Members
   }

 $array += $Object

 $completed = [Math]::Round(($count/$totalcount * 100), 1)
 Write-Progress -Activity "Processing.." -Status "Progress: ` $completed%"
-Percentcomplete ($count/$totalcount * 100)

 }

 $array | Export-Csv -NoTypeInformation -Path C:\Scripts\DGs.csv `
 -Encoding UTF8
```

With the complete preceding script, a short description of it is probably needed. It will help us to extract all distribution groups and their members. The variety of amounts of distribution groups is huge; therefore a counter with a progress bar is also added into the script; it helps to track the progress of the script.

How it works...

The script will start by creating a variable named $groups and then utilize `Get-DistributionGroup` to fetch all distribution groups.

We created a few variables, named `$array`, `$totalcount` which are based on the count of distribution groups and creating `$count` and setting it to 0. They will be used to build a proper input to the progress bar that will be shown during the extraction/backup of the distribution groups.

Then we will loop through the `$groups` variable and collect all distribution groups into the variable. We will then collect some attributes, examples of these are `DisplayName`, `PrimarySmtpAddress`, `EmailAddresses`, `RecipientTypeDetails`, `LegacyExchangeDN`, `ManagedBy/ManagerSmtp`, and `Members`.

The script will then loop through the `$groups` variable, and, for each distribution group save all the attributes listed in the preceding paragraph, into the array variable named `$array`. During the loop, a progress bar is shown to track its progress. To extract the Manager of each distribution group, we need to utilize the cmdlet

`Get-Recipient` to fetch the `PrimarySmtpAddress`. This needs to be done because during the restoration of the admin, a unique identifier needs to be used. All members are listed with a semi-colon to separate them.

The contents of `$array` is saved into a CSV file using the cmdlet Export-Csv, we also use the parameters `-NoTypeInformation` and we want to encode the contents to UTF8, this is to ensure that all non-English characters are formatted correctly.

There's more...

Let us assume that you've recently extracted all the distribution group information and saved it into the CSV file. This is quite useless if we don't use it for restoring the information into the target environment during a cross-forest migration or a cutover migration from Exchange on-premises to Exchange Online when the full synchronization using Azure AD Connect isn't being used.

The distribution groups will get restored to their original states and also add the members back to them. If you're using this method to backup and restore the distribution groups, it's recommended to keep the gap between the backup and the restore as short as possible to prevent potential changes.

In the following script we can find the rows, copy the text into a file named `Restore-DistributionGroups.ps1`:

```
[array]$groups = Import-Csv -Path C:\Scripts\DGs.csv -Delimiter ` "," -
Encoding UTF8

$totalcount = $groups.Count$count = 0

$groups | foreach {
$count++    $groupexists = Get-DistributionGroup -Identity $_.GroupMail `
-ea silentlycontinue

if (!($groupexists))
{
[array]$members = $_.Members.Split(";")
New-DistributionGroup -Name $_.GroupName -DisplayName ` $_.GroupName -
PrimarySmtpAddress $_.GroupMail `
-OrganizationalUnit "OU=Groups,OU=Sales,DC=testlabs,DC=se" `
-ManagedBy $_.Manager

foreach ($member in $members)
{
$identity = $_.GroupName
if ($member -ne "") { Add-DistributionGroupMember -Identity ` $identity -
Member $member }
}
}

$completed = [Math]::Round(($count/$totalcount * 100), 1)

Write-Progress -Activity "Processing data.." -Status ` "Processing..
$completed%" -Percentcomplete ($count/$totalcount ` * 100)

}
```

The preceding script will start by reading/importing the contents of the file `C:\Scripts\DGs.csv` and saving the contents into the array variable `$groups`.

A variable named $totalcount and $count are also created, they will be used to build a proper input to the progress bar that will be shown during the restoration. We will loop through the $groups variable and validate that the distribution group in the loop doesn't exist already, if it exists then it will be skipped and the script will continue to the next item in the loop.

If the distribution group doesn't exist it will be created using the cmdlet New-DistributionGroup. The script will name it equal to the contents we extracted previously, same goes for the variables Name, DisplayName, ManagedBy, PrimarySmtpAddress while OrganizationalUnit is a static value configured in the script. For adding members, we loop through all saved members and add them using the cmdlet Add-DistributionGroupMember.

Update the values in the script to match your own environment. The value for OrganizationalUnit could of course also be put into the CSV file, if you want to differentiate between the distribution groups.

Keep in mind if you want to edit the input for distribution groups, it can easily be edited in the CSV file using notepad or any editor of your choice.

The restoration will look similar to the following screenshot:

See also

- The *Reporting on distribution group membership* recipe in this chapter
- The *Adding members to a distribution group from an external file* recipe in this chapter
- The *Exporting address list membership to a CSV file* recipe in this chapter

Excluding hidden recipients from a dynamic distribution group

When creating dynamic distribution groups through the Exchange Management Console, you can specify which recipients should be included in the group using a basic set of conditions. If you want to do more advanced filtering, such as excluding hidden recipients, you will need to configure OPATH filters for your dynamic distribution groups through the Exchange Management Shell. In this recipe, you'll learn how to use the shell to create a recipient filter that excludes hidden recipients from dynamic distribution groups.

How to do it...

Let's say that we need to set up a distribution group for our TechSupport department. The following commands can be used to create a dynamic distribution group that includes all the mailboxes for the users in the TechSupportOU that are not hidden from address lists:

```
New-DynamicDistributionGroup -Name TechSupport `
-RecipientContainer contoso.com/TechSupport `
-RecipientFilter {
  HiddenFromAddressListsEnabled -ne $true
}
```

How it works...

When you want to exclude a mailbox, contact, or distribution group from an address list, you set the `HiddenFromAddressListsEnabled` property of the recipient to `$true`. This is often done for special purpose recipients that are used for applications or services that should not be visible by the general end-user population. While this takes care of address lists, it does not affect your dynamic distribution groups, and if you want to exclude these recipients, you'll need to use a similar filter to the one shown in the previous example. When we created the `TechSupport` dynamic distribution group, we used a very basic configuration that included all the recipients that exist within the `TechSupportOU` in Active Directory. Our custom recipient filter specifies that the `HiddenFromAddressListEnabled` property of each recipient can't be equal to `$true`. With this filter in place, only recipients that are not hidden from Exchange address lists are included as dynamic distribution group members.

Keep in mind that, when you create a dynamic group using the `-RecipientFilter` parameter, any future changes will have to be made through the Exchange Management Shell. If you need to change the recipient filter at any time, you cannot use Exchange Admin Center and will need to use the `Set-DynamicDistributionGroup` cmdlet to make the change.

There's more...

Updating a recipient filter for an existing dynamic distribution group can be a bit tricky. This is because the recipient filters are automatically updated by Exchange to exclude certain types of resource and system mailboxes. Let's go through the process of creating a new dynamic distribution group, and then we'll modify the recipient filter after the fact so that you can understand how this process works.

First, we'll create a new dynamic distribution group for the `Marketing` department using a basic filter. Only users with email addresses that contain the word `Marketing` will be members of this group:

```
New-DynamicDistributionGroup -Name Marketing `
-RecipientContainer contoso.com/Marketing `
-RecipientFilter {
  EmailAddresses -like '*marketing*'
}
```

Now that the group has been created, let's verify the recipient filter by accessing the `RecipientFilter` property of that object:

```
[PS] C:\>(Get-DynamicDistributionGroup Marketing).recipientfilter
((((EmailAddresses -like '*marketing*') -and (HiddenFromAddressListsEnabled
 -ne 'True'))) -and (-not(Name -like 'SystemMailbox{*')) -and (-not(Name -l
ike 'CAS_{*')) -and (-not(RecipientTypeDetailsValue -eq 'MailboxPlan')) -an
d (-not(RecipientTypeDetailsValue -eq 'DiscoveryMailbox')) -and (-not(Recip
ientTypeDetailsValue -eq 'PublicFolderMailbox')) -and (-not(RecipientTypeDe
tailsValue -eq 'ArbitrationMailbox')) -and (-not(RecipientTypeDetailsValue
-eq 'AuditLogMailbox')) -and (-not(RecipientTypeDetailsValue -eq 'AuxAuditL
ogMailbox')) -and (-not(RecipientTypeDetailsValue -eq 'SupervisoryReviewPol
icyMailbox')))
[PS] C:\>
```

As you can see from the output, we get a lot more back than we originally put in. This is how Exchange prevents the dynamic distribution groups from displaying recipients such as system and discovery mailboxes in your dynamic distribution lists. You do not need to worry about this extraneous code when you update your filters, as it will automatically be added back in for you when you change the recipient filter.

Now that we understand what's going on here, let's update this group so that we can also exclude hidden recipients. To do this, we need to construct a new filter and use the `Set-DynamicDistributionGroup` cmdlet as shown next:

```
Set-DynamicDistributionGroup -Identity Marketing `
-RecipientFilter {
   (EmailAddresses -like '*marketing*') -and
   (HiddenFromAddressListsEnabled -ne $true)
}
```

Using this command, we've specified the previously-configured filter in addition to the new one that excludes hidden recipients. In order for recipients to show up in this dynamic distribution group, they must have the word `Marketing` somewhere in their email address and their account must not be hidden from address lists.

See also

- *Hiding recipients from address lists* recipe from `Chapter 3`, *Managing Recipients*
- *Working with recipient filters* recipe from `Chapter 3`, *Managing Recipients*

Converting and upgrading distribution groups

If you, for some reason, haven't upgraded your legacy distribution groups, this recipe is for you because before migrating to Exchange 2010 from Exchange 2003, you may be carrying over several mail-enabled non-universal groups. These groups will still function, but the administration of these objects within the Exchange tools will be limited. In addition, several distribution group features provided by Exchange 2010, 2013, or 2016 will not be enabled for a group until it has been upgraded. If you somehow haven't upgraded your groups before, now's the time. That's why the recipe is included in this book. This recipe covers the process of converting and upgrading these groups within the Exchange Management Shell.

How to do it...

1. To convert all of your non-universal distribution groups to universal, use the following one-liner:

```
Get-DistributionGroup -ResultSize Unlimited `
-RecipientTypeDetails MailNonUniversalGroup |
  Set-Group -Universal
```

2. Once all of your distribution groups have been converted to universal, you can upgrade them using the following command:

```
Get-DistributionGroup -ResultSize Unlimited |
  Set-DistributionGroup -ForceUpgrade
```

How it works...

The first command will retrieve all the non-universal mail-enabled distribution groups in your organization and pipe the results to the `Set-Group` cmdlet which will convert them using the `-Universal` switch parameter. It may not be a big deal to modify a handful of groups, but if you have hundreds of mail-enabled non-universal groups the command in the previous example can save you a lot of time.

If you have a large number of groups to convert, you may find that some of them are members of another global group and cannot be converted. Keep in mind that a universal group cannot be a member of a global group. If you run into errors because of this, you can convert these groups individually using the `Set-Group` cmdlet. Then you can run the command in the previous example again to convert any remaining groups in bulk.

Even after converting non-universal groups to universal, you'll notice that, when viewing the properties of a distribution group created by Exchange 2003, you cannot manage things such as message moderation and membership approval. In order to fully manage these groups, you need to upgrade them using the `-ForceUpgrade` parameter with the `Set-DistributionGroup` cmdlet. Keep in mind that after the upgrade these objects can no longer be managed using anything other than the Exchange 2010, 2013 or 2016 management tools.

There's more...

The Exchange Management tools, both the graphical console and the shell, can only be used to create distribution groups using universal group scope. Additionally, you can only mail-enable existing groups with universal group scope. If you've recently introduced Exchange into your environment, you can convert existing non-universal, non-mail enabled groups in bulk using a one-liner:

```
Get-Group -ResultSize Unlimited `
-RecipientTypeDetails NonUniversalGroup `
-OrganizationalUnit Sales |
  Where-Object {$_.GroupType -match 'global'} |
    Set-Group -Universal
```

As you can see in this example, we are retrieving all non-mail enabled, non-universal global groups from the `Sales` OU and converting them to universal in a single command. See the following screenshot for the outcome of the preceding cmdlets:

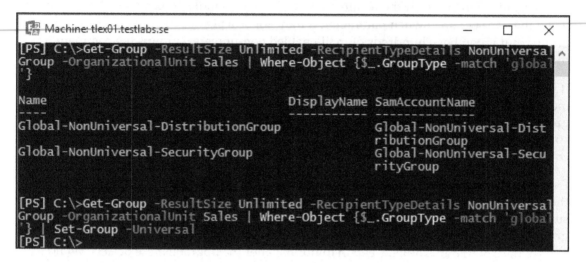

You can change the OU or use additional conditions in your filter based on your needs. Once the group is converted it can be mail-enabled using the `Enable-Distribution` group cmdlet and it will show up in the list of available groups when creating new distribution groups.

See also

- The *Managing distribution groups* recipe in this chapter
- The *Allowing managers to modify group membership* recipe in this chapter

Allowing managers to modify group permissions

Many organizations like to give specific users rights to manage the membership of designated distribution groups. This has been a common practice for years in previous versions of Exchange. While users have typically modified the memberships of the groups they have rights to from within Outlook, they now have the added capability to manage these groups from the web-based **ExchangeControlPanel** (**ECP**). Exchange 2010 introduced a new security model that changed the way you can delegate these rights. In this recipe, we'll take a look at what you need to do in Exchange 2016 to allow managers to modify the memberships of distribution groups.

How to do it...

1. The first thing you need to do is assign the built-in `MyDistributionGroups` role to the Default Role Assignment Policy:

```
New-ManagementRoleAssignment –Role MyDistributionGroups `
-Policy "Default Role Assignment Policy"
```

2. Next, set the `ManagedBy` property of the distribution group that needs to be modified:

```
Set-DistributionGroup Sales –ManagedBy bobsmith
```

After running the given command, Bob Smith has the ability to modify the membership of the `Sales` distribution group through ECP, Outlook, or the Exchange Management Shell.

How it works...

In order to allow managers to modify the membership of a group, we need to do some initial configuration through the Exchange 2016 security model called **Role Based Access Control** (**RBAC**). The `MyDistributionGroups` role is an RBAC management role that allows end-users to view, remove, and add members to distribution groups where they have been added to the `ManagedBy` property.

By default, the `MyDistribitionGroups` management role is not assigned to anyone. In the first step, we added this role to the Default Role Assignment Policy that is assigned to all users by default.

In addition to using the shell, you can assign the `MyDistributionGroups` management role to the Default Role Assignment Policy using ECP.

In the next step, we assigned a user to the `ManagedBy` property of the `Sales` distribution group. The `ManagedBy` attribute is a multi-valued property that will accept multiple users if you need to allow several people to manage a distribution group.

The reason that the `MyDistributionGroups` role is not enabled by default is because, in addition to allowing users to modify the groups that they own, it also allows them to create new distribution groups from within the ECP. While some organizations may like this feature, others may not be able to allow this since the provisioning of groups may need to be tightly controlled. Make sure you keep this in mind before implementing this solution.

There's more...

If you need to prevent users from creating their own distribution groups, then you do not want to assign the `MyDistributionGroups` role. Instead, you'll need to create a custom RBAC role. This can only be accomplished using the Exchange Management Shell.

To implement a custom RBAC role that will only allow users to modify distribution groups that they own, we need to perform a few steps. The first thing we need to do is create a child role based on the existing `MyDistributionGroups` management role, as shown next:

```
New-ManagementRole -Name MyDGCustom -Parent MyDistributionGroups
```

After running this command, we should now have a new role called `MyDGCustom` that contains all of the cmdlets that will allow the user to add and remove distribution groups. Using the following commands, we'll remove those cmdlets from the role:

```
Remove-ManagementRoleEntry MyDGCustom\New-DistributionGroup
Remove-ManagementRoleEntry MyDGCustom\Remove-DistributionGroup
```

This modifies the role so that only the cmdlets that can get, add, or remove distribution group members are available to the users.

Finally, we can assign the custom role to the Default Role Assignment Policy, which, out-of-the-box, is already applied to every mailbox in the organization:

```
New-ManagementRoleAssignment -Role MyDGCustom `
-Policy "Default Role Assignment Policy"
```

Now that this custom RBAC role has been implemented, we can simply add users to the `ManagedBy` property of any distribution group and they will be able to add members to and remove members from that group. However, they will be unable to delete the group, or create a new distribution group, which accomplishes the goal.

See also

- *Working with RBAC* recipe from `Chapter 10`, *Compliance and Audit Logging*
- *Troubleshooting RBAC* recipe from `Chapter 10`, *Compliance and Audit Logging*

Removing disabled users from distribution groups

A standard practice amongst most organizations when users leave or have been let go is to disable their associated Active Directory user account. This allows an administrator to easily re-enable the account in the event that the user comes back to work, or if someone else needs access to the account. Obviously, this has become a common practice because the process of restoring a deleted Active Directory user account is a much more complex alternative. Additionally, if these user accounts are left mailbox-enabled, you can end up with distribution groups that contain multiple disabled user accounts. This recipe will show you how to remove these disabled accounts using the Exchange Management Shell.

How to do it...

To remove disabled Active Directory user accounts from all distribution groups in the organization, use the following code:

```
$groups = Get-DistributionGroup -ResultSize Unlimited

foreach($group in $groups){
 Get-DistributionGroupMember $group |
  ?{$_.RecipientTypeDetails -like '*User*'} |
   Get-User | ?{$_.UserAccountControl -match 'AccountDisabled'} |
    Remove-DistributionGroupMember $group -Confirm:$false
}
```

How it works...

This code uses a `foreach` loop to iterate through each distribution group in the organization. As each group is processed, we retrieve only the members whose recipient type contains the word `User`. We're also filtering out all non-user mailboxes as these are tied to disabled Active Directory accounts. These filters will ensure that we only pipe objects with Active Directory user accounts down to the `Get-User` cmdlet, which will determine whether or not the account is disabled by checking the `UserAccountControl` property of each object. If the account is disabled, it will be removed from the group. See the following screenshot as an example:

```
Machine: tlex01.testlabs.se                                    —   □   ×

[PS] C:\>$groups = Get-DistributionGroup -ResultSize Unlimited
[PS] C:\>foreach($group in $groups){
>>   Get-DistributionGroupMember $group |
>>     ?{$_.RecipientTypeDetails -like '*User*'} |
>>       Get-User | ?{$_.UserAccountControl -match 'AccountDisabled'}}

Name                    RecipientType
----                    -------------
Terrance Randolph       UserMailbox
Tomas Dawson            UserMailbox
Cassandra Peck          UserMailbox


[PS] C:\>foreach($group in $groups){
>>   Get-DistributionGroupMember $group |
>>     ?{$_.RecipientTypeDetails -like '*User*'} |
>>       Get-User | ?{$_.UserAccountControl -match 'AccountDisabled'} |
>>         Remove-DistributionGroupMember $group -Confirm:$false
>> }
[PS] C:\>
```

There's more...

Instead of performing the remove operation, we can use a slightly modified version of the previous code to simply generate a report based on disabled Active Directory accounts that are members of a specific distribution group. Use the following code to generate this report:

```
$groups = Get-DistributionGroup -ResultSize Unlimited

$report = foreach($group in $groups){
  Get-DistributionGroupMember $group |
    ?{$_.RecipientTypeDetails -like '*User*'} |
      Get-User | ?{$_.UserAccountControl -match 'AccountDisabled'} |
```

```
    Select-Object `
Name,RecipientTypeDetails,@{n='Group';e={$group}}
}

$report | Export-CSV c:\disabled_group_members.csv -NoType
```

After running this code, a report will be generated using the specified file name that will list the disabled account name, Exchange recipient type, and associated distribution group for which it is a member.

See also

- The *Managing distribution groups* recipe from `Chapter` 3, *Managing Recipients*

Working with distribution group naming policies

Using group naming policies, you can require that the distribution group names in your organization follow a specific naming standard. For instance, you can specify that all distribution group names are prefixed with a certain word and you can block certain words from being used within group names. In this recipe, you'll learn how to work with group naming policies from within the Exchange Management Shell.

How to do it...

To enable a group naming policy for your organization, use the `Set-OrganizationConfig` cmdlet, as shown next:

```
Set-OrganizationConfig -DistributionGroupNamingPolicy `
"DL_<GroupName>"
```

How it works...

Since Exchange 2010 gives your users the ability to create and manage their own distribution groups, you may want to implement a naming policy that matches your organization's naming standards. In addition, you can implement naming policies so that your administrators are required to follow a specific naming convention when creating groups.

Your distribution group naming policy can be made up of text you specify, or it can use specific attributes that map to the user who creates the distribution group. In the previous example, we specified that all distribution groups should be prefixed with DL_ followed by the group name. The <GroupName> attribute indicates that the group name provided by the user should be used. So, if someone were to create a group named Help Desk, Exchange would automatically configure the name of the group as DL_HelpDesk.

The following attributes can be used within your group naming policies:

- Company
- CountryCode
- CountryorRegion
- CustomAttribute1 - 15
- Department
- Office
- StateOrProvince
- Title

Let's take a look at another example to see how we could implement some of these attributes within a group naming policy. Using the following command, we'll update the group naming policy to include both the Department and the State of the user creating the group:

```
Set-OrganizationConfig -DistributionGroupNamingPolicy `
"<Department>_<GroupName>_<StateOrProvince>"
```

Now let's say that we have an administrator named Dave who works in the IT department in the Arizona office. Based on this information, we know that his Department attribute will be set to IT and his State attribute will be set to AZ. When Dave uses the New-DistributionGroup cmdlet to create a group for the maintenance department, specifying Maintenance for the -Name parameter value, Exchange will automatically apply the group naming policy, and the distribution group name will be IT_Maintenance_AZ.

In addition, we can exclude a list of names that can be used when creating distribution groups. This is also specified by running the `Set-OrganizationConfig` cmdlet. For example, to block a list of words we can use the following syntax:

```
Set-OrganizationConfig `
-DistributionGroupNameBlockedWordsList badword1,badword2
```

If a user tries to create a group using one of the blocked names, they'll receive an error that says the group name contains a word which isn't allowed in group names in your organization. Please rename your group. There is one more parameter to be aware of, which could be very useful.

It's used for providing a default organization unit where the distribution groups are placed by default. See the command example:

```
Set-OrganizationConfig `
-DistributionGroupDefaultOU "contoso.com/Test"
```

This setting can be overridden by using the parameter `-OrganizationalUnit` when creating the distribution groups.

There's more...

When a group naming policy is applied in your organization, it is possible to override it from within the Exchange Management Shell. Both the `New-DistributionGroup` and the `Set-DistributionGroup` cmdlets provides an `-IgnoreNamingPolicy` switch parameter that can be used when you are creating or modifying a group. To create a distribution group that will bypass the group naming policy, use the following syntax:

```
New-DistributionGroup -Name Accounting -IgnoreNamingPolicy
```

The graphical management tools (ECP) can be used to create distribution groups, but if a naming policy is applied to your organization and you need to override it, you must use the shell as shown previously.

You can force administrators to use group naming policies, even if they have access to the Exchange Management Shell. If you plan on doing this, you need to assign them to the `New-DistributionGroup` and `Set-DistributionGroup` cmdlets using a custom RBAC role that does not allow them to use the `-IgnoreNamingPolicy` switch parameter.

See also

- The *Managing distribution groups* recipe from `Chapter 3`, *Managing Recipients*

Working with distribution group membership approval

You can allow end-users to request distribution group membership through the ECP. Additionally, you can configure your distribution groups so that users can join a group automatically without having to be approved by a group owner. We'll take a look at how to configure these options in this recipe.

How to do it...

To allow end-users to add and remove themselves from a distribution group, you can set the following configuration using the `Set-DistributionGroup` cmdlet:

```
Set-DistributionGroup -Identity CompanyNews `
-MemberJoinRestriction Open `
-MemberDepartRestriction Open
```

This command will allow any user in the organization to join or leave the `CompanyNews` distribution group without requiring approval by a group owner.

How it works...

The two parameters that control the membership approval configuration for a distribution group are `-MemberJoinRestriction` and `-MemberDepartRestriction`. The parameter `-MemberJoinRestriction` can be set to one of the following values:

- `Open`: Allows the user to add or remove their account from the group without requiring group owner approval
- `Closed`: Users cannot join or leave the group
- `ApprovalRequired`: Requests to join or leave a group must be approved by a group owner

While the parameter `-MemberDepartRestriction` can only be set to the following values:

- `Open`: Allows the user to add or remove their account from the group without requiring group owner approval
- `Closed`: Users cannot join or leave the group

These settings are not mutually exclusive. For example, you can allow users to join a group without approval, but you can require approval when users try to leave the group, or vice versa. By default, the `MemberJoinRestriction` property is set to `Closed` and the `MemberDepartRestriction` is set to `Open`.

There's more...

When member join or depart restrictions are set to `ApprovalRequired`, a group owner will receive a message informing them of the request, and they can approve or deny the request using the **Accept** or **Reject** buttons in Outlook or OWA. The user who created the distribution group will automatically be the owner, but you change the owner, if needed, using the `-ManagedBy` parameter when running the `Set-DistributionGroup` cmdlet, as shown:

```
Set-DistributionGroup -Identity AllEmployees `
-ManagedBy dave@contoso.com, john@contoso.com
```

As you can see, the `-ManagedBy` parameter will accept one or more values. If you are setting multiple owners, just separate each one with a comma, as shown previously.

See also

- The *Reporting on distribution group membership* recipe in this chapter
- The *Managing distribution groups* recipe from `Chapter 3`, *Managing Recipients*

Creating address lists

Just like dynamic distribution groups, Exchange address lists can be comprised of one or more recipient types and are generated using a recipient filter or using a set of built-in conditions. You can create one or more address list(s), made up of users, contacts, distribution groups, or any other mail-enabled objects in your organization. This recipe will show you how to create an address list using the Exchange Management Shell.

How to do it...

Let's say we need to create an address list for the sales representatives in our organization. We can use the `New-AddressList` cmdlet to accomplish this, as shown next:

```
New-AddressList -Name 'All Sales Users' `
-RecipientContainer contoso.com/Sales `
-IncludedRecipients MailboxUsers
```

How it works...

This example uses the `New-AddressList` cmdlet's built-in conditions to specify the criteria for the recipients that will be included in the list. You can see from the command that, in order for a recipient to be visible in the address list, they must be located within the `Sales` OU in Active Directory and the recipient type must be `MailboxUsers`, which only applies to regular mailboxes and does not include other types such as resource mailboxes, distribution groups, and so on.

There's more...

When you need to create an address list based on a more complex set of conditions, you'll need to use the `-RecipientFilter` parameter to specify an OPATH filter. For example, the following OPATH filter is not configurable when creating or modifying an address list in EAC/ECP:

```
New-AddressList -Name MobileUsers `
-RecipientContainer contoso.com `
-RecipientFilter {
  HasActiveSyncDevicePartnership -ne $false
}
```

You can see here that we're creating an address list for all the mobile users in the organization. We've set the `RecipientContainer` to the root domain, and, within the recipient filter, we've specified that all recipients with an ActiveSync device partnership should be included in the list.

A small reminder: update the address list after it's created so that it applies and updates the list with accurate members. This is done by using the `Update-AddressList` cmdlet.

You can create global address lists using the `New-GlobalAddresslist` cmdlet.

You can combine multiple conditions in your recipient filters using PowerShell's logical operators. For instance, we can extend our previous example to add an additional requirement in the OPATH filter:

```
New-AddressList -Name MobileUsers `
-RecipientContainer contoso.com `
-RecipientFilter {
  (HasActiveSyncDevicePartnership -ne $false) -and
  (Phone -ne $null)
}
```

This time, in addition to having an ActiveSync device partnership, the user must also have a number defined within their `Phone` attribute in order for them to be included in the list.

 If you need to modify a recipient filter after an address list has already been created, use the `Set-AddressList` cmdlet.

Exchange supports a various number of both common and advanced properties that can be used to construct OPATH filters, as shown in the previous example. To view a list of common filterable properties that can be used with the `-RecipientFilter` parameter, see Appendix A at the end of this book.

See also

- The *Working with recipient filters* recipe from Chapter 3, *Managing Recipients*
- The *Exporting address list membership to a CSV file* recipe in this chapter

Exporting address list membership to a CSV file

When it comes to working with address lists, a common task is exporting the list of members to an external file. In this recipe, we'll take a look at the process of exporting the contents of an address list to a CSV file.

How to do it...

Let's start off with a simple example. The following commands will export the `allUsers` address list to a CSV file:

```
$allusers = Get-AddressList "All Users"
Get-Recipient -RecipientPreviewFilter $allusers.RecipientFilter |
  Select-Object DisplayName,Database |
    Export-Csv -Path c:\allusers.csv -NoTypeInformation
```

When the command completes, a list of user display names and their associated mailbox databases will be exported to `c:\allusers.csv`.

How it works...

The first thing we do in this example is create the `$allusers` variable that stores an instance of the `allUsers` address list. We can then run the `Get-Recipient` cmdlet and specify the OPATH filter, using the `$allusers.RecipientFilter` object as the value for the `-RecipientPreviewFilter` parameter. The results are then piped to the `Select-Object` cmdlet that grabs the `DisplayName` and `Database` properties of the recipient. Finally, the data is exported to a CSV file.

Of course, the given example may not be that practical, as it does not provide the email addresses for the user. We can also export this information, but it requires some special handling on our part. Let's export only the `DisplayName` and `EmailAddresses` for each user. To do so, use the following code:

```
$allusers = Get-AddressList "All Users"
Get-Recipient -RecipientPreviewFilter $allusers.RecipientFilter |
  Select-Object DisplayName,
    @{n="EmailAddresses";e={$_.EmailAddresses -join ";"}} |
      Export-Csv -Path c:\allusers.csv -NoTypeInformation
```

Since each recipient can have multiple SMTP email addresses, the `EmailAddresses` property of each recipient is a multi-valued object. This means we can't simply export this value to an external file, since it is actually an object and not a simple string value. In the given command, we're using the `Select-Object` cmdlet to create a calculated property for the `EmailAddresses` collection. Using the `-Join` operator within the calculated property expression, we are adding each address in the collection to a single string that will be delimited with the semi-colon (;) character.

There's more...

The given method will work for any of the address lists in your organization. For example, you can export the recipients of the **Global Address List (GAL)** using the following code:

```
$GAL = Get-GlobalAddressList "Default Global Address List"
Get-Recipient -RecipientPreviewFilter $GAL.RecipientFilter |
   Select-Object DisplayName,
     @{n="EmailAddresses";e={$_.EmailAddresses -join ";"}} |
       Export-Csv -Path c:\GAL.csv -NoTypeInformation
```

As you can see here, the main difference is that this time we are using the `Get-GlobalAddressList` cmdlet to export the default global address list. You can use this technique for any address list in your organization: just specify the name of the address list you want to export when using either the `Get-AddressList` or `Get-GlobalAddress` list cmdlets. The exported csv file will be similar to the following screenshot:

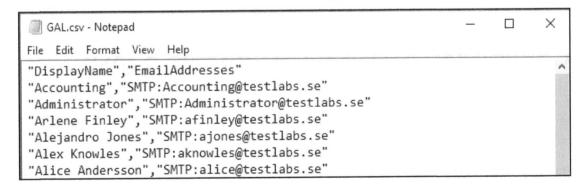

If you are in a situation where you need to extract all users from a distribution group, as shown in the preceding code, besides exporting these into CSV format, they can also be exported into XML format. This is easily done by running the following one-liner:

```
$dl = Get-DistributionGroupMember -Identity DL_Marketing
$dl | Export-Clixml -Path C:\Temp\dl.xml
```

The first row in the preceding command is used to collect all distribution group members from a group called DL_Marketing, by using the cmdlet Get-DistributionGroupMember, the result is saved into the variable $dl. On our next row, we are using the variable to export the distribution group members into an XML file. Use Get-Help Export-Clixml `-Detailed to see all the details regarding the cmdlet Export-Clixml.

If we want to have a look at our recent; exported content, we can use the cmdlet:

```
Import-Clixml -Path C:\Temp\dl.xml
```

See also

- The *Exporting reports to text and CSV files* recipe from Chapter 2, *Exchange Management Shell Common Tasks*
- The *Working with recipient filters* recipe from Chapter 3, *Managing Recipients*
- The *Creating address lists* recipe in this chapter

Configuring hierarchical address books

The idea with hierarchical address books is that you can give your users the ability to search for recipients based on your organization's structure, HAB versus the Global Address List which only provides a flat view. HAB was introduced back in Exchange 2010 SP1. The configuration can only be done using the Exchange Management Shell, and, in this recipe, we'll take a look at an example of how you can configure this feature in your organization. If you're planning on using Outlook with Exchange 2016, it requires at least Outlook version 2010 with KB2965295 or newer.

How to do it...

1. It is recommended that you create an OU in Active Directory to store the root HAB objects. You can create a new OU using your Active Directory administration tools, or using PowerShell. The following code can be used to create an OU in the root of the Contoso domain called **HAB**:

```
$objDomain = [ADSI]''
$objOU = $objDomain.Create('organizationalUnit', 'ou=HAB')
$objOU.SetInfo()
```

2. Next, create a root distribution group for the HAB:

```
New-DistributionGroup -Name ContosoRoot `
 -DisplayName ContosoRoot `
 -Alias ContosoRoot `
 -OrganizationalUnit contoso.com/HAB `
 -SamAccountName ContosoRoot `
 -Type Distribution `
-IgnoreNamingPolicy
```

3. Configure the Contoso distribution group as the root organization for the HAB:

```
Set-OrganizationConfig -HierarchicalAddressBookRoot ContosoRoot
```

4. At this point, you need to add subordinate groups to the root organization group. These can be existing groups or you can create new ones. In this example, we'll add three existing groups called Executives, Finance, and Sales to the root organization in the HAB:

```
Add-DistributionGroupMember -Identity ContosoRoot -Member Executives
Add-DistributionGroupMember -Identity ContosoRoot -Member Finance
Add-DistributionGroupMember -Identity ContosoRoot -Member Sales
```

5. Finally, we'll designate each of the groups as hierarchical groups and set the seniority index for the subordinate groups:

```
Set-Group -Identity ContosoRoot -IsHierarchicalGroup $true
Set-Group Executives -IsHierarchicalGroup $true -SeniorityIndex 100
Set-Group Finance -IsHierarchicalGroup $true -SeniorityIndex 50
Set-Group Sales -IsHierarchicalGroup $true -SeniorityIndex 75
```

6. After this configuration has been completed, Outlook 2010+ users can click on the **AddressBook** button and view a new tab called **Organization** that will list our HAB:

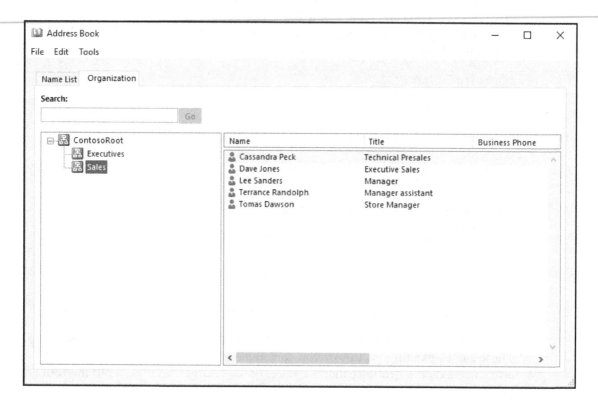

How it works...

The root organization of a HAB is used as the top tier for the organization. Under the root, you can add multiple tiers by adding other distribution groups as members of this root tier and configuring them as hierarchical groups. This allows you to create a HAB that is organized by department, location, or any other structure that makes sense for your environment.

In order to control the structure of the HAB, you can set the SeniorityIndex of each sub group under the root organization. This index overrides the automatic sort order based on the DisplayName which would otherwise be used if no value was defined. This also works for individual recipients within each group. For example, you can set the SeniorityIndex on each member of the Executives group using the Set-User cmdlet:

```
Set-User cmunoz -SeniorityIndex 100
Set-User awood -SeniorityIndex 90
Set-User ahunter -SeniorityIndex 80
```

The users will be displayed in order, with the highest index number first. This allows you to further organize the HAB and override the default sort order if needed.

There's more...

You may notice that after configuring a HAB, Outlook 2010+ users are not seeing the **Organization** tab when viewing the **AddressBook**. If this happens, double check the Active Directory schema attribute ms-Exch-HAB-Root-Department-Link using ADSIEdit. The isMemberOfPartialAttributeSet attribute should be set to True. If it is not, change this attribute to True, ensure that this has replicated to all DCs in the forest, and restart the Microsoft Exchange Active Directory Topology service on each Exchange server. Of course, this is something you'll want to do out of hours to ensure there is no disruption of service for end-users. After this change has been completed, Outlook 2010+ users should be able to view the Organization tab in the Address Book.

We can make a basic script for the preceding tasks, save it to a file called hab.ps1:

```
$objDomain = [ADSI]''
$objOU = $objDomain.Create('organizationalUnit', 'ou=HAB')
$objOU.SetInfo()
$hab = Read-Host "Type a name for the HAB root"
New-DistributionGroup -Name $hab -DisplayName $hab `
 -OrganizationalUnit "contoso.com/HAB" -SAMAccountName $hab `
 -Type Distribution
Set-Group -Identity $hab -IsHierarchicalGroup $true
$File = Import-Csv ".\hab.csv"
$File | foreach {
  New-DistributionGroup -Name $_.GroupName -OrganizationalUnit `
    "contoso.com/HAB" -Type Distribution -SAMAccountName $_.GroupName   Set-
Group -Identity $_.GroupName -SeniorityIndex $_.Seniority `
    -IsHierarchicalGroup $true
  Add-DistributionGroupMember -Identity $hab -Member $_.GroupName
}
Set-OrganizationConfig -HierarchicalAddressBookRoot $hab
```

The script starts with creating an OU called HAB. A variable is created with the name $hab; the prompt will ask for a name for the HAB root. This name is used when creating the initial distribution group. A CSV file called hab.csv is imported to the variable $File; a foreach loop is used for processing each row in the CSV file.

The CSV includes names of the distribution groups and what SeniorityIndex value they should be configured with. The script also makes sure that these groups are configured as hierarchical groups. Finally, the users need to be added into the corresponding groups for forming the organization.

See also

- The *Managing distribution groups* recipe from Chapter 3, *Managing Recipients*

6

Mailbox Database Management

In this chapter, we will cover:

- Managing the mailbox databases
- Moving databases and logs to another location
- Configuring the mailbox database limits
- Reporting on mailbox database size
- Finding the total number of mailboxes in a database
- Determining the average mailbox size per database
- Reporting on database backup status
- Restoring data from a recovery database

Introduction

In this chapter, we will focus on several scenarios in which PowerShell scripting can be used to increase your efficiency when managing databases, which are the most critical resources in your Exchange environment. We will look at how you can add and remove mailbox databases, configure database settings, generate advanced reports on database statistics, and more from within the Shell.

Performing some basic steps

To work with the code samples in this chapter, follow these steps to launch the Exchange Management Shell:

1. Log onto a workstation or server with the Exchange Management Tools installed.
2. You can connect using remote PowerShell if you, for some reason, don't have Exchange Management Tools installed. Use the following command:

```
$Session = New-PSSession -ConfigurationName Microsoft.Exchange `
-ConnectionUri http://servername/PowerShell/ `
-Authentication Kerberos
Import-PSSession $Session
```

3. Alternatively, open the Exchange Management Shell by clicking the Windows button and go to **Microsoft Exchange Server 2016 | Exchange Management Shell**.

If any additional steps are required they will be listed at the beginning of the recipe in the *Getting ready* section.

Remember to start the Exchange Management Shell using **Run As Administrator** to avoid permission problems.

In the chapter, notice that in the examples of cmdlets, I have used the back tick (`) character for breaking up long commands into multiple lines. The purpose with this is to make it easier to read. The back ticks are not required and should only be used if needed.

Managing the mailbox databases

The Exchange Management Shell provides a set of cmdlets for mailbox database management. In this recipe, we will take a look at how you can use these cmdlets to create, change, or delete mailbox databases. We will also take a look at how the automatic mailbox distribution works.

How to do it...

The process for managing mailbox databases is pretty straightforward. We'll start with creating a new mailbox database:

1. To create a mailbox database, use the `New-MailboxDatabase` cmdlet, as shown in the following example:

```
New-MailboxDatabase -Name DB4 `
-EdbFilePath E:\Databases\DB4\Database\DB4.edb `
-LogFolderPath E:\Databases\DB4\Logs `
-Server EX01
```

   You can mount the database after it has been created using the `Mount-Database` cmdlet:

```
Mount-Database -Identity DB4
```

2. The name of a database can be changed using the Set-`MailboxDatabase` cmdlet:

```
Set-MailboxDatabase -Identity DB4 -Name Database4
```

3. And, finally, you can remove a mailbox database using the `Remove-MailboxDatabase` cmdlet:

```
Remove-MailboxDatabase -Identity Database4 `
-Confirm:$false
```

How it works...

The `New-MailboxDatabase` cmdlet requires that you provide a name for your database and specify the server name where it should be hosted. In the previous example, you can see that we created the `DB4` database on the `EX01` server. The `-EdbFilePath` parameter specifies the location for your database file, however it is not required for creating the database. Additionally, you can use the `-LogFolderPath` variable to identify the directory that should hold the transaction logs for this database. If no value is provided for either of these parameters, the database and log directories will be set to the default location within the Exchange installation directory.

Mounting a database is done as a separate step. If you want to create the database and mount it in one operation, pipe your `New-MailboxDatabase` command to the `Mount-Database` cmdlet, as shown in the following line of code:

```
New-MailboxDatabase -Name DB10 -Server EX01 | Mount-Database
```

The `Mount-Database` cmdlet can be used with mailbox databases. The same is true for its counterpart, `Dismount-Database`, which allows you to dismount a mailbox database.

As you saw previously, to rename a mailbox database, we used the `Set-MailboxDatabase` cmdlet with the `-Name` parameter. It's important to note that, while this will change the database name in the Active Directory and therefore in Exchange, it does not change the filename or path of the database.

Before running the `Remove-MailboxDatabase` cmdlet, you will need to move any regular mailboxes, archive mailboxes, or arbitration mailboxes to another database; using the `New-MoveRequest` or `New-MigrationBatch` cmdlet. The arbitration mailboxes can be found by using the `Get-Mailbox -Arbitration` command, these can be found on the first created database.

Keep in mind that the removal of a database is only done logically in the Active Directory. Later on, you will need to manually delete the files and directories used by the database running the `Remove-MailboxDatabase` cmdlet.

 There are only two required parameters for creating the mailbox database, which are `Name` and `Server`. However, the others like `EdbFilePath` and `LogFolderPath` are nice to use for specifying the configuration.

There's more...

The `-Database` parameter allows you to omit the `-Database` parameter when creating or moving a Mailbox and an agent determines the most appropriate target database based on a number of factors.

The Mailbox Resources Management Agent, a cmdlet extension agent, is an, application that runs in the background that handles this, and it is enabled by default. The benefit of this is that if you provision multiple mailboxes or move multiple mailboxes at one time without specifying a target database, the mailboxes will be distributed across all of the available mailbox databases in the current Active Directory site from where you are running the commands.

Understanding automatic mailbox distribution

Each mailbox database has three properties called `IsExcludedFromProvisioning`, `IsExcludedFromInitialProvisioning` and `IsSuspendedFromProvisioning`. These control whether or not a database can be used for automatic mailbox distribution. By default, all are set to `$false`, which means that every mailbox database you create is available for automatic distribution out-of-the-box. If you intend to create a mailbox database used strictly for archiving mailboxes, or you don't want mailboxes to be placed in a particular database automatically, you can exclude the database from being automatically used. To do so, use the following command syntax after the database has been created:

```
Set-MailboxDatabase -Identity DB1 -IsExcludedFromProvisioning ` $true
```

When the `IsExcludedFromProvisioning` property is set to `$true`, you can still manually create mailboxes in the database, but it will not be used for automatic distribution.

Taking it a step further

Let's look at an example of creating mailbox databases in bulk. This can be helpful when creating many databases. The following code can be used for doing the job:

```
$data = Import-CSV .\DBs.csv
foreach($row in $data) {
  $DBName = $row.DBName
  $LogPath = 'E:\Databases\' + $DBName + '\Logs'
  $DBPath = 'E:\Databases\' + $DBName + '\Database\' + $DBName + '.edb'
  $Server = $row.Server
New-MailboxDatabase -Name $DBName -Server $Server -Edbfilepath ` $DBPath -
Logfolderpath $LogPath
}

foreach($row in $data) {
    $DBName = $row.DBName
Mount-Database $DBName
}
```

In this example, we create an array by importing a CSV file. We start looping through each row in the file; also in the loop we create new variables named DBName, LogPath, DBPath and Server. These variables are then used in the cmdlet New-MailboxDatabase. Finally, with this small script we'll loop through each row again and create a new variable named DBName and try to mount each database in the CSV file.

The resource called `MSFT_xExchMailboxDatabase` in xExchange module for Desired State Configuration can be used for creating databases.

 When creating databases in larger environments it can be impossible to mount the databases immediately, in these cases let the Active Directory replication finish. When it's completed the databases can be mounted.

See also

- The *Reporting on mailbox database size* recipe in this chapter

- The *Moving databases and logs to another location* recipe in this chapter

Moving databases and logs to another location

As your environment grows or changes over time, it may be necessary to move one or more databases and their log streams to another location. This is one of those tasks that's required to be done from the Exchange Management Shell. The advantage is, the Shell gives you some more flexibility. In this recipe, you will learn how to move database and log files to another location.

How to do it...

To move the database file and log stream for the `DB1` database to a new location, use the following command syntax:

```
Move-DatabasePath -Identity DB1 `
-EdbFilePath F:\Databases\DB1\Database\DB1.edb `
-LogFolderPath F:\Databases\DB1\Logs `
-Confirm:$false `
-Force
```

After executing the preceding command, the `DB1` database and log files will be moved to the `F:\Databases\DB1\Database` directory, without prompting you for confirmation.

How it works...

In this example, you can see that we are moving both the database file and the transaction logs to the same directory. You can use different directories or even separate disk spindles as the locations for the database and log folder paths if needed.

To remove the confirmation prompts, we need to set the −Confirm parameter to $false and also use the −Force switch parameter. This may be an important detail if you are running this cmdlet from an automated script. If not used, the cmdlet will not make any changes until an operator confirms it in the Shell.

Obviously, in order to move the database file or the logs, the database will need to be taken offline for the duration of the move. The Move-DatabasePath cmdlet will automatically dismount the database and remount it when the move process is complete. If the database is already dismounted at the time that you initiate a move, the database will not be automatically mounted upon completion of the command and you will need to mount it manually using the Mount-Database cmdlet. Obviously, any users with a mailbox in a dismounted database will be unable to connect to their mailbox. If you need to move a database, ensure that this can be done during a time that will not impact end users.

Keep in mind that databases that are replicated within a **Database Availability Group (DAG)** cannot be moved. Each database copy in a DAG needs to use the same local path for the database and logs, so you cannot change this after copies have already been created. If you need to change the paths for a replicated database, you will need to remove all database copies and perform the move. Once this process has been completed, you can create new database copies that will use the new path.

There's more...

Before changing the EdbfilePath or the LogFolderPath locations for a database, you may want to check the existing configuration. To do so, use the Get-MailboxDatabase cmdlet, as shown in the following screenshot:

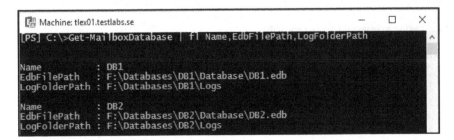

Here you can see that we are piping the `Get-MailboxDatabase` cmdlet to `Format-List` (using the `fl` alias) and selecting the `Name`, `EdbFilePath`, and `LogFolderPath` properties, which will display the relevant information for every database in the organization. You can retrieve this information for a single database by specifying the name of the database using the `-Identity` parameter.

Manually moving databases

In certain situations, you may prefer to manually copy or move the database and log files instead of allowing the `Move-DatabasePath` cmdlet to move the data for you. In this case, you can use the following process:

1. Let's say that you need to move the DB2 database to the `F:\` drive. To do this manually, the first thing you will want to do is dismount the database:

    ```
    Dismount-Database -Identity DB2 -Confirm:$false
    ```

2. Next, use whatever method you prefer to copy the data to the new location on the `F:\` drive. After the data has been copied, use the `Move-DatabasePath` cmdlet, as shown next, to update the configuration information in Exchange:

    ```
    Move-DatabasePath -Identity DB2 `
    -EdbFilePath F:\Databases\DB2\Database\DB2.edb `
    -LogFolderPath F:\Databases\DB2\Logs `
    -ConfigurationOnly `
    -Confirm:$false `
    -Force
    ```

3. The preceding command uses the `-ConfigurationOnly` switch parameter when running the `Move-DatabasePath` cmdlet. This ensures that only the configuration of the database paths is updated and that there is no attempt to copy the data files to the new location.

4. After the files are manually moved or copied and the configuration has been changed, you can remount the database, as shown next:

    ```
    Mount-Database -Identity DB2
    ```

At this point, the database will be brought online and the move operation will be complete.

Taking it a step further

Let's look at an example of how we can use the Shell to move databases in bulk. Let's say we have added a new disk to the EX01 server using the S:\ drive letter and all the databases need to be moved to this new disk under the Databases root directory. The following code can be used to perform the move:

```
foreach($i in Get-MailboxDatabase -Server EX01) {
  $DBName = $i.Name

  Move-DatabasePath -Identity $DBName `
  -EdbFilePath "S:\Databases\$DBName\Database\$DBName.edb" `
  -LogFolderPath "S:\Databases\$DBName\Logs" `
  -Confirm:$false `
  -Force
}
```

In this example, we use the Get-MailboxDatabase cmdlet to retrieve a list of all the mailbox databases on the EX01 server. As we loop through each mailbox database, we move the EDB file and log path under the S:\Database folder in a subdirectory that matches the name of the database.

You can type the preceding code straight into the Shell or save it in an external .ps1 file and execute it as a script.

See also

- The *Looping through items* in Chapter 1, *PowerShell Key Concepts*
- The *Working with variables and objects* in Chapter 1, *PowerShell Key Concepts*

Configuring the mailbox database limits

The Exchange Management Shell provides cmdlets that allow you to configure the storage limits for mailbox databases. This recipe will show you how to set these limits interactively in the shell or in bulk using automated script.

How to do it...

To configure the storage limits for a mailbox database, use the `Set-MailboxDatabase` cmdlet, for example:

```
Set-MailboxDatabase -Identity DB1 `
-IssueWarningQuota 2gb `
-ProhibitSendQuota 2.5gb `
-ProhibitSendReceiveQuota 3gb
```

How it works...

In the example, we have configured the `IssueWarningQuota`, `ProhibitSendQuota`, and `ProhibitSendReceieveQuota` limits for the `DB1` mailbox database. These are the storage limits that will be applied to each mailbox that is stored in this database. Based on the values used with the command, you can see that users will receive a warning once their mailbox reaches 2 GB in size. When their mailbox reaches 2.5 GB, they will be unable to send outbound email messages and when they hit the 3 GB limit they will be unable to send or receive email messages.

You can override the database limits on a per mailbox basis using the `Set-Mailbox` cmdlet.

There's more...

Mailbox databases support deleted item retention, which allows you to recover items that have been removed from the deleted items folder. By default, the retention period for mailbox databases is set to 14 days, but this can be changed using the `-DeletedItemRetention` parameter when using the appropriate cmdlet. For example, to increase the deleted item retention period for the `DB1` database, use the following command:

```
Set-MailboxDatabase -Identity DB1 -DeletedItemRetention 30
```

In this example, we have set the deleted item retention to 30 days. This parameter will also accept input in the form of a time span, and therefore can be specified using the `dd.hh:mm:ss` format. For example, we could have also used `30.00:00:00` as the parameter value, indicating that the deleted item retention should be 30 days, zero hours, zero minutes, and zero seconds, but that would be pointless in this example. However, this format is useful when you need to be specific about hours or minutes, for instance, using `12:00:00` would indicate that deleted items should only be retained for 12 hours.

In addition to the deleted item retention, mailbox databases also retain deleted mailboxes for 30 days by default. You can change this value using the `-MailboxRetention` parameter as shown next:

```
Set-MailboxDatabase -Identity DB1 -MailboxRetention 90
```

Like the value used for the `-DeletedItemRetention` parameter, you can specify a time span as the value for the `-MailboxRetention` parameter. Both of these parameters will accept a maximum of 24,855 days.

Finally, you can configure mailbox databases so that items will not be permanently deleted until a database backup has been performed. This is not enabled by default. To turn it on for a particular database, use the `-RetainDeletedItemsUntilBackup` parameter with the `Set-MailboxDatabase` cmdlet. For example:

```
Set-MailboxDatabase -Identity DB1 `
-RetainDeletedItemsUntilBackup $true
```

Taking it a step further

To configure these settings in bulk, we can make use of the pipeline to update the settings for a group of databases. For example, the following command will set the database limits for all mailboxes in the organization:

```
Get-MailboxDatabase | Set-MailboxDatabase `
-IssueWarningQuota 2gb `
-ProhibitSendQuota 2.5gb `
-ProhibitSendReceiveQuota 3gb `
-DeletedItemRetention 30 `
-MailboxRetention 90 `
-RetainDeletedItemsUntilBackup $true
```

In this command, we are piping the results of the `Get-MailboxDatabase` cmdlet to the `Set-MailboxDatabase` cmdlet and changing the default settings to the desired values for all databases in the organization.

See also

- The *Determining the average mailbox size per database* recipe in this chapter

Reporting on mailbox database size

In this recipe, we are going to take a look at how we can verify the size of the mailbox databases. This is fairly simple and the information can easily be retrieved using the Get-MailboxDatabase cmdlet. In this recipe, we will take a look at how to report on mailbox database size using the Exchange Management Shell for Exchange 2016.

How to do it...

To retrieve the total size for each mailbox database, use the following command:

```
Get-MailboxDatabase -Status | select-object Name,DatabaseSize
```

The output from this command might look something like this:

```
Machine: tlex01.testlabs.se                                    —    □    ×
[PS] C:\>Get-MailboxDatabase -Status | Select-Object Name,DatabaseSize

Name DatabaseSize
---- ------------
DB1  247.9 MB (259,981,312 bytes)
DB2  247.9 MB (259,981,312 bytes)
```

How it works...

When running the Get-MailboxDatabase cmdlet, we can use the -Status switch parameter to receive additional information about the database, such as the mount status, the backup status, and the total size of the database, as shown in the previous example. To generate a report with this information, simply pipe the command to the Export-CSV cmdlet and specify the path and filename, as shown:

```
Get-MailboxDatabase -Status |
   select-object Name,Server,DatabaseSize,Mounted |
     Export-CSV -Path c:\databasereport.csv -NoTypeInformation
```

This time, we have added the server name that the database is currently associated with and the mount status for that database.

There's more...

When viewing the value for the database size, you probably noticed that we see the total size in megabytes and in parentheses we see the value in bytes, rather than just seeing a single integer for the total size. The `DatabaseSize` property is of the type `ByteQuantifiedSize`, and we can use several methods provided by this type to convert the value if all we want to retrieve is a numeric representation of the database size.

For example, we can use the `ToKB`, `ToMB`, `ToGB` and `ToTB` methods of the `DatabaseSize` object to convert the value to kilobytes, megabytes, gigabytes, or terabytes. For example:

```
Get-MailboxDatabase -Status |
    Select-Object Name,
        @{n="DatabaseSize (MB)";e={$_.DatabaseSize.ToMb()}}
```

As you can see, this time we have created a calculated property for the `DatabaseSize` and we are using the `ToMB` method to convert the value of the database. The output we get from the command would look something like this:

```
Machine: tlex01.testlabs.se                                    —    □    ×

[PS] C:\>Get-MailboxDatabase -Status | Select-Object Name,@{n="DatabaseSize
(MB)";e={$_.DatabaseSize.ToMb()}}

Name DatabaseSize (MB)
---- -----------------
DB1                247
DB2                247
```

This technique may be useful if you are looking to generate basic reports and you don't need all of the extra information that is returned by default. For instance, you may already know that your databases will always be in the range of hundreds of gigabytes. You can simply use a calculated property as shown in the previous example and call the `ToGB` method for each `DatabaseSize` object.

See also

- The *Formatting output* from recipe `Chapter 1`, *PowerShell Key Concepts*

Finding the total number of mailboxes in a database

You can retrieve all kinds of information about a mailbox database using the Exchange Management Shell cmdlets. Surprisingly, the total number of mailboxes in a given mailbox database is not one of those pieces of information. We need to retrieve this data manually. Luckily, PowerShell makes this easy, as you will see in this recipe.

How to do it...

1. There are two ways that you can retrieve the total number of mailboxes in a database. First, we can use the Count property of a collection of mailboxes:

```
@(Get-Mailbox -Database DB1).count
```

2. Another way to retrieve this information is to use the Measure-Object cmdlet using the same collection from the preceding example:

```
Get-Mailbox -Database DB1 | Measure-Object
```

How it works...

In both steps, we use the Get-Mailbox cmdlet and specify the -Database parameter, which will retrieve all of the mailboxes in that particular database. In the first example, we have wrapped the command inside the @() characters to ensure that PowerShell will always interpret the output as an array. The reason for this is that if the mailbox database contains only one mailbox, the resulting output object will not be a collection, and thus will not have a Count property.

 Remember, the default result size for Get-Mailbox is 1000. Set the -ResultSize parameter to Unlimited to override this.

The second step makes use of the `Measure-Object` cmdlet. You can see that, in addition to the `Count` property, we also get a number of other details. Consider the output as shown in the following screenshot:

```
Machine: tlex01.testlabs.se                          —    □    ✕
[PS] C:\>Get-Mailbox -Database DB1 | Measure-Object

Count     : 16
Average   :
Sum       :
Maximum   :
Minimum   :
Property  :
```

To retrieve only the total number of mailboxes, we can extend this command further in two ways. First, we can enclose the entire command in parentheses and access the `Count` property:

```
(Get-Mailbox -Database DB1 | Measure-Object).Count
```

In this case, the preceding command would return only the total number of mailboxes in the `DB1` database.

We can also pipe the command to `Select-Object`, and use the `-ExpandProperty` parameter to retrieve only the value of the `Count` property:

```
Get-Mailbox -Database DB1 |
    Measure-Object |
        Select-Object -ExpandProperty Count
```

This command would again only return the total number of mailboxes in the database.

One of the most common questions that comes up when people see both of these methods is, of course, which way is faster? Well, we can use the `Measure-Command` cmdlet to determine this information, but the truth is that your results will vary greatly and there probably won't be a huge difference in this case. The syntax to measure the time it takes to run a script or command is shown next:

```
Measure-Command -Expression {@(Get-Mailbox -Database DB1).Count}
```

Simply supply a script block containing the commands you want to measure and assign it to the -Expression parameter as shown previously. The Measure-Command cmdlet will return a TimeSpan object that reports on the total milliseconds, seconds, and minutes that it took to complete the command. You can then compare these values to other commands that produce the same result but use alternate syntax or cmdlets.

> To report on the total number of archive mailboxes, use Get-Mailbox -Filter {ArchiveName -ne $null} | Measure-Object.

There's more...

We can easily determine the total number of mailboxes in each database using a single command. The key to this is using the Select-Object cmdlet to create a calculated property. For example:

```
Get-MailboxDatabase |
    Select-Object Name,
        @{n="TotalMailboxes";e={@(Get-Mailbox -Database $_).count}}
```

This command would generate output similar to the following:

```
Machine: tlex01.testlabs.se                                    —   □   ×
[PS] C:\>Get-MailboxDatabase |
>>     Select-Object Name,
>>        @{n="TotalMailboxes";e={@(Get-Mailbox -Database $_).count}}

Name  TotalMailboxes
----  --------------
DB1               16
DB2               13
```

This command pipes the output from Get-MailboxDatabase to the Select-Object cmdlet. For each database output by the command, we select the database name and then use the $_ object when creating the calculated property to determine the total number of mailboxes, using the Get-Mailbox cmdlet. This command can be piped further down to the Out-File or Export-CSV cmdlets that will generate a report saved in an external file.

See also

- The *Creating custom objects* recipe from `Chapter 1`, *PowerShell Key Concepts*

Determining the average mailbox size per database

PowerShell is very flexible and gives you the ability to generate very detailed reports. When generating mailbox database statistics, we can utilize data returned from multiple cmdlets provided by the Exchange Management Shell. This recipe will show you an example of this, and you will learn how to calculate the average mailbox size per database using PowerShell.

How to do it...

To determine the average mailbox size for a given database, use the following one-liner:

```
Get-MailboxStatistics -Database DB1 |
  ForEach-Object {$_.TotalItemSize.Value.ToMB()} |
    Measure-Object -Average |
      Select-Object -ExpandProperty Average
```

How it works...

Calculating an average is as simple as performing some basic math, but PowerShell gives us the ability to do this quickly with the `Measure-Object` cmdlet. The example uses the `Get-MailboxStatistics` cmdlet to retrieve all the mailboxes in the `DB1` database. We then loop through each one, retrieving only the `TotalItemSize` property, and inside the `ForEach-Object` script block we convert the total item size to megabytes. The result from each mailbox can then be averaged using the `Measure-Object` cmdlet. At the end of the command, you can see that the `Select-Object` cmdlet is used to retrieve only the value for the `Average` property.

The number returned here will give us the average mailbox size in total for regular mailboxes, archive mailboxes, as well as any other type of mailbox that has been disconnected. If you want to be more specific, you can filter out these mailboxes after running the `Get-MailboxStatistics` cmdlet:

```
Get-MailboxStatistics -Database DB1 |
    Where-Object{!$_.DisconnectDate -and !$_.IsArchive} |
        ForEach-Object {$_.TotalItemSize.Value.ToMB()} |
            Measure-Object -Average |
                Select-Object -ExpandProperty Average
```

Notice that, in the preceding example, we have added the `Where-Object` cmdlet to filter out any mailboxes that have a `DisconnectDate` defined or where the `IsArchive` property is `$true`.

Another thing that you may want to do is round the average. Let's say the `DB1` database contained 16 mailboxes and the total size of the database was around 512 megabytes. The value returned from the preceding command would roughly look something like `4.33333333333333`. Rarely are all those extra decimal places of any use. Here are a couple of ways to make the output a little cleaner:

```
$MBAvg = Get-MailboxStatistics -Database DB1 |
    ForEach-Object {$_.TotalItemSize.value.ToMB()} |
        Measure-Object -Average |
            Select-Object -ExpandProperty Average
[Math]::Round($MBAvg,2)
```

You can see that this time, we stored the result of the one-liner in the `$MBAvg` variable. We then used the `Round` method of the `Math` class in the .NET Framework to round the value, specifying that the result should only contain two decimal places. Based on the previous information, the result of the preceding command would be `4.35`.

We can also use string formatting to specify the number of decimal places to be used:

```
[PS] "{0:n2}" -f $MBAvg
4.35
```

The `-f` format operator is documented in PowerShell's help system in `about_operators`.

Keep in mind that this command will return a string, so if you need to be able to sort on this value, cast it to `double`:

```
[PS] [double]("{0:n2}" -f $MBAvg)
4.35
```

There's more...

The previous examples have only shown how to determine the average mailbox size for a single database. To determine this information for all mailbox databases, we can use the following code (save it to a file called size.ps1):

```
foreach($DB in Get-MailboxDatabase) {
  Get-MailboxStatistics -Database $DB |
  ForEach-Object{$_.TotalItemSize.value.ToMB()} |
  Measure-Object -Average |
  Select-Object @{n="Name";e={$DB.Name}},
  @{n="AvgMailboxSize";e={[Math]::Round($_.Average,2)}} |
  Sort-Object AvgMailboxSize -Desc
}
```

The result of this command would look something like this:

This example is very similar to the one we looked at previously. The difference is that, this time, we are running our one-liner using a `foreach` loop for every mailbox database in the organization. When each mailbox database has been processed, we sort the output based on the `AvgMailboxSize` property.

See also

- The *Creating custom objects* recipe from Chapter 1, *PowerShell Key Concepts*

Reporting on database backup status

Using the Exchange Management Shell, we can write scripts that will check on the last full backup time for a database that can be used for monitoring and reporting. In this recipe, you will learn how to check the last backup time for each database and use this information to generate statistics and find databases that are not being backed up on a regular basis.

How to do it...

To check the last full backup time for a database, use the Get-MailboxDatabase cmdlet, as shown:

```
Get-MailboxDatabase -Identity DB1 -Status | fl Name,LastFullBackup
```

How it works...

When you run the Get-MailboxDatabase cmdlet, you must remember to use the -Status switch parameter or else the LastFullBackup property will be $null. In the previous example, we checked the last full backup for the DB1 database and piped the output to the Format-List (using the fl alias) cmdlet. When viewing the LastFullBackup for each database, you might find it helpful to pipe the output to the Select-Object cmdlet, as shown in the following screenshot:

```
[PS] C:\>Get-MailboxDatabase -Status | Select-Object Name,LastFullBackup

Name LastFullBackup
---- --------------
DB1  4/10/2017 11:22:10 PM
DB2  4/10/2017 11:22:10 PM
```

In addition to simply checking the date, it may be useful to schedule this script to run daily and report on the databases that have not recently been backed up. For example, the following command will only retrieve databases that have not had a successful full backup in the last 24 hours:

```
Get-MailboxDatabase -Status |
  ?{$_.LastFullBackup -le (Get-Date).AddDays(-1)} |
    Select-object Name,LastFullBackup
```

Here you can see that the `Get-MailboxDatabase` output is piped to the `Where-Object` cmdlet (using the `?` alias) and we check the value of the `LastFullBackup` property for each database. If the value is less than or equal to 24 hours ago, the database name and last full backup time are returned.

There's more...

Since the `LastFullBackup` property value is a `DateTime` object, not only can we use comparison operators to find databases that have not been backed up within a certain time frame, but we can also calculate the number of days since that time. This might be a useful piece of information to add to a reporting or monitoring script. The following code will provide this information:

```
Get-MailboxDatabase -Status | ForEach-Object {
  if(!$_.LastFullBackup) {
    $LastFull = "Never"
  }
  else {
    $LastFull = $_.LastFullBackup
  }
  New-Object PSObject -Property @{
    Name = $_.Name
    LastFullBackup = $LastFull
    DaysSinceBackup = if($LastFull-is [datetime]) {
      (New-TimeSpan $LastFull).Days
    }
    Else {
      $LastFull
    }
  }
}
```

When running this code in the Exchange Management Shell, you would see output similar to the following:

```
[PS] C:\Scripts>.\lastbackup.ps1

DaysSinceBackup Name LastFullBackup
--------------- ---- --------------
              0 DB1  4/10/2017 11:24:37 PM
              0 DB2  4/10/2017 11:24:37 PM
```

As you can see, we are simply looping through each mailbox database and retrieving the LastFullBackup time. If a database has never been backed up, the value will be $null. With that in mind, this code will return the string Never for those databases when reporting on the status. If a value is present for LastFullBackup, we use the New-TimeSpan cmdlet to determine the number of days since the last backup and include that in the data returned.

See also

- The *Creating custom objects* recipe from Chapter 1, *PowerShell Key Concepts*

Restoring data from a recovery database

When it comes to recovering data from a failed database, you have several options depending on what kind of backup product you are using or how you have deployed Exchange 2016. The ideal method for enabling redundancy is to use a DAG, which will replicate your mailbox databases to one or more servers and provide automatic failover in the event of a disaster. However, you may need to pull old data out of a database restored from a backup. In this recipe, we will take a look at how you can create a recovery database and restore data from it using the Exchange Management Shell.

How to do it...

First, restore the failed database using the steps required by your current backup solution. For this example, let's say that we have restored the DB1 database file to E:\Recovery\DB1 and the database has been brought to a clean shutdown state. We can use the following steps to create a recovery database and restore mailbox data:

1. Create a recovery database using the New-MailboxDatabase cmdlet:

```
New-MailboxDatabase -Name RecoveryDB `
-EdbFilePath E:\Recovery\DB1\DB1.edb `
-LogFolderPath E:\Recovery\DB1 `
-Recovery `
-Server MBX1
```

2. When you run the preceding command, you will see a warning that the recovery database was created using the existing database file. The next step is to check the state of the database, followed by mounting the database:

```
Eseutil /mh .\DB1.edb
Eseutil /R E00 /D
Mount-Database -Identity RecoveryDB
```

3. Next, query the recovery database for all mailboxes that reside in the database `RecoveryDB`:

```
  Get-MailboxStatistics -Database RecoveryDB | fl
DisplayName,MailboxGUID,LegacyDN
```

4. Lastly, we will use the `New-MailboxRestoreRequest`cmdlet to restore the data from the recovery database for a single mailbox:

```
New-MailboxRestoreRequest -SourceDatabase RecoveryDB `
-SourceStoreMailbox "Joe Smith" `
-TargetMailbox joe.smith
```

When running the `eseutil` commands, make sure to be in the folder where the restored mailbox database and logs are placed.
Also make sure that the name of the recovery database is unique.

How it works...

When you restore the database file from your backup application, you may need to ensure that the database is in a clean shutdown state. For example, if you are using Windows Server Backup for your backup solution, you will need to use the `Eseutil.exe` database utility to play any uncommitted logs into the database to get it in a clean shutdown state.

Once the data is restored, we can create a recovery database using the `New-MailboxDatabase` cmdlet, as shown in the first example. Notice that when we ran the command we used several parameters. First, we specified the path to the EDB file and the log files, both of which are in the same location where we restored the files. We have also used the `-Recovery` switch parameter to specify that this is a special type of database that will only be used for restoring data and should not be used for production mailboxes.

Finally, we specified which mailbox server the database should be hosted on using the `-Server` parameter. Make sure to run the `New-MailboxDatabase` cmdlet from the mailbox server that you are specifying in the `-Server` parameter, and then mount the database using the `Mount-Database` cmdlet.

The last step is to restore data from one or more mailboxes. As we saw in the previous example, the `New-MailboxRestoreRequest` is the tool to use for this task. This cmdlet was introduced in Exchange 2010 SP1, so if you have used this process in the past, the procedure is the same with Exchange 2013.

There's more...

When you run the `New-MailboxRestoreRequest` cmdlet, you need to specify the identity of the mailbox you wish to restore using the `-SourceStoreMailbox` parameter. There are three possible values you can use to provide this information: `DisplayName`, `MailboxGuid` and `LegacyDN`. To retrieve these values, you can use the `Get-MailboxStatistics` cmdlet once the recovery database is online and mounted:

```
Get-MailboxStatistics -Database RecoveryDB | `
    fl DisplayName,MailboxGUID,LegacyDN
```

Here we have specified that we want to retrieve all three of these values for each mailbox in the `RecoveryDB` database.

Understanding target mailbox identity

When restoring data with the `New-MailboxRestoreRequest` cmdlet, you also need to provide a value for the `-TargetMailbox` parameter. The mailbox needs to already exist before running this command. If you are restoring data from a backup for an existing mailbox that has not changed since the backup was done, you can simply provide the typical identity values for a mailbox for this parameter.

If you want to restore data to a mailbox that was not the original source of the data, you need to use the `-AllowLegacyDNMismatch` switch parameter. This will be useful if you are restoring data to another user's mailbox, or if you've recreated the mailbox since the backup was taken.

Learning about other useful parameters

The New-MailboxRestoreRequest cmdlet can be used to granularly control how data is restored out of a mailbox. The following parameters may be useful to customize the behavior of the restores:

- **ConflictResolutionOption**: This parameter specifies the action to take if multiple matching messages exist in the target mailbox. The possible values are KeepSourceItem, KeepLatestItem or KeepAll. If no value is specified, KeepSourceItem will be used by default.
- **ExcludeDumpster**: Use this switch parameter to indicate that the dumpster should not be included in the restore.
- **SourceRootFolder**: Use this parameter to restore data only from a root folder of a mailbox.
- **TargetIsArchive**: You can use this switch parameter to perform a mailbox restore to a mailbox archive.
- **TargetRootFolder**: This parameter can be used to restore data to a specific folder in the root of the target mailbox. If no value is provided, the data is restored and merged into the existing folders, and, if they do not exist, they will be created in the target mailbox.

These are just a few of the useful parameters that can be used with this cmdlet, but there are more. For a complete list of all the available parameters and full details on each one, run Get-Help New-MailboxRestoreRequest –Detailed

Understanding mailbox restore request cmdlets

There is an entire cmdlet set for mailbox restore requests in addition to the New-MailboxRestoreRequest cmdlet. The remaining available cmdlets are outlined as follows:

- Get-MailboxRestoreRequest: Provides detailed status of mailbox restore requests
- Remove-MailboxRestoreRequest: Removes fully or partially completed restore requests
- Resume-MailboxRestoreRequest: Resumes a restore request that was suspended or failed

- `Set-MailboxRestoreRequest`: Can be used to change the restore request options after the request has been created
- `Suspend-MailboxRestoreRequest`: Suspends a restore request any time after the request was created but before the request reaches the status of `Completed`

For complete details and examples for each of these cmdlets, use the `Get-Help` cmdlet with the appropriate cmdlet using the `-Full` switch parameter.

Taking it a step further

Let's say that you have restored your database from backup, you have created a recovery database, and now you need to restore each mailbox in the backup to the corresponding target mailboxes that are currently online. We can use the following script to accomplish this:

```
$mailboxes = Get-MailboxStatistics -Database RecoveryDB
foreach($mailbox in $mailboxes) {
  New-MailboxRestoreRequest -SourceDatabase RecoveryDB `
  -SourceStoreMailbox $mailbox.DisplayName `
  -TargetMailbox $mailbox.DisplayName
}
```

Here you can see that first, we use the `Get-MailboxStatistics` cmdlet to retrieve all the mailboxes in the recovery database and store the results in the `$mailboxes` variable. We then loop through each mailbox and restore the data to the original mailbox. You can track the status of these restores using the `Get-MailboxRestoreRequest` cmdlet and the `Get-MailboxRestoreRequestStatistics` cmdlet.

See also

- The *Managing disconnected mailboxes* from `Chapter 4`, *Managing Mailboxes*
- The *Importing and exporting mailboxes* from `Chapter 4`, *Managing Mailboxes*

7
Managing Client Access

In this chapter, we will cover the following:

- Managing ActiveSync, OWA, POP3, and IMAP4 mailbox settings
- Setting internal and external CAS URLs
- Managing Outlook Anywhere settings
- Blocking Outlook clients from connecting to Exchange
- Reporting on Active OWA and RPC connections
- Controlling ActiveSync device access
- Reporting on ActiveSync devices

Introduction

While we had the option to split roles between servers in previous versions of Exchange Server, we don't have that anymore. Instead, the Exchange server roles are divided between Mailbox and Edge Transport server roles now. As you will understand, the previous role called Client Access Role is not a role anymore; instead, it's renamed to Client Access services, which makes sense when thinking about it. It basically serves our end users with its services.

Under the hood of Client Access services, we still have underlying services for Outlook on the Web/**Outlook Web App (OWA)**, ActiveSync, POP3, and IMAP4.

By default, all MAPI clients now connects by using MAPI over HTTP instead of the MAPI over RPC version. This is now enabled by default in Exchange 2016; the MAPI over RPC has now been discontinued.

With the new CAS architecture, the connection procedure has been simplified; a request is sent from the user to Active Directory where the mailbox is actively located. Outlook is then sends the request to this specific Mailbox server to take care of the connection. This is now possible since we have Client Access services included in the Mailbox role.

When it comes to the load balancing, the Mailbox role is still stateless, which means that it does not save any data.

Some benefits with this new architecture can, for example, be:

- Faster reconnection times after communication breaks, because it's only using TCP connections.
- The Layer-7 load balancer is not required anymore, which means cheaper deployment and investments.
- The CAS servers are not required to be on the same installation build/version, even though they need to be on Exchange 2016. This means that upgrades can be done more easily done and this would also help with troubleshooting and verifying that a new build is working in the way it should.

The Client Access services and the Exchange Management Shell cmdlets used to manage it provide plenty of opportunities for automating repetitive tasks from PowerShell one-liners, scripts, and functions.

In this chapter, we'll take a look at how you can control access to the CAS services in your environment, customize their settings, and generate usage reports using the Exchange Management Shell.

Performing some basic steps

To work with the code samples in this chapter, follow these steps to launch the Exchange Management Shell:

1. Log onto a workstation or server with the Exchange Management Tools installed.
2. You can connect using remote PowerShell if you, for some reason, don't have Exchange Management Tools installed. Use the following command:

```
$Session = New-PSSession -ConfigurationName Microsoft.Exchange `
-ConnectionUri http://servername/PowerShell/ `
-Authentication Kerberos
Import-PSSession $Session
```

3. Alternatively, open the Exchange Management Shell by clicking the Windows button and go to **Microsoft Exchange Server 2016 | Exchange Management Shell**.

If any additional steps are required, they will be listed at the beginning of the recipe in the *Getting ready* section.

Remember to start the Exchange Management Shell using **Run As Administrator** to avoid permission problems.
In the chapter, notice that in the examples of cmdlets, I have used the back tick (` ` `) character for breaking up long commands into multiple lines. The purpose of this is to make it easier to read. The back ticks are not required and should only be used if needed.

Managing ActiveSync, OWA, POP3, and IMAP4 mailbox settings

You can use the Exchange Management Shell to configure a user's ability to access services such as ActiveSync, OWA, POP3, and IMAP4. You can also allow or disallow MAPI connectivity and the ability to connect to Exchange using Outlook Anywhere. In this recipe, you'll learn techniques used to control these settings, whether it is done interactively through the Shell or using an automated script.

How to do it...

To control access to Client Access services for a mailbox, use the `Set-CasMailbox` cmdlet. Here's an example of how you might use this cmdlet:

```
Set-CasMailbox -Identity 'Charlene Munoz' `
-OWAEnabled $false `
-ActiveSyncEnabled $false `
-PopEnabled $false `
-ImapEnabled $false
```

This command will disable OWA, ActiveSync, POP3, and IMAP4 for the mailbox belonging to Charlene Munoz.

How it works...

When you create a mailbox, OWA, ActiveSync, POP3, IMAP4, and MAPI access are enabled by default. For most organizations, these default settings are acceptable, but, if that is not the case for your environment, you can use the Set-CASMailbox cmdlet to enable or disable access to these services. This can be done for individual users as needed, or you can do this in bulk.

For example, let's say that all of the users in the Sales department should only access Exchange internally through Outlook using MAPI, POP, and IMAP. We can use a simple pipeline command to make this change:

```
Get-Mailbox -Filter {Office -eq 'Sales'} |
    Set-CasMailbox -OWAEnabled $false `
    -ActiveSyncEnabled $false `
    -PopEnabled $true `
    -ImapEnabled $true
```

As you can see, we use the Get-Mailbox cmdlet and specify a filter that limits the results to users that have their Office attribute in Active Directory set to Sales. The results are then piped to the Set-CASMailbox cmdlet and access to the CAS services is modified for each mailbox. Notice that this time we've used additional parameters to allow POP and IMAP access.

Alternatively, you may want to block MAPI access and only allow users in your organization to connect through OWA. In this case, use the following one-liner:

```
Get-Mailbox -RecipientTypeDetails UserMailbox |
    Set-CasMailbox -OWAEnabled $true `
    -ActiveSyncEnabled $false `
    -PopEnabled $false `
    -ImapEnabled $false `
    -MAPIEnabled $false
```

This time we use Get-Mailbox to retrieve all the mailboxes in the organization. We're using the -RecipientTypeDetails parameter to specify that we want to find user mailboxes and exclude other types such as discovery and resource mailboxes. The results are piped to the Set-CASMailbox cmdlet and access to CAS services is configured with the required settings. You'll notice that this time we've included the -MAPIEnabled parameter and set its value to $false so that users will only be able to access Exchange through OWA.

There's more...

If you are planning on provisioning all of your new mailboxes through an automated script, you may want to configure these settings at mailbox creation time. Consider the following script named New-MailboxScript.ps1:

```
param(
  $name,
  $password,
  $upn,
  $alias,
  $first,
  $last
)

$pass = ConvertTo-SecureString -AsPlainText $password -Force

$mailbox = New-Mailbox -UserPrincipalName $upn `
-Alias $alias `
-Name "$first $last" `
-Password $pass `
-FirstName $first `
-LastName $last

Set-CasMailbox -Identity $mailbox `
-OWAEnabled $false `
-ActiveSyncEnabled $false `
-PopEnabled $false `
-ImapEnabled $false
```

This script can be used to create a mailbox and configure access to Client Access services based on your requirements. If the script is saved in the root of the C: drive, the syntax would look like this:

```
[PS] C:\>.\New-MailboxScript.ps1 -first John -last Smith -alias jsmith
-password P@ssw0rd01 -upn jsmith@contoso.com
```

There are basically two phases to the script. First, the mailbox for the user is created using the New-Mailbox cmdlet. In this example, the New-Mailbox result is saved in the $mailbox variable, and the mailbox is created using the parameters provided by the user running the script. Once the mailbox is created, the Set-CASMailbox cmdlet is used to configure access to CAS services and uses the $mailbox variable to identify the mailbox to modify when the command executes.

See also

- The *Adding, modifying, and removing mailboxes* recipe from Chapter 3, *Managing Recipients*

Setting internal and external CAS URLs

Each Mailbox server has multiple virtual directories, some of which can only be modified through the Exchange Management Shell. Scripting the changes made to both the internal and external URLs can be a big time-saver, especially when deploying multiple servers. In this recipe, you will learn how to use the set of cmdlets that are needed to modify both the internal and external URLs for each CAS server virtual directory.

How to do it...

To change the external URL of the OWA virtual directory for a server named CAS1, use the following command:

```
Set-OwaVirtualDirectory -Identity 'TLEX01\owa (Default Web Site)' `
-ExternalUrl https://mail.contoso.com/owa
```

After the change has been made, we can view the configuration using the Get-OwaVirtualDirectory cmdlet:

```
[PS] C:\>Get-OwaVirtualDirectory -Server TLEX01 | fl ExternalUrl
ExternalUrl : https://mail.contoso.com/owa
```

Notice that if changing the URL for OWA, the ECP URL should be changed as well. You will see a warning text in the Exchange Management Shell about this.

How it works...

Each Mailbox server hosts virtual directories in IIS that support OWA, **Exchange Control Panel (ECP)**, ActiveSync, **Offline Address Book (OAB)**, and **Exchange Web Services (EWS)**. Each of these services has an associated cmdlet set that can be used to manage the settings of each virtual directory. One of the most common configuration changes made during the deployment process is modifying the internal and external URLs for each of these services. The required configuration varies greatly depending on a number of factors in your environment, especially in larger, multi-site environments.

The following cmdlets can be used to modify several settings for each virtual directory, including the values for the internal and external URLs:

- `Set-ActiveSyncVirtualDirectory`: Used to configure the internal and external URL values for the /Microsoft-Server-ActiveSync virtual directory. Use the `InternalUrl` and `ExternalUrl` parameters to change the values.
- `Set-EcpVirtualDirectory`: Used to configure the internal and external URL values for the /ECP virtual directory. Use the `InternalUrl` and `ExternalUrl` parameters to change the values.
- `Set-OabVirtualDirectory`: Used to configure the internal and external URL values for the /OAB virtual directory. Use the `InternalUrl` and `ExternalUrl` parameters to change the values.
- `Set-OwaVirtualDirectory`: Used to configure the internal and external URL values for the /OWA virtual directory. Use the `InternalUrl` and `ExternalUrl` parameters to change the values.
- `Set-WebServicesVirtualDirectory`: Used to configure the internal and external URL values for the /EWS virtual directory. Use the `InternalUrl` and `ExternalUrl` parameters to change the values.

When running each of these cmdlets, you need to identify the virtual directory in question. For example, when modifying the external URL for the ECP virtual directory, the command might look similar to this:

```
Set-EcpVirtualDirectory -Identity 'TLEX01\ecp (Default Web Site)' `
-ExternalUrl https://mail.contoso.com/ecp
```

The syntax is similar to the first example where we modified the OWA virtual directory; the only difference is that the cmdlet name and `ExternalUrl` value have changed. Notice that the identity for the virtual directory is in the format of `ServerName\VirtualDirectoryName (WebsiteName)`. The reason this needs to be done is because it's possible, but not very common, for a particular CAS server to be running more than one site in IIS containing virtual directories for each of these CAS services.

If you are like most folks and have only the default website running in IIS, you can also take advantage of the pipeline if you forget the syntax needed to specify the identity of the virtual directory. For example:

```
Get-EcpVirtualDirectory -Server TLEX01 |
    Set-EcpVirtualDirectory -ExternalUrl ` https://mail.contoso.com/ecp
```

The given pipeline command makes the same change as shown previously. This time we're using the `Get-EcpVirtualDirectory` cmdlet with the `-Server` parameter to identify the Mailbox server. We then pipe the resulting object to the `Set-EcpVirtualDirectory` cmdlet that makes the change to the `ExternalUrl` value.

> It is important to configure the URLs correctly, since this will have an end-user impact. If they are not correctly configured and are using a name that is not included in the certificate, then the end users will be prompted when they are trying to reach the services, or even worse, the services will be broken and not reachable.

There's more...

If you are allowing access to Exchange through Outlook Anywhere, you'll need to configure the external URLs that will be handed to Outlook clients for services such as ECP, OAB, and EWS. These URLs may need to point to a FQDN that resolves to a load balancer VIP or to your reverse proxy infrastructure solution.

In addition, you'll probably want to configure your internal URLs to point to a FQDN that resolves to your internal load balancer VIP. In this situation, you want to make sure you do not modify the internal URL for both the OWA and ECP virtual directories in non-internet-facing sites. This is because OWA and ECP connections from the internet-facing CAS server will be proxied to the servers in the non-internet facing sites, and, if the internal FQDN of the CAS server is not set on each of these virtual directories, Kerberos authentication will fail and the user will not be able to access their mailbox.

Finally, for load-balanced CAS servers, you'll want to configure the `AutoDiscover` internal URL so that it also points to a FQDN that resolves to your load balancer VIP. The syntax for this would look like the following:

```
Set-ClientAccessServer -Identity TLEX01 `
-AutoDiscoverServiceInternalUri `
https://mail.contoso.com/Autodiscover/Autodiscover.xml
```

Of course, you'll need to make all changes to internal and external URLs on all CAS servers.

Command syntax for the remaining virtual directories

We've already looked at the syntax for modifying both OWA and ECP and internal and external URLs; now let's look at how we can do this for the remaining virtual directories. In these examples, we'll configure the external URL value using the `-ExternalUrl` parameter. If you need to modify the internal URL, simply use the `-InternalUrl` parameter.

To configure the external URL for the OAB, use the following syntax:

```
Set-OABVirtualDirectory -Identity "TLEX01\oab (Default Web Site)" `
-ExternalUrl https://mail.contoso.com/oab
```

To configure the external URL for the `ActiveSync` virtual directory, use the following syntax:

```
Set-ActivesyncVirtualDirectory -Identity `
"TLEX01\Microsoft-Server-ActiveSync (Default Web Site)" `
-ExternalURL https://mail.contoso.com/Microsoft-Server-Activesync
```

To configure the `EWS` virtual directory, use the following syntax:

```
Set-WebServicesVirtualDirectory -Identity `
"TLEX01\EWS (Default Web Site)" `
-ExternalUrl https://mail.contoso.com/ews/exchange.asmx
```

In each example, we're setting the value on the TLEX01 server. When running these commands or using them in a script, replace the server name with the name of the appropriate Mailbox server name.

See also

- The *Generating a certificate request* recipe from `Chapter 10`, *Exchange Security*
- The *Installing certificates and enabling services* recipe from `Chapter 10`, *Exchange Security*
- The *Importing certificates on multiple exchange servers* recipe from `Chapter 10`, *Exchange Security*

Managing Outlook Anywhere settings

Now with the new CAS architecture in place, Outlook Anywhere is used as a fallback method if the used Outlook version doesn't support MAPI over HTTP. Outlook Anywhere is also being used when clients are connecting from the internet.

By default, Outlook Anywhere is enabled, but it's only configured with default settings which means that the `-InternalUrl` parameter is configured to FQDN of the server. Outlook Anywhere allows Outlook clients to connect to Exchange through RPCs encapsulated into an HTTPS connection. This allows external clients to access Exchange from Outlook, as there is no need to open RPC ports on firewalls. In this recipe, we'll take a look at how you can use the Exchange Management Shell to manage Outlook Anywhere settings.

How to do it...

By default, the Outlook Anywhere feature is enabled, but it needs to be configured with the correct hostname and authentication values. This is done by using the `Set-OutlookAnywhere` cmdlet. See the following example:

```
Set-OutlookAnywhere -Identity 'TLEX01\Rpc (Default Web Site)' `
    -ExternalHostname mail.contoso.com `
    -ExternalClientRequireSsl $true `
 -InternalHostname mail.contoso.com `
    -InternalClientRequireSsl $true `
 -ExternalClientAuthenticationMethod Basic `
 -InternalClientAuthenticationMethod Ntlm `
    -SSLOffloading $false
```

In this example, Outlook Anywhere is configured on the `TLEX01` server.

How it works...

Before enabling Outlook Anywhere, there are two prerequisites that need to be met. First, you need to ensure that your server has a valid SSL certificate installed from a **certificate authority (CA)** that is trusted by your client machines. Exchange installs a self-signed certificate by default, but this will not be trusted by client workstations.

During the installation of Exchange 2016, the RPC over HTTP Proxy component is installed on the server. When running the `Set-OutlookAnywhere` cmdlet, you can see that we specified the `ExternalHostname`. This will be the FQDN that Outlook clients use to connect to Exchange. You'll need to make sure that you have a DNS record created for this FQDN that resolves to your Mailbox server or to your reverse proxy solution.

An appreciated feature with Exchange 2013 and 2016 is that `InternalHostname` can be configured. This means that the `InternalUrl` can be something else which most likely is pointed to the internal load balancer VIP, for spreading the load.

When specifying a value for the `ExternalClientAuthenticationMethod` and `InternalClientAuthenticationMethod` parameters, you'll want to use either `Basic`, `NTLM`, or `Negotiate`. These settings determine how users authenticate to Outlook Anywhere. When using `Basic` authentication, the user's password is sent to the server in plain text, but the connection is secured by SSL. If you have workstations that are not domain-joined, which will be connecting to Exchange through Outlook Anywhere, you'll need to use `Basic` authentication.

If only domain-joined clients will be connecting to Outlook Anywhere, such as roaming users with laptops who connect from home, using `NTLM` authentication is a much more secure option for the `ClientAuthenticationMethod`. When using `NTLM`, a user's password is not sent to the server; instead, `NTLM` sends a hashed value of the user's credentials to the server. Another benefit to using `NTLM` is that Outlook clients will not be prompted for their credentials when connecting with Outlook Anywhere.

Keep in mind that if you are publishing Outlook Anywhere with a reverse proxy solution, you'll need to use **Kerberos Constrained Delegation (KCD)**, which allows the reverse proxy to request a Kerberos service ticket from Active Directory on behalf of the user. Also, remember that `NTLM` authentication may not work correctly through some firewalls; check with your firewall manufacturer's documentation for details.

Instead when setting the setting to Negotiate, it means that it automatically selects between Kerberos protocol and NTLM authentication pending on availability. Kerberos is used if it's available or else NTLM will be used.

Finally, SSLOffloading allows the server to offload the encryption and decryption of the SSL connections to a third-party device, unless you have an SSL offloading solution in place, which is normally located on the reverse proxy solution or load balancer solution. By default, this setting is set to $true, which changes the require SSL setting automatically to $false. With the SSL Offloading configured to $false, the require SSL configuration automatically is being set to $true.

There's more...

In addition to enabling Outlook Anywhere from the Shell, we can also perform some other routine tasks. For example, to view the Outlook Anywhere configuration, use the Get-OutlookAnywhere cmdlet:

```
    [PS] C:\>Get-OutlookAnywhere | fl ServerName,ExternalHostname,
InternalHostname
    ServerName        : TLEX01
    ExternalHostname : mail.contoso.com
 InternalHostname : mail.contoso.com
```

The Get-OutlookAnywhere cmdlet will return configuration information for servers that have the Outlook Anywhere feature enabled.

If you at any time need to change the authentication method or external hostname for Outlook Anywhere, you can use the Set-OutlookAnywhere cmdlet:

```
    Set-OutlookAnywhere -Identity 'TLEX01\Rpc (Default Web Site)' `
    -ExternalHostname 'outlook.contoso.com'
```

Notice that the identity of the server needs to be specified in the format of ServerName\VirtualDirectoryName (WebsiteName).

With the new architecture, we have a new way of controlling the settings for MAPI; this is being used with the Set-MapiVirtualDirectory cmdlet.

To view the MAPI configuration, we can see the default configuration using the `Get-MapiVirtualDirectory` cmdlet:

```
[PS] C:\>Get-MapiVirtualDirectory | fl `
Server,ExternalUrl,ExternalAuthenticationMethods,InternalUrl, `
InternalAuthenticationMethods
    Server                       : TLEX01
    ExternalUrl                  :
    ExternalAuthenticationMethods : {Ntlm, OAuth, Negotiate}
    InternalUrl                  : https://tlex01.contoso.com/mapi
    InternalAuthenticationMethods : {Ntlm, OAuth, Negotiate}
```

With the preceding settings, you probably want to configure the `InternalUrl` and `ExternalUrl` parameters with something similar to the following example:

```
Set-MapiVirtualDirectory -Identity 'TLEX01\mapi (Default Web Site)' `
-ExternalUrl https://mail.testlabs.se/mapi `
-InternalUrl https://mail.testlabs.se/mapi
```

When having this configuration in place, we will rely on the DNS name, `mail.testlabs.se`. With that said, we are required to have a certificate containing that specific name to have a working solution. This means that Outlook will connect using MAPI to the specified URLs.

See also

- The *Managing ActiveSync, OWA, POP3, and IMAP4 mailbox settings* recipe from `Chapter 7`, *Managing Client Access*
- The *Generating a certificate request* recipe from `Chapter 9`, *Exchange Security*
- The *Importing certificates on multiple exchange servers* recipe from `Chapter 9`, *Exchange Security*

Blocking Outlook clients from connecting to Exchange

Exchange gives you plenty of options to block clients from connecting to mailboxes, depending on the version of the Outlook client and the method used to access the mailbox. In this recipe, you'll learn how to configure these options using the Exchange Management Shell.

How to do it...

1. The `Set-CASMailbox` can be used to block access to mailboxes based on several factors. For example, we can prevent an individual user from using Outlook to connect using Outlook Anywhere:

```
Set-CASMailbox -Identity dsmith -MAPIBlockOutlookRpcHttp $true
```

2. In addition, we can also prevent a user whose Outlook is not configured in cached mode from connecting to their mailbox using the following command:

```
Set-CASMailbox -Identity dsmith `
-MAPIBlockOutlookNonCachedMode $true
```

> In both cases, the user can still access their mailbox using OWA, as long as the OWAEnabled property is set to $true.

3. You can also block users from connecting from clients based on their version. The following command will block all Outlook versions earlier than 2013 or later for every mailbox in the organization:

```
Get-CASMailbox -Resultsize Unlimited |
  Set-CASMailbox -MAPIBlockOutlookVersions '-14.9.9'
```

4. To find all mailboxes in an organization that have MAPIBlockOutlookVersions defined, run the following command:

```
Get-CASMailbox -ResultSize Unlimited |
  ?{$_.MAPIBlockOutlookVersions}
```

5. To remove the restriction for a single mailbox, use the following command:

```
Set-CASMailbox dsmith -MAPIBlockOutlookVersions $null
```

6. To remove the restriction for the entire organization, use the following command:

```
Get-CASMailbox -ResultSize Unlimited |
  Set-CASMailbox -MAPIBlockOutlookVersions $null
```

How it works...

The `Set-CASMailbox` cmdlet allows you to configure which protocols and services a particular mailbox user can access. To determine the existing settings, we can use the `Get-CASMailbox` cmdlet. For instance, if you need to retrieve all users that have been blocked from connecting to their mailboxes in non-cached mode, use the following command:

```
Get-CASMailbox | Where-Object{$_.MAPIBlockOutlookNonCachedMode}
```

To find all mailboxes blocked from using Outlook Anywhere, the command is almost identical, just reference the correct property name:

```
Get-CASMailbox | Where-Object{$_.MAPIBlockOutlookRpcHttp}
```

In both examples, we pipe the `Get-CASMailbox` to the `Where-Object` cmdlet. Inside the filter, we're checking to see if the property values evaluate as `$true`. If that is the case, the command will return a list of users who have the corresponding setting enabled.

As always, we can use pipelining to enable or disable these settings for multiple users in a single command. Let's say that we want to block all of the users in the `Sales` OU from using Outlook Anywhere:

```
Get-CASMailbox -OrganizationalUnit contoso.com/Sales |
    Set-CASMailbox -MAPIBlockOutlookRpcHttp $true
```

To remove this restriction, use the same command but this time set the parameter value to `$false`:

```
Get-CASMailbox -OrganizationalUnit contoso.com/Sales |
    Set-CASMailbox -MAPIBlockOutlookRpcHttp $false
```

In both cases, the `Get-CASMailbox` cmdlet retrieves every mailbox from the `Sales` OU and pipes the object's output by the command to the `Set-CASMailbox` cmdlet that then makes the change.

As we saw earlier, Outlook client versions can be blocked on a per-mailbox basis using the `Set-CASMailbox` cmdlet. This is done by specifying the client version using the `MAPIBlockOutlookVersions` parameter.

To determine the specific client versions in your environment, you can use the **Help** | **About** screen in Outlook to determine the exact version number. On the server side level, this information can be found in the logs located in: `%ExchangeInstallPath%Logging\RPC Client Access`.

A version number is made up of a Major, Minor, and Build number. Here are a few version numbers for some commonly used versions of Outlook:

- Outlook 2010 RTM-14.0.7147.5001
- Outlook 2013 RTM-15.0.4420.1000
- Outlook 2016 RTM-16.0.4266.1003

The Major build numbers are consistent across the entire Office suite and never change. For example, for Office 2010 the Build number is 14, for Office 2013 the Build number is 15, and for Office 2016 the Build number is 16 and so on.

The Minor and Build numbers will change depending on the hotfixes and service packs deployed to the clients. Therefore, the -MAPIBlockOutlookVersions parameter will accept a range of values that will allow you to be very specific about which versions should be blocked. You can even specify multiple version ranges and separate each one using a semi-colon.

For example, the following command can be used to block access to Exchange for all versions of Outlook below 2013:

```
Set-CASMailbox dsmith -MAPIBlockOutlookVersions '-14.9.9'
```

Keep in mind that when you are making these changes, they will not take effect right away. If you want to force a change so it is effective immediately, restart the Microsoft Exchange RPC Client Access service on the Mailbox server used to access the mailbox. Make sure to do this outside of production hours as it will affect every user connected to this specific server.

There's more...

In addition to blocking Outlook versions at the mailbox level, we can also block them at the server level, which is the preferred choice to control it on a wide scale. Since the MAPI client endpoint is now at the Mailbox role again, we can use the Set-RPCClientAccess cmdlet to accomplish this:

```
Set-RpcClientAccess -Server tlex01 `
-BlockedClientVersions '-14.9.9'
```

You can see here that we use the `BlockedClientVersions` parameter to define the client versions that should be blocked, and it works in exactly the same way as it does when using the `Set-CASMailbox` cmdlet. In this example, all client versions below Outlook 2013 will be blocked at the server level. Notice that the server name has been specified with this command and you'll need to run it against each Mailbox server that should block specific Outlook versions.

Reporting on active OWA and RPC connections

One of the nice things about using PowerShell to manage Exchange is that you have a great deal of flexibility when it comes to solving problems. When the Exchange Management Shell does not provide a cmdlet that specifically meets your needs, you can often tap into other resources accessible through PowerShell. This recipe provides a great example for this. In this section, we'll use PowerShell to query performance counter data to determine the number of active OWA and HTTP/RPC (Outlook Anywhere) connections on one or more Mailbox servers.

How to do it...

1. To determine the number of users currently logged into OWA on a Mailbox server, use the following command syntax:

```
Get-Counter -Counter '\ASP.NET Apps
v4.0.30319(_LM_W3SVC_1_ROOT_OWA)\Requests Executing'
```

This retrieves the total number of users logged into OWA on the TLEX01 server. The output from this command will look similar to the following:

Viewing the output, we can see that two users are currently logged on to OWA.

2. To find the total number of MAPI connections (users), we simply need to use another performance counter:

```
Get-Counter '\\tlex01\MSExchange MapiHttp Emsmdb\User Count'
```

Similar to the previous example, the total number of HTTP/RPC connects will be reported, as shown in the following screenshot:

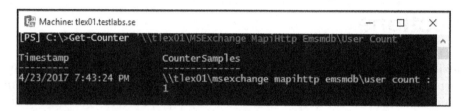

3. To find the total number of HTTP/RPC (Outlook Anywhere) connections, we simply need to use another performance counter:

```
Get-Counter '\\tlex01\MSExchange RpcClientAccess\User Count'
```

Similar to the previous example, the total number of HTTP/RPC connects will be reported, as shown in the following screenshot:

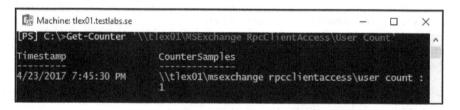

How it works...

The `Get-Counter` cmdlet can be used to retrieve performance counter data from both local and remote machines. In the previous example, we collected the total of number current OWA users using the `\MSExchange OWA\CurrentUsers` counter and the total number of HTTP/RPC connections using the `MSExchangeRpcClientAccess\User Count` counter on the `TLEX01` server. We also had a look at the counter `MSExchangeMapiHttp Emsmdb\User Count` to see how many users were connected using MAPI.

In the preceding examples, we've specified the computer name in the counter name assigned to the -Counter parameter. Another way to gather performance counter data from a remote computer is to use the -ComputerName parameter:

```
Get-Counter 'ASP.NET Apps ` v4.0.30319(_LM_W3SVC_1_ROOT_OWA)\Requests
Executing' `
    -ComputerName tlex01,tlex02
```

Notice that in the alternate syntax used previously, we've removed the computer name from the counter name and have assigned a list of server names using the -ComputerName parameter. This is a quick way to check the number of connections on multiple computers.

There are many Exchange-related performance counters on each Exchange server. You can also use the Get-Counter cmdlet to discover these counters:

```
Get-Counter -ListSet *owa* -ComputerName cas1 |
    Select-Object -expand paths
```

This will do a wildcard search and return a list of counters on the specified server that have the letters owa in their name. You can use this syntax to quickly find counter names that can be used with the Get-Counter cmdlet.

There's more...

To create more advanced and customizable reports, we can create a PowerShell function that returns a custom object with only the information we're interested in. Add the following function to your Shell session:

```
function Get-ActiveUsers {
  [CmdletBinding()]
  param(
    [Parameter(Position=0,
      ValueFromPipelineByPropertyName=$true,
      Mandatory=$true)]
    [string[]]
    $Name
  )

  process {
    $Name | %{
      $RPC = Get-Counter "\MSExchange RpcClientAccess\User Count"`
        -ComputerName $_
$MAPI = Get-Counter "\MSExchange MapiHttp Emsmdb\User ` Count" -
ComputerName $_
```

```
$OWA = Get-Counter "\ASP.NET Apps v4.0.30319(_LM_W3SVC_1_ROOT_OWA)\Requests
Executing" `
      -ComputerName $_
      New-Object PSObject -Property @{
        Server = $_
        'MAPI users' = $MAPI.CounterSamples[0].CookedValue
  'HTTP/RPC users' = $RPC.CounterSamples[0].CookedValue
  'Outlook Web App users' = `
$OWA.CounterSamples[0].CookedValue
      }
    }
  }
}
```

You can call the function and provide one or more Mailbox server names that you'd like to
generate the report for, as shown in the following screenshot:

If you look closely at the code in the function, you'll notice that we've added some attributes
to the $Name parameter. As you can see, in addition to being a mandatory parameter, it also
accepts its value from the pipeline by property name. This means that, instead of calling the
function and providing a list of server names, we can leverage the objects that are returned
by the Get-MailboxServer cmdlet to quickly generate a report using a pipeline command:

You can continue to pipe this command down to Export-CSV or ConvertTo-Html to
generate an external report file that can be viewed outside of the Shell.

See also

- The *Understanding the pipeline* recipe from `Chapter 1`, *PowerShell Key Concepts*

Controlling ActiveSync device access

Together with the increase of smartphones being deployed, ActiveSync can now be used pretty much on all mobile devices. Using device access rules, we can define the specific devices or device types that can form an ActiveSync partnership with an Exchange server. This recipe will explore the options that can be used to allow, block, or quarantine ActiveSync devices using the Exchange Management Shell for Exchange 2016.

How to do it...

By default, there is an organization-wide configuration setting that will allow any ActiveSync device to connect to Exchange. You can modify this so that all devices are initially quarantined, and need to be approved by an administrator before they can gain access. To implement this, first run the following command:

```
Set-ActiveSyncOrganizationSettings -DefaultAccessLevel `
Quarantine -AdminMailRecipients administrator@contoso.com
```

After the previous command completes, all devices that attempt to form an ActiveSync device partnership will be quarantined. When a device is quarantined, the address provided by the `-AdminMailRecipients` parameter will be notified via email. The user will also receive a message on their mobile device informing them that access needs to be granted by an administrator before they'll be able to access any content. Based on the information in the email message, the administrator can choose to enable the device using the `Set-CASMailbox` cmdlet:

```
Set-CASMailbox -Identity dsmith -ActiveSyncAllowedDeviceIDs `
GDI18O09516R350JE2A3DU4BD9
```

Once the command has been run, the user will be able to connect.

How it works...

In Exchange 2016, you can manage the devices in the **Exchange Control Panel** (**ECP**), and, of course, the cmdlets can still be used if you want to do this work from the Shell.

When configuring the ActiveSync organization settings, you have the option of adding a custom message that will be sent to the user when they receive the email notification, explaining that their device has been quarantined. Use the `-UserMailInsert` parameter when running the `Set-ActiveSyncOrganizationSettings` cmdlet to configure this setting:

```
Set-ActiveSyncOrganizationSettings -DefaultAccessLevel `
Quarantine -AdminMailRecipients helpdesk@contoso.com `
   -UserMailInsert 'Call the Help Desk for immediate assistance'
```

In addition to the administrative email notifications, you can find all the devices that are currently in a quarantined state using the `Get-ActiveSync` device cmdlet:

```
Get-MobileDevice | ?{$_.DeviceAccessState -eq 'Quarantined'} |
   fl UserDisplayName,DeviceAccessState,DeviceID
```

The output from the command will be similar to the following screenshot:

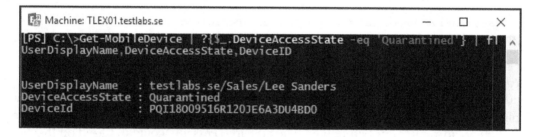

The command retrieves ActiveSync devices and is filtered on the `DeviceAccessState` property. The output will provide the username, device access state, and the `DeviceID` that can be used to allow access using the `Set-CASMailbox` cmdlet.

There's more...

Manual approval of ActiveSync devices may not be something you want to take on as an administrative task. An alternative to this is to use device access rules. For instance, let's say that you want to block all ActiveSync devices that are not iPhone devices. You could set the `DefaultAccessLevel` for the organization to `Block` and create a device access rule allowing only those devices:

```
New-ActiveSyncDeviceAccessRule -Characteristic DeviceType `
-QueryString iPhone -AccessLevel Allow
```

You can create multiple access rules for different types of devices if needed. To determine the device type, you can use the `Get-MobileDevice` cmdlet. The property values for `DeviceModel`, `DeviceType`, `DeviceOS`, `DeviceUserAgent` and `XMSWLHeader` can be used with the `-QueryString` parameter to define the device type when creating a device access rule.

See also

- The *Reporting on ActiveSync devices* recipe from `Chapter 7`, Managing Client Access
- The *Managing ActiveSync, OWA, POP3, and IMAP4 mailbox settings* recipe from `Chapter 7`, Managing Client Access

Reporting on ActiveSync devices

The Exchange Management Shell provides several cmdlets that can be used for generating reports. We can obtain information about users and their devices and we can also generate reports based on enduser activity and server usage. In this recipe, we'll take a look at how we can use these cmdlets to generate multiple ActiveSync reports from the Exchange Management Shell.

How to do it...

1. To generate a report for an individual user's device synchronization status, use the following command:

```
Get-MobileDeviceStatistics -Mailbox lsanders
```

2. This cmdlet will output a lot of information, some of which may not be very interesting. You can limit the data returned by selecting only the properties that provide useful information:

```
Get-MobileDeviceStatistics -Mailbox lsanders |
select LastSuccessSync,Status,DevicePhoneNumber,`
DeviceType
```

The output for the previous command will look similar to the following screenshot:

```
Machine: TLEX01.testlabs.se                              —    □    ×

[PS] C:\>Get-MobileDeviceStatistics -Mailbox lsanders | select LastSuccessS ^
ync,Status,DevicePhoneNumber,DeviceType

LastSuccessSync             Status DevicePhoneNumber DeviceType
---------------             ------ ----------------- ----------
2017-05-01 19:38:46 DeviceOk                         iPhone
```

3. To export this information, you can pipe the command even further to the `Export-CSV` cmdlet:

```
Get-MobileDeviceStatistics -Mailbox lsanders |
    select LastSuccessSync,Status,DevicePhoneNumber,`
DeviceType | Export-CSV -Path c:\report.csv -NoType
```

How it works...

Using the `Get-MobileDeviceStatistics` cmdlet, we can retrieve the mobile phones that are configured to synchronize with a particular user's mailbox. As you can see from the previous examples, it's quite easy to generate a report for an individual user. This cmdlet requires that you either specify the identity of the ActiveSync device or the mailbox of the owner. In order to generate reports based on statistics for multiple devices, we have a couple of options.

First, we can use the `Get-MobileDevice` cmdlet to retrieve a list of allowed devices and then pipe the results to the `Get-MobileDeviceStatistics` cmdlet:

```
$dev = Get-MobileDevice | ?{$_.DeviceAccessState -eq 'Allowed'}
$dev | ForEach-Object {
  $mailbox = $_.UserDisplayName
  $stats = Get-MobileDeviceStatistics -Identity $_
  $stats | Select-Object @{n="Mailbox";e={$mailbox}},
```

```
    LastSuccessSync,
    Status,
    DevicePhoneNumber,
    DeviceType
}
```

This code retrieves all the ActiveSync devices with the `Allowed` access state. We loop through each device, retrieve the device statistics for each one, and return several properties that provide details about the user and the status of their device. Notice that, in the example, we're using a calculated property to return the mailbox name since that information is not included in the output of the `Get-MobileDeviceStatistics` cmdlet.

The other method for obtaining this information is by using the `Get-CASMailbox` cmdlet to find all users with an ActiveSync device partnership, and then sending those objects down the pipeline to the `Get-MobileDeviceStatistics` cmdlet:

```
$mbx = Get-CASMailbox | ?{$_.HasActiveSyncDevicePartnership}
$mbx | ForEach-Object {
  $mailbox = $_.Name
  $stats = Get-MobileDeviceStatistics -Mailbox $mailbox
  $stats | Select-Object @{n="Mailbox";e={$mailbox}},
    LastSuccessSync,
    Status,
    DevicePhoneNumber,
    DeviceType
}
```

Similarly to the previous example, we loop through each mailbox, retrieve the ActiveSync statistics, and then return the same properties as before. This version is considerably slower since it has to first check every mailbox to determine if a device partnership exists, but if you need specific filtering capabilities based on the properties returned by the `Get-CASMailbox` cmdlet, this may be a useful method. This will also filter out system mailboxes.

There's more...

The Exchange Management Shell also provides the `Export-ActiveSyncLog` cmdlet that can be used to generate reports based on ActiveSync usage. The cmdlet generates reports based on IIS log files and then outputs six separate CSV files that contain detailed information about the usage of ActiveSync devices:

- `Users.csv`: Provides details on ActiveSync usage for each user that includes the number of sent and received items

- `UserAgents.csv`: Provides details on the various user agents used by devices to access Exchange
- `StatusCodes.csv`: Provides the HTTP response codes issued to ActiveSync clients
- `Servers.csv`: Provides details on server usage including total bytes sent and received
- `PolicyCompliance.csv`: Provides details on ActiveSync device compliance such as the total number of compliant, non-compliant, and partially compliant devices
- `Hourly.csv`: Provides an hourly breakdown of device synchronization activity

The cmdlet supports a number of parameters that can be used to generate reports. For example, the following command generates reports for ActiveSync activity taking place on May 1, 2017:

```
Export-ActiveSyncLog `
-Filename C:\inetpub\logs\LogFiles\W3SVC1\u_ex170501.log `
-OutputPath c:\report
```

When running this command, make sure that the directory specified for the output path has already been created. The given command generates the six CSV files discussed previously in the `c:\report` folder.

To generate reports for multiple log files, you'll need to do a little extra work. For example:

```
$path = "C:\inetpub\logs\LogFiles\W3SVC1\"
Get-ChildItem -Path $path -Filter u_ex1705*.log | %{
  Export-ActiveSyncLog -Filename $_.fullname `
  -OutputPrefix $_.basename `
  -OutputPath c:\report
}
```

Here we're using the `Get-ChildItem` cmdlet to retrieve a list of log files from May of 2017. Each time we run the `Export-ActiveSyncLog` cmdlet for a log file, a new set of six CSV reports will be generated. Since we can only define one `OutputPath`, we use the log file base name as a prefix for each CSV report file generated. After the cmdlet has been run, six CSV reports for each day of the month will be located in the `c:\report` directory. You can read these reports in the Shell using the `Import-CSV` cmdlet, or open them in **Excel** or **Notepad** for review.

See also

- The *Creating custom objects* recipe from `Chapter 1`, *PowerShell Key Concepts*
- The *Controlling ActiveSync device access* recipe from `Chapter 7`, *Managing Client Access*
- The *Managing ActiveSync, OWA, POP3, and IMAP4 mailbox settings* recipe from `Chapter 7`, *Managing Client Access*

8

Managing Transport Servers

In this chapter, we will cover the following topics:

- Configuring transport limits
- Managing connectors
- Allowing application servers to relay emails
- Checking if the IP address is in a receive connector
- Comparing receive connectors
- Adding IP address to receive connectors
- Working with custom DSN messages
- Managing connectivity and protocol logs
- Searching message tracking logs
- Determining which email client sent an email
- Working with messages in transport queues
- Searching anti-spam agent logs
- Implementing a header firewall
- Configuring the Edge Transport server role

Introduction

In Exchange 2013 SP1 (CU4), the Edge Transport was reintroduced and it remains present in Exchange 2016. But, unlike Exchange 2013, there are now only two server roles- Edge Transport servers and Mailbox servers. This means the Mailbox server role now includes both the client access services that accept client connections for all protocols, as well as the transport services that are used to route email.

In addition to routing messages, you can apply rules, configure settings, and enforce limits on messages as they pass through the servers in your environment. Transport agents can be used to provide basic anti-spam protection, and both roles implement detailed logging capabilities that can be leveraged from the shell. In this chapter, we'll take a look at several useful scripting techniques that include imposing limits and rules on messages and generating detailed reports on mail flow statistics.

Performing some basic steps

To work with the code samples in this chapter, follow these steps to launch the Exchange Management Shell:

1. Log on to a workstation or server with the Exchange Management tools installed.
2. You can connect using a remote PowerShell if you, for some reason, don't have Exchange Management tools installed. Use the following command:

```
$Session = New-PSSession -ConfigurationName `
Microsoft.Exchange -ConnectionUri `
  http://servername/PowerShell/ -Authentication Kerberos
  Import-PSSession $Session
```

3. Alternatively, open the Exchange Management Shell by navigating to **Start | All Apps | Microsoft Exchange Server 2016**.
4. Click on the **Exchange Management Shell** shortcut.

 Remember to start the Exchange Management Shell using Run as administrator to avoid permission problems. In this chapter, you might notice that in the examples of cmdlets I have used the back tick (`` ` ``) character to break up long commands into multiple lines. The purpose of this is to make it easier to read. The back ticks are not required and should only be used if needed.

Configuring transport limits

Depending on your requirements, transport limits can be configured in multiple ways. We can configure limits on individual mailboxes, on specific connectors, on servers, and even at the organization level. In this recipe, you'll learn how to use the Exchange Management Shell to configure limits based on the total number of acceptable recipients for a message, and also the total maximum size of each message that passes through your organization.

How to do it...

To configure mail flow restrictions for an individual mailbox, use the `Set-Mailbox` cmdlet, as shown next:

```
Set-Mailbox dsmith `
-MaxSendSize 10mb `
-MaxReceiveSize 10mb `
-RecipientLimits 100
```

Here, you can see that we've set limits for Dave Smith so that the maximum send and receive size for messages sent to or from his mailbox is limited to 10 MB. In addition, the maximum number of recipients that can be addressed when he sends an email message is limited to 100.

To validate these changes, you can use the `Get-Mailbox` cmdlet to ensure the limits were indeed applied:

```
Get-Mailbox dsmith | `
Select MaxSendSize, MaxReceiveSize, RecipientLimits
```

How it works...

All Exchange recipients provide some type of mail flow settings that can be applied on an individual basis. In the previous example, we applied limits on a mailbox, but you also have the option of applying the `MaxReceiveSize` property on distribution groups and contacts. You may want to implement individual mail flow limits on a subset of recipients, and to do this in bulk, we can take advantage of PowerShell's flexible pipelining capabilities.

For example, let's say that we'd like to configure the mail flow limits shown in the previous example for all the mailbox-enabled users in the `Marketing` OU. The following command would take care of this:

```
Get-Mailbox -ResultSize Unlimited `
-OrganizationalUnit contoso.com/Marketing | `
Set-Mailbox -MaxSendSize 10mb `
-MaxReceiveSize 20mb `
-RecipientLimits 100
```

Here, you can see that we're simply retrieving a list of mailboxes from the `Marketing` OU using the `Get-Mailbox` cmdlet. To configure the limits, we pipe those objects to the `Set-Mailbox` cmdlet, and each user is then updated with the new settings.

There's more...

In addition to setting limits on individual recipients, we have the option to configure limits organization-wide. To do this, we use the `Set-TransportConfig` cmdlet:

```
Set-TransportConfig -MaxReceiveSize 10mb `
-MaxRecipientEnvelopeLimit 1000 `
-MaxSendSize 10mb
```

This command will enforce a `10` megabyte send and receive limit for messages passing through all servers in the organization, as well as limit the total number of recipients per message to `1000`.

Limits can also be set on a per-connector basis. To set the limits on an internet receive connector, the command might look something like this:

```
Set-ReceiveConnector EX1\Internet `
-MaxMessageSize 20mb `
-MaxRecipientsPerMessage 100
```

Notice that the identity is referenced using the format of `ServerName\ConnectorName`. This command will update the `Internet` connector on the `EX1` server. If you have multiple servers with this receive connector, you can update the settings for each server with one command:

```
Get-ReceiveConnector *\Internet | `
Set-ReceiveConnector -MaxMessageSize 20mb `
-MaxRecipientsPerMessage 100
```

This time, we use the `Get-ReceiveConnector` cmdlet, using an asterisk (`*`) as a wildcard so that any connector in the organization named `Internet` will be retrieved. We pipe the output down to the `Set-ReceiveConnector` cmdlet and the change is made in bulk.

Modifying send connectors is a little easier because they are defined at the organization level, so you don't need to iterate through connectors on multiple servers. To modify the maximum message size limits on a send connector named `Internet`, you can run the following command:

```
Set-SendConnector Internet -MaxMessageSize 50mb
```

In this example, outbound messages through the `Internet` send connector are limited to `50` MB in size.

Implementing restrictions at the organization, server, connector, and user levels should give you plenty of options. However, you can also use transport rules to set a maximum attachment size per message, if needed.

It is important to be aware of the order of precedence in which message size limits are applied: the most restrictive limit is enforced. As such, it is recommended to reject large messages as early in the transport pipeline as possible. By ensuring that your organization, server, connector, and mailbox limits are properly configured, you minimize any unnecessary processing of messages. You do this by either configuring identical limits in all locations, or by configuring more restrictive limits where messages enter your Exchange organization.

Message size limits between authenticated users (typically, internal users) are exempt from the organizational limit. This means that you can configure specific users to exceed the organization's default message size limit. However, messages sent between anonymous users (typically, internet senders or recipients), are still subject to the organizational limit. For example, suppose your organization message size limit is 20 MB, but you configured users in the legal department with a 40 MB limit. These users will be able to exchange large messages with each other, but not with internet senders and recipients.

See also

- *Managing transport rules* recipe in this chapter
- The *Managing connectors* recipe in this chapter

Managing connectors

Just like in previous editions, Exchange 2016 uses both send and receive connectors to transmit and accept messages from other servers. Receive connectors are maintained at the server level, while send connectors are maintained at an organization level.

These connectors can be managed from within the **Exchange Admin Center (EAC)**, but the addition, configuration, and removal of these connectors can also be completely managed from the Exchange Management Shell. In this recipe, we'll take a look at the various cmdlets that can be used to manage send and receive connectors.

How to do it...

Let's see how to create send and receive connectors using the following steps:

1. To create a send connector, use the `New-SendConnector` cmdlet:

```
New-SendConnector -Name Internet `
-Usage Internet `
-AddressSpaces 'SMTP:*;1' `
-IsScopedConnector $false `
-DNSRoutingEnabled $false `
-SmartHosts smtp.contoso.com `
-SmartHostAuthMechanism None `
-UseExternalDNSServersEnabled $False `
-SourceTransportServers EX1
```

2. Receive connectors can be created on each Exchange server using the `New-ReceiveConnector` cmdlet:

```
New-ReceiveConnector -Name 'Inbound from DMZ' `
-Usage 'Custom' `
-Bindings '192.168.1.245:25' `
-Fqdn mail.contoso.com `
-RemoteIPRanges '172.16.23.0/24' `
-PermissionGroups AnonymousUsers `
-Server EX2
```

How it works...

By default, Exchange does not create a send connector for routing messages to the internet, so it needs to be created manually using either EAC or the shell. However, there is a hidden implicit send connector that is used to send a mail between servers within the organization, and you don't need to worry about creating send connectors for internal mail flow.

In the previous example, we used the `New-SendConnector` cmdlet to create an internet send connector on a Mailbox server. This cmdlet provides a number of options that control how the connector is configured. In this case, we've configured an address space of `SMTP:*;1`, which specifies that all messages addressed to recipients outside the organization will be sent through this connector. Instead of using DNS to route the messages, we're forwarding all messages to a smart host called `smtp.contoso.com` which in this case, would be an SMTP gateway in the perimeter network.

The source Mailbox server has been configured using the server name EX1, which means that any message destined for the internet will be first routed through this server before being forwarded to the smart host. There are over 30 parameters available with this cmdlet, so you'll want to review the `help` file to determine how to configure the settings based on your needs. To do this, run `Get-Help New-SendConnector -Full`.

After a send connector has been created, its settings can be modified using the `Set-SendConnector` cmdlet. The following example will modify our previous internet send connector by replacing the associated address spaces:

```
Set-SendConnector -Identity Internet `
-AddressSpaces 'SMTP:*.litwareinc.com;5',
'SMTP:corp.contoso.com;10'
```

To view all of the properties of a send connector, use the `Get-SendConnector` cmdlet and pipe the command to `Format-List`:

```
Get-SendConnector -Identity Internet | FL
```

To disable the connector, we can use the following syntax:

```
Set-SendConnector Internet -Enabled $False
```

Finally, the connector can be removed using the `Remove-SendConnector` cmdlet:

```
Remove-SendConnector Internet -Confirm:$False
```

Each Mailbox server will initially be configured during the installation of Exchange with five receive connectors-two for client connections named `Client Proxy <Server Name>` and `Client Frontend <Server Name>`, two for server connections called `Default <Server Name>` and `Default Frontend <Server Name>`, and finally, one for Outbound Proxy called `Outbound Proxy Frontend <Server Name>`. When installing an Exchange 2016 Mailbox server, you don't need to modify any of the default connectors for the internal mail flow to work. A design change regarding inbound mail was made in Exchange 2013 and it remains the same in 2016-it now accepts mail from external senders by default using the `Default Frontend <ServerName>` receive connector, which can be useful. However, if your inbound email first come through a mail relay solution, for example, you should limit this receive connector to only accept emails from that mail relay IP address. If you need to send anonymous mail from applications or servers, you can create a new connector (recommended) or update this one, so it isn't open for everyone to use anonymously. You can read more about this in the *Allowing application servers to relay mail* recipe in this chapter.

There's more...

Receive connectors are created on a per server basis. In step 2, we used the New–
ReceiveConnector cmdlet to create a receive connector on the EX2 server that will be used
to accept messages from a remote SMTP server in the perimeter network. You can see that
we configured the connector so that the EX2 server is listening on the IP address
192.168.1.245 on TCP port 25 for incoming messages. Based on the RemoteIPRanges
and PermissionGroups parameters, any host in the 172.16.23.0/24 subnet will be able
to make an unauthenticated connection to EX2 and submit messages to any recipient within
the organization. Like send connectors, there are a number of parameters that can be used
to create a receive connector. Review the help file for this cmdlet using Get–Help New–
ReceiveConnector–Full to determine all of the available options.

Similar to send connectors, receive connectors have the Set–* and Remove–* cmdlets that
can be used to modify, disable, or remove a receive connector.

To change the settings of a receive connector, use the Set–ReceiveConnector cmdlet:

```
Set-ReceiveConnector 'EX2\Inbound from DMZ' `
-Banner '220 SMTP OK' `
-MaxInboundConnection 2500 `
-ConnectionInactivityTimeout '00:02:30'
```

Here, you can see that we've modified a number of properties on the receive connector.
Each of the settings modified here can only be managed from the shell. To view all of the
properties available, use the Get–ReceiveConnector cmdlet and pipe the command to
Format–List:

```
Get-ReceiveConnector 'EX2\Inbound from DMZ' |
FL
```

To disable a receive connector, use the Set–ReceiveConnector cmdlet:

```
Set-ReceiveConnector 'EX2\Inbound from DMZ' `
-Enabled $False
```

You can remove a receive connector using the following command:

```
Remove-ReceiveConnector 'EX2\Inbound from DMZ' `
-Confirm:$false
```

See also

- The *Configuring transport limits* recipe in this chapter
- The *Allowing application servers to relay mail* recipe in this chapter

Allowing application servers to relay emails

When you deploy Exchange 2016, you may be required to allow applications or physical devices, such as printers, to relay mail off of your servers. In order to allow these systems to anonymously relay mail, you should configure a dedicated receive connector on your Mailbox servers to support this. Although the `Default Frontend <Server Name>` receive connector accepts anonymous emails from any IP address on port 25 by default, this connector should be locked down to your inbound mail relay service or devices only.

In this recipe, we'll take a look at how you can create a dedicated receive connector for this purpose using the Exchange Management Shell.

How to do it...

When implementing an unauthenticated relay, it is wise to use a dedicated receive connector for this purpose:

```
New-ReceiveConnector -Name Relay `
-Usage Custom `
-Bindings '192.168.1.245:25' `
-Fqdn mail.contoso.com `
-RemoteIPRanges 192.168.1.110 `
-Server EX1 `
-PermissionGroups ExchangeServers `
-AuthMechanism TLS, ExternalAuthoritative
```

This command creates a receive connector on the EX1 server named Relay. The settings used here specify that the connector listens on the server IP address of 192.168.1.245 on TCP Port 25, and will allow the host at 192.168.1.110 to relay mail, either internally or externally, without requiring authentication.

How it works...

When creating a relay connector using this technique, you want to ensure that only certain hosts are allowed to relay mail using the `RemoteIPRanges` property. If this connector was configured with a remote IP range of `0.0.0.0-255.255.255.255`, this would effectively turn the Exchange server into an open relay. This is because the `AuthMechanism` parameter has been set to `ExternalAuthoritative`, which means that the connection is considered externally secured by using a security mechanism external to Exchange, so Exchange bypasses all security and fully trusts all messages received from hosts in the `RemoteIPRanges` list. Additionally, messages accepted through this connector will not be scanned by anti-spam agents or be restricted by any of the system-wide message size limits.

There's more...

If the devices or application servers in your environment only need to submit messages to internal recipients and do not need to be completely trusted, creating a receive connector with the following settings is a better option:

```
New-ReceiveConnector -Name Relay `
-Usage Custom `
-Bindings '192.168.1.245:25' `
-Fqdn mail.contoso.com `
-RemoteIPRanges 192.168.1.110 `
-Server EX1 `
-PermissionGroups AnonymousUsers
```

As you can see, we've removed the `AuthMechanism` parameter from the command and assigned `AnonymousUsers` to the permission groups. This is a more secure approach, since messages submitted from applications or devices will now be subjected to anti-spam agents and message restrictions. If you need to allow these devices to route mails to external recipients through this connector, you'll also need to assign the anonymous users the extended right `ms-Exch-SMTP-Accept-Any-Recipient`:

```
Get-ReceiveConnector EX1\Relay |
Add-ADPermission -User "NT AUTHORITY\ANONYMOUS LOGON" `
-ExtendedRights ms-Exch-SMTP-Accept-Any-Recipient
```

After the previous command has been executed, the `Relay` connector on the `EX1` server will be updated and the host at `192.168.1.110` will be able to route messages through the server using an unauthenticated relay; but it will still pass through the anti-spam agents and message restriction settings.

If you want to ensure that a single user or a domain is bypassing the anti-spam agents, you need to configure content filtering. This can easily be accomplished by running the following command:

```
Set-ContentFilterConfig -BypassedSenders sending-user@contoso.com
Set-ContentFilterConfig -BypassedSenderDomains contoso.com
```

By running these commands, the user `sending-user@contoso.com` is bypassed by the anti-spam agents. The last command makes sure that the whole domain `contoso.com` is bypassed.

See also

- The *Configuring transport limits* recipe in this chapter
- The *Managing connectors* recipe in this chapter

Checking if the IP address is in a receive connector

In large environments, maintaining receive connectors across multiple servers can be hard work. Imagine an organization with dozens of Exchange servers, each with a receive connector that allows applications or devices to relay emails. If we are lucky, all connectors will have the same list of IPs, which makes them easier to manage. However, if the organization is geographically dispersed, this might not be the case. When troubleshooting mail flow issues, it might be required to check if a particular application's IP address is configured in any receive connector. If all connectors are configured identically, this can easily be done using the EAC, but if they are not or if we want to check all connectors (including default ones), PowerShell is the way to go.

In this recipe, we will see how we can easily check if a particular IP address is configured on any receive connectors and, if yes, which ones.

How to do it...

1. To check all receive connectors in the environment to see if a particular IP address is listed, we can use the following script:

```
Param (
        [Parameter(Mandatory = $True)]
        [IPAddress] $IP
)


Function CheckRangeForIP {
    Param (
            [IPAddress] $IPaddress,
            [IPAddress] $from,
            [IPAddress] $to
    )

    $ip = [System.Net.IPaddress]::Parse($ipAddress).GetAddressBytes()
    [Array]::Reverse($ip)
    $ip = [System.BitConverter]::ToUInt32($ip, 0)

    $lowerIP = [System.Net.IPaddress]::Parse($from).GetAddressBytes()
    [Array]::Reverse($lowerIP)
    $lowerIP = [System.BitConverter]::ToUInt32($lowerIP, 0)

    $upperIP = [System.Net.IPaddress]::Parse($to).GetAddressBytes()
    [Array]::Reverse($upperIP)
    $upperIP = [System.BitConverter]::ToUInt32($upperIP, 0)

    Return $lowerIP -le $ip -and $ip -le $upperIP
}


Get-ReceiveConnector | % {
        ForEach ($entry in $_.RemoteIPRanges) {
                If ($entry.LowerBound -eq "::" -or $entry.LowerBound -eq
"0.0.0.0") {Continue}

                If (CheckRangeForIP $IP $entry.LowerBound $entry.UpperBound)
{
                        Write-Host $_.Identity -ForegroundColor Green -
NoNewline
                        Write-Host " ($($entry.Expression))"
                }
        }
}
```

2. Save the script in a `.ps1` file, such as `CheckIPRecCon.ps1` for example, and run it as:

```
./ CheckIPRecCon.ps1 -IP 192.168.140.146
```

How it works...

The script accepts one IP address as an argument, which is the IP address we will search for. We start by retrieving a list of all receive connectors across all servers using the `Get-ReceiveConnector` cmdlet. We then process each one individually by using `ForEach`'s alias `%`, and retrieve their `RemoteIPRanges` properties which contains all the IPs configured for that particular connector. Using another `ForEach`, we go through all the entries in the `RemoteIPRanges` list and start by checking if their `LowerBound` IP is `::` (IPv6) or `0.0.0.0` so we can exclude default connectors otherwise our comparison later on would always match. After all, any IP address is included in `0.0.0.0-255.255.255.255`, so that is why we exclude these.

 In a `For`, `ForEach`, or `While` loop, a `Continue` statement will jump to the top of the innermost loop, effectively skipping everything after it to the next iteration of the look.

Next, we call a `CheckRangeForIP` function where we compare our IP address with the lower and upper IP addresses in the current `RemoteIPRanges` entry. Single entries will have the same lower and upper IP addresses, but range entries will not, such as `192.168.140.146-192.168.140.149`.

The function basically takes all three IPs and converts them to a 32-bit unsigned integer so we can easily compare them. We check if our IP is between the lower and upper IPs and return either `True` or `False`.

Finally, if the function returns `True`, it prints the receive connector's name and the expression that matched the IP address. If it matched a single IP, it will print that IP. If it matched a range, it will print the range.

There's more...

To easily check all the IP addresses configured on a particular receive connector, we can use the following command:

```
(Get-ReceiveConnector EX1\Relay).RemoteIPRanges.Expression | Sort
```

Just be aware that this is a numeric sort, so the following will happen (notice the 70 before the 9):

```
172.20.64.7
172.20.64.70
172.20.64.8
172.20.64.9
```

See also

- The *Managing connectors* recipe in this chapter

Comparing receive connectors

Continuing with our previous scenario, maintaining receive connectors across multiple servers can be challenging. Ensuring that two or more connectors have the exact same list of IP addresses using the EAC is not easy, especially if the list of IPs is extensive.

In this recipe, we will look at a simple script to compare the list of IP addresses configured in two receive connectors and print any differences.

How to do it...

To compare the list of IP addresses configured in two receive connectors, we need to compare their RemoteIPRanges properties. The following script does exactly that:

```
$recCon1 = "EX1\Relay"
$recCon2 = "EX2\Relay"
$recCon1IPs = (Get-ReceiveConnector $recCon1).RemoteIPRanges
$recCon2IPs = (Get-ReceiveConnector $recCon2).RemoteIPRanges
$comparison = Compare-Object -ReferenceObject $recCon1IPs -
DifferenceObject $recCon2IPs
$comparison | Select InputObject, @{n="Connector"; e={If
($_.SideIndicator -eq "<=") {$recCon1} ElseIf ($_.SideIndicator -eq "=>")
```

```
{$recCon2}}}
```

How it works...

We start by specifying which two receive connectors we want to compare and save their names into two variables (this will be useful at the end). Then we gather the list of IP addresses configured on these two connectors and save them into two other variables.

The next part is the actual comparison. Here, we use the `Compare-Object` cmdlet which compares two objects and lets us know what differences, if any, exist between the two. If we print the output of the `$comparison` variable at this stage, we would get something like this:

The output shows, for example, that IP `172.28.125.248` is configured on the second object we compared, in this case `EX1\Relay`, and not on `EX2\Relay`.

To make it easier to understand, we finish our little script by replacing <= and => with the name of the receive connector where that IP is present:

See also

- The *Managing connectors recipe* in this chapter
- The *Checking if IP address is in receive connector* recipe in this chapter

Adding IP address to receive connectors

When using custom receive connectors to allow applications to relay emails, there will eventually come a time when we need to add an IP address to such a connector. In small environments, this is typically not an issue, but if the IP address needs to be added to multiple connectors, then it can take a long time to do this using the EAC. Especially if this needs to happen frequently. In such cases, PowerShell is the best option.

In this recipe, we will see how to add IP addresses to one or more receive connectors.

How to do it...

To add one or more IP address to a single receive connector, we can use the following code:

```
$recCon = Get-ReceiveConnector "EX1\Relay"
$recCon.RemoteIPRanges += "172.28.125.239", "172.28.125.242",
"172.28.125.249"
Set-ReceiveConnector $recCon -RemoteIPRanges $recCon.RemoteIPRanges
```

How it works...

We start off by getting the entire configuration of the receive connector we want to update and saving it into the `$recCon` variable. Then we update the `RemoteIPRanges` property of the receive connector (stored in the variable, not in the actual connector) and add our new IP addresses. Finally, we update the `RemoteIPRanges` property of the receive connector itself with the updated list of IPs stored in `$recCon.RemoteIPRanges`.

It is important to note the use of += to **add** the new IPs to the existing ones already configured. If we had used = instead, or if we had used the following code, all the existing IPs would have been deleted and the receive connector configured with only these three new IPs:

```
Set-ReceiveConnector "EX1\Relay" -RemoteIPRanges "172.28.125.239",
"172.28.125.242", "172.28.125.249"
```

There's more...

To update multiple receive connectors, the code is almost identical. All we have to do is retrieve all the connectors we want to update, and then update them one by one. In the following example, we are updating the Relay receive connector across all servers in the environment:

```
Get-ReceiveConnector "*\Relay" | % {
        $_.RemoteIPRanges += "10.0.0.99", "10.0.0.100", "10.0.0.101"
        Set-ReceiveConnector $_ -RemoteIPRanges $_.RemoteIPRanges
}
```

If we have a long list of IP addresses to add, typing all of them can be out of the question. In this case, it is much easier to put them all in a text file, in this case named IPlist.txt, and use that file to update the receive connectors:

```
$recCon = Get-ReceiveConnector "EX1\Relay"
cat .\IPlist.txt | % {$recCon.RemoteIPRanges += $_}
Set-ReceiveConnector $recCon -RemoteIPRanges $recCon.RemoteIPRanges
```

To convert this to a one-liner, and to work with multiple connectors, we can use the following cmdlet:

```
Get-ReceiveConnector "*\Application Relay" | % {Set-ReceiveConnector $_
-RemoteIPRanges ($_.RemoteIPRanges + (cat .\IPlist.txt) | Sort -Unique)}
```

See also

- The *Managing connectors* recipe in this chapter

Working with custom DSN messages

Delivery Status Notification (**DSN**) messages are system messages generated by the Transport service that inform the sender of a message about its status. When a message cannot be delivered to a recipient, Exchange will respond to the sender with a message that is associated with a status message. Sometimes, these status messages may not be detailed enough for your liking. In those cases, you can create new messages associated with the DSN code to provide more details to the sender. This is something that has to be done from the Exchange Management Shell.

How to do it...

You can use the `New-SystemMessage` cmdlet to create a custom DSN message:

```
New-SystemMessage -DSNCode 5.1.1 `
-Text "The mailbox you tried to send an email message to
does not exist. Please contact the Help Desk at extension
4112 for assistance." `
-Internal $True `
-Language En
```

In this example, a **Non Delivery Report** (**NDR**) with the custom DSN message will be delivered to senders that try to send messages to an invalid internal recipient.

How it works...

When creating a custom DSN message, you want to check whether it will be used for internal or external use. The previous example configured a custom message for `DSNCode` `5.1.1` for internal use. In addition to this, you could create a separate custom DSN message for external users only; just set the `-Internal` parameter to `$False`.

Custom DSN messages can also support basic HTML tags. This can be useful when creating an internal custom DSN that directs users to an internal help desk site. Here's another way we could have created the custom DSN message:

```
New-SystemMessage -DSNCode 5.1.1 `
-Text "The mailbox you tried to send an e-mail message to does not
exist. Please visit the <a href='http://support.contoso.com'>help desk
site</a>
for assistance" `
-Internal $True `
-Language En
```

In this example, we've included a hyperlink within the custom DSN message, so users can click on the link and visit an internal help desk website for additional assistance.

There's more...

To view custom DSN messages, use the `Get-SystemMessage` cmdlet:

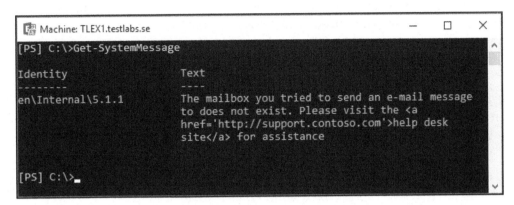

You can also view the default system messages that were installed with Exchange. To do this, run the previous cmdlet with the `-Original` switch parameter:

```
Get-SystemMessage -Original
```

To modify a system message, use the `Set-SystemMessage` cmdlet:

```
Set-SystemMessage 'en\Internal\5.1.1' `
-Text "Sorry, but this recipient is no longer available
or does not exist."
```

As you can see here, we've modified the custom internal 5.1.1 message with a new message using the `-Text` parameter.

To remove a custom DSN message, use the `Remove-SystemMessage` cmdlet:

```
Remove-SystemMessage 'en\Internal\5.1.1' -Confirm:$False
```

The previous command removes the custom message created for the 5.1.1 DSN code without confirmation.

System-generated messages for mailbox and public folder quota warnings can also be customized:

```
New-SystemMessage -QuotaMessageType WarningMailbox `
-Text "Your mailbox is getting too large. Please delete some messages
to free up space or call the help desk at extention 3391." `
-Language En
```

When creating a custom quota message, as shown previously, there is no need to specify a DSN code. Actually, this parameter can't be used when the -DsnCode parameter is specified. The -QuotaMessageType parameter is used to modify the messages for the various warnings supported by the system. The -QuotaMessageType parameter accepts the following values that can be used to customize warning messages:

- ProhibitSendReceiveMailBox
- ProhibitSendMailbox
- WarningMailbox
- WarningMailboxUnlimitedSize
- ProhibitPostPublicFolder
- WarningPublicFolder
- WarningPublicFolderUnlimitedSize
- ProhibitReceiveMailboxMessagesPerFolderCount
- WarningMailboxMessagesPerFolderCount
- WarningMailboxMessagesPerFolderUnlimitedCount
- ProhibitReceiveFolderHierarchyChildrenCountCount
- WarningFolderHierarchyChildrenCount
- WarningFolderHierarchyChildrenUnlimitedCount
- WarningFoldersCount
- ProhibitReceiveFoldersCount
- WarningFoldersCountUnlimited
- ProhibitReceiveFolderHierarchyDepth
- WarningFolderHierarchyDepth
- WarningFolderHierarchyDepthUnlimited

When creating a custom quota message, you cannot use the -Internal parameter. This is not a problem since quota messages are only intended for internal recipients.

Managing connectivity and protocol logs

Every Exchange Mailbox server is capable of logging connection activities and SMTP conversations that take place between servers. You can configure the retention settings for these logs and then use them to diagnose mail flow issues within your environment. In this recipe, you'll learn how to configure the logging options on your servers, and how to examine the data when troubleshooting problems.

How to do it...

To view the connectivity logging configuration for the Transport service of a Mailbox server, use the Get-TransportService cmdlet:

Get-TransportService tlex1 | FL ConnectivityLog*

The previous command retrieves the default connectivity logging settings for a Mailbox server named TLEX1. The output returned will be similar to the following screenshot:

```
Machine: TLEX1.testlabs.se                                    —    □    ✕
[PS] C:\>Get-TransportService TLEX1 | FL ConnectivityLog*


ConnectivityLogEnabled          : True
ConnectivityLogMaxAge           : 30.00:00:00
ConnectivityLogMaxDirectorySize : 1000 MB (1,048,576,000 bytes)
ConnectivityLogMaxFileSize      : 10 MB (10,485,760 bytes)
ConnectivityLogPath             : C:\Program Files\Microsoft\Exchange Serv
                                  er\V15\TransportRoles\Logs\Hub\Connectiv
                                  ity



[PS] C:\>_
```

How it works...

Connectivity logs record connection details about outbound message delivery queues on a Mailbox server. Connectivity logging is enabled by default on Exchange 2016 servers. Based on the output of the `Get-TransportService` cmdlet in the previous example, we can see that by default, the maximum age for connectivity log files is 30 days. Once a log file reaches 10 MB, a new log file will be created. The directory for connectivity logging will hold up to 1 GB of logs. Mailbox servers use circular logging for connectivity logs, so once the directory reaches its maximum size, or the log files reach their maximum age, those log files will be removed to make space for new log files.

You can control these settings using the `Set-TransportService` cmdlet. Here's an example of modifying the connectivity log's maximum age and directory size on a Mailbox server named `tlex1`:

```
Set-TransportService tlex1 `
-ConnectivityLogMaxAge 45 `
-ConnectivityLogMaxDirectorySize 5gb
```

If you change these settings on a Mailbox server, it is recommended that you also update the remaining Mailbox servers in your organization with a matching configuration.

To make this change to all the Mailbox servers at once, use the following commands:

```
Get-TransportService |
Set-TransportService -ConnectivityLogMaxAge 45 `
-ConnectivityLogMaxDirectorySize 5gb
```

There's more...

You can configure protocol logging to record the SMTP conversations between your Mailbox servers and other mail servers or clients. Protocol logging can be enabled on a per connector basis, but just like the connectivity logging options, the configuration of the protocol log file settings is made using the `Set-TransportService` cmdlet. The following screenshot shows these available properties:

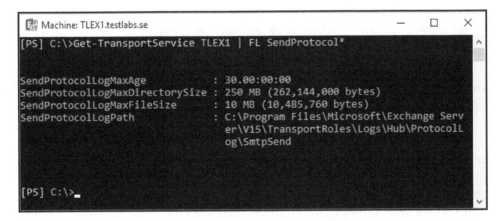

Here, you can see that we've got protocol log settings for receive connectors. The settings shown here are the default values.

The send connectors will use the following protocol log configurations by default:

Just like connectivity logs, the send and receive protocol logs have a maximum age and directory size and are controlled by circular logging. The default settings can be changed with the `Set-TransportService` cmdlet:

```
Set-TransportService tlex1 `
-SendProtocolLogMaxAge 45 `
-ReceiveProtocolLogMaxAge 45
```

Again, if you plan on changing this setting, make sure you update all of the servers in your organization with the same information.

Before you can capture protocol logging information, you need to enable verbose protocol logging on each connector that you want to report on:

```
Set-SendConnector Internet -ProtocolLoggingLevel Verbose
```

In the previous command, you can see that we've configured the `Internet` send connector for verbose protocol logging. You can do the same for a receive connector using the `Set-ReceiveConnector` cmdlet:

```
Get-ReceiveConnector *\Relay |
Set-ReceiveConnector -ProtocolLoggingLevel Verbose
```

Here, we are using an asterisk (*) as a wildcard to retrieve the `Relay` connector from each server in the organization. We can pipe the output to the `Set-ReceiveConnector` cmdlet to enable verbose protocol logging for the connector on each server.

All Mailbox servers use an invisible intra-organization send connector that is used to transmit messages internally to other mailbox servers. You can configure verbose logging for this connector using the `Set-TransportService` cmdlet:

```
Set-TransportService tlex1 `
-IntraOrgConnectorProtocolLoggingLevel Verbose
```

The protocol log files for the intra-org connector will be saved in the send protocol log path.

The connectivity and protocol log files are stored in the CSV format and, by default, are organized in subdirectories under the following path:

```
<install path>\V15\TransportRoles\Logs\
```

The connectivity logs are stored in a subdirectory called `Connectivity` of the `Hub`, `Mailbox`, and `FrontEnd` folders, and the log file naming convention is in the format of `CONNECTLOGyyyymmdd-nnnn.log`, where `yyyymmdd` is the date that the log file was created, and where `nnnn` is an instance number, starting with 1 for each day. The instance number will be incremented by one as each log file reaches the default 10 MB limit, and a new log file is created.

The protocol logs are stored in subdirectories named `ProtocolLog\SmtpReceive` and `ProtocolLog\SmtpSend` of the `Hub`, `Mailbox` and `FrontEnd` folders. The files in these folders use a naming convention in the format of `prefixyyyymmdd-nnnn.log`. The prefix for the log filename will be `SEND` for send connectors and `RECV` for receive connectors. Like connectivity logs, `yyyymmdd` is the date when the log file was created, and `nnnn` is the instance number that starts with 1 and is incremented as each new log file is created.

The connectivity logs store details about messages transmitted from local queues to the destination server. For example, a record in a connectivity log file will log the source queue, destination server, DNS resolution details, connection failures, and the total number of messages and bytes transferred.

The protocol logs store SMTP conversations that take place when either sending or receiving a message. The details logged will contain connector and session IDs, the local and remote endpoints of the servers involved, and the SMTP verbs used in the conversation.

Parsing log files

Even though connectivity and protocol logs are stored in a CSV format, each log file has a header information prepended to the file. The following screenshot shows an example of a connectivity log file in Excel:

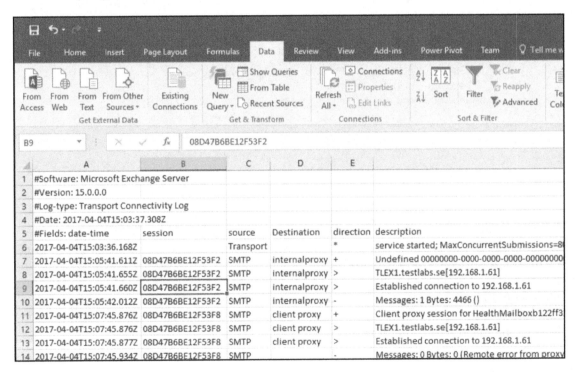

As you can see, the header information includes the date and the fields used in the log files. This header information, makes it impossible to read these files into the Shell using the `Import-CSV` cmdlet. Luckily, PowerShell is so flexible that we can work around this with a little creativity.

Let's say that you are interested in finding all the errors in the connection log on a server named `tlex1`. Start the Exchange Management Shell on the `tlex1` server and run the following command:

```
$logpath = (Get-TransportService tlex1).ConnectivityLogPath
```

This will store a reference to the connectivity log folder path that will make the following code easier to read and work with. Now let's say that you want to parse the connectivity logs from the past 24 hours for failures. We'll parse each log file in the directory and perform a wildcard search based on a keyword:

```
$logs = Get-ChildItem $logpath *.log | ? {$_.LastWriteTime -gt (Get-
Date).AddDays(-1)}
$data = $logs | % {
  Get-Content $_.Fullname | % {
    $IsHeaderParsed = $False
    If ($_ -like '#Fields: *' -and !$IsHeaderParsed) {
      $_ -replace '^#Fields: '
      $IsHeaderParsed = $True
    }
    Else {
      $_
    }
  } | ConvertFrom-Csv
}
$data | Where-Object {$_.description -like '*fail*'}
```

This code will loop through each log file in the connectivity log folder that has been written to within the past 24 hours. For each log file, we'll read the content into the Shell, excluding the header information, and convert the information to properly-formed CSV data using the `ConvertFrom-CSV` cmdlet. The result will be stored in the `$data` variable that can then be filtered on. In this example, any record in each of the log files where the description contains the word `fail` will be returned. You can adjust the `Where-Object` filter based on the information you are searching for.

POP and IMAP logging

Using the Shell, you can also enable, disable, or modify protocol logging settings for POP3 and IMAP4. Protocol logging, as already mentioned, allows you to review the POP3 and IMAP4 connections in your Exchange environment, which is extremely useful for troubleshooting issues, or even to gather statistics about POP and IMAP usage.

In order to enable protocol logging for IMAP4 or POP3 on server EX1 (by default, logging is not enabled for these two protocols) you use the following cmdlet:

```
Set-ImapSettings -Server EX1 -ProtocolLogEnabled $True
Set-PopSettings -Server EX1 -ProtocolLogEnabled $True
```

To modify logging settings, you use the `Set-ImapSettings` or `Set-PopSettings` cmdlets. In the following example, we change the location for the POP3 protocol log files and specify that Exchange should create a new log every hour:

```
Set-PopSettings -Server EX1 -ProtocolLogEnabled $true -LogFileLocation
"C:\Pop3Logging" -LogFileRollOverSettings Hourly -LogPerFileSizeQuota 0
```

Searching message tracking logs

The `Get-MessageTrackingLog` cmdlet is a versatile tool that can be used to search the message tracking logs on Mailbox servers. In this recipe, you'll learn how to use this Exchange Management Shell cmdlet to generate detailed reports on various aspects of mail flow within your organization.

How to do it...

The `Get-MessageTrackingLog` cmdlet has a number of available parameters that can be used to perform a search. To retrieve all the messages sent from a Mailbox server during a specified time frame, use the following syntax:

```
Get-MessageTrackingLog -Server tlex1 `
-Start (Get-Date).AddDays(-1) `
-End (Get-Date) `
-EventId Send
```

Using this command, all the messages sent through SMTP from the `tlex1` server in the past 24 hours will be returned. If the `-End` parameter is not used, Exchange will search all the logs from the start date and time until now, so in this particular case we do not really need to specify it.

How it works...

Each Mailbox server role generates and collects message tracking logs. Message tracking is enabled by default, and the logs are stored in the `<install path>\V15\TransportRoles\Logs\MessageTracking` directory.

Log files are limited to 10 MB by default, and when they reach its maximum size, a new log file is created. Log files are kept for either 30 days, or until the maximum size configured for the directory has been reached. Like connectivity and protocol logs, the message tracking logs are removed as needed using circular logging.

You can configure all of these options using the `Set-TransportService` cmdlet.

In the previous example, we ran the `Get-MessageTrackingLog` cmdlet and specified a Mailbox server to execute the search. Depending on your network topology, you may need to search several servers in order to get accurate results.

For instance, let's say that you've got multiple servers in your organization. You might want to generate a report for all the messages sent by a specific user within a certain time frame. You can search the logs on each Mailbox server using the following syntax:

```
Get-TransportService | Get-MessageTrackingLog `
-ResultSize Unlimited `
-Start (Get-Date).AddDays(-1) `
-EventId Send `
-Sender dmsith@contoso.com
```

Here, you can see that we're using the `Get-TransportService` cmdlet to retrieve a list of all the Mailbox servers in the organization. Those objects are piped to the `GetMessageTrackingLog` cmdlet where we set the `-ResultSize` parameter to `Unlimited` because, by default, this cmdlet will only return the first 1,000 results. Then we specify the start and end time for the search, the event ID, and the sender. The records returned by the previous command will provide a number of useful properties, such as the sender and recipients of the message, the total size of the message, the IP address of the destination server, the subject of the message, and more. These records can be piped out to `Export-CSV` or `ConvertTo-Html` to generate an external report, or you can pipe the command to `Format-List` to view all of the properties for each log entry.

There's more...

The –EventID parameter can be used to specify the event category used to classify a tracking log entry when you perform a search. The following are some possible event categories that can be used:

- BadMail: The message was submitted through the pickup or replay directories but cannot be delivered
- Deliver: The message was delivered to a local mailbox
- DSN: A DSN was generated
- Expand: Expansion of a distribution group
- Fail: Message delivery failed
- PoisonMessage: The message was added or removed from the poison message queue
- Receive: The message was received either through SMTP or by StoreDriver
- Redirect: The message was redirected to an alternate recipient
- Resolve: After an Active Directory lookup, the recipients listed in the message were resolved to another email address
- Send: The message was sent through SMTP to another mail server
- Submit: The message was transmitted by the Mailbox Transport Submission service
- Transfer: The recipients were moved to a forked message because of content conversion, recipient limits, or agents

As shown in the previous example, you can search message tracking logs based on the sender or recipient:

```
Get-TransportService | Get-MessageTrackingLog `
-ResultSize Unlimited `
-Sender sales@litwareinc.com -EventId Receive
```

In this example, we're searching the message tracking logs for an external sender address and specifying Receive as the event category. This would allow us to track all inbound messages from this external sender.

In addition, you can use the `-Recipients` parameter to find messages sent to one or more email addresses, as shown in the following command:

```
Get-TransportService | Get-MessageTrackingLog `
-ResultSize Unlimited `
-Recipients dave@contoso.com, john@contoso.com
```

In order to count the number of emails received by a user in the last 48 hours, you can use the following cmdlet:

```
(Get-TransportService | Get-MessageTrackingLog `
-ResultSize Unlimited `
-Start (Get-Date).AddDays(-2) `
-Recipients john@contoso.com -EventID DELIVER).Count
```

If you know the subject of the message you want to track, use the `-MessageSubject` parameter when running the command:

```
Get-TransportService | Get-MessageTrackingLog `
-ResultSize Unlimited `
-MessageSubject 'Financial Report for Q4'
```

When it comes to message tracking, you may need to generate reports based on the total number of messages sent or received. Let's say that your boss has asked you to determine the number of individual email messages received by your Mailbox servers from the internet in the past week. Let's start with the following command:

```
Get-TransportService | Get-MessageTrackingLog | `
-EventId Receive `
-Start (Get-Date).AddDays(-7) `
-ResultSize Unlimited |
Where-Object {$_.ConnectorId -like '*\Internet'}
```

Here, we're specifying that the event category of the logs returned should be set to `Receive` with the `-EventID` parameter. Next, we specify the date 7 days ago as the start time for the search, and the current date for the end time. We set the `-ResultSize` parameter to `Unlimited` and finally we filter the output using the `Where-Object` cmdlet based on the connector. Since we have a dedicated receive connector for inbound internet email, we filter the results so that only received messages by this connector are returned.

Now that we've got an idea of how to construct this command, let's take it a step further. Again, to ensure that we're getting all of the required information, we'll search the logs on each Mailbox server and then output the total number of email items and their total size for the past week:

```
$results = Get-TransportService |
Get-MessageTrackingLog -EventId Receive `
-Start (Get-Date).AddDays(-7) `
-ResultSize Unlimited | `
Where-Object {$_.ConnectorId -like '*\Internet'}
$results | Measure-Object `
-Property TotalBytes -Sum | `
Select-Object @{n="Total Items";e={$_.Count}},
@{n="Total Item Size (MB)";e={[math]::Round($_.Sum /1mb,2)}}
```

Although this could be done on one line, we've separated it out here into two phases for the sake of readability. First, we gather the message tracking logs on each Mailbox server using the desired settings, and the output is stored in the `$results` variable.

Next, we pipe `$results` to the `Measure-Object` cmdlet that is used to sum up the `TotalBytes` for all the messages accepted from the `Internet` receive connector.

The command is piped further to the `Select-Object` cmdlet, where we create a custom object with calculated properties that display the total number of email items and the total number of bytes represented in megabytes. The results from the previous code would look something like the following screenshot:

```
Machine: TLEX1.testlabs.se                                    —    □    ×

[PS] C:\>$results | Measure-Object -Property TotalBytes -Sum | Select-Objec
t @{n="Total Items";e={$_.Count}}, @{n="Total Item Size (MB)";e={[math]::Ro
und($_.Sum /1mb,2)}}

Total Items Total Item Size (MB)
----------- --------------------
       7484               802.76

[PS] C:\>
```

Taking it a step further

Message tracking logs can be used to create some pretty advanced reports. Let's say that you want to create a report that shows the total number of messages sent from your organization per external domain. This is possible using the following command:

```
$report = Get-TransportService |
Get-MessageTrackingLog -EventId Send `
-ResultSize Unlimited `
-Start (Get-Date).AddDays(-30) `
Where-Object {$_.ConnectorId -eq 'Internet'}
if($report) {
   $domains = $report | % {$_.Recipients | % {$_.Split("@")[1]}}
$domains | Group | Sort Count -Descending | FT Name, Count -AutoSize
   }
```

You can see here that first, we use the `Get-MessageTrackingLog` cmdlet to build a report for all of the messages sent in the past 30 days using a send connector named `Internet`. Next, we loop through the recipients and retrieve only the domain name from their email addresses and store the results in the `$domains` array. We then use the `Group-Object` cmdlet (here we are using its `Group` alias) to group identical objects, in this case identical domain names. Finally, we print the result in descending order based on the total number of emails sent to each particular domain. Here's an example of the type of output you might get from the previous code:

```
Machine: TLEX1.testlabs.se                                    —   □   ✕

[PS] C:\>$domains | Group | Sort Count -Descending | FT Name, Count -Auto

Name             Count
----             -----
gmail.com        2170
hotmail.com      673
jpmorgan.com     309
yahoo.com        231
me.com           157
barclays.com     87


[PS] C:\>_
```

From the preceding output, we can see that, for example, 2170 emails were sent out to Gmail recipients.

See also

- The *Managing connectivity and protocol logs* recipe in this chapter
- The *Working with messages in transport queues* recipe in this chapter
- The *Determining which email client sent an email* recipe in this chapter

Determining which email client sent an email

There might be times where determining which email client (Outlook, OWA, or ActiveSync) sent a particular email is important. In this recipe, we will see how we can do this using Message Tracking Logs.

How to do it...

To check which email client was used to send an email, we check the `SourceContext` property of the email using the following cmdlet:

```
Get-TransportService | Get-MessageTrackingLog `
-ResultSize Unlimited -Start 04/04/2017 `
-Sender dave@contoso.com -Recipients john@contoso.com `
-MessageSubject "Financial Report" -EventID SUBMIT | `
Select SourceContext
```

How it works...

Every email sent has a `SourceContext` property which contains, amongst other information, the `ClientType` used to send the email. The important thing is to check this property for `SUBMIT` events, that is, when the Mailbox Transport Submission service successfully transmits the email to the Transport service.

For `SUBMIT` events, the `SourceContext` property contains the following details:

- MDB: The mailbox database GUID;
- Mailbox: The mailbox GUID;
- Event: The event sequence number;
- MessageClass: The type of message. for example, `IPM.Note`;

- CreationTime: Date and time of the message submission;
- ClientType: For example, OWA or ActiveSync.

The following is an example of the content of the SourceContext field:

```
Machine: TLEX1.testlabs.se                              —    □    ×

SourceContext : MDB:02176f42-32bd-4e99-b5fc-bfe79ccf12ce,
                Mailbox:7a126ca0-9acc-49a5-8119-ab4e8087b70b, Event:7025,
                MessageClass:IPM.Note,
                CreationTime:2017-04-04T16:44:40.067Z, ClientType:MOMT, Su
                bmissionAssistant:MailboxTransportSubmissionEmailAssistant


[PS] C:\>_
```

In this case, **MAPI on the Middle Tier** (**MOMT**), basically clients that connect using Outlook or any other application that connects using RPC/HTTP or MAPI/HTTP.

 Please note that this only applies to emails sent by internal users. There is no SUBMIT event when an external sender sends an email to an internal user, meaning there is no ClientType property for these emails. In these cases, the only information we have regarding the sender is what the email headers contain, which does not include information regarding the email client.

There's more...

To count the total number of emails sent using OWA within the past 24 hours, we can use the following cmdlet:

```
(Get-TransportService | Get-MessageTrackingLog `
-ResultSize Unlimited -Start (Get-Date).AddHours(-24) `
-EventID SUBMIT | `
? {$_.SourceContext -match "OWA"}).Count
```

See also

- *Search Message Tracking Logs* recipe in this chapter

Working with messages in transport queues

Transport queues are a temporary storage location for messages that are in transit. Each mailbox server can have multiple queues at any given time, depending on the destination of the message. In this recipe, we'll cover several methods that can be used to view queued messages, remove messages from queues, and more.

How to do it...

To view the transport queues that are currently in use on a specific server, use the Get-Queue cmdlet:

```
Get-Queue -Server tlex1
```

In this example, the transport queues on the tlex1 server will be returned. The output might look similar to the following screenshot:

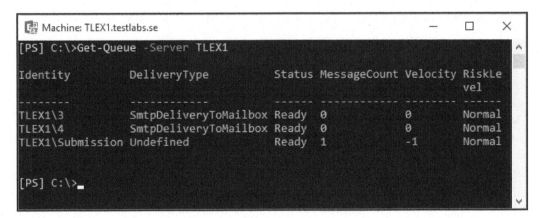

In this example, there is one message awaiting to be delivered.

How it works...

When running the Get-Queue cmdlet, the queues displayed will vary depending on what types of messages are currently awaiting delivery. The following queue types are used on the Mailbox servers:

- **Submission queue**: All messages received by a Mailbox server are first processed in the submission queue. After categorization, each message is moved to either a delivery queue or the retry queue. The queue identity will be listed as <ServerName>\Submission, for example, tlex1\Submission.

- **SMTP delivery to Mailbox queue**: All messages destined for direct delivery to a Mailbox server using SMTP will go through this queue. The queue identity will be listed as <ServerName>\Unique Number, for example, tlex1\15.

- **Remote delivery queue**: All messages being routed to another server through SMTP will go through this queue. The queue identity will be listed as <ServerName>\Unique Number, for example, tlex1\6.

- **Poison message queue**: Messages that are determined to be potentially harmful will be placed in this queue. The queue identity will be listed as <ServerName>\Poison, for example, tlex1\Poison.

- **Unreachable queue**: Messages that cannot be routed to their destination server will be placed in this queue. The queue identity will be defined as <ServerName>\Unreachable, for example, tlex1\Unreachable.

In addition to viewing the queues on a single server, you can use the following command to view the queues on all servers in the organization:

```
Get-TransportService | Get-Queue
```

If you work with busy servers, you may want to take advantage of the filtering capabilities of the Get-Queue cmdlet. For example, to filter by delivery type, you can use the following command:

```
Get-TransportService |
Get-Queue -Filter {DeliveryType -eq ' SmtpDeliveryToMailbox'}
```

This example filters the results based on the DeliveryType parameter. The following values can be used with this filter:

- DeliveryAgent
- DNSConnectorDelivery
- NonSMTPGatewayDelivery
- SmartHostConnectorDelivery

- SmtpDeliveryToMailbox
- SmtpRelayToConnectorSourceServers
- SmtpRelayToDag
- SmtpRelayToMailboxDeliveryGroup
- SmtpRelayToRemoteActiveDirectorySite
- SmtpRelayToServers
- SmtpRelayWithinAdSitetoEdge
- Heartbeat
- ShadowRedundancy
- Undefined
- Unreachable

The Get-Queue cmdlet also supports several other properties that can be used to construct a filter:

- Identity: This specifies the queue identity in the format of server\destination, where destination is a remote domain, server, or queue name
- LastError: This is used to search by the last error message recorded for a queue
- LastRetryTime: This specifies the time when a connection was last tried for a queue
- MessageCount: This allows you to search by the total number of items in a queue
- NextHopConnector: This specifies the identity of the connector used to create a queue
- NextHopDomain: The next hop, such as an SMTP domain, server name, AD site, or mailbox database
- NextRetryTime: This is used to search by when a connection will next be tried by a queue
- Status: This shows the status of a queue, such as Active, Ready, Retry, or Suspended

For example, if you want to view queues that have a total message count of more than a certain number of messages, use the MessageCount property with the greater than (-gt) operator:

```
Get-Queue -Server tlex1 -Filter {MessageCount -gt 25}
```

Another useful method of finding backed up queues is to use the `Status` filter:

```
Get-Queue -Server tlex1 -Filter {Status -eq 'Retry'}
```

This example searches the queues on the `tlex1` server for queues that have messages with a status of `Retry`. Notice that this time, we've used the equals (`-eq`) comparison operator in the filter to specify the status type.

 To learn all about the available comparison operators supported by PowerShell, run the `Get-Helpabout_comparison_operators` command.

There's more...

To view messages that are queued for delivery, you can use the `Get-Message` cmdlet. If you want to view all of the messages that are sitting in queues with a status of `Retry`, use the following command:

```
Get-TransportService | `
Get-Queue -Filter {Status -eq 'Retry'} | `
Get-Message
```

The `Get-Message` cmdlet also provides a `-Filter` parameter that can be used to find messages that match some specific criteria:

```
Get-TransportService | Get-Message `
-Filter {FromAddress -like '*contoso.com'}
```

The previous command returns all queued messages from every server in the organization where the sender domain is `contoso.com`.

If you know which server the message is queued on, and you just want to view the properties of the message, you can use the following syntax:

```
Get-Message -Server tlex1 -Filter {Subject -eq 'test'} | FL
```

This example filters the `Subject` parameter of queued messages on the `tlex1` server. If you want to view all the messages queued on a server, you can simply remove the `-Filter` parameter and value.

To prevent the delivery of a message in a queue, you can use the Suspend-Message cmdlet:

```
Get-Message -Server tlex1 -Filter {Subject -eq 'test'} | `
Suspend-Message -Confirm:$False
```

To suspend all messages in a particular queue, use the following command:

```
Get-Message -Queue tlex1\7 | `
Suspend-Message -Confirm:$False
```

Keep in mind that messages in the submission or poison message queue cannot be suspended. When the time comes to allow delivery, you can use the Resume-Message cmdlet:

```
Get-Message -Server tlex1 -Filter {Subject -eq 'test'} | `
Resume-Message
```

Or, we can resume all the messages in a particular queue using the following command:

```
Get-Message -Queue tlex1\7 | Resume-Message
```

When you need to force a retry for a queue, you can use the Retry-Queue cmdlet:

```
Get-Queue tlex1\7 | Retry-Queue
```

Or simply:

```
Retry-Queue tlex1\7
```

The Retry-Queue cmdlet can also be used to resubmit messages to the submission queue, which will allow the categorizer to reprocess the messages. You can resubmit messages with a status of Retry in the mailbox or remote delivery queues, or messages that are stored in the unreachable or poison message queues.

For example, to resubmit all the messages in queues with a Retry status on all servers in the organization, use the following command:

```
Get-TransportService | `
Get-Queue -Filter {Status -eq 'Retry'} | `
Retry-Queue -Resubmit $True
```

Or, to resubmit messages in the unreachable queue on a specific server, use the following command:

```
Retry-Queue tlex1\Unreachable -Resubmit $True
```

 Messages with a suspended status cannot be resubmitted using the Retry-Queue cmdlet.

You can purge messages from transport queues using the Remove-Message cmdlet:

```
Get-TransportService | Get-Queue `
-Filter {DeliveryType -eq 'DnsConnectorDelivery'} | `
Get-Message | Remove-Message -Confirm:$False
```

The preceding command retrieves queued messages on all servers with a specified delivery type and removes them without confirmation. An NDR will be generated and sent to the originator of the message advising them that they'll need to resend the message.

The Remove-Message cmdlet provides multiple parameters that can be used to either identify the message based on the message identity, or using a filter with the -Filter parameter when you only want to remove a single message:

```
Remove-Message -Identity tlex01\10\67095979098886 `
-WithNDR $False -Confirm:$False
```

The previous command removes a single message based on its MessageIdentity value. Notice that this time, we've set the -WithNDR parameter to $False, and the sender will not be notified that the message will not be delivered.

See also

- The *Configure the Edge Transport server role* recipe in this chapter
- The *Implementing a header firewall* recipe in this chapter

Searching anti-spam agent logs

Exchange 2016 Mailbox servers are capable of using several anti-spam agents to reduce the amount of unwanted email messages that enter your organization. All anti-spam activity is logged by Mailbox servers, and this data can be used to troubleshoot issues and generate reports. In this recipe, you'll learn how to search the anti-spam agent logs using the Exchange Management Shell. Notice that these anti-spam agents are not installed by default.

How to do it...

The Get-AgentLog cmdlet can be used to parse the anti-spam agent logs. To find all the log entries for a particular agent, filter the output based on the Agent property:

```
Get-AgentLog | ? {$_.Agent -eq 'Content Filter Agent'}
```

When running this command in a busy environment, you may get back a large number of results, so you may want to consider refining your filter and perhaps limiting the date range to a specific period of time.

How it works...

All of the anti-spam agents use a series of log files on each Mailbox server with the anti-spam agents installed. By default, Mailbox servers do not have the anti-spam agents installed, but you can install them manually using the following commands:

```
cd $exscripts
.\Install-AntiSpamAgents.ps1
Restart-Service MSExchangeTransport
```

After performing the preceding commands, the agents will be installed, and the Transport service needs to be restarted.

By default, the agent log file directory is set to a maximum size of 250 MB. Each individual log file is limited to 10 MB in size and will be kept for a maximum of 7 days, or until the directory reaches its maximum size. These values can be adjusted using the Set-TransportService cmdlet along with the AgentLogMaxAge, AgentLogMaxDirectorySize, and AgentLogMaxFileSize parameters.

The following anti-spam filters are available on Mailbox servers:

- **Content filtering**: This agent uses the Microsoft SmartScreen technology to process the contents of each message and determine whether or not the content of the message is appropriate.
- **Sender ID**: This agent determines the action to be taken based on whether or not the sender of a message is transmitting the message from a mail server associated with the sender's domain. This is used to combat domain spoofing.
- **Sender filtering**: This agent allows you to configure one or more blocked senders and the action that should be taken if a message is received from a specific address.
- **Protocol analysis**: This agent is the underlying agent for sender reputation functionality.

Although **Recipient Filter** is also available on Mailbox servers, it should not be configured. This is because it will reject an entire message when it detects one invalid or blocked recipient in a message with several other valid recipients. When anti-spam agents are installed, **Recipient Filter** is enabled, but it is not configured to reject or block any recipients.

 Please note that from November 2016, Microsoft stopped generating updates for the SmartScreen spam filters in Exchange 2007 to 2016, as well as Outlook 2007 to 2016, and Outlook 2011 for Mac. Microsoft has also stated that the SmartScreen spam filter will be removed from future versions of Exchange and Outlook.

In turn, the following anti-spam filters are available on Edge Transport servers:

- **Connection filtering:** This agent uses an IP block and allow lists, and list providers to determine whether a connection should be blocked or allowed.
- **Recipient filtering**: This agent determines the action to be taken based on the recipients of an email message.
- **Attachment filtering:** This agent blocks messages or attachments based on the attachment file name, extension, or MIME content type.

When viewing agent log entries in the Shell, several properties are available that can be used to determine the status of the message, as shown in the following screenshot:

```
Machine: TLEX1.testlabs.se                                    —    □    ×

[PS] C:\>Get-AgentLog | ? {$_.Agent -eq 'Sender Filter Agent'}


RunspaceId         : 71b361bb-64ca-4892-88be-1597da8d3315
Timestamp          : 04/04/2017 18:46:38
SessionId          : 08D47B825645C668
IPAddress          : 192.168.1.2
MessageId          :
P1FromAddress      : spammer@nunomota.pt
P2FromAddresses    : {}
Recipients         : {}
Agent              : Sender Filter Agent
Event              : OnMailCommand
Action             : RejectCommand
SmtpResponse       : 554 5.7.105 SenderFilterAgent; Sender denied as
                     sender's email address is on SenderFilterConfig list
Reason             : ExactMatch
ReasonData         : spammer@nunomota.pt
Diagnostics        :
NetworkMsgID       : 00000000-0000-0000-0000-000000000000
TenantID           : 00000000-0000-0000-0000-000000000000
Directionality     : Undefined



[PS] C:\>_
```

In this example, you can see that the message was blocked because the `P1FromAddress` property was configured as a blocked sender on `Sender Filtering Agent` with the action set to `RejectCommand`.

There's more...

When you run the `Get-AgentLog` cmdlet, every entry in the log file will be returned. In an environment that receives a lot of emails, this can be a little overwhelming and slow. To narrow your searches, you can specify a time frame using the `-StartDate` and `-EndDate` parameters:

```
Get-AgentLog -StartDate (Get-Date).AddDays(-7) -EndDate (Get-Date)
```

The previous command retrieves the agent logs for the past 7 days. In this example, the start and end dates are specified using the `Get-Date` cmdlet, but if needed, you can manually type the date and time for the search, as shown in the following command:

```
Get-AgentLog -StartDate "1/4/2015 9:00 AM" `
-EndDate "1/9/2015 11:00 PM"
```

You can also create searches based on the agent, as shown in the first example of this recipe. You can combine this technique with a time frame as well to refine your searches, as shown in the following command:

```
Get-AgentLog -StartDate (Get-Date).AddDays(-7) `
-EndDate (Get-Date) | `
? {$_.Agent -eq 'Sender Filter Agent'}
```

This command pulls the agent logs from the past 7 days. The output is piped to the `Where-Object` cmdlet (using the `?` alias) to filter based on the `Agent` property of the log entry. In this example, only the logs for `Sender Filter Agent` are retrieved.

The agent logs provide properties that identify both the sender and recipient addresses for the message. To search based on the sender, use the following command:

```
Get-AgentLog | `
? {$_.P1FromAddress -or $_.P2FromAddress -eq `'sales@litwareinc.com'}
```

This command checks both the `P1FromAddress` and `P2FromAddress` properties, and only returns the log entries where the sender address is `sales@litwareinc.com`.

You can use a similar filter using the `-Like` comparison operator and a wildcard to find all the messages in the log from a particular sending domain:

```
Get-AgentLog | `
? {$_.P1FromAddress -or $_.P2FromAddress -like '*@litwareinc.com'}
```

To retrieve the logs for specific recipients, filter on the `Recipients` property:

```
Get-AgentLog | ? {$_.Recipients -eq 'dsmith@contoso.com}
```

You can export the agent logs to a CSV file that can be used in another application, such as Excel. To do this, pipe the desired logs to the `Export-CSV` cmdlet:

```
Get-AgentLog -StartDate (Get-Date).AddDays(-3) | `
? {$_.Agent -eq 'Content Filter Agent' -and $_.ReasonData -ge 4} | `
Export-CSV C:\contentfilter.csv -NoType
```

In this example, agent logs from the past 3 days processed by the `Content Filter Agent` and with an SCL rating of 4 or higher are exported to a CSV file.

You can use the `-Location` parameter to search agent log files that are located in an alternate directory. This may be useful when you have specific retention requirements and still need to report on old data that is no longer on your production servers. When using this parameter, specify the full path to the directory containing the log files:

```
Get-AgentLog -Location E:\logs
```

Keep in mind that this parameter requires a local path, so a UNC path to a shared network folder will not work.

See also

- The *Exporting reports to text and CSV files* recipe from `Chapter 2`, *Exchange Management Shell Common Tasks*

Implementing a header firewall

When messages are passed from one server to another through SMTP, Exchange Edge, and Mailbox servers, add custom `X-Header` fields are added to the message header. These headers can contain a variety of information, such as mail server IP addresses, **spam confidence levels** (SCL), content filtering results, and rule processing statuses. Header firewalls are used to remove these custom `X-Header` fields so that unauthorized sources cannot obtain detailed information about your messaging environment. In this recipe, you'll learn how to use the Exchange Management Shell to implement a header firewall that prevents the disclosure of internal information sent to an external source.

How to do it...

One of the most common uses of a header firewall is to remove the internal server infrastructure details from SMTP email message headers destined for an external recipient. To do this, on an Edge Transport server, you need to modify the permissions for the internet send connector using the `Remove-ADPermission` cmdlet:

```
Remove-ADPermission "EdgeSync - Litware to Internet" `
-User "MS Exchange\Edge Transport Servers" `
-ExtendedRights Ms-Exch-Send-Headers-Routing `
```

```
-Confirm:$False
```

In this example, the Edge server's Internet send connector, named `EdgeSync - Litware to Internet`, is modified. The `Ms-Exch-Accept-Headers-Routing` permission is removed from the internet send connector for the `MS Exchange\Edge Transport Servers` account.

How it works...

By default, all connectors are configured to include routing headers in SMTP email messages. This can be a security concern for many organizations, as it exposes Exchange server names and versions in the message header. In addition, for Mailbox servers that are configured to send messages directly to the internet, the internal IP addresses of the servers that handle the messages are included in the headers.

When viewing the headers of a message received from the `contoso.com` mail server, the following information is available:

```
Received: from tlex1.contoso.com ([x.x.x.x]) by tlex01.c
([10.100.100.20]) with mapi id 15.1.845.32; Wed, 8 Apr
```

Here, we can see the internal IP address of the Contoso mail server at `10.100.100.20` and the version number is `15.1.845.32`, which tells us that the server is running Exchange 2016 CU5. When implementing a header firewall for routing headers, this information will not be sent to external recipients.

There's more...

If you do not use an Edge Transport server to send internet emails, and instead send messages to the internet directly from the Mailbox server, then you'll need to specify a different user when running the `Remove-ADPermission` cmdlet:

```
Remove-ADPermission Internet `
-User "NT Authority\Anonymous Logon" `
-ExtendedRights Ms-Exch-Send-Headers-Routing `
-Confirm:$False
```

Again, you'll need to specify the name of the send connector that is used to send outbound internet emails. When dealing with Mailbox servers, you can remove the permission for the `NT Authority\Anonymous Logon` account, since the `MS Exchange\Edge Transport Servers` user is specific only to Edge Transport servers.

See also

- The *Configuring the Edge Transport server role recipe* in this chapter
- The *Working with messages in transport queues recipe* in this chapter

Configuring the Edge Transport server role

The Exchange Edge Transport role is responsible for handling mail flow from and to your organization and can be used to secure and filter messages sent to and received from the internet. In addition to routing messages, you can apply rules, configure settings, and enforce limits on messages as they pass through the servers in your environment. Transport agents can be used to provide basic anti-spam protection, and both the roles implement detailed logging capabilities that can be leveraged from the Shell.

The Edge Transport role was reintroduced in Exchange 2013 Service Pack 1 (CU4) and remains part of Exchange 2016's architecture. In this recipe, we will take a look at how to install the Edge Transport role and how to configure the Edge subscription.

 Please note that, at the time of writing this book, Exchange 2016 Edge is not supported on Windows Server 2016. This is due to a conflict with the SmartScreen Filters shipped for Windows, Microsoft Edge and Internet Explorer browsers. Hopefully this is resolved in the future.

The Edge subscription is the procedure for exporting information from the Edge Transport server(s) and importing it into the Mailbox server(s). This is to allow them to use the EdgeSync service.

EdgeSync is a scheduled synchronization task. For example, it synchronizes the available email addresses from Active Directory into the ADLDS directory instance of the Edge server(s). The replication of data is performed in only one direction, from Mailbox to Edge. The information that's being synchronized is used in order to allow the Edge servers to filter and secure emails based on, for example, recipient filtering, which means it drops emails that are being sent to non-existing mailboxes.

 It is fully supported to use Exchange 2010 SP3 RU11 (and above) or 2013 CU10 (and above) Edge Transport servers together with Exchange 2016. In the future, this may change.

How to do it...

1. To be able to install the Edge Transport role on Windows 2012 Server and Windows 2012 R2 Server, there is a technical prerequisite, which is to install the Windows feature called **Active Directory Lightweight Directory Services (AD LDS)** by running the following PowerShell cmdlet:

```
Install-WindowsFeature ADLDS
```

2. After the operating system roles and features have been installed, it is time to install .NET Framework 4.6.2. This is recommended for any Exchange 2016 version, but a hard requirement starting from CU5.

3. Another thing to consider and solve prior to starting the installation is to make sure that the Exchange 2016 Mailbox servers can resolve the names of the Edge servers and vice versa. Since the Edge servers are placed in DMZ, they are not joined to the domain, and most customers don't have any DNS servers in DMZ for doing name lookups to internal resources. If this is the case, you can easily go ahead and use the hosts file by just adding each Mailbox server with its corresponding IP address.

   > The DNS suffix should be added to the Edge servers for the internal domain; so, for example, if contoso.com is the internal domain name, then add contoso.com as the DNS suffix to the Edge servers.

4. Last but not least, verify that traffic is allowed between Mailbox servers and the Edge servers. It's using TCP/25 (SMTP), and TCP/50636 (Secure LDAP).

5. Also make sure that the traffic for sending and receiving emails is allowed from external (internet) to the Edge servers, and also that the Edge servers are allowed to send emails externally.

6. Once the prerequisites have been installed, proceed with installing the Edge Transport role on the server; this is done by using the following command:

```
Setup.exe /mode:Install /role:EdgeTransport `
/IAcceptExchangeServerLicenseTerms
```

7. After the installation is completed successfully, it's time to create the Edge subscription. This is first done from the Edge server, by creating the following XML file:

```
New-EdgeSubscription -FileName C:\Edge.xml
```

8. Once the subscription file is generated, copy it to the Mailbox servers, and run the following cmdlet to complete the subscription:

```
New-EdgeSubscription -FileData ([byte[]]$(Get-Content `
-Path "C:\temp\Edge.xml" -Encoding Byte -ReadCount 0)) -Site `
"Default-First-Site-Name"
```

9. When the subscription is configured, two send connectors are created: `EdgeSync – Default-First-Site-Name to Internet` and `EdgeSync – Inbound to Default-First-Site-Name`. If you had any send connectors for sending emails to external recipients created prior to configuring Edge subscription, make sure to remove these to only allow the Edge servers to send emails to external recipients. Verify your send connectors by running the following cmdlet:

```
Get-SendConnector | FT -AutoSize
```

The output will look similar to the following screenshot:

```
Machine: TLEX1.testlabs.se                                        —    □    ×
[PS] C:\>Get-SendConnector

Identity                                        AddressSpaces Enabled
--------                                        ------------- -------
EdgeSync - Default-First-Site-Name to Internet {smtp:*;100}  True
EdgeSync - Inbound to Default-First-Site-Name  {smtp:--;100} True


[PS] C:\>
```

 The `--` value in `AddressSpaces` represents all of Exchange's authoritative and internal relay accepted domains. Any emails the Edge server receives for these domains are routed to this send connector and relayed to the configured smart hosts.

How it works...

Most of the preceding information is described during the steps; some information can be added.

When creating the initial Edge subscription, the `Site` parameter is used for specifying the site where the Mailbox server is placed. In the preceding example, I've used the default value called `Default-First-Site-Name`, which is the initially created Active Directory site.

If you have multiple Edge servers, which is recommended for high availability, you do have to create multiple Edge subscriptions, one per Edge server.

When a new Mailbox server is added to the messaging environment, it needs to be added to the subscription by running the same procedure for it.

There's more...

Once you have created the subscription and you want to see whether everything works as expected, you can run the following cmdlets:

```
Start-EdgeSynchronization
Test-EdgeSynchronization
```

The first cmdlet will start the synchronization of the recipient information and the result will be shown once it's completed.

Running the second cmdlet will show `SyncStatus`, which should be stated as `Normal`. It will also show you at what time the synchronization was last run and when it's scheduled to run the next time.

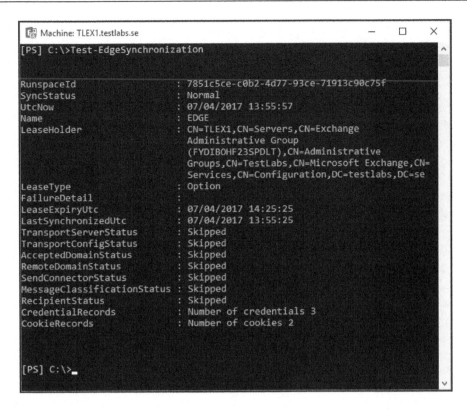

If you, for any reason, want to force a full synchronization, once the synchronization is set up and running, you can use the following cmdlet:

```
Start-EdgeSynchronization -ForceFullSync
```

A Telnet client and network monitor of your choice are both great tools when the Edge role is being implemented and also during troubleshooting.

See also

- The *Implementing a header firewall recipe* in this chapter
- The *Working with messages in transport queues recipe* in this chapter

9
Exchange Security

In this chapter, we will cover the following topics:

- Granting users full access permissions to mailboxes
- Finding users with full access to mailboxes
- Sending email messages as another user or group
- Throttling client connections
- Working with Role Based Access Control
- Creating a custom RBAC role for administrators
- Creating a custom RBAC role for end users
- Troubleshooting RBAC
- Generating a certificate request
- Installing certificates and enabling services
- Importing certificates on multiple Exchange servers
- Configuring Domain Security
- Configuring S/MIME for OWA
- Configuring Windows Defender Exclusions

Introduction

When it comes to managing security in Exchange 2016, you have several options depending on the resources that you're dealing with. For example, you can allow multiple users to open a mailbox by assigning them full access permissions to a mailbox object, but granting administrators the ability to create recipient objects needs to be done through **Role Based Access Control (RBAC)**. Obviously, since the security for both components is handled differently, we have unrelated sets of cmdlets that need to be used to get the job done, and managing each of them through the Shell requires a different approach.

In this chapter, we'll take a look at several solutions implemented through the Exchange Management Shell that address each of the components described previously, as well as some additional techniques that can be used to improve your efficiency when dealing with Exchange security.

Performing some basic steps

To work with the code samples in this chapter, follow these steps to launch the Exchange Management Shell:

1. Log on to a workstation or server with the Exchange Management tools installed.
2. You can connect using a remote PowerShell. If you, for some reason, don't have the Exchange Management tools installed, use the following command:

```
$Session = New-PSSession -ConfigurationName '
Microsoft.Exchange -ConnectionUri '
http://servername/PowerShell/ -Authentication Kerberos
Import-PSSession $Session
```

3. Alternatively, open the Exchange Management Shell by navigating to **Start** | **All Apps** | Microsoft **Exchange Server 2016**.
4. Click on the **Exchange Management Shell** shortcut.

5. To launch a standard PowerShell console, open a standard PowerShell console by navigating to **Start** | **All Apps**, and click on the **Windows PowerShell** shortcut.

Unless specified otherwise in the *Getting ready* section, all of the recipes in this chapter will require the use of the Exchange Management Shell.

 Remember to start the Exchange Management Shell using **Run as Administrator** to avoid permission problems. In this chapter, you might notice that, in the examples of cmdlets, I have used the back tick (') character to break up long commands into multiple lines. The purpose of this is to make it easier to read. The back ticks are not required and should only be used if needed.

Granting users full access permissions to mailboxes

One of the most common administrative tasks that Exchange administrators perform is to manage access rights to mailboxes. For example, you may have several users that share access to an individual mailbox, or you may have administrators and help desk staff that need to be able to open end users' mailboxes when troubleshooting a problem or providing technical support. In this recipe, you'll learn how to assign the permissions required to perform these tasks through the Exchange Management Shell.

How to do it...

To assign full access rights for an individual user to a specific mailbox, use the Add-MailboxPermission cmdlet:

```
Add-MailboxPermission dsmith '
-User hlawson '
-AccessRights FullAccess '
-InheritanceType All
```

After running this command, the user hlawson will be able to open the mailbox that belongs to dsmith and read or modify the data within the mailbox.

How it works...

When you assign full access rights to a mailbox, you may notice that the change does not take effect immediately, and the user that has been granted permissions to a mailbox still cannot access that resource. This is because the Information Store service uses a cached mailbox configuration that, by default, is refreshed every two hours. You can force the cache to refresh by restarting the Information Store service on the mailbox server that is hosting the active database where the mailbox resides. Obviously, this is not something that should be done during business hours on production servers, as it will disrupt mailbox access for end users.

Since we can grant permissions to a mailbox using the `Add-MailboxPermission` cmdlet, you would be correct in assuming that this change can also be reversed if needed. To remove the permissions assigned in the previous example, use the `Remove-MailboxPermission` cmdlet:

```
Remove-MailboxPermission dsmith '
-User hlawson '
-AccessRights FullAccess '
-Confirm:$False
```

In addition to assigning full access permissions to individual users, you can also assign this right to a group:

```
Add-MailboxPermission dsmith '
-User "IT Help Desk" '
-AccessRights FullAccess
```

In this example, the `ITHelpDesk` is a mail-enabled universal security group, and it has been granted full access to the `dsmith` mailbox. All users who are members of this group will be able to open the mailbox and access its contents through Outlook or OWA.

Of course, you may need to do this for multiple users, and doing so one mailbox at a time is not very efficient. To make this easier, we can make use of the pipeline. For example, let's say that you want to grant full access rights to all the mailboxes in the organization:

```
Get-Mailbox -ResultSize Unlimited -RecipientTypeDetails UserMailbox | '
Add-MailboxPermission -User "IT Help Desk" '
-InheritanceType All
-AccessRights FullAccess
-AutoMapping $False
```

The given command retrieves all the user mailboxes in the organization, and sends them down the pipeline to the `Add-MailboxPermission` cmdlet, where full access rights are assigned to the `IT Help Desk` group. When a user is granted `Full Access` permissions to a shared mailbox or to another user's mailbox, Outlook automatically loads all mailboxes to which the user has full access to by using Autodiscover. When granting a user access to multiple mailboxes, this might not be desired so, in this example, we used the `AutoMapping` parameter to ensure the mailboxes are not automatically added to the users' Outlook profile.

There's more...

If you need to assign access permissions to all the mailboxes in your organization, you probably should consider doing this at the database level, rather than on an individual mailbox basis. In the previous example, we used a pipeline operation to apply the permissions to all mailboxes with a command. The limitation with this is that the command only sets the permissions on existing mailboxes; any new mailbox created afterwards will not inherit these permissions. You can solve this problem by assigning the `Generic-All` extended right to a user or group on a particular database.

For example, if all of our mailboxes are located in the `DB01` database, we can allow user access to every mailbox in the database using the following command:

```
Add-ADPermission DB01 '
-User svcBackup '
-AccessRights GenericAll
```

After running this command, the backup service account will be able to log on to every mailbox in the `DB01` database, as well as any mailboxes created in that database in the future.

Of course, you'll likely have more than one database in your organization. If you want to apply this setting to every mailbox database in the organization, pipe the output from the `Get-MailboxDatabase` cmdlet to the `Add-ADPermission` cmdlet using the appropriate parameters:

```
Get-MailboxDatabase | '
Add-ADPermission -User svcBackup '
-AccessRights GenericAll
```

Once this command has been run, the service account will be able to connect to any mailbox in the Exchange organization.

See also

- The *Sending email messages as another user or group* recipe in this chapter

Finding users with full access to mailboxes

One of the issues with assigning full mailbox access to users and support personnel is that things change over time. People change roles, move to other departments, or even leave the organization. Keeping track of all of this and removing full access permissions when required can be challenging in a fast-paced environment. This recipe will allow you to solve these issues using the Exchange Management Shell to find out exactly who has full access permissions to the mailboxes in your environment.

How to do it...

To find all users or groups who have been assigned full access rights to a mailbox, use the Get-MailboxPermission cmdlet:

```
Get-MailboxPermission admin | `
Where-Object {$_.AccessRights -match "FullAccess"}
```

You can see here that we are limiting the results using a filter by piping the output to the Where-Object cmdlet. Only the users with the FullAccess access rights will be returned.

How it works...

The previous command is useful for quickly viewing the permissions for a single mailbox while working interactively in the Shell. The first problem with this approach is that it also returns a lot of information that we're probably not interested in. Consider the truncated output from our previous command:

```
Machine: TLEX1.testlabs.se                              —    □    ×

[PS] C:\>Get-MailboxPermission admin | Where-Object {$_.AccessRights -match
 "FullAccess"}

Identity            User                   AccessRights     IsInherited Deny
--------            ----                   ------------     ----------- ----
testlabs.se/Users... NT AUTHORITY\SELF     {FullAccess...   False       False
testlabs.se/Users... TESTLABS\it.servi...  {FullAccess}     False       False
testlabs.se/Users... TESTLABS\Domain A...  {FullAccess}     True        True
testlabs.se/Users... TESTLABS\Enterpri...  {FullAccess}     True        True
testlabs.se/Users... TESTLABS\admin        {FullAccess}     True        True
testlabs.se/Users... TESTLABS\Organiza...  {FullAccess}     True        True
testlabs.se/Users... NT AUTHORITY\SYSTEM   {FullAccess}     True        False
testlabs.se/Users... TESTLABS\Domain A...  {FullAccess...   True        False
testlabs.se/Users... TESTLABS\Enterpri...  {FullAccess...   True        False
testlabs.se/Users... TESTLABS\admin        {FullAccess...   True        False
testlabs.se/Users... TESTLABS\Organiza...  {FullAccess...   True        False
testlabs.se/Users... TESTLABS\Exchange...  {FullAccess...   True        False
testlabs.se/Users... TESTLABS\Exchange...  {FullAccess...   True        False
testlabs.se/Users... TESTLABS\auditor      {FullAccess...   True        False


[PS] C:\>_
```

Notice that both IT ServiceDesk and auditor users have full access permissions to the administrator mailbox. This is useful because we know that someone assigned these permissions to the mailbox, as this is not something Exchange is going to do on its own. What is not so useful is that we also see all the built-in full access permissions that apply to every mailbox, such as the NT AUTHORITY\SELF user and other default permissions. To filter out this information, we can use a more complex filter:

```
Get-MailboxPermission admin |
Where-Object {
  ($_.AccessRights -match "FullAccess") '
  -and ($_.User -notmatch "SELF") '
  -and ($_.IsInherited -eq $False)
} | FT User, AccessRights, Inherited -AutoSize
```

You can see that we're still filtering based on the `AccessRights` property, but now we're excluding the `SELF` account and any other accounts that receive their permissions through inheritance. The output now gives us something that's easier to work with when reviewing a report:

```
Machine: TLEX1.testlabs.se                                    —    □    ✕

[PS] C:\>Get-MailboxPermission admin | Where-Object {($_.AccessRights -matc
h "FullAccess") -and ($_.User -notmatch "SELF") -and ($_.IsInherited -eq $F
alse)} | FT User, AccessRights, IsInherited -AutoSize

User                     AccessRights IsInherited
----                     ------------ -----------
TESTLABS\it.servicedesk {FullAccess}        False


[PS] C:\>_
```

This is an easy way to figure out which accounts have been directly assigned full access to a mailbox via the `Add-MailboxPermission` cmdlet. Keep in mind that users who have been assigned these permissions at the database level receive their permissions through inheritance, so you may need to adjust the filter to meet your specific needs. The user `auditor` in the first screenshot is a good example of this.

There's more...

Finding out which users have full access rights to an individual mailbox can be useful for quick troubleshooting, but chances are that you're going to need to figure this out for all the mailboxes in your organization. The following code will generate the output that provides this information:

```
ForEach ($mailbox in Get-Mailbox -ResultSize Unlimited) {
  Get-MailboxPermission $mailbox |
  Where-Object {
    ($_.AccessRights -match "FullAccess") '
    -and ($_.User -notmatch "SELF") '
    -and ($_.IsInherited -eq $False)
  }
}
```

As you can see here, we use a ForEach loop to process all the mailboxes in the organization. Inside the loop, we're using the same filter from the previous example to determine which users have full access rights to each mailbox.

Sending email messages as another user or group

In some environments, it may be required to allow users to send email messages from a mailbox as if the owner of that mailbox had actually sent that message. This can be accomplished by granting Send-As permissions to a user on a particular mailbox. In addition, you can also allow a user to send email messages that are sent using the identity of a distribution group. This recipe explains how you can manage these permissions from the Exchange Management Shell.

How to do it...

To assign Send-As permissions to a mailbox, we use the Add-ADPermission cmdlet:

```
Add-ADPermission "Frank Howe" '
-User "Eric Cook" '
-AccessRights ExtendedRight '
-ExtendedRights "Send As"
```

After running the previous command, Eric Cook can send messages from the mailbox of Frank Howe.

How it works...

Using the Add-ADPermission cmdlet, you start by specifying the object to which you will set permissions on. Unlike many of the Exchange cmdlets, you cannot use the alias of the mailbox. You can use the user's name or display name, as shown previously, as long as they are unique, or you can use the distinguished name of the object. If you do not know a user's full name, you can use the Get-Mailbox cmdlet and pipe the object to the Add-ADPermission cmdlet:

```
Get-Mailbox fhowe | '
Add-ADPermission -User ecook '
-AccessRights ExtendedRight '
-ExtendedRights "Send As"
```

You might find this syntax useful when assigning `Send-As` rights in bulk. For example, to grant a user `Send-As` permission for all users in a particular OU, use the following syntax:

```
Get-Mailbox -OrganizationalUnit contoso.com/Sales | '
Add-ADPermission -User ecook '
-AccessRights ExtendedRight '
-ExtendedRights "Send As"
```

If you ever need to remove these settings, simply use the `Remove-ADPermission` cmdlet. This command will remove the permissions assigned in the first example:

```
Remove-ADPermission "Frank Howe" '
-User ecook '
-ExtendedRights "Send As" '
-Confirm:$False
```

There's more...

To assign `Send-As` permissions to a distribution group, the process is exactly the same as for a mailbox. Use the `Add-ADPermission` cmdlet, as shown in the following command:

```
Add-ADPermission Marketing '
-User ecook '
-AccessRights ExtendedRight '
-ExtendedRights "Send As"
```

You can also provide the identity of the group to the `Add-ADPermission` cmdlet via a pipeline command, just as we saw earlier with the `Get-Mailbox` cmdlet. To do this with a distribution group, use the `Get-DistributionGroup` cmdlet:

```
Get-DistributionGroup -ResultSize Unlimited | '
Add-ADPermission -User ecook '
-AccessRights ExtendedRight '
-ExtendedRights "Send As"
```

In the given example, the user `ecook` is given `Send-As` rights to all distribution groups in the organization.

To list which users have `Send-As` permissions to a particular mailbox, you use the `Get-ADPermission` cmdlet:

```
Get-ADPermission "Jonas" | `
Where-Object { `
  ($_.ExtendedRights -match "Send-As") `
  -and ($_.User -notmatch "SELF") `
```

```
    -and ($_.IsInherited -eq $False)} | `
FT User, ExtendedRights
```

Besides `Send-As` permissions, you can instead assign `Send-On-Behalf` permissions to mailboxes using the `Set-Mailbox` cmdlet with the `GrantSendOnBehalfTo` parameter:

```
Set-Mailbox fhowe -GrantSendOnBehalfTo ecook
```

Using `Send-on-Behalf` will show the recipient that the email was sent from a specific user on behalf of another user.

If you already gave `Send-on-Behalf` permissions to a user and want to also give it to another user on the same mailbox, you can use the `Add` method to ensure the existing permissions are not lost:

```
Set-Mailbox fhowe -GrantSendOnBehalfTo @{add="auditor", "admin"}
```

Throttling client connections

Client Throttling Policies are used to manage client access performance by stipulating, for example, the number of concurrent connections for each client access protocol, the percentage of time that a client session can use to perform certain operations, and so on. There is a default client throttling policy named `GlobalThrottlingPolicy_<GUID>` with a throttling scope of `Global` that is perfectly adequate to manage the load placed on client access services for most environments. However, if this is not the case for your environment, you can modify this default policy or create additional custom policies to meet your requirements.

Client throttling policies are available for **ActiveSync (EAS)**, **Exchange Web Services (EWS)**, **Outlook on the web (OWA)**, and **RPC Client Access (RCA)**, among a few others. At the time of writing this book (Exchange 2016 CU5), there were still no throttling policies specific for MAPI over HTTP.

In this recipe, you will create a new throttling policy that allows for more concurrent OWA and mobile device connections and assign it to a user.

How to do it...

1. Use the following cmdlets to create a new throttling policy and configure it to allow 25 OWA and ActiveSync concurrent connections against an Exchange server at one time per user:

```
New-ThrottlingPolicy -Name "High Connection Mailbox" -OwaMaxConcurrency
25 -EasMaxConcurrency 25
```

2. Next, assign the policy to one or more users using the following cmdlet:

```
Set-ThrottlingPolicyAssociation John -ThrottlingPolicy "High Connection
Mailbox"
```

How it works...

We start by using the New-ThrottlingPolicy cmdlet to create a non-default user throttling policy. Then, we used the OwaMaxConcurrency and EasMaxConcurrency parameters to specify how many concurrent connections an OWA or ActiveSync user can have against an Exchange server at one time.

Each one of these connections is held from the moment a request is received until a response is sent to the requestor. If a user attempts to make more concurrent requests than their throttling policy allows, the new connection fails (but existing connections remain valid). The default value for OwaMaxConcurrency is 5, while EasMaxConcurrency is 10.

> Any parameters that you omit when creating a new policy, inherit the values from the default throttling policy GlobalThrottlingPolicy_<GUID>.

Once the policy is created, we associate it with the mailbox of the user John by using the Set-ThrottlingPolicyAssociation cmdlet. You don't necessarily need to use this cmdlet to associate a user with a policy. The following cmdlet achieves the exact same result:

```
Set-Mailbox John -ThrottlingPolicy "High Connection Mailbox"
```

There's more...

There are many other parameters that can be used to limit resource consumption. For example, you can use the `PowerShellMaxCmdlets` parameter to control the number of cmdlets that can be run within a 2-minute interval:

```
New-ThrottlingPolicy -Name "Limit Max Cmdlets" -PowerShellMaxCmdlets 10
-PowerShellMaxCmdletsTimePeriod 2
```

Another example is the `RecipientRateLimit` parameter that is used to limit the number of recipients a user can address in a 24-hour period.

You can also create a policy that applies to all users in the organization automatically using the following cmdlet:

```
New-ThrottlingPolicy -Name "Limit Recipient Rate" -RecipientRateLimit
1000 -ThrottlingPolicyScope Organization
```

The `ThrottlingPolicyScope` parameter, as the name suggests, specifies the scope of the policy. This can be `Regular`, for custom policies that apply to specific users, or `Organization` for custom policies that apply to all users in the organization. The scope of `Global` is reserved for the default throttling policy.

See also

- The *Transport Throttling Policies* recipe from Chapter 8, *Managing Transport Servers*

Working with Role Based Access Control

The security model that was introduced in Exchange 2010 is still present in Exchange 2016. With the introduction of the RBAC permissions model, you can essentially control which cmdlets administrators and end users are allowed to run. This recipe will show you how to work with RBAC permissions in Exchange 2016.

How to do it...

Let's say that you need to allow a member of your staff to manage the settings of the Exchange servers in your organization. This administrator only needs to manage server settings and should not be allowed to perform any other tasks, such as recipient management.

Exchange 2016 provides a large set of predefined permissions that can be used to address common tasks such as this one. In this case, we can use the Server Management role group that allows administrators to manage servers in the organization.

All we need to do to assign the permission is to add the required user account to this role group:

```
Add-RoleGroupMember "Server Management" -Member bwelch
```

At this point, the user can use the Exchange Admin Center or the Exchange Management Shell to perform server-related management tasks.

How it works...

Exchange 2016 implements RBAC by grouping sets of cmdlets used to perform specific tasks in management roles. Think of a management role simply as a list of cmdlets. For example, one of the roles assigned via the Server Management role group is called Exchange Servers. This role allows an assigned user the ability to use over 30 separate cmdlets that are specifically related to managing servers, such as Get-ExchangeServer, Set-ExchangeServer, and more.

There are a number of built-in role groups that you can use to delegate typical management tasks to administrators in your environment. You can view all the built-in role groups using the Get-RoleGroup cmdlet.

Role groups can assign many different management roles to a user. In the previous example, we were working with the Server Management role group, which assigns a number of different management roles to any user that is added to this group. To view a list of these roles, we can use the Get-ManagementRoleAssignment cmdlet:

```
Get-ManagementRoleAssignment -RoleAssignee 'Server Management' |
Select Role
```

The output of this command is shown in the following screenshot:

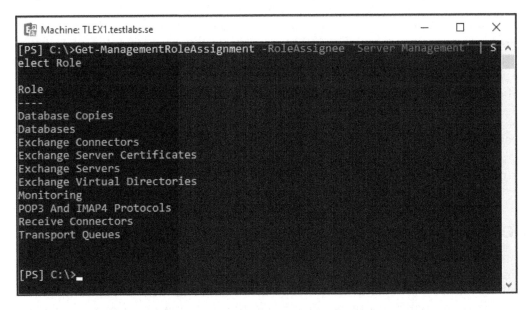

As you can see, each management role assigned through this role group is returned. To determine which cmdlets are made available by each of these roles, we can run the Get-ManagementRoleEntry cmdlet against each of them individually. An example of this can be seen in the following screenshot:

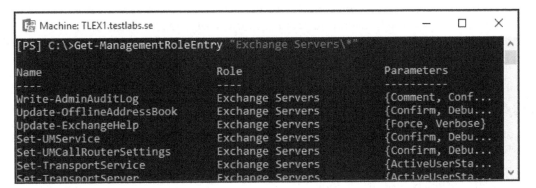

Management role entries are listed in the format of `<Role Name>\<Cmdlet Name>`. The `Get-ManagementRoleEntry` cmdlet can be used with wildcards, as shown in the previous command. The output of the `Get-ManagementRoleEntry` command in the previous example is truncated for readability, but as you can see, there are several cmdlets that are part of the `Exchange Servers` management role, which can be assigned via the `Server Management` role group. If only this role is assigned to a user, they are given access to these specific cmdlets and will not see other cmdlets, such as `New-Mailbox`, as that is part of another management role.

To view all the management roles that exist in the organization, use the `Get-ManagementRole` cmdlet. You can then use the `Get-ManagementRoleEntry` cmdlet to determine which cmdlets belong to that role.

There's more...

Many of the management roles installed with Exchange 2016 can be assigned to users by adding them to a role group. Role groups are associated with management roles through something called role assignments. Although the recommended method of assigning permissions is through role groups, you can still directly assign a management role to a user with the `New-ManagementRoleAssignment` cmdlet:

```
New-ManagementRoleAssignment -Role 'Mailbox Import Export' '
-User administrator
```

In this example, the administrator is assigned the `MailboxImportExport` role, which is not associated with any of the built-in role groups. In this case, we can create a direct assignment as shown previously, or use the `-SecurityGroup` parameter to assign this role to an existing role group, or a custom role group created with the `New-RoleGroup` cmdlet.

RBAC for end users

Everything we've discussed so far is related to RBAC for administrators, but end users need to be able to run cmdlets too. Now, this doesn't mean that they need to fire up EMS and start executing commands, but some things that they can change require the use of PowerShell cmdlets behind the scenes.

A good example of this is the **Exchange Control Panel** (**ECP**). When a user logs into the ECP, the very first thing they see is the **Account Information** screen, which allows them to change various settings that apply to their user account, such as their address, city, state, zip code, and phone numbers. When users change this information in ECP, these changes are carried out in the background with PowerShell cmdlets.

Here's the confusing part. End users are also assigned permissions from management roles, but not through role groups or role assignments, as they are applied to administrators. Instead, end users are assigned their management roles through something called a role assignment policy.

When you install Exchange, a single role assignment policy is created. Mailboxes that are created or moved over to Exchange 2016 will use the DefaultRoleAssignmentPolicy property which gives users some basic rights, such as modifying their contact information, creating inbox rules through ECP, and more.

To determine which management roles are applied to the Default Role Assignment Policy, use the following command:

```
Get-RoleAssignmentPolicy "Default Role Assignment Policy" |
Format-List AssignedRoles
```

See also

- The *Creating a custom RBAC role for administrators* recipe in this chapter
- The *Creating a custom RBAC role for end users* recipe in this chapter
- The *Troubleshooting RBAC* recipe in this chapter

Creating a custom RBAC role for administrators

Sometimes, the management roles that are installed by Exchange are not specific enough to meet your needs. When you are faced with this issue, the solution is to create a custom RBAC role. The process can be a little tricky, but the level of granular control that you can achieve is quite astounding. This recipe will show you how to create a custom RBAC role that can be assigned to administrators based on a very specific set of requirements.

How to do it...

Let's say that your company has decided that a group of support personnel should be responsible for the creation of all new Exchange recipients. You want to be very specific about what type of access this group will be granted, and you plan on implementing a custom management role based on the following requirements:

- Support personnel should be able to create Exchange recipients in the Employees OU in the Active Directory, and in this OU alone
- Support personnel should not be able to remove recipients in the Employees OU, or any other OU in the Active Directory

Use the following steps to implement a custom RBAC role for the support group based on the previous requirements:

1. First, we need to create a new custom management role:

```
New-ManagementRole -Name "Employee Recipient Creation" '
-Parent "Mail Recipient Creation"
```

2. Next, we need to modify the role so that the support staff cannot remove recipients from the organization:

```
Get-ManagementRoleEntry "Employee Recipient Creation\*" | `
Where-Object {$_.name -like "remove-*"} | `
Remove-ManagementRoleEntry -Confirm:$False
```

3. Now we need to scope this role to a specific location in the Active Directory:

```
New-ManagementScope -Name Employees '
-RecipientRoot contoso.com/Employees '
-RecipientRestrictionFilter {
   (RecipientType -eq "UserMailbox") -or
   (RecipientType -eq "MailUser") -or
   (RecipientType -eq "MailContact")
}
```

4. Finally, we can create a custom role group and add the support staff as members:

```
New-RoleGroup -Name Support '
-Roles "Employee Recipient Creation" '
-CustomRecipientWriteScope Employees '
-Members bjacobs, dgreen, jgordon
```

How it works...

The built-in management roles cannot be modified, so when we want to customize an existing role to meet our needs, we need to create a new custom role based on an existing parent role. Since we know that the built-in `Mail Recipient Creation` role provides the cmdlets that our support group will need, the first thing we must do is create a new role by copying the `Mail Recipient Creation` role, called `Employee Recipient Creation`.

One of the requirements in our scenario was that support personnel should not be able to remove recipients from the organization, so we edited our custom role to get rid of any cmdlets that could be used to remove recipients from the `Employees` OU, or from any other location in the Active Directory. We used the `Remove-ManagementRoleEntry` cmdlet to delete all the `Remove-*` cmdlets from our custom role, therefore preventing users assigned the custom role from removing recipient objects.

Next, we created a management scope that defines what the support group can access. We used the `New-ManagementScope` cmdlet to create the `Employees` management scope. As you can see from the command, we specified the recipient root as the `Employees` OU, as per the requirements in our scenario. When specifying `RecipientRoot`, we are also required to specify `RecipientRestrictionFilter`, which will be limited to the `UserMailbox`, `MailUser`, and `MailContact` recipient types.

Finally, we created our management role group using the `New-RoleGroup` cmdlet. The command used created a role group named `Support`, which created a universal security group in the Microsoft Exchange Security Groups OU in Active Directory. The role group was created using the `Employees` management scope, limiting the access to the `Employees` OU. Also, notice that we added three users to the group using the `-Members` parameter. Doing it this way automatically creates the management role assignment for us. You can view the management role assignments using the `Get-ManagementRoleAssignment` cmdlet.

There's more...

One of the things that make custom RBAC role assignments so powerful is the use of the management scope. When we created the `Employees` management scope, we used the `-RecipientRestrictionFilter` parameter to limit the types of recipients that would apply to that scope. When creating the role group, we specified this scope using the `-CustomRecipientWriteScope` parameter. This locks the administrator down to only writing to recipient objects that match the scope's filter and recipient root.

Keep in mind that scopes can be created with a `ServerRestrictionFilter` parameter and role groups and role assignments can be configured to use these scopes by assigning them to the `CustomConfigWriteScope` parameter. This can be useful when assigning custom RBAC roles for administrators who will be working on servers, as opposed to recipients. For example, instead of limiting your staff to working with recipient objects in a specific OU, you could create a custom role that only applies to specific servers in your organization, such as ones located in another city or another Active Directory site.

See also

- The *Working with Role Based Access Control* recipe in this chapter
- The *Creating a custom RBAC role for end users* recipe in this chapter
- The *Troubleshooting RBAC* recipe in this chapter

Creating a custom RBAC role for end users

Like custom RBAC roles for administrators, you can also create custom roles that apply to your end users. This may be useful when you need to allow them to modify additional configuration settings that apply to their own accounts through the ECP. This recipe will provide a real-world example of how you might implement a custom RBAC role for end users in your Exchange organization.

How to do it...

When users log on to ECP, they have the ability to modify their work phone number, fax number, home phone number, and mobile phone number, among other things. Let's say that you need to limit this so that they can only update their home phone number, as their work, fax, and mobile numbers will be managed by the administrators in your organization.

Since built-in roles cannot be modified, we need to create a custom role based on one of the existing built-in roles. Use the following steps to implement a custom RBAC role for end users based on the previous requirements:

1. The `MyContactInformation` role allows end users to modify their contact information, so we'll create a new custom role based on this parent role:

```
New-ManagementRole -Name MyContactInfo '
-Parent MyContactInformation
```

2. The `Set-User` cmdlet is what executes in the background when users modify their contact information. This is done using several parameters made available through this cmdlet. We'll create an array that contains all these parameters so that we can modify them later:

```
$parameters = Get-ManagementRoleEntry "MyContactInfo\Set-User" |
Select-Object -ExpandProperty parameters
```

3. Next, we'll create a new array that excludes the parameters that allow the end users to change their business-related phone numbers:

```
$parameters = $parameters | Where-Object{ `
    ($_ -ne "Phone") -and '
    ($_ -ne "MobilePhone") -and '
    ($_ -ne "Fax")
}
```

4. Now, we'll modify the `Set-User` cmdlet so that it only includes our custom list of parameters:

```
Set-ManagementRoleEntry "MyContactInfo\Set-User" '
-Parameters $parameters
```

5. The `MyContactInformation` role is assigned to end users through the default role assignment policy, so we need to remove that assignment from the policy:

```
Remove-ManagementRoleAssignment '
"MyContactInformation-Default Role Assignment Policy" '
-Confirm:$False
```

6. Finally, we can add our custom RBAC role to the default role assignment policy:

```
New-ManagementRoleAssignment -Role MyContactInfo -Policy "Default Role
Assignment Policy"
```

When users log in to the ECP, they'll only be able to modify their home phone number.

How it works...

As you can see from these steps, not only do management roles provide users with access to cmdlets, but also specific parameters available on those cmdlets. We're able to limit the use of the Set-User cmdlet by removing the access to the parameters that allow users to modify properties of their account that we do not want them to change.

End user management roles are assigned through a role assignment policy. By default, only one role assignment policy is created when you deploy Exchange 2016, called the DefaultRoleAssignmentPolicy. In the first example, we created a custom role based on the existing MyContactInformation role, which allows end users to update their personal contact details.

One of the questions that you may ask at this point is how did we determine that the MyContactInformation role was the one that was needed to be modified? Well, we can come to this conclusion by first checking which roles assign the Set-User cmdlet with the -Phone parameter:

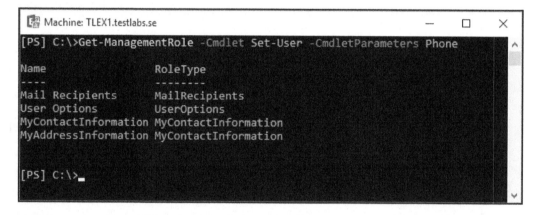

All the built-in end user management roles are prefixed with `My`, and as you can see from the preceding screenshot, the only two roles that apply here are listed at the bottom. Now we need to check the default role assignment policy:

```
Machine: TLEX1.testlabs.se                                    —    □    ×

[PS] C:\>Get-RoleAssignmentPolicy "Default Role Assignment Policy" | FL Ass
ignedRoles


AssignedRoles : {MyTeamMailboxes, MyDistributionGroupMembership, My
                Custom Apps, My Marketplace Apps, My ReadWriteMailbox
                Apps, MyBaseOptions, MyContactInformation,
                MyTextMessaging, MyVoiceMail}


[PS] C:\>
```

As you can see from the preceding screenshot, the only roles assigned to end users that contain the `Set-User` cmdlet are assigned by the `MyContactInformation` role, so we know that this is the role that needs to be replaced with a custom role.

There's more...

If you don't want to modify the existing role assignment policy, you can create a new role assignment policy that can be applied to individual users. This may be useful if you need to test things without affecting other users. To do this, use the `New-RoleAssignmentPolicy` cmdlet and specify a name for the policy and all the roles that should be applied via this role assignment policy:

```
New-RoleAssignmentPolicy -Name MyCustomPolicy '
-Roles MyDistributionGroupMembership, '
MyBaseOptions, MyTeamMailboxes, MyTextMessaging, '
MyVoiceMail, MyContactInfo
```

Once this is complete, you can assign the role assignment policy to an individual user with the `Set-Mailbox` cmdlet:

```
Set-Mailbox "Ramon Shaffer" '
-RoleAssignmentPolicy MyCustomPolicy
```

If you later decide that this new policy should be used for all your end users, you'll need to do two things. First, you'll need to set this role assignment policy as the default policy for new mailboxes:

```
Set-RoleAssignmentPolicy MyCustomPolicy -IsDefault
```

Then, you'll need to modify the existing users so that they are assigned the new role assignment policy:

```
Get-Mailbox -ResultSize Unlimited | '
Set-Mailbox -RoleAssignmentPolicy MyCustomPolicy
```

See also

- The *Working with Role Based Access Control* recipe in this chapter
- The *Creating a custom RBAC role for administrators* recipe in this chapter
- The *Troubleshooting RBAC* recipe in this chapter

Troubleshooting RBAC

Troubleshooting permission issues can be challenging, especially if you've implemented custom RBAC roles. In this recipe, we'll take a look at some useful techniques that can be used to troubleshoot issues related to RBAC.

How to do it...

There are several scenarios in which you can use the Exchange Management Shell cmdlets to solve problems with RBAC, and there are a couple of cmdlets that you'll need to use to do this. The following steps outline the solutions for some common troubleshooting situations:

1. To determine which management roles have been assigned to a user, use the following command syntax:

```
Get-ManagementRoleAssignment -GetEffectiveUsers | '
Where-Object {$_.EffectiveUserName -eq 'sysadmin'}
```

2. To retrieve a list of users that have been assigned a specific management role, run the following command and specify a role name, such as the `Legal Hold` role:

```
Get-ManagementRoleAssignment -Role 'Legal Hold' '
-GetEffectiveUsers
```

3. You can also determine whether a user has write access to a recipient, server, or database. For example, use the following syntax to determine whether the `sysadmin` account has the ability to modify Dave Jones' mailbox:

```
Get-ManagementRoleAssignment -WritableRecipient djones '
-GetEffectiveUsers |
Where-Object {$_.EffectiveUserName -eq 'sysadmin'}
```

After running the previous command, any roles that give the `sysadmin` write access to the specified recipient will be returned.

How it works...

The `Get-ManagementRoleAssignment` cmdlet is a useful tool when it comes to troubleshooting RBAC issues. If an administrator is unable to modify a recipient or make a change against a server, it is possible that the role assignment is either incorrect or it might not exist at all. In each step shown previously, we used the `-GetEffectiveUsers` parameter with this cmdlet, which provides a quick way to find out if certain roles have been assigned to a specific user.

In addition to the `-WritableRecipient` parameter, you have the option of using either the `-WritableServer` or `-WritableDatabase` parameters. These can be used to determine whether an administrator has write access to a server or database object. This can be useful to determine if a role assignment has not been made for an administrator that would be able to modify one of these objects. You can also use this as a method to determine whether some administrators have been granted too much control in your environment.

There's more...

If someone is not receiving the permissions you think they should, they may not be a member of the required role group. The steps outlined previously should help you determine if this is the case, but it may be as simple as making sure the administrator has been added to the right role group that will assign the appropriate roles. You can retrieve the members of a role group in the Shell using the `Get-RoleGroupMember` cmdlet. This command will return all the members of the `Organization Management` role group:

```
Get-RoleGroup 'Organization Management' | Get-RoleGroupMember
```

You can also use these cmdlets to generate a report of all the members of each role group. For example, the following code will display the member of each role group in the Shell:

```
ForEach ($rg in Get-RoleGroup) {
  Get-RoleGroupMember $rg |
  Select-Object Name, @{n="RoleGroup";e={$rg.Name}}
}
```

A new and very useful cmdlet in Exchange 2016 is `Get-RbacDiagnosticInfo`:

```
Machine: TLEX1.testlabs.se                                      —    □    ×

[PS] C:\>Get-RbacDiagnosticInfo -UserName nuno
WARNING: User name is nuno

Name                          Value
----                          -----
CombinedScripts               {GetAppMarketplaceUrl, InstallApp}
UserSid                       S-1-5-21-1411203154-1084355696-209206089...
TokenSids                     {S-1-5-21-1411203154-1084355696-20920608...
RbacUserId                    TESTLABS\nuno
AllRoleEntries                {RoleEntry: GetAppMarketplaceUrl ...
IdentityName                  testlabs.se/Users/Nuno
MachineName                   TLEX1
CombinedCmdlets               {(Microsoft.Exchange.Management.PowerShe...


[PS] C:\>
```

For example, this cmdlet allows you to easily determine exactly which `Set-*` cmdlets a particular user is allowed to run by checking the `CombinedCmdlets` property:

```
(Get-RbacDiagnosticInfo -UserName nuno).CombinedCmdlets | Where {$_.Na
me -like "Set-*"} | Select Name, Parameters
```

```
Machine: TLEX1.testlabs.se                                    —    □    ×

[PS] C:\>(Get-RbacDiagnosticInfo -UserName nuno).CombinedCmdlets | ? {$_.Na
me -like "Set-*"} | Select Name, Parameters
WARNING: User name is nuno


Name                              Parameters
----                              ----------
Set-CalendarNotification          {CalendarUpdateNotification, Calendar...
Set-CalendarProcessing            {AddAdditionalResponse, AdditionalRes...
Set-CASMailbox                    {ActiveSyncDebugLogging, ActiveSyncSu...
Set-ConsumerGroup                 {Confirm, Identity, MembersToAdd, Wha...
Set-ConsumerMailbox               {Confirm, DefaultFromAddress, Deliver...
```

In the screenshot above, you can see that the user nuno is able to run, among other cmdlets, the Set-CASMailbox cmdlet, as well as some of the parameters he can run. To check all the parameters the user is allowed to run, you simply filter the cmdlet you want and print its Parameters property:

```
((Get-RbacDiagnosticInfo -UserName nuno).CombinedCmdlets | Where
{$_.Name -eq "Set-CASMailbox"}).Parameters
```

```
Machine: TLEX1.testlabs.se                                    —    □    ×

[PS] C:\>((Get-RbacDiagnosticInfo -UserName nuno).CombinedCmdlets | ? {$_.N
ame -eq "Set-CASMailbox"}).Parameters
WARNING: User name is nuno
ActiveSyncDebugLogging
ActiveSyncSuppressReadReceipt
Confirm
ErrorAction
ErrorVariable
Identity
ImapForceICalForCalendarRetrievalOption
ImapMessagesRetrievalMimeFormat
ImapSuppressReadReceipt
ImapUseProtocolDefaults
OutBuffer
OutVariable
PopForceICalForCalendarRetrievalOption
PopMessagesRetrievalMimeFormat
PopSuppressReadReceipt
PopUseProtocolDefaults
ShowGalAsDefaultView
WarningAction
WarningVariable
WhatIf
[PS] C:\>_
```

Does this mean that user `nuno` can run this cmdlet against all mailboxes in the environment? Let's find out! To determine this, we need to check the `AllRoleEntries` property for the user, which gives us more details about all the cmdlets and parameters a user can run:

```
(Get-RbacDiagnosticInfo -UserName nuno).AllRoleEntries | Where {$_ -match "Set-CASMailbox"}
```

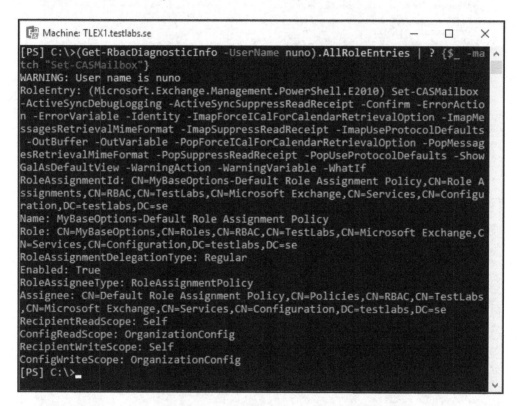

The output of this cmdlet has all the information we need. `RoleEntry` lists the cmdlet and all its parameters the user can run. Under `Name` and `Role`, we can see that this cmdlet is assigned to the user through the `MyBaseOptions` role, and finally, if we look at `RecipientReadScope` and `RecipientWriteScope`, we can see that the user can only run this cmdlet against his own mailbox and no other mailboxes in the environment.

See also

- The *Working with Role Based Access Control* recipe in this chapter
- The *Creating a custom RBAC role for administrators* recipe in this chapter
- The *Creating a custom RBAC role for end users* recipe in this chapter

Generating a certificate request

In order to create a new certificate, you first need to generate a certificate request using either the Exchange Admin Center, or through the Shell using the `New-ExchangeCertificate` cmdlet. Once you have a certificate request generated, you can then obtain a certificate from an internal **Certificate Authority** (**CA**) or from a third-party external CA (recommended). In this recipe, we'll take a look at the process of generating a certificate request from the Exchange Management Shell.

How to do it...

Let's see how to generate a certificate request using the following steps:

1. In this example, we'll generate a request using two **Subject Alternative Names** (**SANs**). This will allow us to support multiple URLs with one certificate:

```
$cert = New-ExchangeCertificate -GenerateRequest '
-SubjectName "c=US, o=Contoso, cn=mail.contoso.com" '
-DomainName autodiscover.contoso.com, mail.contoso.com '
-PrivateKeyExportable $True
```

2. After the request has been generated, we can export it to a file that can be used to submit a request to a CA:

```
$cert | Out-File C:\cert_request.txt
```

How it works...

When you install Exchange 2016, self-signed certificates are automatically generated and installed to encrypt data passed between servers. Since these self-signed certificates will not be trusted by your client machines when accessing Exchange services, it is recommended that you replace them with new certificates issued from a trusted CA. If you do not replace these certificates, Outlook and Outlook on the Web users will receive certificate warnings informing them that the certificates are not issued from a trusted source. This can create some confusion for end users and could generate calls to your help desk.

You can get around these certificate warnings by installing the server's self-signed certificates in the **Trusted Root Certificate Authorities** store on the client machines, but even in a small environment, this can become an administrative headache. That's why it is recommended that you replace the self-signed certificates before placing your Exchange 2016 servers into production.

When using the `New-ExchangeCertificate` cmdlet to generate a certificate request, you can use the `-SubjectName` parameter to specify the common name of the certificate. This value is set using an X.500 distinguished name, and as you saw in step 2, the common name for the certificate was set to `mail.contoso.com`. If you do not provide a value for the `-SubjectName` parameter, the hostname of the server where the cmdlet is run to generate the request will be used.

The `-DomainName` parameter is used to define one or more FQDNs that will be listed in the **Subject Alternative Name** field of the certificate. This allows you to generate certificates that support multiple FQDNs that can be installed on multiple Exchange servers. For example, you may have several servers in your environment across multiple geographic locations, and instead of generating multiple certificates for each one, you can simply add **Subject Alternative Name** to cover all the possible FQDNs that users will need to access, and then install the same single certificate on all servers.

The `New-ExchangeCertificate` cmdlet outputs a certificate request in Base64 format. In the previous example, we saved the output of the command in a variable so that we could simply output the data to a text file. Once the request is generated, you'll need to supply the data from this request to the issuing CA. This is usually done through a web form hosted by the CA where you submit the certificate request. You can simply open the request file in Notepad, copy the data, and paste it into the submission form on the CA website. Once the information is submitted, the CA will generate a certificate that can be downloaded and installed on your servers. Refer to the next recipe in this chapter titled *Installing certificates and enabling services* for steps on how to complete this process.

There's more...

It's recommended as a best practice that you limit the number of Subject Alternative Names on your certificates, so your name space design should be completely defined before creating your certificates. For example, let's say that you've got four servers in a load-balanced configuration located in a single Active Directory site. Even though you have multiple servers, you only need to include the FQDNs that your end users will use to access these servers. If you configure your namespace appropriately, there's no need to include the server's FQDN or hostname as a Subject Alternative Name.

If you plan on installing a certificate on multiple servers, make sure that you mark the certificate as exportable by setting the `-PrivateKeyExportable` parameter to `$True`. This will allow you to export the certificate and install it on the remaining servers in your environment.

 It's recommended that you use either the Exchange Management Shell or the Exchange Admin Center for generating the certificate, and not the MMC snap-in or IIS management console.

See also

- The *Installing certificates and enabling services* recipe in this chapter
- The *Importing certificates on multiple Exchange servers* recipe in this chapter

Installing certificates and enabling services

After you've generated a certificate request and have obtained a certificate from a CA, you will need to install the certificate on your server using the `Import-ExchangeCertificate` cmdlet. This recipe will show you how to install certificates issued from a certificate authority and how to assign services to the certificate using the Exchange Management Shell.

How to do it...

Let's see how to install and enable services using the following steps:

1. Let's say that you have requested and downloaded a certificate from an Active Directory Enterprise CA and downloaded the file to the root of the C:\ drive. First, read the certificate data into a variable in the Shell using the following command:

```
$certificate = Get-Content -Path C:\certnew.cer '
-Encoding Byte -ReadCount 0
```

2. Next, we can import the certificate and complete the pending request:

```
Import-ExchangeCertificate -FileData $certificate
```

3. Now that the certificate is installed, we can enable it for specific services:

```
Get-ExchangeCertificate -DomainName mail.contoso.com | '
Enable-ExchangeCertificate -Services IIS, SMTP
```

At this point, the certificate has been installed and will now be used for client access services, such as Outlook on the Web and the Exchange Admin Center, as well as for securing **Simple Mail Transfer Protocol (SMTP)** traffic.

How it works...

Since the Exchange Management Shell uses remote PowerShell sessions, the Import-ExchangeCertificate cmdlet cannot use a local file path to import a certificate file. This is because the cmdlet could be running on any server within your organization and a local file path may not exist. Therefore, we need to use the -FileData parameter to provide the actual data of the certificate. In step 1, we read the certificate data into a byte array using the Get-Content cmdlet, which is a PowerShell core cmdlet, and is not run through the remote PowerShell on the Exchange server. The content of the certificate is stored as a byte array in the $certificate variable, and we can assign this data to the -FileData parameter of the Import-ExchangeCertificate cmdlet, which allows us to import the certificate to any Exchange server through the remote PowerShell.

Use the `-Server` parameter with the Get-ExchangeCertificate cmdlet to target a specific server. Otherwise, the cmdlet will run against the server you are currently connected to.

There's more...

As shown previously, once the certificate has been imported, it needs to have one or more services assigned before it can be used by an Exchange server. After importing a certificate, you can use the Get-ExchangeCertificate cmdlet to view it:

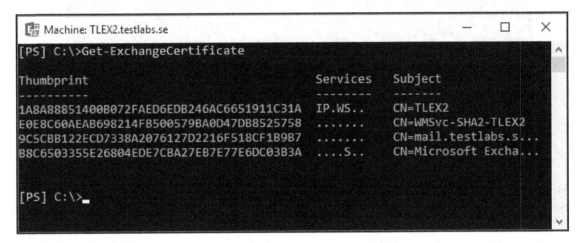

You can see that there are several certificates installed. When assigning services to a certificate, we need to be specific about which one needs to be modified. We can do this either by specifying the thumbprint of the certificate when running the Enable-ExchangeCertificate cmdlet, or using the method shown previously, where we used the Get-ExchangeCertificate cmdlet with the `-DomainName` parameter to retrieve a specific certificate, and send it down the pipeline to the Enable-ExchangeCertificate cmdlet. No matter which method you use, make sure it is the right certificate.

Let's say that we're connected to a server named TLEX2. We've imported a certificate, and now we need to view all the installed certificates so that we can figure out which one needs to be enabled and assigned the appropriate services. We can do this by viewing a few key properties of each certificate using the Get-ExchangeCertificate cmdlet:

```
Machine: TLEX2.testlabs.se                                    —    □    ×

[PS] C:\>Get-ExchangeCertificate | FL Thumbprint, CertificateDomains, Servi
ces, IsSelfSigned


Thumbprint          : 1A8A88851400B072FAED6EDB246AC6651911C31A
CertificateDomains  : {TLEX2, TLEX2.testlabs.se}
Services            : IMAP, POP, IIS, SMTP
IsSelfSigned        : True

Thumbprint          : E0E8C60AEAB698214FB500579BA0D47DB8525758
CertificateDomains  : {WMSvc-SHA2-TLEX2}
Services            : None
IsSelfSigned        : True

Thumbprint          : 9C5CBB122ECD7338A2076127D2216F518CF1B9B7
CertificateDomains  : {mail.testlabs.se, autodiscover.testlabs.se}
Services            : None
IsSelfSigned        : False
```

Here, you can see that we've retrieved the Thumbprint, CertificateDomains, and assigned Services for each installed Exchange certificate in the list format. We also selected the IsSelfSigned property that will tell us whether or not the certificate was issued from a CA or installed by Exchange as a self-signed certificate. It's clear from the output that the third certificate in the list is the one that was issued from a certificate authority, since the IsSelfSigned property is set to False. At this point, we can use the certificate's thumbprint to assign services to this certificate using the following command:

```
Enable-ExchangeCertificate '
-Thumbprint 9C5CBB122ECD7338A2076127D2216F518CF1B9B7 '
-Services IIS, SMTP
```

If you have multiple certificates installed, especially with duplicate domain names, use the method shown here to assign services based on the certificate thumbprint. Otherwise, you may find it easier to enable certificates based on the domain name, as shown in the first example.

See also

- The *Importing certificates on multiple Exchange servers* recipe in this chapter
- The *Generating a certificate request* recipe in this chapter

Importing certificates on multiple Exchange servers

If your environment contains multiple Exchange servers, you'll likely want to use the same certificate on multiple servers. If you have a large number of servers, importing certificates one at a time, even with the Exchange Management Shell, could end up being quite time-consuming. This recipe will provide a method to automate this process using the Exchange Management Shell.

How to do it...

Once you've gone through the process of generating a certificate request, installing a certificate and assigning the services on one server, you can export that certificate and deploy it to your remaining servers.

The following steps outline the process of exporting an installed certificate on a server named TLEX01 and importing that certificate into a server named TLEX02:

1. In order to export a certificate, we'll first need to assign a password to secure the private key that will be exported with the certificate:

```
$password = ConvertTo-SecureString -String P@ssword '
-AsPlainText -Force
```

2. Now we can export the certificate data with the Export-ExchangeCertificate cmdlet. We'll retrieve the certificate from the TLEX01 server and export the data to a binary-encoded value stored in a variable:

```
$cert = Get-ExchangeCertificate '
-DomainName mail.contoso.com -Server TLEX01 | '
Export-ExchangeCertificate -BinaryEncoded:$True '
-Password $password
```

3. Next, we can import the certificate file data into the TLEX02 server as a certificate:

```
Import-ExchangeCertificate -FileData $cert.FileData '
-Password $password -Server TLEX02
```

4. Finally, we can assign the services to the certificate that was recently imported on the TLEX02 server:

```
Get-ExchangeCertificate '
-DomainName mail.contoso.com -Server TLEX02 | '
Enable-ExchangeCertificate -Services IIS, SMTP
```

How it works...

As you can see from these steps, exporting a certificate from one server and importing it on an additional server is rather complex and would be even more so if you want to do this on 5 or 10 servers. If this is a common task that needs to be done frequently, then it makes sense to automate it even further. The following PowerShell function will automate the process of exporting a certificate from a source server and will import the certificate on one or more target servers:

```
Function Deploy-ExchangeCertificate {
  param (
    $SourceServer,
    $Thumbprint,
    $TargetServer,
    $Password,
    $Services
  )
  $password = ConvertTo-SecureString -String $Password '
  -AsPlainText    -Force
  $cert = Get-ExchangeCertificate -Thumbprint $Thumbprint '
  -Server $SourceServer |
    Export-ExchangeCertificate -BinaryEncoded:$True '
    -Password $Password
  ForEach ($Server in $TargetServer) {
    Import-ExchangeCertificate -FileData $cert.FileData '
    -Password $Password    -Server $Server
    Enable-ExchangeCertificate -Thumbprint $Thumbprint '
    -Server $Server    -Services $Services '
    -Confirm:$False    -Force
}
```

This function allows you to specify a certificate that has been properly set up and installed on a source server, and then deploy that certificate and enable a specified list of services on one or more servers. The function accepts several parameters and requires that you specify the thumbprint of the certificate that you want to deploy.

Let's say that you've got six servers. You've gone through the certificate generation process, obtained the certificate from a trusted certificate authority, and installed the certificate on the first server. Now you can add the `Deploy-ExchangeCertificate` function to your PowerShell session and deploy the certificate to the remaining servers.

First, you need to determine the thumbprint on the source server you want to deploy, and you can do this using the `Get-ExchangeCertificate` cmdlet. The next step is to run the function with the following syntax:

```
Deploy-ExchangeCertificate -SourceServer TLEX01 '
-TargetServer TLEX02,TLEX03,TLEX04,TLEX05,TLEX06 '
-Thumbprint DE4382508E325D27D2D48033509EE5F9C621A07B '
-Services IIS,SMTP '
-Password P@ssw0rd
```

The function will export the certificate on the `TLEX01` server with the thumbprint value assigned to the `-Thumbprint` parameter. The value assigned to the `-Password` parameter will be used to secure the private key when the certificate data is exported. The certificate will then be installed on the five remaining servers and will have the IIS and SMTP services assigned.

There's more...

You may want to export your certificates to an external file that can be used to import the certificate on another server at a later time. To do this, use the following command:

```
$password = ConvertTo-SecureString '
-String P@ssword -AsPlainText -Force
$file = Get-ExchangeCertificate '
-Thumbprint DE4382508E325D27D2D48033509EE5F9C621A07B -Server '
TLEX01 | Export-ExchangeCertificate -BinaryEncoded:$True '
-Password $password
Set-Content -Path C:\cert.pfx -Value $file.FileData -Encoding Byte
```

This is similar to the previous examples, except that this time we're exporting the certificate data to an external .pfx file.

You can use the following commands to import this certificate at a later time into another server in your environment:

```
$password = ConvertTo-SecureString '
-String P@ssword -AsPlainText -Force
$filedata = Get-Content -Path C:\cert.pfx -Encoding Byte -ReadCount 0
Import-ExchangeCertificate -FileData ([Byte[]]$filedata) '
-Password $password -Server TLEX02
```

This will import the certificate from the external .pfx file to the TLEX02 server. Once this is complete, you can use the Enable-ExchangeCertificate cmdlet to assign the required services to the certificate.

See also

- The *Generating a certificate request* recipe in this chapter
- The *Installing certificates and enabling services* recipe in this chapter

Configuring Domain Security

Securing SMTP traffic has been a concern for many years. Nowadays, many servers support opportunistic **Transport Layer Security (TLS)** where the sending server first attempts to secure the path that emails take when they travel to recipient email systems by using encryption. However, this is not always possible and emails end up being sent in clear text.

As you will see in the last recipe of this chapter, S/MIME can be used to digitally sign and encrypt emails, but if certificates from an internal PKI are used, external recipients will likely not trust them. Additionally, implementing S/MIME on an enterprise scale is not always easy.

Domain security provides a low-cost alternative to S/MIME and other message-level security solutions, by helping secure SMTP traffic between two Exchange organizations. Its advantage is that it is configured on a server level and works without any client-side configuring. Domain security uses mutual TLS authentication to provide session-based authentication and encryption.

With mutual TLS, each server verifies the connection with the other server by validating a certificate that is provided by that other server, so clients are not included in the process. A secure SMTP channel between two Exchange servers is then established, usually over the internet. Outlook is aware of Domain Security and will display a green check icon on emails exchanged between servers on which Domain Security is implemented.

> The Exchange self-signed certificate for TLS is only for opportunistic TLS and not for mutual TLS. As such, it cannot be used for Domain Security.

Domain Security does not protect all SMTP traffic in and out of your organization, but it efficiently protects SMTP traffic between you and one or more partner organizations.

This recipe shows how to configure Domain Security between two organizations.

How to do it...

Let's see how to configure Domain Security between two organization domains: contoso.com and fabrikam.com.

> For organizations that have Exchange Edge servers implemented, the following tasks should be performed on these servers.

1. The first step is to establish a certificate trust between the two organizations. If both organizations use publicly trusted certificates on their Exchange servers, it is likely that nothing needs to be done in this step.

    If that is not the case, and certificates from an internal PKI or self-signed certificates are used, you will have to import root CA certificates on both sides using one of the methods previously demonstrated or by using the Certificate MMC to export and import certificates.

    Alternatively, you can also issue certificates for SMTP for both Exchange organizations from a single trusted root CA, if there is one. In any case, the objective here is that each Exchange server trusts the certificate installed (and assigned to the SMTP service) on the other Exchange server.

2. Next, you configure both organizations with the domains from which you want to send and receive domain secured email by using mutual TLS authentication. For Contoso, you run the following cmdlets:

```
Set-TransportConfig -TLSSendDomainSecureList contoso.com
Set-TransportConfig -TLSReceiveDomainSecureList fabrikam.com
```

For Fabrikam, these are the other way around:

```
Set-TransportConfig -TLSSendDomainSecureList fabrikam.com
Set-TransportConfig -TLSReceiveDomainSecureList contoso.com
```

3. The final step is to configure `Send` and `Receive` connectors. For this, it is strongly recommended to use dedicated connectors for Domain Security. The following steps are performed on Contoso's side, but the same will also have to be performed on Fabrikam's, obviously updating the cmdlets with the correct information.

```
New-SendConnector -Partner -Name "To Fabrikam" -AddressSpaces
fabrikam.com -Fqdn mail.contoso.com -ProtocolLoggingLevel Verbose -
FrontendProxyEnabled $True
```

4. Using the cmdlet above, the new send connector should be automatically configured for Domain Security. Ensure this is the case by running the following cmdlet which displays further configuration details to help ensure everything is configured as it should be:

```
Get-SendConnector "To Fabrikam" | Select Name, DNSRoutingEnabled,
FQDN,DomainSecureEnabled
```

5. If, for some reason, the connector is not enabled for Domain Security, set the following parameter to `$True`:

```
Set-SendConnector "To Fabrikam" -DomainSecureEnabled $True
```

6. We now need to configure a Receive connector to accept domain secured emails from Fabrikam's public IP address:

```
New-ReceiveConnector -Partner -Name "From Fabrikam" -TransportRole
FrontEndTransport -Bindings 0.0.0.0:25 -RemoteIPRanges 10.10.1.1 -Fqdn
mail.contoso.com -ProtocolLoggingLevel Verbose
```

7. Ensure that `TLS` and domain security are both enabled by running the following cmdlet:

```
Get-ReceiveConnector "<server>\From Fabrikam" | Select AuthMechanism,
DomainSecureEnabled
```

You are now ready to send domain secured emails between the two organizations.

How it works...

As mentioned, domain security uses digital certificates to secure the SMTP channel between two organizations. As such, a certificate trust between the two organizations needs to be in place. This can be done by using publicly trusted certificates or by exporting and importing the certificates used for SMTP into both organizations.

The bottom line here is: each Exchange server has to trust the certificate installed and assigned to the SMTP service on the other organization's Exchange server. Besides establishing this trust, it is important to make sure that the certificate common name is the same as the name that Exchange provides in the HELO/EHLO greeting.

Then we specify for which domains we will be sending and receiving domain secured emails using mutual TLS authentication. This is done using the `Set-TransportConfig` with the `TLSSendDomainSecureList` and `TLSReceiveDomainSecureList` parameters.

We completed the configuration by creating dedicated Send and Receive connectors.

For the send connector, we start by setting the `Partner` usage type, which specifies the permissions and authentication methods assigned to the connector. Then we specify that it should only be used for emails sent to `fabrikam.com` addresses, the `FQDN` that will be presented in the HELO/EHLO greeting, and we set the protocol logging level to `Verbose` so we can validate and/or troubleshoot any possible issues.

Please note that when using domain security, you can't specify smart hosts in the send connector, it has to use MX records to determine where to send emails to. This means that emails sent to the partner organization might bypass any smart host or mail relay you might have for outbound email.

Next, you must configure the receive connector on each Edge Transport server that accepts mail from the domain from which you want to receive domain-secured emails. If Edge servers are not used, then this is performed on the internal Exchange servers. We set the receive connector with a `Partner` usage type, specify that the connector accepts connections on TCP port `25` on all IP addresses configured on all network adapters in the server by setting the `-Bindings` parameter to `0.0.0.0:25`, and finally we specify that this connector should only accept messages from the IP address `10.10.1.1` (which is the public IP from which Fabrikam's Exchange servers send emails from).

The easiest way to test if Domain Security is working is by sending an email and checking if the email is displayed in the recipient's Outlook with a green check mark:

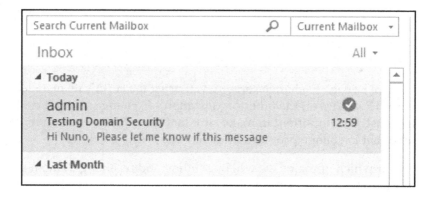

By opening the email and clicking on the green check mark, we are informed that the email was securely received:

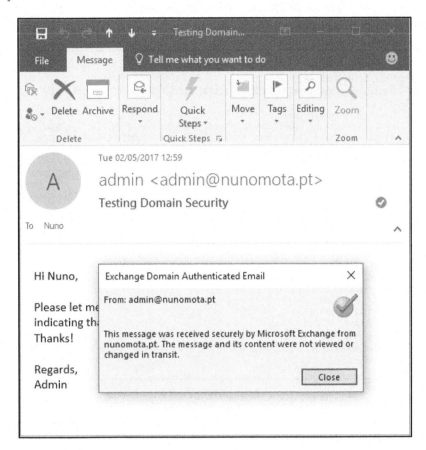

If the email is not received, and since we already enabled both send and receive connectors with verbose logging, we can analyze the protocol logs to determine whether TLS negotiation was successful. These logs will contain information that is extremely useful when troubleshooting Domain Security.

If all is working well, you should see certificates being exchanged during the authentication process. In the following screenshot, you can see this happening. More precisely, you can see that `testlabs.se` uses a self-signed certificate, but `nunomota.pt` uses a publicly-trusted certificate from DigiCert:

```
,+,,
,>,,"220 mail.nunomota.pt Microsoft ESMTP MAIL Service ready at Tue, 2 May 2017 13:24:0
,<,EHLO tlex1.testlabs.se,
,>,,250  mail.nunomota.pt Hello [192.168.1.161] SIZE 37748736 PIPELINING DSN ENHANCEDST
,<,STARTTLS,
,>,,220 2.0.0 SMTP server ready,
,*," CN=mail.nunomota.pt, OU=IT, O=Nuno Mota, L=London, C=GB CN=DigiCert SHA2 Secure 9
,*, CN=TLEX1 CN=TLEX1 17A753A2E0CB0C9D41EEBFC4ED83EDA8 7D099306C5F30E401CF42B0DC3EDF48
,*,,"TLS protocol SP_PROT_TLS1_2_SERVER negotiation succeeded using bulk encryption al
,<,EHLO tlex1.testlabs.se,
,*, CN=TLEX1 CN=TLEX1 17A753A2E0CB0C9D41EEBFC4ED83EDA8 7D099306C5F30E401CF42B0DC3EDF48
,*,,TlsDomainCapabilities='None'; Status='Success'; Domain=''
,*, CN=TLEX1 CN=TLEX1 17A753A2E0CB0C9D41EEBFC4ED83EDA8 7D099306C5F30E401CF42B0DC3EDF48
,*,,TlsDomainCapabilities='None'; Status='Success'; Domain=''
,>,,250  mail.nunomota.pt Hello [192.168.1.161] SIZE 37748736 PIPELINING DSN ENHANCEDST
,<,MAIL FROM:<admin@testlabs.se> SIZE=5346,
,*, CN=TLEX1 CN=TLEX1 17A753A2E0CB0C9D41EEBFC4ED83EDA8 7D099306C5F30E401CF42B0DC3EDF48
,*,SMTPSubmit AcceptRoutingHeaders,Set Session Permissions
,*,SMTPSubmit AcceptRoutingHeaders,Set Session Permissions
,*,08D491548CAD3D49;2017-05-02T12:24:03.469Z;1,receiving message
,<,RCPT TO:<admin@nunomota.pt>,
,>,,250 2.1.0 Sender OK,
,>,,250 2.1.5 Recipient OK,
,<,BDAT 1702 LAST,
,*,,Proxy destination(s) obtained from OnProxyInboundMessage event
,>,,"250 2.6.0 <0dff7003d376447880ed4b890f4cf7bf@testlabs.se> [InternalId=1541893259282
,<,QUIT,
,-,,Local
```

The most common error you might see in these logs is `454 4.7.5 Certificate validation failure, Reason:UntrustedRoot` when one of the organizations does not trust the other organization's certificate.

See also

- The *Managing connectivity and protocol logs* recipe from `Chapter 8`, *Managing Transport Servers*

Configuring S/MIME for OWA

For those of you who might not be aware of what **S/MIME (Secure/Multipurpose Internet Mail Extensions)** is, this short description might be helpful.

As most of you are aware, emails in general are mostly insecure if they are not digitally signed and their transport isn't encrypted. With S/MIME, the messages can be digitally signed, which can be seen as a guarantee that the sender is the person they claim to be and not someone else. With the use of S/MIME, the contents and attachments of messages can also be encrypted.

In Exchange 2013 RTM, the support for S/MIME was removed for OWA, but it was brought back when Service Pack 1 was released and it is still available in Exchange 2016.

For this recipe, I've decided to use an internal PKI solution based on Windows Server 2016 for issuing certificates to users for securing their emails and ensuring their identities. The important thing to keep in mind, when implementing this in production, is that it's recommended that you use certificates from a third-party trusted root issuer. However, the internal PKI solution is great in lab or training environments. The reason why it is not recommended to use the internal PKI solution in production, is that the root certificate created for the PKI infrastructure is not known by anyone outside the domain, which means that the recipients of our encrypted messages don't know about the trusted root certificate, so they cannot decrypt the contents of the messages.

Let's start with the configuration and take a look at the results in this recipe.

How to do it...

1. To verify the current configuration, we can easily run the following cmdlet:

    ```
    Get-SMIMEConfig
    ```

2. In this example, I've configured my environment to give the user the option to select the user certificate themselves. For the encryption algorithm, I've used the option of RC2 with 128-bit encryption. These options are configured using the following cmdlet:

    ```
    Set-SmimeConfig -OWAAllowUserChoiceOfSigningCertificate $True '
    -OWAEncryptionAlgorithms 6602:128
    ```

3. Once this configuration is in place, the root certificate of the internal PKI solution needs to be exported and configured as a S/MIME, issuing CA. You do this by configuring a virtual certificate collection, set up as a certificate store file type with an SST extension, that will be used to validate S/MIME certificates. This SST file contains all the root and intermediate certificates used when validating an S/MIME certificate.

```
Get-ChildItem -Path '
"Cert:\LocalMachine\CA\175AC872CA60AAD30FBBC66228A706CDA8E4B787" '
| Export-Certificate -Type SST '
-FilePath C:\Scripts\SMIME\testlabsca.sst
Set-SmimeConfig -SMIMECertificateIssuingCA (Get-Content
C:\Scripts\SMIME\testlabsca.sst -Encoding Byte)
```

4. With the configuration in place, I logged into my Windows 10 client using two of the users called Nuno and Jonas, and requested a certificate from the local CA for securing messages. This can easily be done by using, for example, the Microsoft Management Console (MMC).

5. With the certificate in place, it should look similar to the following screenshot:

At this point, the user can use Outlook to send emails digitally signed without any further configuration. When using OWA, the S/MIME control needs to be deployed to the clients. This can be downloaded and installed by the end users by going to the **Options** of OWA and then **S/MIME**:

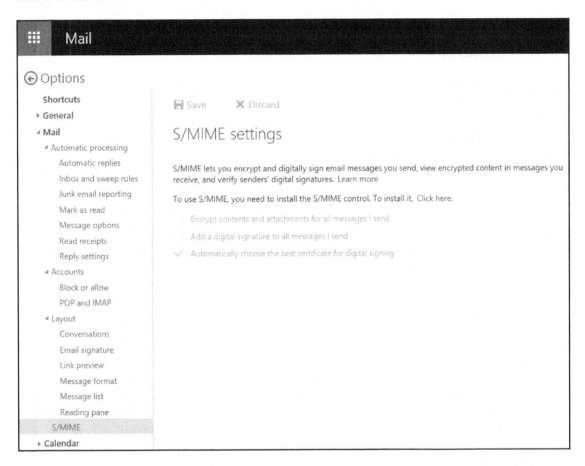

However, it is recommended to get this deployed using any existing deployment solution or using a group policy for getting it installed.

This recipe is just an example of how S/MIME can be used in Exchange 2016 together with OWA. When deploying this in your lab and production environments, make sure to investigate all the requirements and make decisions based on them.

How it works...

At the time of writing this book, there were three options to use S/MIME: Outlook, Outlook on the Web, and Exchange ActiveSync.

When the user certificate is issued, it gets published to its Active Directory user object under the `userSMIMECertificate` and `userCertificate` attributes (visible through the `Get-Mailbox` cmdlet).

Digital signatures are the most commonly used service of S/MIME. As the name suggests, digital signatures are the digital counterpart to the traditional, legal signature on a paper document. As with a legal signature, digital signatures provide the following security capabilities: **authentication** (a signature validates an identity), **nonrepudiation** (the uniqueness of a signature prevents the owner of the signature from disowning the signature), and **data integrity** (when the recipient of a digitally signed email validates the digital signature, the recipient is assured that the email received is, in fact, the same email that was signed and sent, and has not been altered while in transit).

Continuing with our previous example, if Nuno wants to send Jonas a digitally signed email, he first generates a message digest of the original plaintext message using a hashing algorithm. Then, he encrypts only the message digest using his private key from the certificate he just requested. This encrypted message digest is the digital signature. He appends the signed message digest to the plaintext message, and transmits the entire message to Jonas.

When Jonas receives the digitally signed message, he reverses the process performed by Nuno: he uses the same hashing function to create a message digest of the full plaintext message received from Nuno. Jonas decrypts the digital signature using Nuno's public key (retrieved from Active Directory), compares the decrypted message digest he received from Nuno with the message digest he computed himself. If the two digests match, he can be assured that the message he received was sent by Nuno and was not altered in-between. If they do not match, either the message was not sent by Nuno or the message was modified while in transit.

The difference between only using digital signature and encryption is that when the message is not encrypted, the contents are sent in clear text. However, the digital signature ensures the unique identity of the sender and that the contents were not altered while in transit.

When sending confidential contents, it's recommended that you encrypt the message together with digitally signing it. If anyone comes across an encrypted message, they will not be able to open or read it.

When receiving a digitally signed and encrypted message, it will look similar to the following screenshot:

See also

- The *Searching message tracking logs* recipe in this chapter
- The *Managing connectivity and protocol logs* recipe from `Chapter 8`, *Managing Transport Service*

Configuring Windows Defender Exclusions

It is always recommended to install antivirus software on Exchange servers, or any server for that matter, to help enhance the security and health of the Exchange organization. However, this will cause issues in Exchange if it is not configured correctly. For example, the antivirus might lock an open log or database file that Exchange needs to access or modify, thus possibly causing severe failures.

For this reason, it is crucial to properly configure folder, process and file name extension exclusions on any antivirus program running on Exchange servers.

When installing Exchange 2016 on Windows Server 2016, *Windows Defender* is installed by default. The good news is that it contains PowerShell cmdlets that we can use to easily configure these exclusions.

In this recipe, we will have a look at how to configure Exchange exclusions in Windows Defender.

How to do it...

Use the following cmdlets to exclude the Exchange install directory, the Exchange Transport service, and some extensions of files used by Exchange from being scanned by Windows Defender:

```
Add-MpPreference -ExclusionPath $ExInstall
Add-MpPreference -ExclusionProcess
"$($ExInstall)Bin\MSExchangeTransport.exe"
Add-MpPreference -ExclusionExtension ".chk", ".edb", ".log", ".que"
```

How it works...

In order to configure Windows Defender, we use the `Set-MpPreference` or the `Add-MpPreference` cmdlets. In this example, we want to `add` exclusions, so we use the latter with the following parameters:

- `ExclusionPath`: It specifies an array of file paths to exclude from scheduled and real-time scanning. Any subfolder will also be excluded.
- `ExclusionProcess`: It excludes any files opened by the processes that you specify from scheduled and real-time scanning. It excludes files opened by executable programs only, it does not exclude the processes themselves. To exclude a process, use the `ExclusionPath` parameter instead.
- `ExclusionExtension`: It specifies an array of file name extensions to exclude from scheduled, custom, and real-time scanning.

 This is nowhere near the complete list of exclusions that should be configured for Exchange 2016! For a complete list, please visit the following TechNet article:
https://technet.microsoft.com/en-us/library/bb332342%28v=exchg.160%29.aspx.

There's more...

Using PowerShell, we can do much more with Windows Defender. For example:

- We can get the status of anti-malware software on the server by running the following cmdlet:

`Get-MpComputerStatus`

- We can also get the history of threats detected on the server using the `Get-MpThreat` cmdlet.
- As a last resort, we can disable real-time protection by running:

`Set-MpPreference -DisableRealtimeMonitoring $True`

10
Compliance and Audit Logging

In this chapter, we will cover the following topics:

- Configuring journaling
- Managing archive mailboxes
- Configuring archive mailbox quotas
- Creating retention tags and policies
- Applying retention policies to mailboxes
- Placing mailboxes on retention hold
- Placing mailboxes on in-place hold or litigation hold
- Searching and placing a hold on public folders
- Performing eDiscovery searches
- Performing Compliance searches
- Configuring data loss prevention
- Configuring administrator audit logging
- Searching the administrator audit logs
- Configuring mailbox audit logging
- Searching mailbox audit logs

Introduction

One of the significant changes introduced in Exchange 2010 was the development of the feature called **Litigation Hold**; this was further developed and ended up in a feature called **In-Place Hold in Exchange 2013** and **2016**. One more welcomed feature is that it's possible to archive the contents from Lync or Skype for business into mailboxes.

This came together with the new search engine called FAST, which made searches across platforms available (Exchange, SharePoint, and Skype).

The compliance and audit logging features that were introduced in Exchange 2010 still apply to Exchange 2016, with some improvements. Over the years, many organizations have relied on third-party products for archiving and retaining email messages for legal protection and regulatory compliance. Fortunately, this function is now built into the product, along with some very powerful auditing capabilities that can track which users are accessing and modifying items in mailboxes and which administrators are making changes throughout the Exchange organization.

In this chapter, we'll take a look at some of the most common tasks related to compliance and audit logging that can be performed and automated through the Exchange Management Shell. This includes managing retention polices, performing legal searches, and configuring data loss prevention, along with generating detailed reports based on mailbox and administrator audit logs.

Performing some basic steps

To work with the code samples in this chapter, follow these steps to launch the Exchange Management Shell:

1. Log on to a workstation or server with the Exchange Management tools installed.
2. You can connect using a remote PowerShell if, for some reason, you don't have the Exchange Management tools installed. To do so, use the following command:

```
$Session = New-PSSession -ConfigurationName ' Microsoft.Exchange -
ConnectionUri '
    http://servername/PowerShell/ -Authentication Kerberos
    Import-PSSession $Session
```

3. Alternatively, open the Exchange Management Shell by navigating to **Start** | **All Apps** | **Microsoft Exchange Server 2016**.
4. Click on the **Exchange Management Shell** shortcut.
5. To launch a standard PowerShell console, open a standard PowerShell console by navigating to **Start** | **All Apps**, and click on the **Windows PowerShell** shortcut.

   Unless specified otherwise in the Getting ready section, all of the recipes in this chapter will require the use of the Exchange Management Shell.

Remember to start the Exchange Management Shell using **Run as administrator** to avoid permission problems.

In this chapter, you might notice that, in the examples of cmdlets, I have used the back tick (') character to break up long commands into multiple lines. The purpose of this is to make it easier to read. The back ticks are not required and should only be used if needed.

Configuring journaling

Journaling in Exchange 2016 is pretty much unchanged from Exchange 2010, but it is still a crucial feature for many organizations worldwide as it helps respond to legal, regulatory, and organizational compliance requirements by recording all or specific email messages. Exchange provides two types of journaling:

- **Standard journaling** is configured on a mailbox database and journals all messages sent to and from mailboxes located on that database.
- **Premium journaling** provides more granular journaling by using journal rules. Instead of journaling every single email sent or received by all mailboxes in a database, you can restrict journaling based on recipients or members of distribution groups, and scope (internal, external, or all messages). Premium journaling requires an Exchange Enterprise **Client Access License (CAL)**.

In both journaling methods, a `journal report` is generated. This journal report is the message that the `journaling agent` generates when an email is journaled and submitted to the journaling mailbox. The original email is included unaltered as an attachment to the journal report. The body of a journal report contains information regarding the original email such as the sender email address, message subject, message-ID, and recipient email addresses. This is also known as `envelope journaling`, and is the only journaling method supported by Exchange 2016.

In this recipe, we will see how to configure both journaling methods using the Exchange Management Shell.

How to do it...

1. In order to configure standard journaling, we use the following cmdlet to enable journaling on the mailbox database `DB01`, and configure the mailbox named `Journaling` as the journaling mailbox to store all journaled emails:

```
Set-MailboxDatabase DB01 -JournalRecipient journal
```

2. To configure premium journaling to journal external emails from the user `john@contoso.com`, we use the following cmdlet:

```
New-JournalRule -Name "Journal - John" -JournalEmailAddress
journal@contoso.com -Recipient john@contoso.com -Scope External -Enabled
$True
```

How it works...

Configuring standard journaling is straightforward: you use the `Set-MailboxDatabase` cmdlet to update one or more databases, and the `-JournalRecipient` parameter to specify the journal recipient to use for per-database journaling for all mailboxes on the database. Simple as that.

To disable journaling on the same mailbox database, you use the following cmdlet

```
Set-MailboxDatabase DB01 -JournalRecipient $null
```

With premium journaling, we can be more specific. In the previous example, we created a journal rule for the user `John` and stipulated that any email sent or received by John to or from external users should be journaled to the `journal` mailbox.

Premium journaling uses `journal rules` to record emails based on recipients (all recipients or specified recipients) and scope (internal, external, or all emails). The basic components of these rules are:

*   **Journal recipient** is who you want to journal. You can configure a journal rule to journal emails for all senders and recipients in the organization (by not using the `Recipient` parameter), or you can limit a journal rule to a mailbox, group, mail user, or mail contact.
*   **Journal rule scope** specifies what you want to journal: internal emails only (`Internal`), external emails only (`External`), or both (`Global`).
*   **Journaling mailbox** is where you want to store the journaled emails.

There's more...

If a journaling mailbox becomes unavailable (note that you can have one or more journaling mailboxes), journal reports sent to it are rejected and resubmitted for delivery (they are never returned to the original sender for obvious reasons). If you don't want these to remain in the delivery queue, you can configure an alternate journal mailbox to receive the journal reports until the original journaling mailbox becomes available.

Journal reports are delivered to this alternate journaling mailbox as attachments in a **Non-delivery reports** (**NDRs**). When the journaling mailbox becomes available again, you can use the **Send Again** feature in Outlook to resubmit the journal reports for delivery.

 Please note that when you configure an alternate journaling mailbox, it will apply to the entire Exchange organization. Any journal report rejected by any journaling mailbox will be redirected to the same alternate journaling mailbox.

To configure an alternate journaling mailbox, you must use the Shell and the `Set-TransportConfig` cmdlet (since it is a global setting):

```
Set-TransportConfig -JournalingReportNdrTo
alternate.journal@contoso.com
```

If your organization uses **Unified Messaging** (**UM**), Exchange will also journal voice mail notification and missed call notification emails. You can disable journaling for these types of emails, but emails containing faxes generated by the UM service are always journaled. To disable journaling for voice mail and missed call notifications, you use the following cmdlet:

```
Set-TransportConfig -VoicemailJournalingEnabled $False
```

Managing archive mailboxes

In Exchange 2010, a new personal storage concept was introduced, which still remains in Exchange 2016, called an archive mailbox, or in-place archive. The idea is that you can give one or more users a secondary mailbox that can be accessed from anywhere, just like their regular mailbox, and it can be used to store older mailbox data, thus eliminating the need for a PST file. The benefit of this is that archive mailboxes can be located on a database separate from the primary mailbox, allowing administrators to put low-priority, archived mailbox data on an inexpensive lower tier of storage. In this chapter, we'll take a look at how you can manage archive mailboxes for your users through the Exchange Management Shell.

How to do it...

To create an archive mailbox for an existing mailbox, use the `Enable-Mailbox` cmdlet, as shown in the following example:

```
Enable-Mailbox administrator -Archive
```

How it works...

When you create an archive mailbox for a user, they can access their personal archive when connecting to Exchange using Outlook 2010, 2013, and 2016, or Outlook on the Web. In the previous example, we created an archive mailbox for an existing user. We can also do this in bulk for multiple users very easily. For example, to create an archive mailbox for all users in the DB01 database, you could use the following command:

```
Get-Mailbox -Database DB01 | `
Enable-Mailbox -Archive -ArchiveDatabase ARCHIVE01
```

As you can see, we're making use of the pipeline here to perform a bulk operation on all mailboxes in database DB01. The result of the `Get-Mailbox` command is piped to the `Enable-Mailbox` cmdlet. The `-Archive` switch parameter tells the cmdlet that we know this user already has a mailbox, and we just want to create a personal archive for the user. In addition, we've specified the `-ArchiveDatabase` parameter so that the archives for each mailbox are not created in the same database as the primary mailbox, but instead in the ARCHIVE01 database.

When creating the archive mailboxes, they will receive the default size limitation for an archive mailbox, which has a warning quota limit set to 90 GB and the archive quota limit set to 100 GB.

In addition to creating an archive for an existing user, we can enable a personal archive for a mailbox as it is created. For example, the following commands will create a mailbox and a personal archive for a new user:

```
$password = ConvertTo-SecureString P@ssword -AsPlainText -Force
New-Mailbox -Name "Dave Smith" -alias dsmith '
-UserPrincipalName dave@contoso.com '
-Database DB01 -Archive '
-ArchiveDatabase ARCHIVE01 '
-Password $password
```

In this command, we've created the primary mailbox in the DB01 database, and again, we've made use of the -Archive and -ArchiveDatabase parameters so that the archive is created in the ARCHIVE01 database.

There's more...

If you need to turn off an archive mailbox for a user, you can use the Disable-Mailbox cmdlet with the -Archive switch parameter. The command to disable the personal archive for *Dave Smith* is as simple as this:

```
Disable-Mailbox dsmith -Archive -Confirm:$False
```

When you run this command, the archive mailbox for the user goes into a disconnected state, but the user can still access their primary mailbox. The disconnected archive mailbox is retained in the database until the deleted mailbox retention period for the database has elapsed.

 Be aware, as enabling in-place archive requires an Enterprise CAL for the enabled users.

See also

- *Adding, modifying, and removing mailboxes* recipe in Chapter 3, *Managing Recipients*
- *Configuring archive mailbox quotas* recipe in this chapter

Configuring archive mailbox quotas

As you enable archive mailboxes for end users and set up retention policies (shown later in the chapter), you may find that the default limitations configured for archive mailboxes do not meet your needs. In this recipe, you'll learn how to modify archive mailbox quotas using the Exchange Management Shell.

How to do it...

Let's see how to configure archive mailbox quotas by performing the following steps:

1. To modify the archive quota settings for a single mailbox, use the `Set-Mailbox` cmdlet:

```
Set-Mailbox dsmith -ArchiveQuota 10gb -ArchiveWarningQuota 8gb
```

2. To do this in bulk, use the `Get-Mailbox` cmdlet to retrieve the mailboxes that need to be updated and pipe the results to the `Set-Mailbox` cmdlet. For example, this command would update all the users in the DB01 database:

```
Get-Mailbox -Database DB01 -Archive | `
Set-Mailbox -ArchiveQuota 10gb -ArchiveWarningQuota 8gb
```

As you can see here, we're filtering the results of the `Get-Mailbox` cmdlet by using the `-Archive` switch so only archive mailboxes are included in the results, and then setting their quota.

How it works...

There are two settings that can be used to configure quotas for archive mailboxes:

- `ArchiveWarningQuota`: When an archive mailbox exceeds the size set for the archive warning quota, a warning message is sent to the mailbox owner and an event is logged on the mailbox server that hosts the archive mailbox
- `ArchiveQuota`: When an archive mailbox exceeds the size set for the archive quota, a warning message is sent to the mailbox owner and items can no longer be moved to the archive mailbox

In Exchange 2016, archive mailboxes are configured with default limitations. The archive warning quota is set to 90 GB and the archive quota is set to 100 GB. These settings can only be applied on a per-mailbox basis, unlike regular mailboxes, which can receive their limits from the parent database.

If you implement custom archive quotas, you may need to run a script on a regular basis to update any new archives that have been recently created. For example, let's say that you've decided that archive mailboxes should not be larger than 5 GB. You can run a script regularly, either manually or through a scheduled task, that will update any new users:

```
Get-Mailbox -ResultSize Unlimited -Archive |
```

```
Where-Object {$_.ArchiveQuota -ge 100gb} |
Set-Mailbox -ArchiveQuota 5gb -ArchiveWarningQuota 4gb
```

Again, we're using the `-Archive` switch to get only archive mailboxes, plus the `Where-Object` cmdlet to filter those whose `ArchiveQuota` value is greater than or equal to 100 GB. If any are found, we send those mailboxes down the pipeline to the `Set-Mailbox` cmdlet and modify the archive quota settings.

You could remove the `Where` filter which would set every archive to 5 GB and ignore those already set to 5 GB. However, if you have users with a different archive sizes, they would all be set to 5 GB, which might not be desirable. By using the `Where` filter, we ensure only new mailboxes are targeted.

There's more...

You can view the current settings for these values using the `Get-Mailbox` cmdlet. For example, to check the values for a specific user, run the following command:

```
Get-Mailbox <user> | Format-List *archive*
```

You will be presented with the following screenshot:

```
[PS] C:\>Get-Mailbox nuno | Format-List *archive*


ArchiveDatabase               : DB1
ArchiveGuid                   : b5d3eef1-c097-46d3-8eb5-3ae447dd0589
ArchiveName                   : {In-Place Archive - Nuno}
JournalArchiveAddress         :
ArchiveQuota                  : 100 GB (107,374,182,400 bytes)
ArchiveWarningQuota           : 90 GB (96,636,764,160 bytes)
ArchiveDomain                 :
ArchiveStatus                 : None
ArchiveState                  : Local
AutoExpandingArchiveEnabled   : False
DisabledArchiveDatabase       :
DisabledArchiveGuid           : 00000000-0000-0000-0000-000000000000
ArchiveRelease                :
```

The preceding command uses a wildcard to display all the properties of a mailbox that contain the `word` archive. This will provide the quota settings, as well as the database location for the archive mailbox, which may be different from that of the user's primary mailbox.

See also

- *Managing archive mailboxes* recipe in this chapter

Creating retention tags and policies

Retention policies are the recommended method for implementing messaging records management in Exchange 2016. Retention policies use retention tags to apply settings to mailbox folders and individual items. Retention tags are configured with a retention action that can be taken when an item reaches its retention age limit. In this recipe, you'll learn how to create retention tags and policies using the Exchange Management Shell.

How to do it...

There are three types of retention tags that can be used to apply retention settings to a mailbox through a retention policy. The following steps outline the process of creating custom retention tags based on these types and assigning them to a new retention policy:

1. The following command will create a retention policy tag for the `Inbox` folder, specifying that items older than 90 days should be permanently deleted:

```
New-RetentionPolicyTag -Name AllUsers-Inbox '
-Type Inbox '
-Comment "Items older than 90 days are deleted" '
-RetentionEnabled $True '
-AgeLimitForRetention 90 '
-RetentionAction PermanentlyDelete
```

2. In addition, we can create a default policy tag for the entire mailbox. To do this, we need to set the type to `All`. A default retention policy tag of `Type All` will apply to any item that does not have a retention tag applied:

```
New-RetentionPolicyTag -Name AllUsers-Default '
-Type All '
```

```
-Comment "Items older than 120 days are permanently deleted" '
-RetentionEnabled $True '
-AgeLimitForRetention 120 '
-RetentionAction PermanentlyDelete
```

3. We can also create personal tags that can be used by end users for personal items:

```
New-RetentionPolicyTag -Name Critical '
-Type Personal '
-Comment "Use this tag for all critical items" '
-RetentionEnabled $True '
-AgeLimitForRetention 730 '
-RetentionAction DeleteAndAllowRecovery
```

4. After creating these tags, we can create a new retention policy and add the previously created tags:

```
New-RetentionPolicy -Name AllUsers '
-RetentionPolicyTagLinks AllUsers-Inbox, '
AllUsers-Default, Critical
```

At this point, the `AllUsers` retention policy can be assigned to one or more mailboxes, and the settings defined by the retention tags will be applied.

How it works...

The management of retention tags and policies can be done both from the Exchange Admin Center and using the Shell. You might find it easier to manage the policies through the GUI, but in either case, the cmdlets used to create and manage tags and policies can still be used if automation or command-line administration is required.

As we saw from the previous example, there are three types of retention tags that can be used to apply retention settings to mailbox folders and messages. These types are outlined in detail as follows:

- **Retention policy tags**: These are used to apply settings to default folders, such as `Inbox` and `Sent Items`.
- **Default policy tags**: These apply to any item that does not have a retention tag set. A retention policy can contain only one default policy tag.
- **Personal tags**: These can be applied by users who access their mailboxes from Outlook or the Outlook on the Web. Personal tags can be applied to custom folders and individual items.

When you create one or more retention tags to be applied to a policy, you'll need to define the type using one of these settings. Additionally, retention tags have actions that will be used when the age limit for retention is met. The available retention actions are outlined as follows:

- `MarkAsPastRetentionLimit`: This action will mark an item as past the retention limit, displaying the message using strikethrough text in Outlook or OWA.
- `DeleteAndAllowRecovery`: This action will perform a hard delete, sending the message to the dumpster. The user will be able to recover the item using the **Recover Deleted Items** dialog box in Outlook or OWA.
- `PermanentlyDelete`: This action will permanently delete the message. It cannot be restored using the **Recover Deleted Items** dialog box.
- `MoveToArchive`: This action moves the message to the user's archive mailbox.

When working with retention tags and policies, there are a few things you should keep in mind. First, mailboxes can only be assigned one policy at a time, and you cannot have multiple retention policy tags for a single default folder in the same retention policy. For example, you can't have two retention policy tags for the `Inbox` default folder in the same retention policy.

Retention policies can only contain one default policy tag of type `All`. You can assign multiple personal tags to a policy, but be careful not to go overboard, as this can be confusing for users. Also, keep in mind that retention tags are not applied to mailboxes until they have been linked to an enabled retention policy and the managed folder assistant has run against each mailbox.

 Keep in mind that the managed folder assistant is throttle-based in Exchange 2016, which means that it will run whenever there are resources available. It can, however, be forced to start using the `Start-ManagedFolderAssistant` cmdlet.

There's more...

You can create a retention policy without initially linking any retention tags to it. You can also go back and add retention tags to a policy later if needed. If you need to add or remove tags to an existing policy, you can use the `Set-RetentionPolicy` cmdlet. For example, to add the `Sales-Inbox` and `Sales-DeletedItems` retention policy tags to the `Sales-Users` retention policy, your command would look like the following:

```
Set-RetentionPolicy Sales-Users '
-RetentionPolicyTagLinks Sales-Inbox, Sales-DeletedItems
```

The thing to note here is that this command will overwrite the policy's current tag list. If you need to add tags and keep the policy's existing tags, you will need to use a special syntax. For example, run the following command:

```
$Tags = (Get-RetentionPolicy Sales-Users).RetentionPolicyTagLinks
$Tags += Get-RetentionPolicyTag Sales-Critical
Set-RetentionPolicy Sales-Users -RetentionPolicyTagLinks $Tags
```

What we're doing here is saving the existing tag list applied to the Sales-Users policy in the $Tags variable. We then add the new tag to this variable. Finally, we assign $Tags back to the retention policy when running the Set-RetentionPolicy cmdlet.

Understanding default tags

When you install Exchange 2016, several retention tags are created by default. These may be specific enough to meet your needs, so you might want to take a look at these before creating any custom tags. To view the current list of available retention tags, use the Get-RetentionPolicyTag cmdlet:

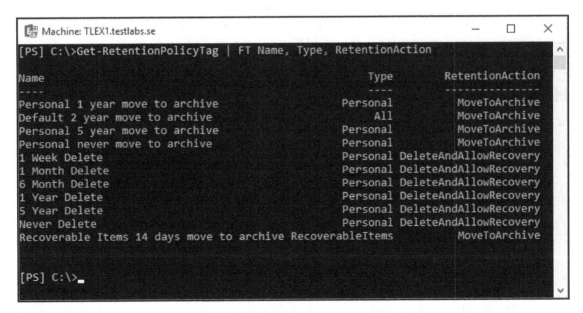

In addition, Exchange automatically creates retention policies for use with personal archives and arbitration mailboxes.

In Exchange 2016, by default, only one retention policy is created, named `Default MRM Policy`. This policy can be applied to mailboxes that contain personal archives and it provides a built-in set of retention tags.

Some of the retention tags used within these policies are considered system tags and, by default, are not visible when running the `Get-RetentionPolicyTag` cmdlet. You can view the tags included with these policies using the `-IncludeSystemTags` switch parameter:

```
Get-RetentionPolicyTag -IncludeSystemTags
```

See also

- *Applying retention policies to mailboxes* recipe in this chapter

Applying retention policies to mailboxes

Retention policies are not automatically applied to end user mailboxes and must be set manually using either the Exchange Admin Center or the Exchange Management Shell. In this recipe, you'll learn how to apply retention policies to mailboxes from the command line, which will be useful when performing a retention policy assignment on a large number of mailboxes, or on a regular basis as new mailboxes are created.

How to do it...

Let's see how to apply retention policies to mailboxes by performing the following steps:

1. To apply a retention policy to a mailbox, you use the `Set-Mailbox` cmdlet, specifying the retention policy name using the `-RetentionPolicy` parameter. For example, to do this for one user, the command would look something like this:

```
Set-Mailbox dsmith -RetentionPolicy AllUsers
```

2. In addition, you may need to perform this operation on all mailboxes at once. In this case, you could use the following command:

```
Get-Mailbox -RecipientTypeDetails UserMailbox `
-ResultSize Unlimited | `
Set-Mailbox -RetentionPolicy AllUsers
```

How it works...

Retention policies are set on a per-mailbox basis. Unfortunately, there is no default setting that allows you to apply retention policies for new mailboxes. This can become a problem if your organization regularly creates new mailboxes and administrators forget to assign a retention policy during the provisioning process.

To get around this, you can schedule the following command to run on a regular basis:

```
Get-Mailbox -RecipientTypeDetails UserMailbox `
-Filter {RetentionPolicy -eq $null} `
-ResultSize Unlimited | `
Set-Mailbox -RetentionPolicy AllUsers
```

The preceding command will retrieve all user mailboxes in the organization that do not have a retention policy setting. This is done by using the `-Filter` parameter to only return those mailboxes without a retention policy applied Any mailboxes retrieved based on this filter will be piped down to the `Set-Mailbox` cmdlet, where a retention policy will be applied.

Another option would be to set the retention policy as mailboxes are created using the scripting agent. See the *Automating tasks with the scripting agent* recipe in `Chapter 2`, *Exchange Management Shell Common Tasks*, for more details.

There's more...

Once a retention policy is set on a mailbox, the retention settings defined by the policy's retention tags will be applied to each mailbox by the **Managed Folder Assistant (MFA)**. MFA is a service that runs on each mailbox server and, by default, it is set to process every mailbox on the server within one day. It is throttle-based, which means that the tasks will be running all the time and it will do its work only when there are resources available. Having said that, it is possible to force the **Managed Folder Assistant** to run immediately, but keep in mind that it could impact the performance of the mailbox server.

To force MFA to process a particular mailbox, use the `Start-ManagedFolderAssistant` cmdlet:

```
Start-ManagedFolderAssistant dsmith@contoso.com
```

To force it to run against all mailboxes in a particular database, use the following command:

```
Get-Mailbox -Database DB01 | Start-ManagedFolderAssistant
```

See also

- *Placing mailboxes on retention hold* recipe in this chapter
- *Scheduling scripts to run at a later time* recipe in `Chapter 2`, *Exchange Management Shell Common Tasks*
- *Automating tasks with the scripting agent* recipe in `Chapter 2`, *Exchange Management Shell Common Tasks*

Placing mailboxes on retention hold

When users go on vacation or are out of the office for an extended period of time, you may need to suspend the processing of the retention policy applied to their mailboxes. This recipe will show you how to use the Exchange Management Shell to place mailboxes on retention hold, as well as how to remove the retention hold and discover which mailboxes are currently configured for retention hold.

How to do it...

Let's see how to place a mailbox on retention hold by performing the following steps:

1. To place a mailbox on retention hold, use the `Set-Mailbox` cmdlet:

   ```
   Set-Mailbox dsmith -RetentionHoldEnabled $True
   ```

2. To remove the retention hold setting from the mailbox, use the same command, but set the `-RetentionHoldEnabled` parameter to `$False`:

   ```
   Set-Mailbox dsmith -RetentionHoldEnabled $False
   ```

How it works...

When retention hold is enabled for a mailbox, the user who owns that mailbox can still open their mailbox, send and receive messages, delete items, and so on. The only difference is that any items that are past the retention period for any assigned tags will not be processed.

You can include a retention comment when placing a user on retention hold. Users running supported versions of Outlook will see the retention comments in the backstage area of Outlook. To add a comment, use the same command used previously, but supply a message using the -RetentionComment parameter:

```
Set-Mailbox dsmith `
-RetentionHoldEnabled $True `
-RetentionComment "You are currently on retention hold"
```

Since the retention hold setting is enabled using the Set-Mailbox cmdlet, you can easily apply this setting to many mailboxes at once with a simple command. Let's say that you need to do this for all users in the Marketing distribution group:

```
Get-DistributionGroupMember Marketing | `
Set-Mailbox -RetentionHoldEnabled $True
```

Or, maybe you need to do this for all users in a particular database:

```
Get-Mailbox -Database DB01 | `
Set-Mailbox -RetentionHoldEnabled $True
```

In addition to simply enabling this setting, you also have the option of configuring a start and end date for the retention hold period using the following command:

```
Set-Mailbox dsmith -RetentionHoldEnabled $True `
-StartDateForRetentionHold '5/1/2017 8:00:00 AM' `
  -EndDateForRetentionHold '5/31/2017 5:00:00 PM'
```

This command will preconfigure the start date for the retention hold period and remove that setting when the end date elapses.

There's more...

If you are not sure which users are currently configured with the retention hold setting, you can use the following command to retrieve all mailboxes that have retention hold enabled:

```
Get-Mailbox -ResultSize Unlimited | `
Where-Object {$_.RetentionHoldEnabled}
```

Any mailboxes with the RetentionHoldEnabled property set to $True will be retrieved using the preceding command.

See also

- *Placing mailboxes on in-place hold or litigation hold* recipe in this chapter

Placing mailboxes on in-place hold or litigation hold

When an organization is dealing with the possibility of a legal action, data such as documents and email messages related to the case will usually need to be reviewed, and an effort to preserve this information must be made. Exchange 2016 allows you to protect and maintain this data by placing mailboxes on **In-Place Hold** or on **Litigation Hold**. This prevents users or retention policies from modifying or removing any messages that may be required during the legal discovery process. In this recipe, you'll learn how to manage hold settings for mailboxes from the Exchange Management Shell.

 Litigation hold was introduced in Exchange 2010, and it still remains in Exchange 2016. Although it is recommended that you use the in-place hold feature instead, which is better suited for most scenarios, we will show you how to use both.

How to do it...

Let's first see how to place a mailbox on litigation hold using the following steps:

```
Set-Mailbox john@contoso.com `
-LitigationHoldEnabled $True `
-LitigationHoldDuration 90
```

To place a mailbox on in-place hold, you use the New-MailboxSearch cmdlet. However, you will need special permissions to do so. By default, no one, not even the user who installed Exchange 2016, is assigned the right to perform searches. Using an account that is a member of the Organization Management role group, you can assign the required permissions in one of the two ways, and then perform a discovery search.

These tasks are outlined in the following steps:

1. For example, if you are using the administrator account that is already a part of the `Organization Management` role group, you can assign yourself the permission to perform discovery searches by adding your account to the `Discovery Management` role group:

```
Add-RoleGroupMember "Discovery Management" `
-Member administrator
```

2. As an alternative, you can also give yourself or another user a direct role assignment to the `Mailbox Search` role:

```
New-ManagementRoleAssignment -Role "Mailbox Search" `
-User administrator
```

3. After restarting the Shell to refresh the permissions assigned to the account, you can use the `New-MailboxSearch` cmdlet to place a mailbox on in-place hold:

```
New-MailboxSearch -Name "InPlace-Hold-dsmith" `
-SourceMailboxes dsmith@contoso.com `
-InPlaceHoldEnabled $True
```

4. To remove the in-place hold setting from the mailbox, we need to disable the in-place hold and remove the mailbox search using the following cmdlet:

```
Set-MailboxSearch "InPlace-Hold-dsmith" `
-InPlaceHoldEnabled $False
Remove-MailboxSearch "InPlace-Hold-dsmith"
```

How it works...

Litigation Hold only allows you to place all items in a mailbox on hold, while in-place hold allows you to search and preserve messages matching query parameters. Both types of hold protect messages from permanent deletion, modification, and tampering and can preserve these indefinitely or for a specified period.

Litigation Hold uses the `LitigationHoldEnabled` property of a mailbox. When Litigation Hold is enabled, all mailbox items are placed on hold. In our example, we also used the `LitigationHoldDuration` parameter to specify that mailbox items should be held for 90 days (the duration is calculated from the date a mailbox item is received or created). The default value is `unlimited`, meaning items are held indefinitely or until the hold is removed.

In our second example, we used in-place hold to achieve the same thing: place a hold on all mailbox items. The advantage of using in-place hold is that we can use the `SearchQuery` parameter to specify keywords for the search query by using **Keyword Query Language (KQL)**. Additionally, we can use the `MessageTypes` parameter to only place a hold on certain message types such as `Contacts`, `Docs`, `Email`, `IM`, `Journals`, `Meetings`, `Notes`, or `Tasks`.

You can place multiple in-place holds on a mailbox, unlike Litigation Hold which is either enabled or disabled for a mailbox. If you remove a litigation hold from a mailbox, but one or more in-place holds are still placed on the mailbox, items matching the in-place hold criteria are held for the period of that hold.

At first glance, it may seem that these two hold types and retention hold are essentially the same, but they are quite different. When you place a mailbox on litigation or in-place hold, retention policies are not suspended, which gives the end user the impression that the policies are still in place and that data can be removed from the mailbox.

When a user empties their `Deleted Items` folder or performs a *Shift + Delete* on messages, these items are moved to the `Recoverable Items` folder. Users can recover these items by default for up to 14 days, but they can also delete items from the `Recoverable Items` folder using the Recover Deleted Items tool in an attempt to permanently purge the data from their mailbox. Deleting items for the `Recoverable Items` folder places the data in the `Purges` sub-folder, which is hidden from the user. When a mailbox is on hold, an administrator can access the items in a folder called `DiscoveryHold` using the Discovery Search, and the mailbox assistant does not purge the items in this folder when the database's deleted item retention period elapses.

During the hold period, each object version is saved, and when a user or process changes an item, each version is saved to a new version and placed in a folder called `Versions`.

Messages located in the Recoverable Items folder do not count against a user's mailbox storage quota, but each mailbox does have a `RecoverableItemsQuota` property that is set to 30 GB by default. This property can be changed at the database level using the `Set-MailboxDatabase` cmdlet, or at the mailbox level using the `Set-Mailbox` cmdlet.

 Keep in mind that when you place a mailbox on hold, it may take up to 60 minutes to take effect. You'll receive a warning message in the Shell explaining this when you enable the setting for a mailbox.

You can include a retention comment when placing a user on hold, as some organizations are required to inform users of this for legal purposes. Users running Outlook will see retention comments in the backstage area of Outlook. To add a comment, you use the same parameters as when configuring retention hold in the previous recipe: you provide a message using the -RetentionComment parameter together with the -RetentionUrl parameter when placing the mailbox on in-place hold:

```
Set-Mailbox dsmith '
-RetentionComment "You are currently on in-place hold, please visit the
provided URL" '
-RetentionUrl http://intranet.contoso.com/in-place-hold/
```

After this setting has been configured, it might take a while before it takes effect; it will show up in Outlook when you click on the **File** button, and it will look similar to the following screenshot:

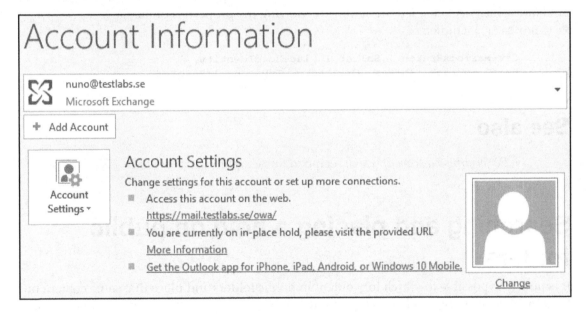

There's more...

To determine which users are currently on litigation hold, who put them on hold, and when, use the following cmdlet:

```
Get-Mailbox -Filter {LitigationHoldEnabled -eq $True} | `
Select Name, LitigationHoldOwner, LitigationHoldDate
```

To determine which users are currently on in-place hold, use the Get-Mailbox cmdlet and retrieve the mailboxes that have a value configured in the InPlaceHolds field using the following cmdlet:

```
Get-Mailbox -ResultSize Unlimited | Where {$_.InPlaceHolds} | `
Select Name, InPlaceHolds
```

When a mailbox has been placed on in-place hold, you can view the date that was placed on hold and which user enabled the setting by viewing the properties of the Get-MailboxSearch cmdlet:

```
Get-MailboxSearch | Select InPlaceHoldIdentity, `
Name, SourceMailboxes, CreatedBy, InPlaceHoldEnabled
```

See also

- *Performing a discovery search* recipe in this chapter

Searching and placing a hold on public folders

It is now also possible to search for content in public folders and place that same content on hold by using eDiscovery. This is important as many organizations still make extensive use of public folders to keep data, and not being able to easily search that data can only bring issues when trying to respond to legal requests.

In this recipe, we will see how to place a hold on public folder content using the Shell.

How to do it...

To place all content in all public folders on in-place hold for an unlimited hold duration, you use the following cmdlet:

```
New-MailboxSearch -Name "All PFs Hold" -AllPublicFolderSources $True -
    AllSourceMailboxes $False -EstimateOnly -InPlaceHoldEnabled $True
        Start-MailboxSearch "All PFs Hold"
```

How it works...

In this example, we are placing a hold on all public folder content, across all public folders, and for an unlimited duration. The `-AllPublicFolderSources` parameter stipulates to include all public folders in the organization in our search, and `-AllSourceMailboxes` excludes any mailboxes. You can use an in-place hold to place public folder content on hold, but if you select the option to search all mailboxes, you can't use the search to place a hold on any of the content sources of the search.

Next, we use the `-EstimateOnly` switch to specify that only an estimate of the number of items that will be returned is provided, and we set the `-InPlaceHoldEnabled` parameter to `True` to enable in-place hold on the search results.

Finally, we use the `Start-MailboxSearch` cmdlet to run the search and place the content on hold.

You can only search or place a hold on all public folders in the organization. There is currently no way of selecting specific public folders to search.

Also, please be aware that you cannot delete a public folder that is on In-Place Hold. To do this, you must remove the hold before you delete the public folder.

There's more...

You can also create an estimate-only search that searches all public folders in the organization for items that match a certain criterion. In the next example, we are searching all public folders for items sent between January 1, 2017 and May 31, 2017 and that contain the phrase "`project x`":

```
New-MailboxSearch -Name "All PFs Project X Search" -
    AllPublicFolderSources $True -AllSourceMailboxes $False -SearchQuery
```

```
"project x" -StartDate "01/01/2017" -EndDate "05/31/2017" -EstimateOnly
    Start-MailboxSearch "All PFs Project X Search"
    Get-MailboxSearch "All PFs Project X Search" | Select
ResultNumberEstimate
```

When compared to the previous example, we are using a few new parameters here. First, we use -SearchQuery to specify the keywords for the search query using the KQL. In this case, we want any item containing the words "project x".

The -StartDate and -EndDate parameter specify the start and end dates of items to include in the search. Here you should use the short date format that is defined in the Regional Options settings on the computer where you are running the command.

Next, we use the -EstimateOnly switch to stipulate that only an estimate of the number of items that will be returned is provided. If you don't use this switch, messages are copied to the target mailbox when the -TargetMailbox parameter is used. Finally, we use the Get-MailboxSearch cmdlet to check how many items the search returned.

See also

- *Placing mailboxes on in-place hold or litigation hold* recipe in this chapter
- *Performing eDiscovery searches* recipe in this chapter

Performing eDiscovery searches

Exchange 2016 provides the ability to search through mailboxes for content that might be required during an investigation, such as a violation of organizational policy or regulatory compliance, or due to a lawsuit. Although this can be done through the Exchange Admin Center, you may need to do this from the command line. In this recipe, you'll learn how to perform discovery searches from the Exchange Management Shell.

How to do it...

To perform an eDiscovery search, we also use the New-MailboxSearch cmdlet. This cmdlet can be used to create a mailbox search and either get an estimate of search results, place search results on in-place hold, or copy them to a **Discovery** mailbox.

After you have been assigned permissions, you can use the `New-MailboxSearch` cmdlet to create a new search:

```
New-MailboxSearch -Name Case1 '
-TargetMailbox "Discovery Search Mailbox" '
-SearchQuery 'Subject:"Corporate Secrets"' '
-StartDate "1/1/2016" '
-EndDate "12/31/2016" '
-MessageTypes Email '
-IncludeUnsearchableItems '
-LogLevel Full
```

The previous command will search all the mailboxes in the organization for messages sent or received in the year 2016 with a subject of `Corporate Secrets`. Any messages found matching this criterion will be copied to the `Discovery Search Mailbox`.

How it works...

One of the benefits of using the Shell instead of the EAC when performing a discovery search is that you can specify the target mailbox. The EAC requires that you use a `Discovery Search Mailbox` to store the results. With the `New-MailboxSearch` cmdlet, you can provide a value for the `-TargetMailbox` parameter and specify another mailbox.

If you perform a search without specifying any source mailboxes by using the `-SourceMailboxes` parameter, all the mailboxes in the organization will be searched, as in our previous example. One thing to keep in mind is that, in order to successfully perform a search, you need to have healthy database indexes, and indexing needs to be enabled (which it is, by default) for each database that contains the mailboxes you are searching.

Let's take a look at another example. This time, we'll search a specific mailbox and store the results in an alternate mailbox using the following command:

```
New-MailboxSearch -Name Case2 '
-SourceMailboxes dsmith, jjones '
-TargetMailbox administrator '
-SearchQuery 'Subject:"Corporate Secrets"' '
-MessageTypes Email, IM, Notes '
-StatusMailRecipients legal@contoso.com
```

This time, we've specified two source mailboxes to search, and the results will be stored in the administrator mailbox. The -StatusMailRecipients parameter is also used to send an email notification to the legal department when the search is complete. Also notice that, this time, we did not specify a start or end date, so the search will be performed against all items of type email, instant messaging, and notes, in each source mailbox.

The key to performing a precise search is using the -SearchQuery parameter. This allows you to use keywords and specific property values when searching for items with the KQL. See Appendix B, *Query Syntaxes*, at the end of this book, for more details on KQL.

Once a discovery search has been completed, you can export the items captured by the search by accessing the target mailbox. Whether it is the discovery search mailbox or an alternate mailbox that you specified when running the command, you can give your account full access permissions to the mailbox and access the items using Outlook or OWA.

There's more...

Once you start a discovery search, it may take some time to complete depending on the size and number of mailboxes you are working with. These searches can be completely managed from the Shell. For example, if you want to remove a search before it completes, you can use the Remove-MailboxSearch cmdlet. You can also stop a search, modify its properties, and then restart it. Let's say that we've just created a new search, we can check its status with the Get-MailboxSearch cmdlet:

```
Get-MailboxSearch | Select Name, Status, Percentcomplete
```

If needed, we can stop the search before it is completed, modify its properties, and then restart the search using the mailbox search cmdlets:

```
Stop-MailboxSearch Case2
Set-MailboxSearch Case2 -SourceMailboxes Finance, HR
Start-MailboxSearch Case2
```

As you can see in these commands, we first stop the Case2 search, then modify the source mailboxes it is configured to run against, and finally restarted the search.

See also

- *Deleting messages from mailboxes* in Chapter 4, *Managing Mailboxes*
- *Performing Compliance searches* recipe in this chapter

Performing Compliance searches

Another new feature introduced in Exchange 2016 is **Compliance Search**, which allows administrators to search all mailboxes in the organization. While In-Place eDiscovery is limited to search only up to 10,000 mailboxes, compliance search does not have such limitation, which is extremely helpful for large organizations that need to perform organization-wide searches.

Compliance search uses the `New-ComplianceSearch` cmdlet we already looked at in the *Deleting messages from mailboxes using Compliance Search* recipe from `Chapter 4`, *Managing Mailboxes*. Using this cmdlet, we can search all mailboxes in the organization and then use in-place eDiscovery to perform other eDiscovery-related tasks, such as placing mailboxes on hold or exporting search results.

In this recipe, we will look at how we can leverage the `New-ComplianceSearch` cmdlet to determine which mailboxes contain items related to an investigation.

How to do it...

To search all mailboxes in the organization for items that match particular criteria, and determine which mailboxes contain such items, use the following cmdlets:

```
New-ComplianceSearch -Name "Search All - Project X" -ExchangeLocation
All -ContentMatchQuery 'sent>=01/01/2017 AND sent<=07/31/2017 AND
subject:"project x"'
Start-ComplianceSearch "Search All - Project X"
Get-ComplianceSearch "Search All - Project X" | FL
```

How it works...

In this example, we used the `New-ComplianceSearch` cmdlet to run an organization-wide search. The `-ExchangeLocation` parameter specifies a distribution group, a single mailbox, or all mailboxes to include in the compliance search. Then we use the `-ContentMatchQuery` parameter to specify our content search filter using the KQL. In this case, we are searching for emails sent or received between January and July 2017 and that have a subject with the phrase `project x`.

Next, we start the actual search by using the `Start-ComplianceSearch` cmdlet. Once the search starts, we can track its progress by running `Get-ComplianceSearch`. When it completes, we can easily check how many items our search criteria matched, and on which mailboxes:

```
Machine: TLEX1.testlabs.se                                      —    □    ✕
[PS] C:\>Get-ComplianceSearch "Search All - Project X" | Select Status, Items, SuccessResult
s, NumFailedSources, NumBindings, ExchangeLocation


Status            : Completed
Items             : 47
SuccessResults    : {Location: admin@testlabs.se, Item count: 11, Total size: 83281,
                    Location: nuno@testlabs.se, Item count: 8, Total size: 68760,
                    Location: ceo@testlabs.se, Item count: 8, Total size: 63432,
                    Location: it.servicedesk@testlabs.se, Item count: 5, Total size: 45315,
                    Location: auditor@testlabs.se, Item count: 5, Total size: 45075,
                    Location: testuser@testlabs.se, Item count: 5, Total size: 45060,
                    Location: jonas@testlabs.se, Item count: 5, Total size: 44950}
NumFailedSources  : 0
NumBindings       : 7
ExchangeLocation  : {All}



[PS] C:\>_
```

There's more...

If you want to place these mailboxes on hold, you can copy their email addresses from the preceding output to a text file and use that file to create the hold. Alternatively, you can use the following code to parse the preceding results and retrieve all the mailboxes:

```
    $results = (Get-ComplianceSearch "Search All - Project
X").SuccessResults
    $mbxs = @()
    $lines = $results -Split '[\r\n]+';
    ForEach ($line in $lines) {
        If ($line -match 'Location: (\S+),.+Item count: (\d+)' -and
$matches[2] -gt 0)
        {
            $mbxs += $matches[1];
        }
    }
```

At the end, the variable $mbxs will contain a list of all the mailboxes that the search returned, which can be easily used to create our In-Place Hold.

See also

- *Deleting messages from mailboxes using Compliance Search* recipe in `Chapter 4`, *Managing Mailboxes*
- *Performing eDiscovery searches* recipe in this chapter

Configuring data loss prevention

Data Loss Prevention (DLP), is a system designed to detect a potential data breach/leakage incident in a timely manner and prevent it. When this happens, sensitive data such as personal or company information (credit card details, social security numbers, and so on) is disclosed to unauthorized users either with malicious intent or by mistake. This has always been crucial for most companies as loss of sensitive data can be very damaging for a business. Since Exchange 2013, and further improved in 2016, Microsoft has made it possible to enforce compliance requirements for such data and control how it is used in email. DLP is the feature that allows administrators to manage sensitive data in Exchange.

In this recipe, we will look at how we can configure DLP using the Shell to help prevent accidental data leakage.

How to do it...

To create a new DLP policy to prevent users from accidentally sending credit card numbers outside of the organization, we use the following cmdlet:

```
New-DlpPolicy -Name "Block Outbound Credit Card Details" -Template
"U.K. Financial Data" -Mode Enforce -State Enabled
```

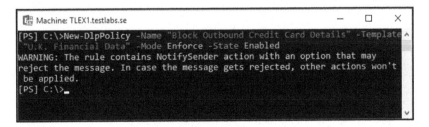

How it works...

DLP works through **DLP Policies**, packages that contain a set of conditions made up of rules, actions, and exceptions. These packages are based on Transport Rules and can be created in the Exchange Administration Center or through the Exchange Management Shell. Once created and activated, they will start analyzing and filtering emails.

To create our DLP policy, we used the New-DlpPolicy cmdlet and gave our policy the name of "Block Outbound Credit Card Details". Using the -Template parameter, we specified that this policy should use the Microsoft-provided template U.K. Financial Data. To know more about this template, or any other template provided by Microsoft, we can use the Get-DlpPolicyTemplate cmdlet:

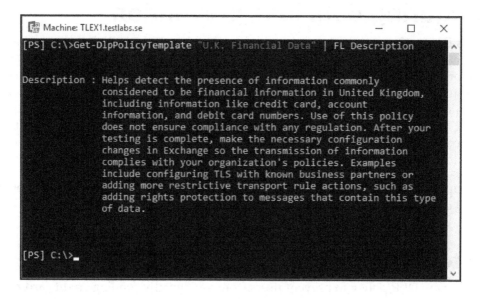

Alternatively, you can use the `-TemplateData` parameter to specify an external DLP policy template file to use in your new DLP policy.

Next, we set the policy's `Mode` to `Enforce`, which means that actions specified by the policy are enforced when a message matches its conditions, and a policy tip (when using a supported email client) is displayed to the user. The other two possible values for the `Mode` parameter are `Audit` (the default value), where the actions specified by the DLP policy are not enforced and a policy tip isn't displayed to the user, and `AuditAndNotify`, where the actions specified by the DLP policy are also not enforced, but a Policy Tip is displayed to the user. This is useful as it allows us to create and test a DLP policy without affecting the mail flow.

Finally, we set the policy's `State` to `Enabled`. By default, any new DLP policy you create is enabled, so we didn't really need to use this parameter.

When a user now tries to send credit card information to an external recipient, they are notified. Depending on how the policy is configured the sender might just get notified and allowed to send the email. This is the default behavior when the number of detected credit card numbers is nine or less:

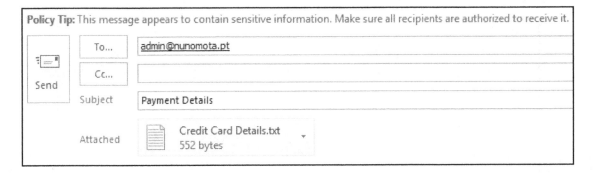

Using message tracking logs, we can see that the transport agent detected three credit card numbers and notified the sender, amongst other details:

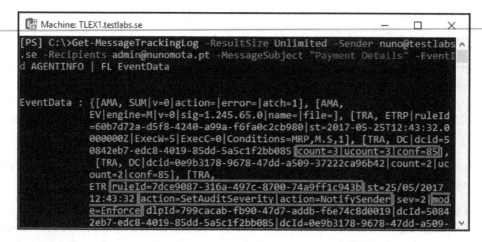

When the number of detected credit cards is 10 or more, the user is prevented from sending the email. If an override is allowed, the user is also notified on how to use it:

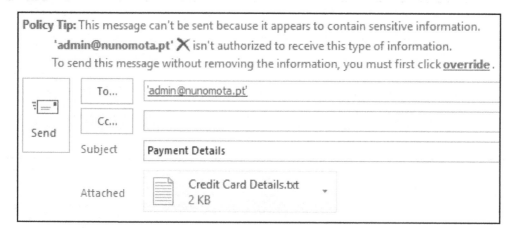

This is shown in the following screenshot:

If the sender is using a mail client that does not support these policies, he/she will receive an NDR:

Delivery has failed to these recipients or groups:

'admin@nunomota.pt' (admin@nunomota.pt)
Unable to deliver your message. You can override this policy by adding the word 'override' to the subject line.

Your message wasn't delivered because the email admin for the organization 'testlabs.se' created an email rule restriction. Please contact the email admin for that organization and ask them to remove or update the rule restriction.
For more information about this error, see DSN code 5.7.1 in Exchange Online - Office 365.

When this happens, message tracking logs also contain information regarding why the email failed to be delivered:

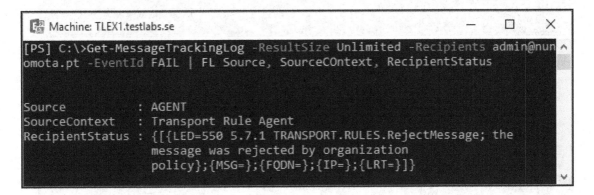

```
[PS] C:\>Get-MessageTrackingLog -ResultSize Unlimited -Recipients admin@nun
omota.pt -EventId FAIL | FL Source, SourceCOntext, RecipientStatus


Source          : AGENT
SourceContext   : Transport Rule Agent
RecipientStatus : {[{LED=550 5.7.1 TRANSPORT.RULES.RejectMessage; the
                  message was rejected by organization
                  policy};{MSG=};{FQDN=};{IP=};{LRT=}]}
```

There's more...

DLP policies are collections of mail flow rules (also known as transport rules) that contain specific conditions, actions, and exceptions that filter messages and attachments based on their content.

After creating our first DLP policy, we can easily check which rules were created for it by using the `Get-TransportRule` cmdlet:

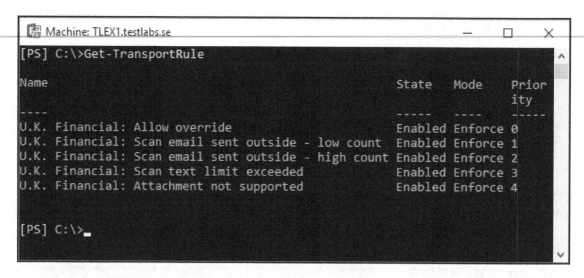

We can further expand on each rule to find out what exactly they do by looking at their `MessageContainsDataClassifications` property:

```
(Get-TransportRule "U.K. Financial: Scan email sent outside - high
count").MessageContainsDataClassifications
```

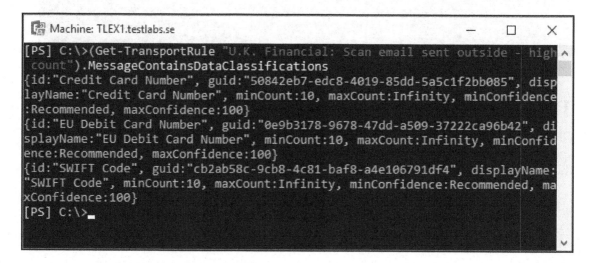

In the preceding screenshot, we can see that the `"U.K. Financial: Scan email sent outside - high count"` rule is triggered when 10 or more credit/debit card numbers are detected inside an email.

A rule to allow users to override the policy is also automatically created. If you do not want users to be able to override this policy, you can easily disable it:

```
Disable-TransportRule "U.K. Financial: Allow override"
```

You can also exempt certain users from this policy so that any emails they send do not trigger the policy:

```
New-TransportRule "Override CEO" -DlpPolicy "Block Outbound Credit Card
Details" -From ceo@testlabs.se -SetHeaderName "X-Ms-Exchange-Organization-
Dlp-SenderOverrideJustification" -SetHeaderValue "TransportRule override" -
Priority 0
```

With this exemption in place, the CEO will never get notified or prevented from sending emails with credit card details to external recipients.

Configuring administrator audit logging

Administrator audit logging allows you to track the cmdlets that are being run within your Exchange organization. The log entries provide details about the cmdlets and parameters used, such as when a command was executed, which objects were affected by the command, and the user who ran the cmdlet. In this recipe, you'll learn how to configure the options used to define the administrator audit logging settings in your environment.

How to do it...

For new installations of Exchange 2016, administrator audit logging is enabled by default. Let's perform the following steps to configure administrator audit logging:

1. To determine the current configuration, use the Get-AdminAuditLogConfig cmdlet, as shown in the following screenshot:

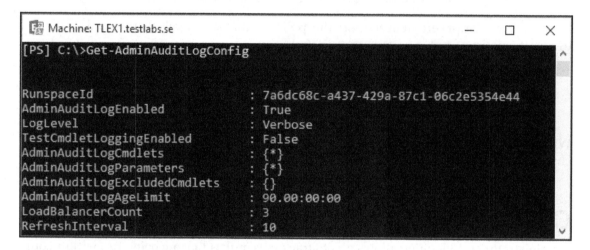

```
Machine: TLEX1.testlabs.se                                    —    □    ✕

[PS] C:\>Get-AdminAuditLogConfig


RunspaceId                      : 7a6dc68c-a437-429a-87c1-06c2e5354e44
AdminAuditLogEnabled            : True
LogLevel                        : Verbose
TestCmdletLoggingEnabled        : False
AdminAuditLogCmdlets            : {*}
AdminAuditLogParameters         : {*}
AdminAuditLogExcludedCmdlets    : {}
AdminAuditLogAgeLimit           : 90.00:00:00
LoadBalancerCount               : 3
RefreshInterval                 : 10
```

2. You can review the output and check the AdminAuditLogEnabled property. If this is set to False, use the Set-AdminAuditLogConfig cmdlet to enable administrator audit logging:

```
Set-AdminAuditLogConfig –AdminAuditLogEnabled $True
```

The administrator audit log settings are an organization-wide setting. The previous command only needs to be run once from a server within the Exchange organization.

How it works...

Once administrator audit logging has been enabled, the default settings are configured so that all cmdlets are audited. Cmdlets ran through the Exchange Management Shell or the Exchange Admin Center are all subject to the administrator audit log settings.

If you take another look at the output of the Get-AdminAuditLogConfig cmdlet, you'll notice that AdminAuditLogCmdlets is set to the asterisk (*) character, which means that all cmdlets by default are configured for auditing.

This is true only for cmdlets that make changes to the environment. Any `Get-*` cmdlets are not subject to auditing, since they do not make any changes and would generate a large number of logs.

You can override this setting using the `Set-AdminAuditLogConfig` cmdlet. For example, if you only want to audit one or two specific cmdlets, you can assign each cmdlet name, separated by a comma, to the `-AdminAuditLogCmdlets` parameter:

```
Set-AdminAuditLogConfig '
-AdminAuditLogCmdlets Set-Mailbox, Set-CASMailbox
```

The same goes for cmdlet parameters. If you want to limit which parameters are audited for each cmdlet, specify a list of parameter names using the `-AdminAuditLogParameters` parameter.

 When making changes to the `Set-AdminAuditLogConfig` cmdlet, you'll receive a warning message that it may take up to 1 hour for the change to take effect. To apply the changes immediately, simply close and reopen the Shell.

You can also exclude specific cmdlets from being audited. To do so, use the following command:

```
Set-AdminAuditLogConfig -AdminAuditLogExcludedCmdlets New-Mailbox
```

In this example, the `New-Mailbox` cmdlet will not be audited. You can exclude multiple cmdlets by supplying a list of cmdlet names separated by a comma.

By default, the administrator audit log will keep up to 90 days of log entries. This setting can also be modified using the `Set-AdminAuditLogConfig` cmdlet. Audit log entries are stored in a hidden, dedicated arbitration mailbox.

There's more...

The Exchange Management Shell provides many troubleshooting cmdlets that use the verb `Test`. By default, these cmdlets are not audited because they can generate a significant amount of data in a short amount of time. If you need to enable logging of the `Test-*` cmdlets, use the `Set-AdminAuditLogConfig` cmdlet:

```
Set-AdminAuditLogConfig -TestCmdletLoggingEnabled $True
```

It is recommended that you only leave test cmdlet logging enabled for short periods of time. Once you are done, you can disable the setting by setting the value back to `False`:

```
Set-AdminAuditLogConfig -TestCmdletLoggingEnabled $False
```

You might have noticed the `-LogLevel` parameter in the initial screenshot. This parameter specifies whether additional properties are included or not in the log entries. When this is set to `Verbose`, the `ModifiedProperties` (old and new) property is also included in the log entries, which can be helpful to determine what a specific setting was before it was changed.

See also

- *Searching the administrator audit logs* recipe in this chapter

Searching the administrator audit logs

You can use the Exchange Management Shell to search the administrator audit logs and generate reports based on the cmdlets and parameters used to modify objects within your Exchange environment. There are two ways in which we can view the audit logs from the Exchange Management Shell, and in this recipe, we'll take a look at both methods.

How to do it...

Let's see how to perform an administrator audit log search by performing the following steps:

1. To perform a synchronous administrator audit log search in the Shell, we can use the `Search-AdminAuditLog` cmdlet:

```
Search-AdminAuditLog -Cmdlets Set-Mailbox '
-StartDate 6/1/2017 '
-EndDate 6/30/2017 '
-IsSuccess $True
```

   This command will return all the log entries for the `Set-Mailbox` cmdlet for the month of June. Only the log entries from successful commands will be returned.

2. To perform an asynchronous search, use the `New-AdminAuditLogSearch`
   cmdlet:

```
New-AdminAuditLogSearch -Name "AdminAuditLogSearch01" '
-Cmdlets Set-Mailbox '
-StartDate 6/1/2017 '
-EndDate 6/30/2017 '
-StatusMailRecipients admin@contoso.com
```

Based on the parameters used here, the results of the search will be the same, the difference is that the search will take place in the background, and instead of displaying the results in the Shell, a message will be emailed to a recipient and the report will be attached in the XML format.

How it works...

The administrator audit log entries provide the complete details of every cmdlet that was used to make a change in your environment. When using the `Search-AdminAuditLog` cmdlet, we can limit the results based on a specific time frame and/or on the name of the cmdlet or the parameters that were used. If you run the cmdlet without any parameters, all of the entries in the administrator audit log will be returned.

One of the most useful things about this cmdlet is that you can quickly determine how and why something has recently been changed. For example, let's say you want to determine who gave permissions to the `IT ServiceDesk` mailbox. In this case, you can consult the administrator audit logs to determine exactly who gave permissions to whom:

```
Machine: TLEX1.testlabs.se                                    —   □   ×

[PS] C:\>Search-AdminAuditLog -Cmdlets Add-MailboxPermission | Where {$_.ObjectModi
fied -match "servicedesk"} | Select Caller -ExpandProperty CmdletParameters

Caller              Name              Value
------              ----              -----
admin@testlabs.se   Identity          it.servicedesk
admin@testlabs.se   AccessRights      FullAccess
admin@testlabs.se   InheritanceType   All
admin@testlabs.se   User              nuno


[PS] C:\>_
```

Using the previous command, we search the administrator audit log for entries where admins ran the `Add-MailboxPermission` cmdlet, and pipe the results to the `Where-Object` cmdlet (in this case it's '?' alias), filtering on the `ObjectModified` property, where the object contains the user's display name. The most recent command used to modify this object will be returned first. In the preceding screenshot, we can see that the `Add-MailboxPermission` cmdlet was run by the user admin to assign `FullAccess` permission to the `it.servicedesk` mailbox to the user `nuno`.

There's more...

The default view of each administrator audit log entry provides a lot of detailed information, but we can work with the properties of each log entry to gain even more insight into what was changed. One good example of this is the ability to view the new and old values that have been set on an object.

For example, let's say that we want to review the audit logs to determine the changes made by the 10 most recent commands. First, we can save the results in a variable:

```
$logs = Search-AdminAuditLog | Select-Object -First 10
```

Each of the log entries are now stored in the `$logs` variable, which at this point is an array of audit log entries. To view the first entry in the list, we can access the zero element of the array:

After reviewing the details, we can see that the `Set-Mailbox` cmdlet modified the `HiddenFromAddressListsEnabled` property of the auditor's mailbox. To determine these values, we can view the `ModifiedProperties` property of the current array element:

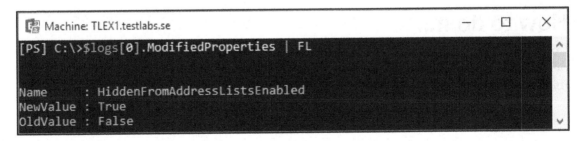

By viewing the output in a list format, we can see that the user was previously not hidden from the Global Address List, and that now it is. In this screenshot, we can see both the new value and the old value of the property. There are additional attributes that change when the `HiddenFromAddressListsEnabled` value gets changed. These have been removed for simplicity's sake, but can be seen in the previous screenshot.

See also

- *Configuring administrator audit logging* recipe in this chapter

Configuring mailbox audit logging

In every organization, there are always mailboxes with sensitive information. These might be the mailboxes of the CEO, directors, users from the HR or Payroll departments, or simply mailboxes for which you have to perform discovery actions to demonstrate compliance with regulatory or legal requirements. Although normally administrators are not concerned with the content of users' mailboxes, there might be someone less honest that attempts to access someone's mailbox in order to obtain information of value for their own benefit.

Administrators can implement Mailbox Audit Logging and run audit reports to obtain details regarding actions taken on a mailbox. After enabling an audit for one or more mailboxes and configuring the level of detail that we want to capture, audit entries are captured in the `Audit` subfolder of the `Recoverable Items` folder (known as Dumpster) and can be interrogated using the Exchange Admin Center, or the Exchange Management Shell, as we will see in this recipe.

How to do it...

Configuring auditing for mailboxes can only be done using the `Set-Mailbox` cmdlet. By default, no mailbox is enabled for auditing. To enable mailbox auditing for the CEO's mailbox, and check what actions are logged by default, you use the following cmdlets:

```
Set-Mailbox CEO -AuditEnabled $True
Get-Mailbox CEO | Select Audit*
```

```
Machine: TLEX1.testlabs.se                                          —    □    ×
[PS] C:\>Set-Mailbox CEO -AuditEnabled $True
[PS] C:\>Get-Mailbox CEO | Select Audit*


AuditEnabled      : True
AuditLogAgeLimit  : 90.00:00:00
AuditAdmin        : {Update, Move, MoveToDeletedItems, SoftDelete,
                    HardDelete, FolderBind, SendAs, SendOnBehalf, Create}
AuditDelegate     : {Update, SoftDelete, HardDelete, SendAs, Create}
AuditOwner        : {}



[PS] C:\>_
```

If the default actions being audited are not ideal, you can easily tweak them to meet your requirements. For example, if you also want to audit the Copy action for admins and the MoveToDeletedItems action for delegates, you use the following cmdlet:

```
Set-Mailbox CEO -AuditAdmin @{Add="Copy"} `
-AuditDelegate @{Add="MoveToDeletedItems"}
```

```
Machine: TLEX1.testlabs.se                                          —    □    ×
[PS] C:\>Set-Mailbox CEO -AuditAdmin @{Add="Copy"} -AuditDelegate @{Add="Mo
veToDeletedItems"}
[PS] C:\>Get-Mailbox CEO | Select Audit*


AuditEnabled      : True
AuditLogAgeLimit  : 90.00:00:00
AuditAdmin        : {Update, Copy, Move, MoveToDeletedItems, SoftDelete,
                    HardDelete, FolderBind, SendAs, SendOnBehalf, Create}
AuditDelegate     : {Update, MoveToDeletedItems, SoftDelete, HardDelete,
                    SendAs, Create}
AuditOwner        : {}



[PS] C:\>_
```

How it works...

Mailbox audit logging is enabled on a per-mailbox basis, by using the `Set-Mailbox` cmdlet. It is possible to configure three levels of auditing:

- Administrative, which audits mailbox moves, imports/exports to and from PSTs, or mailbox discovery searches, for example
- Owner, where actions taken by the owner of the mailbox are audited
- Delegates that have the `SendAs`, `SendOnBehalf` or `FullAccess` permission to someone's mailbox

When we enable mailbox audit logging for a mailbox, access to the mailbox and certain administrator and delegate actions are logged by default as you saw in the first screenshot. Actions taken by the mailbox owner can also be audited, but these are not enabled by default. The following are the actions that can be audited in Exchange 2016:

- `Copy`: An email is copied to another folder or to the Personal Archive
- `Create`: An item (excluding folders) is created in the mailbox (an email is sent, for example)
- `FolderBind`: A `mailbox` folder is accessed
- `HardDelete`: An email is permanently deleted
- `MailboxLogin`: The user signed in to their mailbox (new in Exchange 2016)
- `MessageBind`: An email is opened or viewed in the preview pane
- `Move`: An email is moved to another folder
- `MoveToDeletedItems`: An email is deleted
- `SendAs`: An email is sent using `SendAs` permissions
- `SendOnBehalf`: An email is sent using `SendOnBehalf` permissions
- `SoftDelete`: An email is deleted from the **Deleted Items** and moved to the Dumpster
- `Update`: The properties of an item are updated

The `AuditLogAgeLimit` specifies for how long we want to keep these entries in the mailbox. By default, this is set to 90 days, but can be reduced or increased up to approximately 68 years (or `24855.03:14:07` to be more precise). If set to zero (`00:00:00`), all log entries are deleted the next time the `Managed Folder Assistant` processes the mailbox (automatically or manually by running the `Start-ManagedFolderAssistant` cmdlet).

Searching mailbox audit logs

Similar to searching the admin audit logs, there are two ways to search mailbox audit log entries using the Shell:

1. By using the `Search-MailboxAuditLog` cmdlet to synchronously search mailbox audit log entries for a single mailbox, and displaying the search results in the Shell.
2. Alternatively, you can create a mailbox audit log search to asynchronously search mailbox audit logs for one or more mailboxes, and then have the search results sent to a specified email address as an XML attachment. To create the search, you use the `New-MailboxAuditLogSearch` cmdlet.

In this recipe, we will see how to perform both types of searches.

How to do it...

1. To search all actions performed by delegates on the CEO's mailbox for the month of May, you use the following cmdlet:

```
Search-MailboxAuditLog CEO `
-StartDate 05/01/2017 `
-EndDate 05/31/2017 `
-LogonTypes Delegate -ShowDetails
```

2. To perform the same search asynchronously and send the results by email, you use the following cmdlet instead:

```
New-MailboxAuditLogSearch -Mailboxes CEO `
-StartDate 05/01/2017 `
-EndDate 05/31/2017 `
-LogonTypes Delegate -ShowDetails `
-StatusMailRecipients auditor@contoso.com
```

How it works...

Audit information is written to the `Audit` subfolder of the `Recoverable Items` folder (known as `Dumpster`), which is hidden from Outlook and OWA, meaning normal users cannot access it. To determine if actions are already being audited for a mailbox, we can check if this folder has any logs by using the following cmdlet:

```
Get-MailboxFolderStatistics CEO `
-FolderScope RecoverableItems | `
Where {$_.Name -eq "audits"} | Select ItemsInFolder
```

Assuming there are already items in the folder, we can then use the `Search-MailboxAuditLog` cmdlet and see what actions have been captured so far. In our first example, we specified that we wanted to retrieve actions performed by delegates in the month of May, and we use the `-ShowDetails` switch to retrieve the details of each log entry.

We could have used the `Mailboxes` parameter to search audit logs for multiple mailboxes. However, we cannot use the `ShowDetails` switch together with the `Mailboxes` parameter, so there's not much point, to be honest.

```
Machine: TLEX1.testlabs.se                                    —    □    ×

[PS] C:\>Search-MailboxAuditLog CEO -StartDate 05/01/2017 -EndDate 05/31/20
17 -LogonTypes Delegate -ShowDetails


RunspaceId                        : 7a6dc68c-a437-429a-87c1-06c2e5354e44
Operation                         : SendAs
OperationResult                   : Succeeded
LogonType                         : Delegate
ExternalAccess                    : False
DestFolderId                      :
DestFolderPathName                :
FolderId                          :
FolderPathName                    :
ClientInfoString                  : Client=MSExchangeRPC
ClientIPAddress                   : 192.168.1.171
ClientMachineName                 :
ClientProcessName                 : OUTLOOK.EXE
ClientVersion                     : 16.0.8067.6527
InternalLogonType                 : Owner
MailboxOwnerUPN                   : admin@testlabs.se
MailboxOwnerSid                   : S-1-5-21-1411203154-1084355696-2092060891-
                                    1103
DestMailboxOwnerUPN               :
DestMailboxOwnerSid               :
DestMailboxGuid                   :
CrossMailboxOperation             :
LogonUserDisplayName              : admin
LogonUserSid                      : S-1-5-21-1411203154-1084355696-2092060891-
                                    1103
SourceItems                       : {}
SourceFolders                     : {}
SourceItemIdsList                 :
SourceItemSubjectsList            :
SourceItemAttachmentsList         :
SourceItemFolderPathNamesList     :
SourceFolderPathNamesList         :
ItemId                            : Unknown
ItemSubject                       : Bonus
ItemAttachments                   :
DirtyProperties                   :
OriginatingServer                 : TLEX1 (15.01.1034.013)
MailboxGuid                       : df7a539e-fe4d-4d47-8c65-bad044a9f22a
MailboxResolvedOwnerName          : CEO
LastAccessed                      : 19/05/2017 07:24:56
```

In this example, we can see that the user admin used the Outlook client on a machine with
the IP of 192.168.1.171 and sent an email with the subject Bonus, pretending to be the
CEO.

We can further filter our search. For example, if we are only interested in actions that have deleted an email, we can run:

```
Search-MailboxAuditLog CEO -ShowDetails | `
Where {$_.Operation -match "delete"}
```

```
[PS] C:\>Search-MailboxAuditLog CEO -ShowDetails | Where {$_.Operation -mat
ch "delete"}


RunspaceId                        : 7a6dc68c-a437-429a-87c1-06c2e5354e44
Operation                         : SoftDelete
OperationResult                   : Succeeded
LogonType                         : Delegate
ExternalAccess                    : False
DestFolderId                      :
DestFolderPathName                :
FolderId                          : LgAAAACduxFmtr3NRZPEHNxQZc7oAQD8wlNgaLrbQ6
                                    s8Axuhi8TUAAAAAAEMAAAB
FolderPathName                    : \Inbox
ClientInfoString                  : Client=MSExchangeRPC
ClientIPAddress                   : 192.168.1.171
ClientMachineName                 :
ClientProcessName                 : OUTLOOK.EXE
ClientVersion                     : 16.0.8067.6527
InternalLogonType                 : Owner
MailboxOwnerUPN                   : ceo@testlabs.se
MailboxOwnerSid                   : S-1-5-21-1411203154-1084355696-2092060891-
                                    1691
DestMailboxOwnerUPN               :
DestMailboxOwnerSid               :
DestMailboxGuid                   :
CrossMailboxOperation             : False
LogonUserDisplayName              : admin
LogonUserSid                      : S-1-5-21-1411203154-1084355696-2092060891-
                                    1103
SourceItems                       : {RgAAAACduxFmtr3NRZPEHNxQZc7oBwD8wlNgaLrbQ
                                    6s8Axuhi8TUAAAAAAEMAAD8wlNgaLrbQ6s8Axuhi8T
                                    UAAAAAk2AAAA}
SourceFolders                     : {}
SourceItemIdsList                 : RgAAAACduxFmtr3NRZPEHNxQZc7oBwD8wlNgaLrbQ6
                                    s8Axuhi8TUAAAAAAEMAAD8wlNgaLrbQ6s8Axuhi8TU
                                    AAAAAk2AAAA
SourceItemSubjectsList            : Disciplinary Action
SourceItemAttachmentsList         :
SourceItemFolderPathNamesList     : Inbox
SourceFolderPathNamesList         :
ItemId                            :
ItemSubject                       :
ItemAttachments                   :
DirtyProperties                   :
OriginatingServer                 : TLEX1 (15.01.1034.013)
MailboxGuid                       : df7a539e-fe4d-4d47-8c65-bad044a9f22a
MailboxResolvedOwnerName          : CEO
LastAccessed                      : 19/05/2017 07:24:25
```

Here we can see that `admin` deleted an email with the subject `Disciplinary Action` from the `Inbox` folder of the `CEO`.

In the second search method, we used the `New-MailboxAuditLogSearch` cmdlet to perform the same search on the CEO's mailbox. Remember that this cmdlet performs an asynchronous search, meaning after you execute it, you can close the Shell as the search is performed behind the scenes, just like with the `New-MoveRequest` cmdlet, for example.

The syntax is very similar to our first search, with the main differences being the cmdlet name itself, of course, and the `-StatusMailRecipients` that specifies the email address of one or more recipients to whom the search results should be emailed to.

If no mailboxes are specified by using the `-Mailboxes` parameter, Exchange will perform the search against all mailboxes enabled for auditing. With this cmdlet, we can use the `-Mailboxes` parameter together with the `-ShowDetails` switch.

Once the search is complete, an event entry with ID `4003` is logged in the application event log and an email is sent to the email address(es) specified in the `-StatusMailRecipients` parameter. This email contains the search criteria, such as who requested it, the period searched, and which mailboxes were searched. Attached is the XML file with all the results:

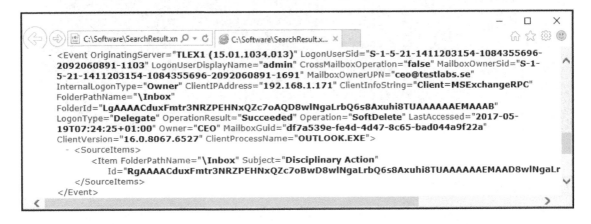

As XML files can be somewhat hard to interpret, you can use PowerShell to make it a lot easier to read and search through:

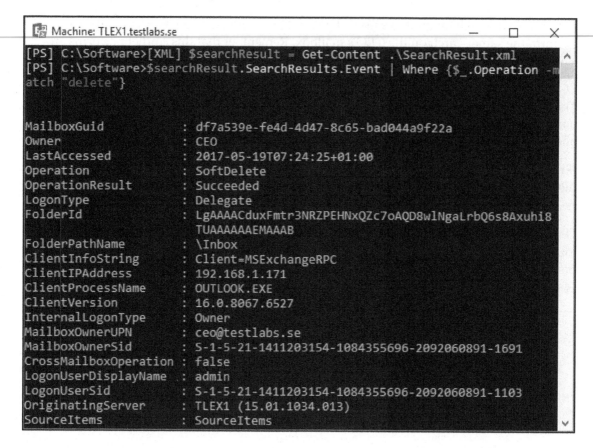

There's more...

In some situations, you might have special accounts such as a backup service account that you want to exclude from auditing. For these cases, you can configure these accounts to bypass mailbox audit logging, so that actions performed by them on any mailbox are not logged. However, you cannot bypass audit logging for an account on a specific mailbox only; this is a global change.

To configure an auditing bypass, you must use the Shell and the following cmdlet:

```
Set-MailboxAuditBypassAssociation svc_Backup `
-AuditBypassEnabled $True
```

Auditing users that have the capability of assigning FullAccess permissions, setting the AuditBypassEnabled option, or enabling/disabling audit is harder. Nothing prevents a user with this level of permissions from assigning himself FullAccess to the CEO's mailbox, bypassing his account from auditing and doing what he wants on the mailbox. For these cases, the only option is to use Auditing Mailbox Access together with Administrator Audit Logging so that, for example, if an admin uses the Set-MailboxAuditBypassAssociation cmdlet, this action is automatically logged.

11

High Availability

In this chapter, we will cover the following topics:

- Creating a Database Availability Group
- Adding mailbox servers to a Database Availability Group
- Configuring Database Availability Group network settings
- Adding mailbox copies to a Database Availability Group
- Activating mailbox database copies
- Working with lagged database copies
- Reseeding a database copy
- Using the automatic reseed feature
- Performing maintenance on Database Availability Group members
- Reporting on database status, redundancy, and replication

Introduction

If you have worked with previous versions of Exchange, you may have been involved in implementing or supporting a highly available solution that required a shared storage model. This allowed multiple server nodes to access the same physical storage, and in the event of an active server node failure, another node in the cluster could take control of the cluster resources, since it had local access to the databases and log files. This was a good model for server availability, but did not provide any protection for data redundancy.

With the release of Exchange 2007, already in end of life, Microsoft still supported this clustering model, rebranded as **Single Copy Clusters (SCC)**, but they also introduced a new feature known as continuous replication.

Among the three types of continuous replication options provided, **Cluster Continuous Replication (CCR)** was the high-availability solution for Exchange 2007 that eliminated the potential risk of a single point of failure at the storage level. With CCR, there were no requirements for shared storage, and database changes were replicated to a passive cluster node using asynchronous log shipping after an initial database seed. Although CCR provided some compelling advantages, there were several limitations. First, you were limited to only two nodes in a CCR cluster. In addition, implementing and managing this configuration required that administrators understand the intricacies of Windows failover clustering.

Microsoft improved their continuous replication technology and introduced **Database Availability Groups (DAGs)** in Exchange 2010. Limitations imposed by CCR in Exchange 2007 were removed by allowing up to 16 nodes to participate within a DAG, while also giving you the option of hosting active copies of individual databases on every server. The reliance on Windows failover clustering administration expertise has been reduced with DAGs, and you can completely manage all aspects of mailbox server high availability using only Exchange's management tools.

The high availability model of the mailbox component in Exchange 2016 has not changed significantly since Exchange 2010 in that the unit of high availability is still the DAG, and continuous replication still supports both file and block mode replication. Nonetheless, there have been some improvements. For example, failover times have been reduced as a result of transaction log code improvements and deeper checkpoints in the passive databases.

, single item recovery, and retention policies, to provide high availability, site resilience, and Exchange-native data protection. The Exchange Information Store and the Extensible Storage Engine (ESE), have also been enhanced to provide greater availability, easier management, and reduced costs.

Exchange 2016 continues to use DAGs and mailbox database copies, along with other features, such as lagged database copies, single item recovery, and retention policies, to provide high availability, site resilience, and Exchange-native data protection. The Exchange Information Store and the Extensible Storage Engine (ESE), have also been enhanced to provide greater availability, easier management, and reduced costs. In terms of providing high availability for client connections, the solution remains load-balanced Mailbox servers running Client Access services. From a load balancing point of view, Exchange 2016 is very similar to Exchange 2013, with the major change being the consolidation of the CAS and Mailbox roles into the Mailbox server. The single-role server provides all the functionality Exchange 2013 multi-role servers provided, effectively allowing inbound client traffic to connect to any mailbox server and then route the request to the server currently hosting the active mailbox being accessed.

With load balancing, the decision comes down to establish a balance between functionality and simplicity. The simplest and easiest solution allows us to use a single namespace, but lacks session affinity management and per-protocol health checking. It is possible to have session affinity management and per-protocol health checking with a single namespace, but at the cost of increased complexity. Another alternative is to deploy a load balancing solution that does not leverage session affinity, but provides per-protocol health checking, at the expense of requiring a unique namespace per-protocol.

As most of this is managed outside of Exchange-that is, in the load balancer solution chosen, DNS, and so on, -load balancing is not covered in this book. However, in Chapter 12, *Exchange Health and Monitoring*, some topics related to high availability are covered, such as health probe checking, which can be used by load balancers to check if Exchange services are healthy or not.

In Exchange 2013, there were other great new features introduced that continue to be present in 2016, such as Managed Store, which in short means that every mailbox database has its own Windows process (`Microsoft.Exchange.Store.Worker.exe`). Another great feature, Managed Availability, provides built-in monitoring and recovery actions in order to preserve the end user experience, such as trying to automatically start up services that have been stopped for one reason or another. Microsoft has made some great developments regarding the lagged copy feature; it now only requires half the amount of IOPS than the active server/disk requires. The lagged copy can also start to play down the logs if the server is running out of disk, which is another great improvement.

In this chapter, we'll cover several aspects of managing Exchange high availability using the shell. You'll learn how to create DAGs, manage database copies, perform maintenance on DAG members, use automatic reseed, and generate reports on mailbox database copies.

Performing some basic steps

To make use of all the examples in this chapter, we'll need to use the Exchange Management Shell, and for one recipe, we have the option of using a standard PowerShell console.

You can launch the Exchange Management Shell using the following steps:

1. Log on to a workstation or server with the Exchange management tools installed.
2. You can connect using a remote PowerShell if you, for some reason, don't have the Exchange management tools installed. Use the following command:

```
$Session = New-PSSession -ConfigurationName '
Microsoft.Exchange -ConnectionUri '
```

```
http://servername/PowerShell/ -Authentication Kerberos
Import-PSSession $Session
```

3. Alternatively, open the Exchange Management Shell by navigating to **Start** | **All Apps** | Microsoft **Exchange Server 2016**.

4. Click on the **Exchange Management Shell** shortcut.

To launch a standard PowerShell console, open a standard PowerShell console by navigating to **Start** | **All Apps**, and click on the **Windows PowerShell** shortcut.

Unless specified otherwise in the *Getting ready* section, all of the recipes in this chapter will require the use of the Exchange Management Shell.

Remember to start the Exchange Management Shell using **Run as Administrator** to avoid permission problems.

In this chapter, you might notice that, in the examples of cmdlets, I have used the back tick (') character to break up long commands into multiple lines. The purpose of this is to make it easier to read. The back ticks are not required and should only be used if needed.

Creating a Database Availability Group

The initial setup and configuration of a Database Availability Group is done using a single cmdlet named New-DatabaseAvailabilityGroup.

First introduced in Exchange 2013 Service Pack 1, the IP-less DAG (also known as a DAG without an administrative access point) is now the norm in Exchange 2016, which is good as it greatly simplifies the creation of DAGs. It generally means that IP addresses are no longer required for the cluster name object, the network name resource, or for the DAG.

The only downside is the third-party vendor support. Before implementing an IP-less DAG it is strongly recommended that you ensure that any third-party software that integrates with Exchange, such as backup solutions, supports IP-less DAGs.

While Windows Server 2012 supports Exchange 2016 DAGs, only 2012 R2 and above support IP-less DAGs.

In this recipe, we'll take a look at how you can automate the creation of a DAG using the Exchange Management Shell.

How to do it...

To create a DAG, use the New-DatabaseAvailabilityGroup cmdlet:

```
New-DatabaseAvailabilityGroup -Name DAG '
-WitnessServer EX1 '
-WitnessDirectory C:\FSW '
-DatabaseAvailabilityGroupIPAddresses ([System.Net.IPAddress]::None)
```

The preceding command creates a new Database Availability Group named DAG. The file share witness server is set to an Exchange server named EX1, and the path for the directory is also specified. Remember that the witness server cannot be a member of the DAG!

In order to create an IP-less DAG, we use ([System.Net.IPAddress]::None) to specify that this DAG will not have an administrative access point. This is because Exchange will attempt to obtain an IP address for the DAG using DHCP if you do not provide an IP address for the DAG (that is, if we do not use the DatabaseAvailabilityGroupIPAddresses parameter). Therefore, we have to use the preceding notation to specify that we do not want an IP address for our DAG.

How it works...

When you run the New-DatabaseAvailabilityGroup cmdlet, the only requirement is that you use a unique name for the DAG of up to 15 characters. In the previous example, we also specified the information for the file share witness , but these values are optional.

The witness server is a quorum resource used by Windows failover clustering as a tie-breaker in DAGs with an even number of nodes.

If you do not provide a value for the witness server or witness server directory, Exchange will attempt to locate an Exchange server in the current Active Directory site. One will be selected automatically and the configuration of the witness server and its directory will be taken care of by Exchange.

There's more...

If you create a DAG using the minimum amount of information, you can always come back later and modify the configuration. For instance, say we first issue the following command:

```
New-DatabaseAvailabilityGroup -Name DAG
```

At this point, the DAG will attempt to automatically configure the witness server details and will try to obtain an IP address using DHCP. You can review the settings of the DAG using the Get-DatabaseAvailabilityGroup cmdlet:

```
Get-DatabaseAvailabilityGroup DAG
```

We can update the DAG using the Set-DatabaseAvailabilityGroup cmdlet to modify the settings:

```
Set-DatabaseAvailabilityGroup DAG '
-WitnessServer EX1 '
-WitnessDirectory C:\FSW '
-DatabaseAvailabilityGroupIPAddresses 192.168.1.55
```

You do not have to place the witness directory on another Exchange server. For example, it's quite common for small- and medium-sized organizations to utilize two Exchange servers as a two-node DAG, along with a hardware load balancer to provide high availability for client connections. In this case, you could use a member server in the domain as the witness server; just make sure that the Exchange Trusted Subsystem security group in Active Directory is a member of the local administrator group on that server. You can now also use a Microsoft Azure file server virtual machine to act as the DAG's witness server!

When you are planning on adding servers that are located in separate IP subnets, and assuming you are using a DAG with an IP address, you'll need to specify an IP address that can be used by the DAG in each of the corresponding networks. For example, run the following command:

```
New-DatabaseAvailabilityGroup -Name DAG '
-DatabaseAvailabilityGroupIPAddresses 10.1.1.10,192.168.1.10
```

In this example, one of the DAG members will be in the 10.1.1.0/24 subnet and the other in the 192.168.1.0/24 subnet. This will allow the cluster IP address to be brought online by a server in either site.

If you have already created the DAG and need to change the addresses, use the `Set-DatabaseAvailabilityGroup` cmdlet:

```
Set-DatabaseAvailabilityGroup -Identity DAG '
-DatabaseAvailabilityGroupIPAddresses 10.1.1.25,192.168.1.25
```

Once again, this is not required when using a DAG without an administrative access point, making it much simpler to create and manage DAGs with members on different subnets.

See also

* *Adding mailbox servers to a Database Availability Group* recipe in this chapter

Adding mailbox servers to a Database Availability Group

Once you've created a Database Availability Group, you'll need to add DAG members. In this recipe, you'll learn how to add mailbox servers to a DAG using the Exchange Management Shell.

How to do it...

To add a mailbox server to a DAG, use the `Add-DatabaseAvailabilityGroupServer` cmdlet:

```
Add-DatabaseAvailabilityGroupServer  DAG '
-MailboxServer MBX1
```

In this example, the `MBX1` server is added to a database availability group named `DAG`.

How it works...

In order to run the `Add-DatabaseAvailabilityGroupServer` cmdlet, the servers being added to the DAG must be running the Standard or Datacenter editions of Windows Server 2012, 2012 R2 or 2016. This is due to the requirement of the Windows failover clustering component, which is required by the DAG. Additionally, the servers must not be a member of an existing DAG for you to successfully run this command.

If you use this cmdlet to add a mailbox server to a DAG, the Windows failover clustering feature will automatically be installed if it has not been already.

When the first mailbox server is added to the DAG, a computer account known as a **cluster network object (CNO)** is added to the Active Directory. The name of the computer account will be created using the same name as the DAG. For this cmdlet to complete successfully, when the first mailbox server is added to the DAG, the **Exchange trusted subsystem** universal security group must have the appropriate permissions in the Active Directory to create the account. In many cases, this should not be an issue, but if you work in an environment where Active Directory security permissions have been modified to restrict access, you may need to prestage this CNO object and ensure that the Exchange trusted subsystem group has been granted full control permissions on the object. If you need to prestage the CNO, you can refer to an official link available at

`https://technet.microsoft.com/en-us/library/ff367878(v=exchg.160).aspx.`

> If you are creating a DAG without an administrative access point with Mailbox servers running Windows Server 2012 R2 or above, you do not need to prestage a CNO for the DAG. IP-less DAGs do not use CNOs, therefore prestaging is not required for those DAGs. This is another advantage of IP-less DAGs.

There's more...

The `Add-DatabaseAvailabilityGroupServer` cmdlet will need to be run for each mailbox server that will be included in the DAG. If you want to automate this process, you have a couple of options.

First, if you simply need to add all of the mailbox servers in the organization to the DAG, use the following command:

```
Get-MailboxServer | Add-DatabaseAvailabilityGroupServer DAG
```

If you are working in a more complex environment with multiple Active Directory sites, you'll need to do a little more work. When adding servers to a DAG, you'll probably need to limit this to the mailbox servers in a particular Active Directory site. The following code will allow you to accomplish this:

```
$mbx = Get-ExchangeServer | ? { `
  $_.Site -match 'Default-First-Site-Name' `
  -and $_.ServerRole -match 'Mailbox'
}
$mbx | % {
  Add-DatabaseAvailabilityGroupServer DAG `
```

```
    -MailboxServer $_
}
```

Here, you can see that we're using the `Get-ExchangeServer` cmdlet to retrieve all the mailbox servers in the default Active Directory site and store the results in the `$mbx` variable. We then pipe this variable to the `Add-DatabaseAvailabilityGroupServer` cmdlet and add each server to the DAG in the site.

See also

- *Adding mailbox copies to a Database Availability Group* recipe in this chapter

Configuring Database Availability Group network settings

The Exchange Management Shell includes several cmdlets that allow you to configure the network connections used by the servers in a DAG. After you have created the DAG networks, or after they've been added automatically by DAG network discovery, you can view the DAG networks and their settings, modify the replication configuration, or remove them completely. This recipe provides multiple examples of how you can perform all of these tasks from the shell.

In previous versions of Exchange, Microsoft recommended at least two networks for DAGs: one MAPI network for client connections, and one replication network. With Exchange 2016, multiple networks are still supported, but Microsoft's recommendation depends on the physical network topology. When there are multiple physical networks between DAG members that are physically separate from one another, using a separate MAPI and replication network provides additional redundancy. However, if there are multiple networks that are partially physically separate but converge into a single physical network, then using a single network for both MAPI and replication traffic is recommended.

How to do it...

To view the configuration settings of your existing DAG networks, use the `Get-DatabaseAvailabilityGroupNetwork` cmdlet:

```
Machine: TLEX1.testlabs.se                              —    □    ×

[PS] C:\>Get-DatabaseAvailabilityGroupNetwork

Identity            ReplicationEnabled Subnets
--------            ------------------ -------
DAG\MapiDagNetwork True                {{192.168.1.0/24,Up}}


[PS] C:\>
```

The output of the preceding cmdlet shows that there are currently two DAG networks in an organization with a single DAG. The identity of the network, the replication state, and the associated subnets are provided.

How it works...

When you create a DAG, Exchange will automatically discover the existing network connections on each server and create a DAG network for the corresponding IP subnet. Although there is a cmdlet called `New-DatabaseAvailabilityGroupNetwork`, you would rarely need to use it, as this is generally done automatically.

If you need to force Exchange to rediscover the DAG network configuration after changes have been made, you can use the `Set-DatabaseAvailabilityGroup` cmdlet:

Set-DatabaseAvailabilityGroup DAG -DiscoverNetworks

Simply provide the name of the DAG and use the `-DiscoverNetworks` switch parameter to indicate that Exchange should search for changes in the network configuration.

There's more...

By default, all DAG networks are used for log shipping and seeding. If you do not want to allow replication on a specific network, use the `Set-DatabaseAvailabilityGroup` cmdlet:

```
Set-DatabaseAvailabilityGroup DAG '
-ManualDagNetworkConfiguration $True
Set-DatabaseAvailabilityGroupNetwork '
DAG\MapiDagNetwork -ReplicationEnabled $False
```

You may consider doing this if you want dedicated DAG networks for replication and heart beating.

> Please note that in the event of a failure affecting the replication network, if the MAPI network is unaffected by the failure, log shipping and seeding operations will revert to using the MAPI network, even if the MAPI network has it's `ReplicationEnabled` property set to `False`.

Additionally, you may have other network connections on your mailbox servers that should not be used by the DAG at all. This is commonly seen with iSCSI network adapters that are used only for connecting to a storage area network. Since Exchange will attempt to discover all network interfaces and add a DAG network for each one, you'll need to completely disable those DAG networks if they are not to be used:

```
Set-DatabaseAvailabilityGroupNetwork DAG\DAGNetwork04 '
-IgnoreNetwork $True
```

In this example, `DAGNetwork04` will be ignored by the DAG. To remove this restriction, use the same cmdlet and set the `-IgnoreNetwork` parameter to `$False` for the required DAG network.

Renaming and removing DAG networks

When making modifications to DAG networks, you may need to rename or remove one or more networks. This can be easily done in the Exchange Management Console, but if you like to work in the shell, you can do this quickly with the built-in cmdlets.

For example, assume that the output of Get-DatabaseAvailabilityGroupNetwork shows the following:

```
Machine: TLEX1.testlabs.se                                    —    □    ×
[PS] C:\>Get-DatabaseAvailabilityGroupNetwork

Identity              ReplicationEnabled Subnets
--------              ------------------ -------
DAG\MapiDagNetwork    True               {{192.168.1.0/24,Up}}
DAG\Replication       True               {{10.0.0.0/8,Misconfigured}}


[PS] C:\>
```

In the preceding screenshot, you can see that DAG\Replication is listed as Misconfigured. In this case, this was a manually added DAG network that is no longer in use by any of the servers in the DAG. Use the Remove-DatabaseAvailabilityGroupNetwork cmdlet to delete the network:

```
Remove-DatabaseAvailabilityGroupNetwork '
DAG\Replication -Confirm:$False
```

Alternatively, we can tell Exchange to automatically configure the DAG's network, which is the default behavior, and this will remove the unwanted network:

```
Set-DatabaseAvailabilityGroup DAG -ManualDagNetworkConfiguration $False
 -DiscoverNetworks
```

If, for any reason, you need or want to rename a network, then this can be done using the following cmdlet:

```
Set-DatabaseAvailabilityGroupNetwork '
DAG\ReplicationDagNetwork03 -Name Replication
```

You can run the Get-DatabaseAvailabilityGroupNetwork cmdlet again to view the DAG network configuration and verify that the changes have been made.

Replication compression and encryption

The Exchange Management Shell allows you to configure some DAG properties that are not available in the EAC. Some of these include the DAG IP addresses (when used), the TCP port used for replication, and the network encryption and compression settings.

DAGs support the use of encryption by leveraging the encryption capabilities of Windows Server. DAGs use Kerberos authentication between Exchange servers and its Security Support Provider (SSP) `EncryptMessage` and `DecryptMessage` APIs to handle encryption and decryption of DAG network traffic. This typically uses Advanced Encryption Standard (AES) 256-bit encryption protocol, potentially with a SHA Hash-based Message Authentication Code (HMAC) to maintain integrity of the data. In order to configure DAG network encryption, you use the `Set-DatabaseAvailabilityGroup` cmdlet with the – `NetworkEncryption` parameter:

`Set-DatabaseAvailabilityGroup DAG -NetworkEncryption Enabled`

The possible encryption settings are:

- `Disabled`: Network encryption is not used.
- `Enabled`: Network encryption is used for both replication and seeding.
- `InterSubnetOnly`: This is the default setting. Network encryption is used when replicating across different subnets.
- `SeedOnly`: Network encryption is only used for seeding.

Similarly to network encryption, DAGs also support built-in compression. When using compression, XPRESS is used for DAG network communication, which is Microsoft's implementation of the LZ77 compression algorithm. This is the same type of compression used in other Microsoft protocols, such as MAPI RPC.

Network compression is also a property of the entire DAG, and of a DAG network. You can configure DAG network compression using the `Set-DatabaseAvailabilityGroup` cmdlet with the `-NetworkCompression` parameter:

`Set-DatabaseAvailabilityGroup DAG -NetworkCompression Enabled`

The possible compression settings for DAG network communications are:

- `Disabled`: Network compression is not used.

- `Enabled`: Network compression is used for both replication and seeding.

- `InterSubnetOnly`: This is the default setting. Network compression is used when replicating across different subnets.

- `SeedOnly`: Network compression is only used for seeding.

Adding mailbox copies to a Database Availability Group

Once your Database Availability Group has been created and configured, the next step is to set up database replication by adding new mailbox database copies of existing databases. In this recipe, we'll take a look at how to add mailbox database copies using the Exchange Management Shell.

How to do it...

Use the `Add-MailboxDatabaseCopy` cmdlet to create a copy of an existing database:

```
Add-MailboxDatabaseCopy DB01 '
-MailboxServer MBX2 '
-ActivationPreference 2
```

When running this command, a copy of the `DB01` database is created on the `MBX2` server.

How it works...

When creating a copy of a database on another mailbox server, you need to ensure that the server is in the same DAG as the mailbox server hosting the source mailbox database. In addition, a mailbox server can only hold one copy of a given database, and the database path must be identical on every server in the DAG, so make sure that the disk path exists on the server you are adding a copy to.

 You can remove a database copy using the Remove-MailboxDatabaseCopy cmdlet. Run `Get-Help Remove-MailboxDatabaseCopy -Full` for details.

When running the `Add-MailboxDatabaseCopy` cmdlet, you need to specify the identity of the database and the destination mailbox server that will be hosting the database copy. The activation preference for a database can optionally be set when you create the database copy. The value of the activation preference is one of the criteria used by the active manager during a failover event to determine the best replicated database copy to activate.

There's more...

In order to create and mount mailbox databases and add database copies to multiple servers in a DAG, several commands must be run from within the shell. If you do deployments on a regular basis or if you build up and tear down lab environments frequently, this is a process that can easily be automated with PowerShell.

The PowerShell function `New-DAGMailboxDatabase` creates new mailbox databases from scratch, mounts them, and then adds passive copies of each database to the remaining servers you specify. The code for this function is as follows:

```
function New-DAGMailboxDatabase {
param (
    $ActiveServer,
    $PassiveServer,
    $DatabasePrefix,
    $DatabaseCount,
    $EdbFolderPath,
    $LogFolderPath
  )
For ($i=1; $i -le $DatabaseCount; $i++) {
    $DBName = $DatabasePrefix + $i
    New-MailboxDatabase -Name $DBName '
    -EdbFilePath "$EdbFolderPath\$DBName\$DBName.edb" '
    -LogFolderPath "$LogFolderPath\$DBName" '
    -Server $ActiveServer
    Mount-Database $DBName
    $PassiveServer | Foreach-Object {
      Add-MailboxDatabaseCopy $DBName '
      -MailboxServer $_
    }
  }
}
```

Once you've added this function to your shell session, you can run it using a syntax similar to the following:

```
New-DAGMailboxDatabase -ActiveServer mbx1 '
-PassiveServer mbx2,mbx3,mbx4,mbx5 '
-DatabaseCount 3 '
-DatabasePrefix MDB '
-EdbFolderPath E:\Database '
-LogFolderPath E:\Database
```

Running this function with the given parameters will do a number of things. First, three new databases will be created using a prefix of MDB. This function will create each database using the same prefix, and then number them in order. In this example, the active server, MBX1, will have three new databases created, called MDB1, MDB2, and MDB3. The -PassiveServer parameter needs to have one or more servers defined. In this case, you can see that we've added database copies of the three new databases to each of the passive servers specified. All databases and log files on each server will be located in a folder under E:\Database in a subdirectory that matches the database name.

In some environments, you might find that trying to mount a database immediately after it was created will fail. What it boils down to is that the mount operation is happening too quickly. If you run into this, add a delay before the mount operation by running Start-Sleep 10 before calling the Mount-Database cmdlet. This will pause the script for 10 seconds, giving Exchange time to catch up and realize that the database has been created before trying to mount it.

See also

- *Reporting on database status, redundancy, and replication* recipe in this chapter

Activating mailbox database copies

After you've created a Database Availability Group and have added multiple database copies to the servers in your organization, you'll need to be able to move the active copies to other servers. In this recipe, you'll learn how to do this using the Exchange Management Shell.

How to do it...

Manually moving the active mailbox database to another server in a DAG is a process known as a database switchover. In order to activate passive mailbox database copies on another server, you'll need to use the Move-ActiveMailboxDatabase cmdlet:

```
Move-ActiveMailboxDatabase DB01 '
-ActivateOnServer MBX2 '
-Confirm:$False
```

In this example, the passive mailbox database copy of DB01 is activated on the MBX2 server.

How it works...

When activating a database copy, you can optionally set the `-MoveComment` parameter to a string value of your choice that will be recorded in the event log entry for the move operation.

You can choose to activate one mailbox database copy at a time, or you can move all the active databases on a particular server to one or more servers in the DAG, as shown in the following command:

```
Move-ActiveMailboxDatabase -Server MBX2 '
-ActivateOnServer MBX1 -Confirm:$False
```

As you can see here, all the active databases on MBX2 will be moved to MBX1. Obviously, this requires that you have the database copies located on MBX1 for every mailbox database on MBX2.

When moving mailbox database copies, you can also override the automount dial settings for the target server by specifying one of the following values for the mount dial override settings:

- None: When using None, the currently configured mount dial setting on the target server will be used.
- Lossless: This is the default value for the `-MountDialOverride` parameter. When performing a lossless mount, all log files from the active copy must be fully replicated to the passive copy.
- GoodAvailability: This specifies that the copy queue length must be less than or equal to six log files in order to activate the passive copy.
- BestEffort: This mounts the database regardless of the copy queue length and could result in data loss.
- BestAvailability: This specifies that the copy queue length must be less than or equal to 12 log files in order to activate the passive copy.

For example, to move the active database of DB01 from MBX2 to MBX1 with good availability, use the `-MountDialOverride` parameter when running the cmdlet:

```
Move-ActiveMailboxDatabase DB01 '
-ActivateOnServer MBX1 '
-MountDialOverride GoodAvailability '
-Confirm:$False
```

There's more...

If you want to forcefully activate an unhealthy database copy, there are a few parameters available with the `Move-ActiveMailboxDatabase` cmdlet that can be used, depending on the situation.

For example, if you have a database copy with a corrupt content index state, you can force the activation of the database using the `-SkipClientExperienceChecks` parameter:

```
Move-ActiveMailboxDatabase DB01 '
-ActivateOnServer MBX1 '
-SkipClientExperienceChecks '
-Confirm:$False
```

At this point, the search catalog on DB01 will need to be recrawled or reseeded.

You also have the option of skipping database health checks when attempting to move the active copy to a database copy in a `Failed` state. It is recommended that you only do this when an initial activation attempt has failed:

```
Move-ActiveMailboxDatabase DB01 '
-ActivateOnServer MBX1 '
-SkipHealthChecks '
-Confirm:$False
```

Finally, you can use the `-SkipLagChecks` parameter to allow the activation of a database copy that has copy and replay queue lengths outside their required thresholds, as shown in the following command:

```
Move-ActiveMailboxDatabase DB01 '
-ActivateOnServer MBX1 '
-SkipLagChecks '
-Confirm:$False
```

It's important to point out here that activating databases that are missing log files will result in data loss and unhappy users.

Another method of moving all active database copies from one server, useful when doing maintenance, for example, is to use the following cmdlet:

```
Set-MailboxServer MBX1 -DatabaseCopyActivationDisabledAndMoveNow $True
```

This cmdlet will prevent databases from being mounted on server MBX1 if there are other healthy copies of the same databases on other servers. Additionally, it immediately moves any mounted databases on server MBX1 to other servers if copies exist and are in a healthy state.

Blocking database moves

We have just seen that using the `-DatabaseCopyActivationDisabledAndMoveNow` parameter will move active database copies to a different server and prevent database copies from being activated on a particular server. Another cmdlet we can use to prevent databases from being automatically activated on a server is the following:

```
Set-MailboxServer MBX1 -DatabaseCopyAutoActivationPolicy Blocked
```

By setting the `-DatabaseCopyAutoActivationPolicy` parameter to `Blocked`, we specify that databases cannot be automatically activated on server `MBX1`. The other possible values for this parameter are `IntrasiteOnly`, where a database copy is allowed to be activated only on Mailbox servers in the same Active Directory site, thus preventing cross-site failover and activation; and the default of `Unrestricted`, where there are no restrictions on activating database copies on the specified server.

We can take it a step further and configure a `Blackout` period during which no mailbox moves should occur by using the `New-SettingOverride` cmdlet:

```
New-SettingOverride -Component WorkloadManagement -Section Blackout -
Parameters @("StartTime=09:00:00", "EndTime=17:00:00") -Name "No DB moves
during business hours" -Reason "Prevent DB moves during peak hours"
```

The `-Component` parameter specifies the name of the component for which the override is being created. There are many available sections in this component, such as `AuditComplianceService`, `AutoDiscover`, `Blackout`, `DiskLatency`, `Eas`, `Ews`, `HADelayedLagPlaydown`, `HASeeding`, `Imap`, `LogExport`, `MailboxReplicationService`, `MdbAvailability`, `MdbReplication`, `OutlookService`, `Owa`, `OwaVoice`, `Pop`, `PowerShell`, `PublicFolderMailboxSync`, `PushNotificationService`, `Transport`, and `TransportSync`, just to name a few.

Next, we specify a `StartTime` and `EndTime` for the blackout and provide a `Name` and `Reason` for the new setting override.

To configure an override on a specific server, you can use the `-Server` parameter and the name of the server (do not use its fully qualified domain name). This method is useful when you want to configure different settings on different Exchange servers.

With the blackout in place, we will receive the following error if we try to activate a database on a different server:

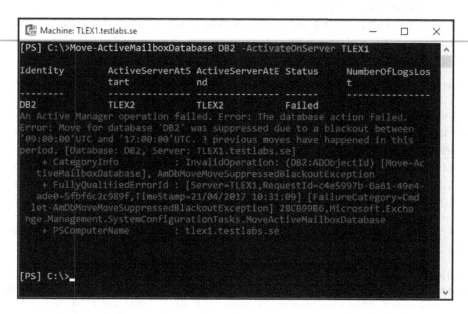

Please note, however, that in the event of a major disaster, databases will be mounted on server TLEX1 if Exchange is unable to mount the database on any other server.

Another alternative is to use the Set-MailboxServer cmdlet to specify how many active databases a particular server can have at any one point in time. To do this, you can use the following two parameters:

- MaximumActiveDatabases: This specifies the maximum number of databases that can be mounted on the server. When the maximum number is reached, the database copies on the server will not be activated if a failover or switchover occurs. If the copies are already active on a server, Information Store will not allow databases to be mounted.

- MaximumPreferredActiveDatabases: This specifies a preferred maximum number of databases that the server should have. This value is only honored during best copy and server selection, database and server switchovers, and when rebalancing the DAG.

See also

- *Reporting on database status, redundancy, and replication* recipe in this chapter
- *Performing maintenance on Database Availability Group members* recipe in this chapter

Reseeding a database copy

There may be times when database replication issues arise in your environment. These issues could be caused by hardware failures, network issues, or, in extremely rare cases, log file corruption, and may leave you with failed database copies that need to be reseeded. This recipe outlines the process of reseeding database copies using the Exchange Management Shell.

How to do it...

Let's see how to reseed a database copy using the following steps:

1. To reseed a database copy, suspend the replication using the following command syntax:

```
Suspend-MailboxDatabaseCopy DB01\MBX2 -Confirm:$False
```

2. Next, you're ready to reseed the database. Use the `Update-MailboxDatabaseCopy` cmdlet, as shown in the following command:

```
Update-MailboxDatabaseCopy DB01\MBX2 -DeleteExistingFiles
```

How it works...

When using the `Update-MailboxDatabaseCopy` cmdlet to reseed a database copy, you can use the `-DeleteExistingFiles` switch parameter to remove the passive database and log files. Depending on the size of the database, it may take a long time to perform the reseed. Once the reseed is complete, replication for the database will automatically resume.

If you don't want replication to resume automatically after a reseed, you can configure it for manual resume:

```
Update-MailboxDatabaseCopy DB01\MBX2 '
-DeleteExistingFiles -ManualResume
```

In this example, we've added the `-ManualResume` switch parameter. After the reseed, we can manually resume replication:

```
Resume-MailboxDatabaseCopy DB01\MBX2
```

There's more...

It is possible to specify the name of a Mailbox server with a copy of the mailbox database to be used as the source of the seed operation. To do this, we use the `-SourceServer` parameter:

```
Update-MailboxDatabaseCopy DB01\MBX2 `
-SourceServer MBX3 `
-DeleteExistingFiles
```

One of the things that you may run into is a database with a corrupt content index state. In this situation, it's not necessary to reseed the entire database, and you can reseed the content index catalog independently:

```
Update-MailboxDatabaseCopy DB01\MBX2 -CatalogOnly
```

The `-CatalogOnly` switch parameter, as shown previously, will allow you to reseed the content index catalog without reseeding the database.

Alternatively, you also have the option of reseeding only the database:

```
Update-MailboxDatabaseCopy DB01\MBX2 -DatabaseOnly
```

In this example, the `DB01` database on the `MBX2` server is reseeded, without having to seed a copy of the content index catalog.

See also

- *Reporting on database status, redundancy, and replication* recipe in this chapter
- *Using the automatic reseed feature* recipe in this chapter

Working with lagged database copies

The concept of a lagged database copy is based on functionality introduced in Exchange 2007 that was included with **standby continuous replication (SCR)**. Using lagged database copies, we can configure a replay lag time in which log files that are replicated to database copies are not committed into the database file, therefore lagging behind the active database, for a given period of time. The benefit of this is that it gives you the ability to recover point-in-time data in the event of a logical database corruption. In this recipe, you'll learn how to use the Exchange Management Shell to work with lagged database copies.

How to do it...

Let's see how to work with lagged database copies using the following steps:

1. To create a lagged database copy, specify a replay lag time value when adding a mailbox database copy:

```
Add-MailboxDatabaseCopy DB03 '
-MailboxServer MBX2 '
-ReplayLagTime 3.00:00:00
```

> In this example, a new lagged database copy is added to the MBX2 mailbox server with a three day replay lag time.

2. You can also change a regular database copy to a lagged copy:

```
Set-MailboxDatabaseCopy DB01\MBX2 '
-ReplayLagTime 12:00:00
```

> This time, the passive database copy of DB01 on the MBX2 server is configured with a lag replay time of 12 hours.

How it works...

When creating lagged database copies, the maximum replay time that can be set is 14 days. In addition to the -ReplayLagTime parameter, both cmdlets shown in the previous example provide a -TruncationLagTime parameter. Setting the truncation lag time on a lagged database copy allows you to configure the amount of time that Exchange will hold on to any log files that have been played into the database before deleting them.

When using either the `-ReplayLagTime` or `-TruncationLagTime` parameters, you need to specify the amount of time in the format of `Days.Hours:Minutes:Seconds`. Alternatively, you can pass a `TimeSpan` object to either of these parameters:

```
Set-MailboxDatabaseCopy DB01\MBX2 '
-ReplayLagTime (New-TimeSpan -Hours 12)
```

The `New-TimeSpan` cmdlet is a PowerShell core cmdlet and has parameters that can be used to create a `TimeSpan` object defined in days, hours, minutes, and seconds.

One of the things you need to keep in mind is that you don't want lagged database copies to be automatically activated in the event of a database failover. The first reason for this is that you lose your point-in-time data recovery options. Secondly, if you have several days of log files that still need to be replayed into a database, the mount time for a lagged database can be very long, taking several hours.

Based on these reasons, you'll want to block activation of your lagged copies after they have been configured. To do this, use the `Suspend-MailboxDatabaseCopy` cmdlet:

```
Suspend-MailboxDatabaseCopy DB01\MBX2 '
-ActivationOnly -Confirm:$False
```

Make sure you use the `-ActivationOnly` switch parameter when running the cmdlet, as shown previously, otherwise it will be suspended indefinitely.

There's more...

Unfortunately, to replay the log files up to a specific point in time, you need to follow a process that cannot be done entirely using the shell. First, you need to suspend the lagged database copy. Next, you have to figure out which log files are required to meet your point-in-time backup requirements, and move any log files that aren't needed out of the log file path to another location. Finally, you delete the checkpoint file for the database and replay any outstanding log files into the database using the `Eseutil` command-line utility.

At this point, the database should be clean, and you should be able to resume and activate the database copy. Fortunately, database logical corruption is an extremely rare occurrence, but if you need to recover from a specific point in time, you may want to consider using Windows Server Backup or a third-party backup solution, or become familiar with the process of recovering from a lagged database copy.

Lagged copy play down

Lagged database copies can invoke automatic log replay to play down the log files in the following scenarios:

- When free disk space is below 10,000 MB
- When the lagged copy has physical corruption and needs to be page patched
- When there are fewer than three available healthy copies for more than 24 hours

Play down based on health copy status requires `ReplayLagManager` to be enabled. From Exchange 2016 CU1 onwards, `ReplayLagManager` is enabled by default. This can be changed by running the following cmdlet:

```
Set-DatabaseAvailabilityGroup DAG -ReplayLagManagerEnabled $False
```

Also starting in Exchange 2016 CU1, playing down logs is subject to the health of the disk, more precisely, the disk's I/O latency. If a disk's read I/O latency is above 35 ms, the play down event is deferred. When this latency drops below 25 ms, the play down event resumes. There is one exception, however: if the disk is running out of free space, the disk latency deferral will be ignored and the lagged copy will play down.

By default, the maximum amount of time that a play down event can be deferred by is 24 hours. This can be changed by using the following cmdlet:

```
Set-MailboxDatabaseCopy DB01\MBX2 -ReplayLagMaxDelay:00.12:00:00
```

In this case, if the disk read I/O latency goes above 25 ms, lagged copy play down is delayed for up to 12 hours for database `DB01` on server `MBX2`. Remember that if the disk is running out of space, this value is ignored and lagged copy play down occurs without delay.

If you want to disable deferred play down, you can set the `ReplayLagMaxDelay` value to (`[TimeSpan]::Zero`).

Using the automatic reseed feature

Automatic reseed, or AutoReseed for short, enables you to quickly restore database redundancy after a disk failure. When a disk fails, the database copy stored on that particular disk is copied from the active database copy to a spare disk on the same server.

In the case of multiple database copies being stored on the failed disk, they can all be automatically reseeded on a spare disk. This minimizes the amount of work an administrator needs to do if a disk is broken and needs to be replaced, or if the database needs to be reseeded. However, be aware of the fact that the administrator needs to replace the broken disk(s).

We will walk you through a simple setup using one mailbox database that uses this feature.

How to do it...

Let's see how to use the automatic reseed feature using the following steps:

1. We'll start with configuring the DAG with the folder structure using the following command:

```
Set-DatabaseAvailabilityGroup DAG '
-AutoDagDatabasesRootFolderPath "C:\ExDbs"
Set-DatabaseAvailabilityGroup DAG '
-AutoDagVolumesRootFolderPath "C:\ExVols"
Set-DatabaseAvailabilityGroup DAG '
-AutoDagDatabaseCopiesPerVolume 1
```

2. Next, verify the changes using the `Get-DatabaseAvailabilityGroup` cmdlet as shown here:

```
Get-DatabaseAvailabilityGroup DAG | Format-List *auto*
```

3. Create the folder structure using Explorer or the Command Prompt:

```
md C:\ExDBs
md C:\ExDBs\DB01
md C:\ExVols
md C:\ExVols\Volume1
md C:\ExVols\Volume2
```

4. Verify the folder structure using the following command:

```
dir C:\ExDBs /s
dir C:\ExVols /s
```

5. Next, add two disks per Mailbox server: one to hold the database and one to act as a spare disk. These two disks should be mounted and used as volumes. The result will be similar to the following screenshot:

Disk 1 Basic 20,00 GB Online	**Volume1 (M:)** 20,00 GB NTFS Healthy (Primary Partition)
Disk 2 Basic 20,00 GB Online	**Volume2 (N:)** 20,00 GB NTFS Healthy (Primary Partition)

6. When the disks have been formatted and added, it is time to mount them into the folder structure that was created in step 3.

   This is done using either disk management or the `mountvol` command:

```
Mountvol.exe C:\ExDBs\DB01 \\?\Volume{43895ac2-a485-11e2-93f5`-
000c2997a8b3}\
    Mountvol.exe C:\ExVols\Volume1 \\?\Volume{53ac38df-68fe-48b6-
ac1f-68a2831fcf50}\
    Mountvol.exe C:\ExVols\Volume2 \\?\Volume{6e762c53-4974-4b06-
b036-940383b09e8a}\
```

   `Volume02` will be used as a spare disk in the preceding example. When the volumes have been mounted into each folder, they will look similar to the following screenshot in Explorer:

7. Verify that the correct volume was mounted into the correct database folder, which can be done using the `Mountvol.exe` command in Command Prompt:

```
Mountvol.exe C:\ExDBs\DB01 /L
Mountvol.exe C:\ExVols\Volume1 /L
Mountvol.exe C:\ExVols\Volume2 /L
```

8. Next, the database folder structure needs to be created, which can be done using either Explorer or the Command Prompt:

```
md C:\ExVols\Volume1\DB01.db
md C:\ExVols\Volume1\DB01.log
```

9. Make sure you verify that the database and log structure was created successfully according to the naming standard, since this is important. You must use the following format for the folder structure:

```
C:\<DatabaseFolderName>\VolumeX\<dbname>.db
C:\<DatabaseFolderName>\VolumeX\<dbname>.log
```

Verify that the folders are named correctly; these folders can be listed using the following command:

```
dir C:\ExDBs /s
dir C:\ExVols /s
```

10. One of the final steps will be to create the mailbox database. This task will be accomplished by running the following command:

```
New-MailboxDatabase -Name DB01 -Server TLEX1 '
-EdbFilePath C:\ExDBs\DB01\DB01.db\DB01.edb '
-LogFolderPath C:\ExDBs\DB01\DB01.log
Mount-Database DB01
```

11. Finally, add a mailbox database copy to the second server. This is done by running the following command:

```
Add-MailboxDatabaseCopy DB01 -MailboxServer TLEX02 `
-ActivationPreference 2
```

How it works...

To start with, we configured the DAG to use the `C:\ExDBs` and `C:\ExVols` folders. These can be changed to the names that suit your environment. The default folder values can also be used, namely `C:\ExchangeDatabases` and `C:\ExchangeVolumes`. We changed them in order to illustrate a basic example of how it can be done.

With the folders in place, we configured the DAG using the `-AutoDagDatabaseCopiesPerVolume` parameter and set it to `1`. This is because we have one database per volume in our example. This means that this parameter should be set to the number of databases that each volume will host.

One of the most important things to remember when configuring AutoReseed, is that the database and log folder structure needs to follow a certain name structure. The database and log folder should be the same as the database name followed by a dot and db or log, depending on whether they should contain the database or the log files.

Refer to the following example of a folder structure for the mailbox database called DB01:

```
C:\ExDBs\DB01\DB01.db\
C:\ExDBs\DB01\DB01.log\
```

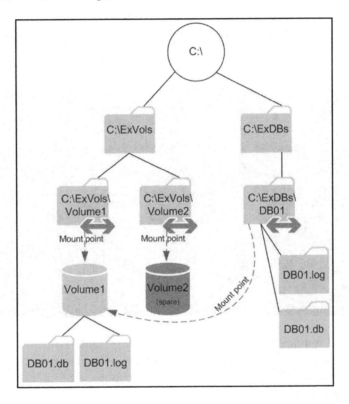

The mailbox database is then created and a copy is also added to the second server.

When the configuration is in place, we are ready to check whether it is working like it should. This can be done simply by disconnecting a physical disk or putting the active volume offline, if using a virtual machine and disks.

In the preceding example, I will put `Volume1` offline for the server that holds the active database. This means the database will failover and then the spare volume should replace the broken drive and the database should receive the database and log files from the other Mailbox server, which now holds the active copy of the mailbox database.

In the earlier example, it took Exchange only a couple of seconds to detect that the database was broken because the disk was offline and to activate it on a second server. Then, it took an additional 20 minutes before the automatic reseed took place.

At this stage, AutoReseed allocates and remaps a spare drive (`Volume2`). If we check where `C:\ExDBs\DB01` is mapped to, we will see that it is no longer `Volume1` but `Volume2`:

```
Machine: TLEX1.testlabs.se                              —    □    ✕

    \\?\Volume{96740b06-04e5-4c4a-bf0d-fe3e4af39e6b}\
        C:\

    \\?\Volume{6e762c53-4974-4b06-b036-940383b09e8a}\
        N:\
        C:\ExVols\Volume2\
        C:\ExDBs\DB01\

    \\?\Volume{9d236651-d862-417d-b460-ae72b7f3f8ca}\
        *** NO MOUNT POINTS ***

    \\?\Volume{8e71f9fa-0357-11e7-841e-00155d01041a}\
        D:\

[PS] C:\>_
```

Because AutoReseed remaps the drive, from an Exchange and Windows perspective, `DB01` is still in the same place as before, as nothing has changed-remember we are using mount points. For this reason, Exchange starts reseeding the database to its "original" location and the database copy will get `Healthy` again.

The information about the automatic reseed can be found in the event viewer by navigating to **Application and Services logs** | **Microsoft** | **Exchange** | **HighAvailability** | **Seeding**. The following is a screenshot showing when the AutoReseed started:

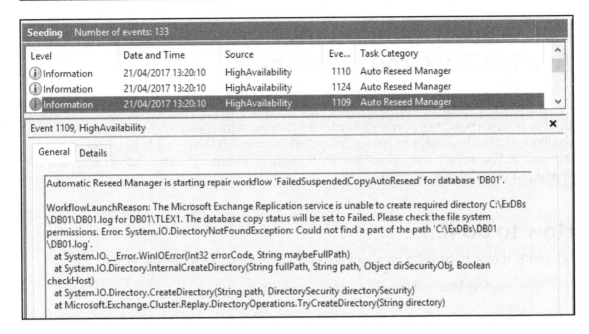

The **Event ID825** and **1109** mean that the reseed progress was started. The **Event ID826** and **1110** mean that the automatic reseed was successfully completed.

However, there is no guarantee that you will have the same time in your environment as the result shown in the preceding screenshot, so you need to verify the function before deploying it into production. In all my tests, the longer it took for AutoReseed to detect a failed and suspended copy was 20 minutes, and the quickest was 3 minutes.
I would recommend that you check how long the whole procedure takes and document every step in detail.

See also

- *Reporting on database status, redundancy, and replication* recipe in this chapter
- *Reseeding a database copy* recipe in this chapter
- *Working with lagged database copies* recipe in this chapter

Performing maintenance on Database Availability Group members

When it comes to performing maintenance on servers that are part of a DAG, you'll need to move any active databases off to another member in the DAG. This will allow you to install patches or take the server down for hardware repairs or upgrades without affecting database availability and user connectivity. This recipe will show you how to use some of the built-in PowerShell scripts installed by Exchange 2016 that can be used to place a server in and out of maintenance mode.

How to do it...

Let's look at how to perform maintenance on a DAG using the following steps:

1. First, switch to the `$exscripts` directory:

```
Set-Location $exscripts
```

2. Next, run the `StartDagServerMaintenance.ps1` script and specify the server name that should be put into maintenance mode:

```
.\StartDagServerMaintenance.ps1 -ServerName MBX1
```

How it works...

When you run the `StartDagMaintenance.ps1` script, it moves all the active databases that are running on the specified server to other members of the DAG and sets the `DatabaseCopyAutoActivationPolicy` mailbox server setting to `Blocked` so that no databases are activated on this server. The script will then pause the server node in the cluster to prevent it from becoming the Primary Active Manager (PAM). The `Suspend-MailboxDatabaseCopy` cmdlet is run for each database hosted by the DAG member, and the cluster core resources are moved to another server in the DAG, if needed.

After the maintenance is complete, run the `StopDagServerMaintenance.ps1` script to take the server out of maintenance mode:

```
.\StopDagServerMaintenance.ps1 -ServerName MBX1
```

This will run the `Resume-MailboxDatabaseCopy` cmdlet for each database located on the specified server and resume the node in the cluster. The autoactivation policy for the mailbox server will then be set back to `Unrestricted` and the server will be back online, ready for production use.

 All the individual steps for placing a server into maintenance mode are fully documented and can be found at `https://technet.microsoft.com /en-us/library/mt697596(v=exchg.160).aspx`.

There's more...

After you've performed maintenance on your DAG members, the databases that were previously active are not moved back, even after running the stop DAG maintenance script.

If you are performing maintenance on multiple servers at the same time, you might end up with an uneven distribution of active databases running on other servers in the DAG.

To correct this, the `RedistributeActiveDatabases.ps1` script, also located in the `$exscripts` folder, can be used to rebalance the active database copies across the DAG. There are two options for balancing active database copies within a DAG: by activation preference, and by site and activation preference.

When using the `-BalanceDbsByActivationPreference` parameter, the script tries to move the databases to their most preferred copy based on the activation preference, regardless of the Active Directory site. If you use the `-BalanceDbsBySiteAndActivationPreference` parameter, the script will attempt to activate the most preferred copy and try to balance them within each Active Directory site.

When running the script, specify the name of the DAG and the preferred method used to rebalance the databases:

```
.\RedistributeActiveDatabases.ps1 -DagName DAG '
-BalanceDbsByActivationPreference '
-ShowFinalDatabaseDistribution '
-Confirm:$False
```

Note that the `-ShowFinalDatabaseDistribution` parameter was also used when we ran this script. This will provide a report that displays the actions taken to balance the databases.

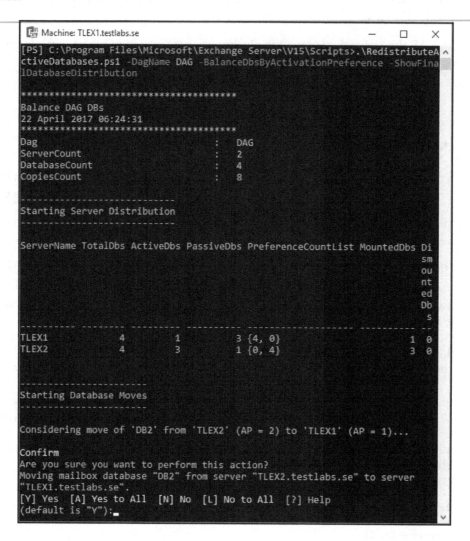

In this screenshot you can see that several key pieces of information are returned, including how many active databases each server has, and that DB2 is being mounted on server TLEX1 as it has a preference of 1 in that server.

Reporting on database status, redundancy, and replication

When dealing with servers and database copies in a DAG, you need to keep a close eye on your database status, including replication health, as well as operational events, such as database mounts, moves, and failovers. In this recipe, you'll learn how to use the Exchange Management Shell, along with some built-in PowerShell scripts to proactively monitor your servers and databases, configured for high availability.

How to do it...

To view the status information about databases that have been configured with database copies, use the Get-MailboxDatabaseCopyStatus cmdlet:

```
Get-MailboxDatabase | `
Get-MailboxDatabaseCopyStatus | `
Select Name, Status, ContentIndexState
```

In this example, we're viewing all the database copies to determine the health and status of the databases. The output of the previous command will look similar to the following screenshot:

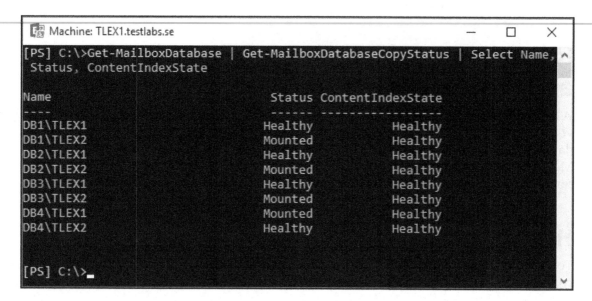

```
Machine: TLEX1.testlabs.se                                    —    □    ✕
[PS] C:\>Get-MailboxDatabase | Get-MailboxDatabaseCopyStatus | Select Name,
  Status, ContentIndexState

Name                              Status ContentIndexState
----                              ------ -----------------
DB1\TLEX1                         Healthy          Healthy
DB1\TLEX2                         Mounted          Healthy
DB2\TLEX1                         Healthy          Healthy
DB2\TLEX2                         Mounted          Healthy
DB3\TLEX1                         Healthy          Healthy
DB3\TLEX2                         Mounted          Healthy
DB4\TLEX1                         Mounted          Healthy
DB4\TLEX2                         Healthy          Healthy


[PS] C:\>_
```

In the preceding screenshot, you can see which server is currently hosting active mailbox databases that are reported with a status of Mounted. All the passive database copies hosted on the servers are reported as Healthy.

How it works...

In our previous example, we selected only a few of the available properties returned by the Get-MailboxDatabaseCopyStatus cmdlet to get an idea of the health of the databases. The default output of the Get-MailboxDatabaseCopyStatus cmdlet will also provide details about the status of your mailbox database copies and show you the CopyQueueLength and ReplayQueueLength values. Keeping an eye on this information is critical to ensure that the database replication is working properly.

If you need to retrieve more detailed information about the database copies on a server, you can pipe this cmdlet to `Format-List` and review several properties that provide details about the copy and replay queue length, log generation and inspection, activation status, and more:

```
Get-MailboxDatabaseCopyStatus -Server MBX1 | Format-List
```

To view the details of a particular database copy, specify the database and server name in the format of `<Database Name>\<ServerName>`, as shown in the following command:

```
Get-MailboxDatabaseCopyStatus DB01\MBX1
```

You can also review the status of networks being used for log shipping and seeding using the `-ConnectionStatus` switch parameter:

```
Get-MailboxDatabaseCopyStatus DB01\MBX2 '
-ConnectionStatus | Format-List
```

When using this parameter, the `IncomingLogCopyingNetwork` and `SeedingNetwork` properties returned in the output will provide the replication networks being used for these operations.

There's more...

Another way to get a quick overview of the replication status of your mailbox database copies is to use the `Test-ReplicationHealth` cmdlet.

When you run this cmdlet, specify the mailbox server that should be tested, as shown in the following screenshot:

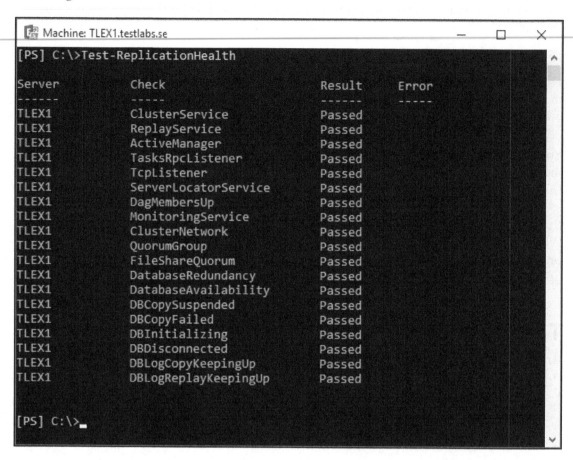

As you can see from the output, all of the cluster services and resources are tested. In addition, several aspects of database copy health will be checked, including log replay, log copy queues, and the status of the database, as well as whether it is suspended, disconnected, or initializing.

To proactively monitor replication health on an ongoing basis, you can schedule the following script to run every hour or so. It will send a message to a specified email address with any errors that are being reported:

```
param(
    $To,
    $From,
    $SMTPServer
```

```
)

$DAGs = Get-DatabaseAvailabilityGroup
$DAGs | Foreach-Object {
  $_.Servers | Foreach-Object {
    $test = Test-ReplicationHealth $_.Name
    $errors = $test | Where-Object {$_.Error}
    If ($errors) {
      $errors | Foreach-Object {
        Send-MailMessage -To $To '
        -From $From '
        -Subject "Replication Health Error" '
        -Body $_.Error '
        -SmtpServer $SMTPServer
      }
    }
  }
}
```

This script iterates through every DAG in your environment and every mailbox server that is a member of a DAG. The `Test-ReplicationHealth` cmdlet is run for each server, and any errors reported will be e-mailed to the specified recipient.

To use this script, save the previous code to a file, such as `ReplicationHealth.ps1`. When you run the script, provide values for the recipient email address, the sender's address, and the SMTP server used to send the message:

```
c:\>.\ReplicationHealth.ps1 -To administrator@contoso.com '
-From sysadmin@contoso.com '
-SMTPServer EX1.contoso.com
```

Remember, depending on where your script is running from, if you are using one of your Mailbox servers as the SMTP server, you may need to configure your receive connectors to allow SMTP relay, or provide credentials.

Understanding switchover and failover metrics

The `CollectOverMetrics.ps1` script can be used to read the event logs from the mailbox servers that are configured in a DAG, and gather information about database mounts, moves, and failovers. This script is installed with Exchange 2016 and is located in the `$exscripts` directory.

To run the script, switch to the $exscripts$ directory:

```
Set-Location $exscripts
```

Next, run the script and specify the name of the DAG you want to receive a report on, and the location where the report should be saved:

```
.\CollectOverMetrics.ps1 -DatabaseAvailabilityGroup DAG '
-ReportPath C:\temp\Report
```

When running this command, you'll see an output similar to the following screenshot:

As you can see, each server in the DAG will be processed and a CSV file will be generated in the specified report path. At this point, you can read the CSV file into the shell using the Import-CSV cmdlet:

```
Import-Csv C:\t
temp\Report\FailoverReport.DAG.2017_04_22_06_47_30.csv
```

You can then view details about switchover or failover events in each database, which will be similar to the following screenshot:

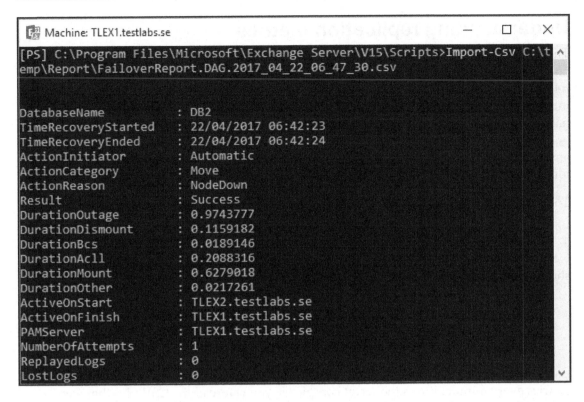

In this example, you can see that database DB2 failed over automatically to server TLEX1 within one second because server TLEX2 was down.

You can limit the reports to specific databases when running the script, and also specify a start and end time so that you can limit the information returned to meet your requirements.

The CollectOverMetrics.ps1 file also has the ability to create a report in an HTML format with additional information by adding the -GenerateHtmlReport parameter.

Understanding replication metrics

The CollectReplicationMetrics.ps1 file is also included in the $exscripts directory on Exchange 2016 servers. This script can be used to collect data from performance counters related to database replication, and it needs to be run for a period of time for it to gather information. Similar to the CollectOverMetrics.ps1 script, you need to specify a DAG name and a path used to save the report in the CSV or HTML format. When running CollectReplicationMetrics.ps1, you need to specify a duration that defines the amount of time for which the script will run. You also need to specify a frequency interval for which metrics will be collected.

To run the script, switch to the $exscripts directory:

```
Set-Location $exscripts
```

Next, run the script and specify the DAG name, duration, frequency, and report path that should be used using the following command:

```
.\CollectReplicationMetrics.ps1 -DagName DAG '
-Duration '01:00:00' '
-Frequency '00:01:00' '
-ReportPath C:\temp\reports
```

Using the given parameter values, the script will run for one hour, and collect replication metrics every minute. When the script completes, you can read the CSV files that were generated into the shell using the Import-CSV cmdlet, or open them up in Excel for review.

See also

- *Scheduling scripts to run at a later time* in Chapter 2, *Exchange Management Shell Common Tasks*

- *Monitoring server and database redundancy* in Chapter 12, *Monitoring Exchange Health*

12
Monitoring Exchange Health

In this chapter, we will cover the following recipes:

- Using Exchange test cmdlets
- Using Health Probe checks
- Checking the server health and health sets
- Monitoring transaction logs
- Monitoring the disk space
- Checking database redundancy

Introduction

In Chapter 11, we explored some aspects of Exchange High Availability using Database Availability Groups, lagged database copies, and automatic reseed, for example. In this chapter, we will provide several recipes to help you monitor the health of your Exchange environment through the built-in Managed Availability feature, test cmdlets, and other methods, hopefully helping you proactively tackle any possible issues before they affect your users.

Performing some basic steps

To make use of all the examples in this chapter, we'll need to use the Exchange Management Shell. You can launch it using the following steps:

1. Log on to a workstation or server with the Exchange Management Tools installed.
2. You can connect using a remote PowerShell if you, for some reason, don't have the Exchange Management Tools installed. Use the following command:

```
$Session = New-PSSession -ConfigurationName '
Microsoft.Exchange -ConnectionUri '
http://tlex01/PowerShell/ -Authentication Kerberos
Import-PSSession $Session
```

3. Alternatively, open the Exchange Management Shell by navigating to **Start** | **All Apps** | **Microsoft Exchange Server 2016**.
4. Click on the **Exchange Management Shell** shortcut.

To launch a standard PowerShell console, open a standard PowerShell console by navigating to **Start** | **All Apps** and click on the **Windows PowerShell** shortcut.

Unless specified otherwise in the *Getting ready* section, all the recipes in this chapter will require the use of the Exchange Management Shell.

Remember to start the Exchange Management Shell using Run as administrator to avoid permission problems.

In this chapter, you might notice that in the examples of cmdlets, I have used the back tick (') character to break up long commands into multiple lines. The purpose of this is to make it easier to read. The back ticks are not required and should be used only if needed.

Using Exchange test cmdlets

Exchange 2016 (CU6 at the time of writing this book) comes with 34 built-in test cmdlets that can be used by both administrators and tools such as Microsoft **System Center Operations Manager** (SCOM), to test and determine the health and functionality of one or more Exchange components or services.

In this recipe, we will look at how to use the Shell to run some of these test cmdlets.

How to do it...

1. First, to get a list of all the test cmdlets you can use, run the following command:

```
Get-Command -Verb Test | Where Module -match $env:ComputerName
```

2. To test whether all the Microsoft Windows services that Exchange depends on have started, use the Test-ServiceHealth cmdlet:

```
Test-ServiceHealth
```

3. To verify server functionality by logging on to a mailbox using MAPI, use the Test-MAPIConnectivity cmdlet:

```
Test-MAPIConnectivity nuno@testlabs.se
```

4. The Test-OutlookWebServices cmdlet allows you to test and verify Autodiscover service settings:

```
Test-OutlookWebServices nuno@testlabs.se -MailboxCredential (Get-Credential)
```

5. Although it can sometimes be confused with the previous cmdlet, Test-WebServicesConnectivity is used to test client connectivity to Exchange Web Services, virtual directories:

```
Test-WebServicesConnectivity -ClientAccessServer TLEX1
```

How it works...

For some of the cmdlets described in this recipe, you can provide a user's e-mail address and credentials to test Exchange connectivity as that user. Alternatively, these cmdlets can use Exchange test accounts to test Exchange connectivity automatically without the need to provide any credentials. Exchange will take care of maintaining these accounts, such as changing their passwords frequently.

In order to use this functionality, you must create one of these test accounts by running the New-TestCasConnectivityUser.ps1 script located at $ExScripts.

Note that this script must be run by an administrator with permissions to create users in the Active Directory.

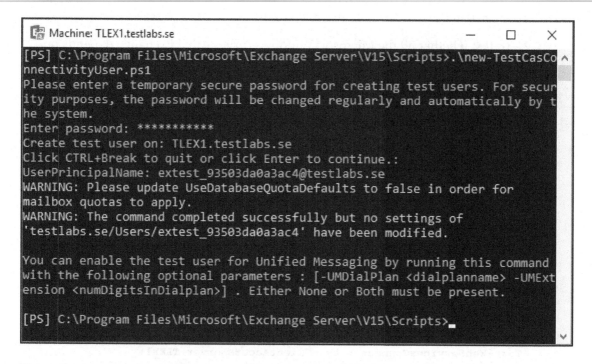

Using the `Test-ServiceHealth` cmdlet, you can check whether all the Windows services that Exchange requires are up and running. If one or more of these services are not running, you will see the `RequiredServicesRunning` result set to `False`, and the `ServicesNotRunning` property will list the service(s) not currently running:

```
Machine: TLEX1.testlabs.se                                    —   □   ×

[PS] C:\>Test-ServiceHealth

Role                        : Mailbox Server Role
RequiredServicesRunning     : True
ServicesRunning             : {IISAdmin, MSExchangeADTopology,
                              MSExchangeDelivery, MSExchangeIS,
                              MSExchangeMailboxAssistants, MSExchangeRepl,
                              MSExchangeRPC, MSExchangeServiceHost,
                              MSExchangeSubmission, MSExchangeThrottling,
                              MSExchangeTransportLogSearch, W3Svc, WinRM}
ServicesNotRunning          : {}

Role                        : Client Access Server Role
RequiredServicesRunning     : True
ServicesRunning             : {IISAdmin, MSExchangeADTopology,
                              MSExchangeMailboxReplication, MSExchangeRPC,
                              MSExchangeServiceHost, W3Svc, WinRM}
ServicesNotRunning          : {}

Role                        : Unified Messaging Server Role
RequiredServicesRunning     : True
ServicesRunning             : {IISAdmin, MSExchangeADTopology,
                              MSExchangeServiceHost, MSExchangeUM, W3Svc,
                              WinRM}
ServicesNotRunning          : {}

Role                        : Hub Transport Server Role
RequiredServicesRunning     : False
ServicesRunning             : {IISAdmin, MSExchangeADTopology,
                              MSExchangeEdgeSync, MSExchangeServiceHost,
                              MSExchangeTransportLogSearch, W3Svc, WinRM}
ServicesNotRunning          : {MSExchangeTransport}


[PS] C:\>_
```

You can also use the −Server parameter to specify a remote server to check. When you don't use this parameter, the cmdlet checks the local server:

```
Test-ServiceHealth -Server TLEX2
```

When it comes to testing Outlook connectivity, there are also several cmdlets available, one of them being `Test-MapiConnectivity`. This cmdlet will log in to the mailbox you specify and retrieve a list of items in the `Inbox` folder, testing both MAPI connectivity and LDAP. If a connection is successfully established to the mailbox, the cmdlet also calculates the time that the operation took to complete (`Latency`):

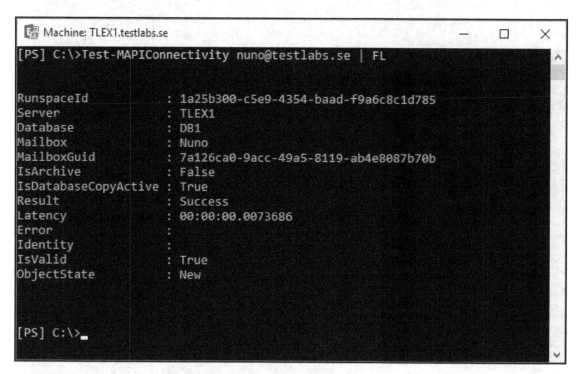

If you do not specify any mailbox or additional parameters, the cmdlet will test all active mailbox databases on the local server using the `SystemMailbox`:

Test-MAPIConnectivity | FT Server, Database, Mailbox, Result, Error

Alternatively, you can use the `-Server` or `-Database` parameters to test a particular server or database, respectively.

In our third example, we used the `Test-OutlookWebServices` cmdlet. This cmdlet uses a specified e-mail address to validate the service information returned to Outlook from Autodiscover for these services: Autodiscover (Outlook Provider), Exchange Web Services, Availability Service, and Offline Address Book. For this cmdlet to work, we must use the `–MailboxCredential` parameter to specify the mailbox credentials to use for the test. We can use `$cred = Get-Credential` to store a credentials object in the `$cred` variable and then use it in the `–MailboxCredential` parameter:

```
Machine: TLEX1.testlabs.se                                    —    □    ✕
[PS] C:\>$cred = Get-Credential

cmdlet Get-Credential at command pipeline position 1
Supply values for the following parameters:
Credential
[PS] C:\>Test-OutlookWebServices nuno@testlabs.se -MailboxCredential $cred
| FT ServiceEndpoint, Scenario, Result, Latency -AutoSize

ServiceEndpoint                              Scenario  Result Latency
---------------                              --------  ------ -------
autodiscover.testlabs.se AutoDiscoverOutlookProvider Success      22
mail.testlabs.se                 ExchangeWebServices Success      10
mail.testlabs.se                 AvailabilityService Success      23
mail.testlabs.se                  OfflineAddressBook Failure      12


[PS] C:\>_
```

In the preceding screenshot, we can see that the connection tests to each service were all successful, except for the Offline Address Book. To get more details on the failure, you just need to include the `Error` field as well.

This cmdlet will also submit a request to the Availability service for the user to determine whether their free/busy information is being returned correctly. This particular response can be seen by running the following cmdlet:

```
Test-OutlookWebServices nuno.mota@adia.ae –MailboxCredential $cred |
Where {$_.Scenario –eq "AvailabilityService"} | FL
```

In our previous example, we used the `Test-WebServicesConnectivity` cmdlet to test client connectivity to Exchange Web Services virtual directories. Once more, we provided a user and credential for the test just like in the previous example. If a user is not specified, then a test account will be used (assuming one has been created, as explained in the beginning of this recipe):

```
Machine: TLEX1.testlabs.se                                    —    □    ×
[PS] C:\>Test-WebServicesConnectivity nuno@testlabs.se -MailboxCredential $
cred | Select ServiceEndPoint, Scenario, Result, Latency

ServiceEndpoint                          Scenario  Result Latency
---------------                          --------  ------ -------
autodiscover.testlabs.se AutoDiscoverSoapProvider Success      15
mail.testlabs.se                       EwsGetFolder Success     15


[PS] C:\>_
```

If you are using self-signed certificates or haven't yet fully configured certificates in your Exchange environment, you can use the `-TrustAnySSLCertificate` switch, which tells the cmdlet to ignore **Secure Sockets Layer** (**SSL**) certificate validation failures. You don't need to specify a value with this switch.

There's more...

This is only a small subset of the 34 test cmdlets available in Exchange 2016. You have a lot more at your disposal to test other Exchange services and features. Some of the most used ones are as follows:

- `Test-ActiveSyncConnectivity`
- `Test-OwaConnectivity`
- `Test-ExchangeSearch`
- `Test-Mailflow`
- `Test-ReplicationHealth`
- `Test-ReplicationHealth`

Using Health Probe checks

Load balancers can run multiple health checks when operating at Layer 7. However, these tests are not necessarily a reliable way of determining whether an Exchange workload is operating correctly. To address this gap, Microsoft introduced two features in Exchange 2013, which are still present in 2016: Managed Availability and a health check web page. Load balancers can take advantage of these health web pages to assess whether or not a particular workload is healthy or not from the perspective of Managed Availability. Additionally, administrators can also take advantage of these to perform their own checks and validations.

In this recipe, you will look at how to use the shell and these health check web pages to check the health of several Exchange workloads.

How to do it...

1. In order to use the Shell to check a health check web page, you use the `Invoke-WebRequest` cmdlet as shown in the next two examples.
2. To use the Shell to check whether Outlook on the Web is healthy, run the following cmdlet:

   ```
   Invoke-WebRequest -Uri "https://mail.testlabs.se/owa/healthcheck.htm"
   ```

3. To perform the same check but for MAPI, simply update the URL being invoked:

   ```
   Invoke-WebRequest -Uri "https://mail.testlabs.se/mapi/healthcheck.htm"
   ```

How it works...

Managed Availability consists of three key components: `Probes`, `Monitors`, and `Responders`. These work closely together to test, detect, and try to resolve possible problems. First, Managed Availability runs a probe. Depending on which probe is run (there are hundreds of different ones), it gathers information about, or executes a series of tests for, a specific component.

Then, a monitor evaluates the results of that probe and uses the gathered information to decide whether the component is healthy or unhealthy. If unhealthy, a responder will take an appropriate action to bring that failed component back to a healthy state. Different actions can be taken depending on the responder and on the type of failure: these can involve restarting a service, failing over a database failover, or even rebooting a server.

After Managed Availability determines a workload's health, Exchange dynamically generates a web page named `healthcheck.htm`. This health check web page exists for each virtual directory:

- `/OWA/healthcheck.htm` for Outlook on the Web
- `/ECP/healthcheck.htm` for Exchange Admin Center
- `/OAB/healthcheck.htm` for Offline Address Book
- `/AutoDiscover/healthcheck.htm` for the Autodiscover process
- `/EWS/healthcheck.htm` for Exchange Web Services
- `/Microsoft-Server-ActiveSync/healthcheck.htm` for Exchange ActiveSync
- `/RPC/healthcheck.htm` for Outlook Anywhere
- `/MAPI/healthcheck.htm` for MAPI over HTTPS

When a workload is healthy, the web page returns a `200 OK` code. When that workload is not healthy, it will return a different code, or the web page might not even get generated. These health web pages can be checked using any internet browser:

Or, we can use PowerShell to get the contents of the web page:

In this example, we used the PowerShell `Invoke-WebRequest` cmdlet, which can be used to send HTTP, HTTPS, FTP, and FILE requests to a web page or web service, parse the response, and return collections of forms, links, images, and other significant HTML elements. For this scenario, we are mainly interested in the `StatusCode` and `StatusDescription` fields. If `StatusCode` is `200`, it means the protocol is up and running. Any other code means Managed Availability marked the protocol as unhealthy or down.

Using the preceding code, you can easily build a basic function to test any of these health web pages:

```
Function Test-URL () {
    Param ($url)
    Try {
        $web = Invoke-WebRequest -Uri "$url/healthcheck.htm" -ErrorAction
Stop
    } Catch {
        Return "page not available"
    }

    If ($web.StatusCode -eq "200") {Return "OK"}
    Else {Return $web.StatusCode}
}
```

The function can then be called using its name and a URL to test just like the following:

```
Test-URL "https://autodiscover.domain.com/autodiscover"
```

There's more...

In the previous examples, we used the generic URL of mail.testlabs.se to check one health web page. This URL might be load balanced, which means we might not know which Exchange server actually returned the page. A way around this is to use the server name in the URL instead, like this:

```
Invoke-WebRequest -Uri "https://tlex1.testlabs.se/owa/healthcheck.htm"
```

The problem with this approach is that it is very likely that your digital certificate does not have the server name in it, which is considered a best practice. This means that Invoke-WebRequest will fail to validate the certificate and will throw this error: "*The underlying connection was closed: Could not establish trust relationship for the SSL/TLS secure channel*". To get around this, you can use .NET Framework class libraries instead and set custom validation of the server certificate by the client, which means you override the certificate trust by telling the command to explicitly trust the certificate presented by the server:

```
[System.Net.ServicePointManager]::ServerCertificateValidationCallback =
{$True}
$wc = New-Object System.Net.WebClient
$wc.DownloadString("https://tlex1.testlabs.se/owa/healthcheck.htm")
```

```
Machine: TLEX1.testlabs.se                                     —    □    ×
[PS] C:\>[System.Net.ServicePointManager]::ServerCertificateValidationCallb
ack = {$true}
[PS] C:\>$wc = New-Object System.Net.WebClient
[PS] C:\>$wc.downloadstring("https://tlex1.testlabs.se/owa/healthcheck.htm"
)
200 OK<br/>TLEX1.TESTLABS.SE
[PS] C:\>_
```

This way, you overcome any certificate errors and can test servers individually.

If you are using these web pages for load balancing health checks, note that you can also manually take a protocol offline (for maintenance or any other reason), thus automatically removing it from the load balancing pool without the need for any changes in the load balancer configuration! As an example, if you want to take the OWA proxy protocol out, you would execute the following cmdlet:

```
Set-ServerComponentState <Server> -Component OwaProxy -Requester
Maintenance -State Inactive
```

Checking the server health and health sets

Exchange includes two built-in health reporting cmdlets that can be used by administrators to perform a variety of tasks related to Managed Availability, such as viewing the health of a server or group of servers; viewing a list of health sets; viewing a list of probes, monitors, and responders associated with a health set; and viewing a list of monitors and their current health.

In this recipe, you will learn how to use the Shell together with these cmdlets to assess the health of an Exchange server.

How to do it...

To determine the health information and the see all the health sets of an Exchange server named TLEX1, you can run either of the following cmdlets:

```
Get-ServerHealth TLEX1
Get-HealthReport TLEX1
```

How it works...

A **health set** is a group of monitors, probes, and responders for a component that determine whether that component is healthy or not. Both these cmdlets return health information for the Exchange server you specify, which can be used to determine the overall state of the server. The Get-ServerHealth cmdlet provides more details, and it returns an AlertValue that provides the specific state of each HealthSet with the following possible values: Degraded, Unhealthy, Repairing, Disabled, Unavailable, or UnInitialized:

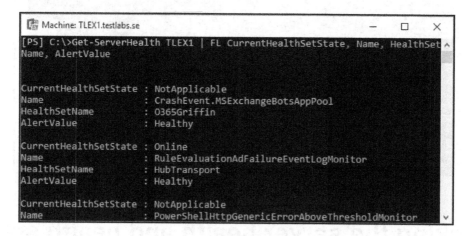

On the other hand, Get-HealthReport cmdlet provides slightly less details but also includes AlertValue for each HealthSet with these possible values: Online, Partially Online, Offline, Sidelined, Functional, or Unavailable:

```
Machine: TLEX1.testlabs.se                                  —    □    ×
[PS] C:\>Get-HealthReport -Server TLEX1 | FT State, HealthSet, AlertValue,
MonitorCount

          State HealthSet              AlertValue MonitorCount
          ----- ---------              ---------- ------------
NotApplicable O365Griffin             Healthy          248
       Online HubTransport            Healthy           67
NotApplicable EDS                     Healthy           43
       Online FrontendTransport       Healthy           20
NotApplicable Search                  Healthy           78
NotApplicable HxService               Healthy          110
NotApplicable StreamingOptics         Healthy           16
NotApplicable Store                   Healthy           90
NotApplicable Xrm                     Healthy           38
NotApplicable PublicFolders           Healthy            9
NotApplicable DataProtection          Healthy           92
```

There's more...

What if a health set is not healthy, as shown in the following example?

```
Machine: TLEX1.testlabs.se                                  —    □    ×
[PS] C:\>Get-HealthReport -Server TLEX1 | Where {$_.AlertValue -ne "Healthy
"} | FT State, HealthSet, AlertValue, MonitorCount

          State HealthSet     AlertValue MonitorCount
          ----- ---------     ---------- ------------
NotApplicable MailboxSpace  Unhealthy           10


[PS] C:\>_
```

In this example, we used the Get-HealthReport cmdlet to view the list of health sets for the TLEX1 server that were not in a Healthy state. We can check all the probes, monitors, and responders associated with this particular health set using the Get-MonitoringItemIdentity cmdlet:

```
Get-MonitoringItemIdentity MailboxSpace -Server TLEX1 | FL Identity,
ItemType, Name
```

However, this will not tell us which monitor triggered the health set to be unhealthy. To see which monitors are healthy and which ones are not for a particular health set, we go back to using the `Get-ServerHealth` cmdlet:

```
Get-ServerHealth -HealthSet MailboxSpace -Server TLEX1 | Sort
AlertValue | FT Name, AlertValue -Auto
```

```
Machine: TLEX1.testlabs.se                              —    □    ×

[PS] C:\>Get-ServerHealth -HealthSet MailboxSpace -Server TLEX1 | Sort Aler
tValue | FT Name, TargetResource, AlertValue -Auto

Name                                    TargetResource AlertValue
----                                    -------------- ----------
DatabaseSizeMonitor                     DB2                Healthy
DatabaseSizeMonitor                     DB3                Healthy
DatabaseSizeMonitor                     DB04               Healthy
DatabaseSizeMonitor                     DB1                Healthy
MaintenanceTimeoutMonitor.MailboxSpace                     Healthy
MaintenanceFailureMonitor.MailboxSpace                     Healthy
StorageLogicalDriveSpaceMonitor         DB1              Unhealthy
StorageLogicalDriveSpaceMonitor         DB04             Unhealthy
StorageLogicalDriveSpaceMonitor         DB3              Unhealthy
StorageLogicalDriveSpaceMonitor         DB2              Unhealthy


[PS] C:\>_
```

We now know that it is the `StorageLogicalDriveSpaceMonitor` monitor that is causing the health set to be unhealthy. So, we now need to get all the probes that are configured for this monitor. Unfortunately, there is no easy way to do that, as we have to check the Event Log Crimson Channel:

```
$monitors = (Get-WinEvent -ComputerName TLEX1 -LogName Microsoft-
Exchange-ActiveMonitoring/MonitorDefinition | ForEach { [XML]
$_.toXml() }).Event.UserData.EventXml
    ($monitors | Where {$_.Name -eq
"StorageLogicalDriveSpaceMonitor"}).SampleMask
```

This will return all the probes defined, such as the following (in this particular example):

MSExchangeDagMgmt/EdbAndLogVolSpace/DB3

MSExchangeDagMgmt/EdbAndLogVolSpace/DB2

MSExchangeDagMgmt/EdbAndLogVolSpace/DB1

MSExchangeDagMgmt/EdbAndLogVolSpace/DB04

Next, we use the crimson channel once more, this time to get the probe results. Let's do this for a single probe, `DB1`, for example:

```
(Get-WinEvent -ComputerName TLEX1 -LogName Microsoft-Exchange-
ActiveMonitoring/ProbeResult -FilterXPath
"*[UserData[EventXML[ResultName='MSExchangeDagMgmt/EdbAndLogVolSpace/DB1']]
]" | ForEach {[XML] $_.toXml()}).Event.UserData.EventXml | Sort
ExecutionEndTime -Descending | Select Error -First 1
```

```
Machine: TLEX1.testlabs.se                          —   □   ×

[PS] C:\>(Get-WinEvent -ComputerName TLEX1 -LogName Microsoft-Exchange-Acti
veMonitoring/ProbeResult -FilterXPath "*[UserData[EventXML[ResultName='MSEx
changeDagMgmt/EdbAndLogVolSpace/DB1']]]" | ForEach {[XML] $_.toXml()}).Even
t.UserData.EventXml | Sort ExecutionEndTime -Descending | Select Error -Fir
st 1 | FL


Error : 'DB1' is low on log volume space [C:\]. Current=9.85 GB,
        Threshold=175.78 GB


[PS] C:\>
```

We finally know that the health set is unhealthy because there is a 175 GB threshold for free space on log volumes.

If you want to lower this threshold, you can use either the `Add-ServerMonitoringOverride` cmdlet to override the thresholds and parameters of Managed Availability probes, monitors, and responders on an Exchange server, or you can use the `Add-GlobalMonitoringOverride` cmdlet to create a similar override but on all Exchange servers in the organization. While global overrides are stored in Active Directory, server-specific ones are stored in the registry of the server itself.

To change this specific threshold on all Exchange 2016 CU6 servers to 5 GB, for example, (value obviously not recommended for production servers!), you can use the following cmdlet:

```
Add-GlobalMonitoringOverride
MailboxSpace\StorageLogicalDriveSpaceMonitor -Item Monitor -PropertyName
MonitoringThreshold -PropertyValue 30 -Duration 180.00:00:00
```

Here, we use the −Duration parameter to specify that the override is only valid for approximately 6 months. If you don't want to specify a duration, you must use the −ApplyVersion parameter, which specifies the version of Exchange to override. This means that when a server gets upgraded, the override will no longer apply, and a new override needs to be created.

You can easily check the health of all Exchange servers by piping these into the Get−HealthReport cmdlet:

```
Get-ExchangeServer | ForEach {Get-HealthReport -Server $_.Name | Where
{$_.AlertValue -ne "Healthy" -and $_.AlertValue -ne "Disabled"}}
```

Alternatively, you can schedule a script to run every day, for example, and report when any healthy set is not healthy:

```
$body = Get-ExchangeServer | ForEach {
  Get-HealthReport -Server $_.Name | Where {$_.AlertValue -ne "Healthy" -
and $_.AlertValue -ne "Disabled"}
}

If ($body) {
Send-MailMessage -From admin@domain.com -To admin@domain.com -Subject
"HealthSetReport" -Body ($body | Out-String ) -SmtpServer mail.domain.com
}
```

See also

- The *Using Exchange test cmdlets* recipe in this chapter
- The *Using Health Probe checks* recipe in this chapter

Monitoring transaction logs

In environments that do not use Circular Logging for their mailbox databases, an issue with Exchange backups can cause the number of transaction logs to keep increasing. If the issue persists for several days, databases might start running out of disk space. As such, it is crucial to keep an eye on the number of transaction logs not yet committed for each database.

In this recipe, you will see how to use the Shell to check and monitor the number of transaction logs across all Exchange servers in the environment.

How to do it...

To monitor the number of transaction logs in the environment and alert if these go above a set limit for any database, use the following code:

```
[Array] $DBcol = @()
[Bool] $alert = $False
[Int] $logThreshold = 3000
Get-MailboxDatabase -Status | Where {$_.Mounted} | ForEach {
    $DBobj = New-Object PSObject -Property @{
        Name    = $_.Name
        Path    = $_.LogFolderPath
        Server  = ($_.MountedOnServer).Split(".")[0]
        Logs    = (Get-ChildItem
"\\$($_.MountedOnServer)\$($_.LogFolderPath -replace ":", "$")").Count    }
    If ($DBobj.Logs -gt $logThreshold) {$alert = $True}
    $DBcol += $DBobj
}

If ($alert) {
    Send-MailMessage -From exchange.alert@domain.com -to admin@domain.com -
Subject "High number of transaction logs!" -Priority High -Body $($DBcol |
Sort Name | FT Name, Server, Logs -Auto | Out-String) -SmtpServer
mail.domain.com
    }

$DBcol | Sort Name | FT Name, Server, Logs -Auto
```

How it works...

We start our little script by instantiating a few variables: $DBcol is a collection (array) of objects that will contain details of all databases, a Boolean $alert to determine at the end of the script if we should send an alert to administrator(s) or not, and $logThreshold to specify the minimum number of logs required for an alert to be sent.

Next, we use the Get-MailboxDatabase cmdlet to retrieve all mailbox databases in the environment. Here, we use the -Status switch to retrieve information about the Mounted status of these databases. We pipe the result of this cmdlet to a filter so that only mounted databases are checked by our script.

Then, for each database, we create a PowerShell object named $DBobj. This object will contain several details of each database:

- **Name:** This is simply the database's name
- **Path:** This property contains the location of the logs for the database. We replace ":" with "$" so we can access the folder remotely using a UNC path (for example, "\\TLEX1\C$\...")
- **Server:** This contains the name of the server where the mailbox is mounted (important when DAGs are used)
- **Logs:** This is the total number of files in the log file directory. Here, we use the Get-ChildItem cmdlet to count not only the number of .log files in the directory, but everything, for the simple reason that it is much faster. Also, the additional files and folders do not make much difference to the total number of logs we are concerned about.

If there are more logs than the number specified for the current database in the $logThreshold variable, we set the Boolean $alert variable to True so we know to send an alert at the end of the script. We then add our $DBobj object to our collection/array of objects $DBcol.

After having processed all the databases, we check whether the $alert variable is set to True. If it is, we use the Send-MailMessage cmdlet to send an alert to one or more administrators. We finish the script by printing the information for all databases in the screen if we are running the script manually:

```
Machine: TLEX1.testlabs.se                                    —    □    ×
[PS] C:\Software>.\countTransactionLogs.ps1

Name Server Logs
---- ------ ----
DB01 TLEX1   488
DB02 TLEX1   509
DB03 TLEX1   474
DB04 TLEX1   474


[PS] C:\Software>_
```

Monitoring the disk space

It goes without saying that having enough disk free space is crucial for Exchange to function correctly. When a disk that is hosting one or more mailbox databases runs out of space, these databases get automatically dismounted and you will not be able to mount them until there is enough disk space, which can turn out to be another problem on its own.

In this recipe, you will learn how to easily check how much free space a database has using the shell.

How to do it...

To check how much free space a database copy (active or passive) has on a particular server, use the following cmdlet:

```
Get-MailboxDatabaseCopyStatus "DB01\TLEX1" | Select DiskTotalSpace,
DiskFreeSpace, DiskFreeSpacePercent
```

How it works...

In Exchange 2010 and previous versions, programmatically checking the available space on a disk holding an Exchange database is not straightforward even when using WMI. In Exchange 2013 and 2016, this is much easier. Get-MailboxDatabaseCopyStatus provides a myriad of information regarding a database copy, including the free space on the disk where the database is located.

As such, you can easily check how much free space all database copies have (unlike the previous example where we checked a single database on a single server) using the following cmdlet:

```
Get-MailboxDatabase | Get-MailboxDatabaseCopyStatus | Sort Name | FT
Name, DiskTotalSpace, DiskFreeSpace -AutoSize
```

```
Machine: TLEX1.testlabs.se                                    —   □   ×

[PS] C:\>Get-MailboxDatabase | Get-MailboxDatabaseCopyStatus | Sort Name |
FT Name, DiskTotalSpace, DiskFreeSpace -AutoSize

Name        DiskTotalSpace                         DiskFreeSpace
----        --------------                         -------------
DB01\TLEX1 69.45 GB (74,567,380,992 bytes) 9.882 GB (10,610,659,328 bytes)
DB01\TLEX2 69.45 GB (74,567,380,992 bytes) 25.96 GB (27,873,320,960 bytes)
DB02\TLEX1 69.45 GB (74,567,380,992 bytes) 9.882 GB (10,610,659,328 bytes)
DB02\TLEX2 69.45 GB (74,567,380,992 bytes) 25.96 GB (27,873,320,960 bytes)
DB03\TLEX1 69.45 GB (74,567,380,992 bytes) 9.882 GB (10,610,659,328 bytes)
DB03\TLEX2 69.45 GB (74,567,380,992 bytes) 25.96 GB (27,873,320,960 bytes)
DB04\TLEX1 4.967 GB (5,333,053,440 bytes) 3.128 GB (3,358,760,960 bytes)
DB04\TLEX2 69.45 GB (74,567,380,992 bytes) 25.96 GB (27,873,320,960 bytes)


[PS] C:\>_
```

In this screenshot, we can see all our database copies (active and passive), the total disk space where they are hosted, and the current free disk space.

There's more...

Reusing the script from our previous recipe, we can easily update the code to also include the free space for each database on the server where they are mounted:

```
[Array] $DBcol = @()
Get-MailboxDatabase -Status | ? {$_.Mounted} | % {
    $DBobj = New-Object PSObject -Property @{
        Name      = $_.Name
        Server    = ($_.MountedOnServer).Split(".")[0]
        Size      = (Get-MailboxDatabase $_.Name -
Status).DatabaseSize.ToGB()
        FreeSpace = (Get-MailboxDatabaseCopyStatus
"$($_.Name)\$(($_.MountedOnServer).Split(".")[0])").DiskFreeSpace.ToGB()
    }
    $DBcol += $DBobj
}
$DBcol | Sort Name | FT -Auto
```

If we add an alert just like the previous recipe, and we can automatically alert administrators when the free disk space for one or more databases goes below a specific threshold.

See also

- The *Monitoring transaction logs* recipe in this chapter

Checking database redundancy

In `Chapter 11`, we saw how to use the `Get-MailboxDatabaseCopyStatus` cmdlet to check the health and status information for one or more database copies across the environment. In Exchange 2016, a new cmdlet named `Get-MailboxDatabaseRedundancy` is available, which lets us view redundancy information about mailbox databases. In this recipe, you will learn how to use this cmdlet.

How to do it...

1. To check the redundancy information regarding a particular database, you can use the following cmdlet:

```
Get-MailboxDatabaseRedundancy DB01 | FL
```

2. Alternatively, you can get the same information for all databases that are part of a DAG:

```
Get-MailboxDatabaseRedundancy -DatabaseAvailabilityGroup DAG1
```

How it works...

In the first example, we specified a particular database to check, which returns the status of all copies of that database. In the second example, we used the – DatabaseAvailabilityGroup parameter, which returns the same information, but for all databases that are part of the DAG1 database availability group. Whichever method you use, the following is the information returned for one or more databases:

In this example, we can see that database DB01 has at least two redundant copies (IsAtLeast2RedundantCopy and AtLeast2RedundantCopy) and that there are at least two available copies (IsAtLeast2AvailableCopy and AtLeast2AvailableCopy). The cmdlet checks up to four copies, and in this example, we can see that this particular database does not have more than two copies.

To make the output of this cmdlet easier to read when checking multiple databases, we can filter some properties we are not interested in and focus on the ones that we are:

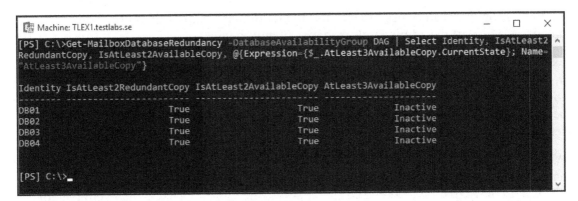

Here, we are taking advantage of PowerShell's calculated properties. A calculated property is a property of an object but not an inherent, built-in property of the object. Instead, it is a property we create by performing a calculation, such as running a script block. In this case, we are taking the `AtLeast3AvailableCopy` property, getting its `CurrentState`, and printing it to a field with the same name.

Let's say we lose our second server in this two-node DAG. In this scenario, the `IsAtLeast2RedundantCopy` and `IsAtLeast2AvailableCopy` properties will go from `True` to `False`:

```
Machine: TLEX1.testlabs.se                                          —  □  ×
[PS] C:\>Get-MailboxDatabaseRedundancy -DatabaseAvailabilityGroup DAG | Sele
ct Identity, IsAtLeast2RedundantCopy, IsAtLeast2AvailableCopy

Identity IsAtLeast2RedundantCopy IsAtLeast2AvailableCopy
-------- ----------------------- ----------------------
DB01                       False                   False
DB02                       False                   False
DB03                       False                   False
DB04                       False                   False


[PS] C:\>_
```

At the same time, the `AtLeast2RedundantCopy` and `AtLeast2AvailableCopy` properties will go from `Active` to `Inactive`.

All these properties can be used to monitor the redundancy and availability of our databases and alert the administrators in case of any changes.

Exchange 2010 introduced a great script named `CheckDatabaseRedundancy.ps1` (located in the Exchange scripts folder `$ExScripts`) that checks whether databases have enough configured and healthy copies. This script is still present in Exchange 2016, but it hasn't been updated for a long time and should not be used since it will not work in certain scenarios.

With the introduction of Managed Availability, this script was replaced with an integrated, native functionality that alerts administrators through event log notifications, such as Event ID `1018` in the `Microsoft-Exchange-HighAvailability/Monitoring` event log, for example:

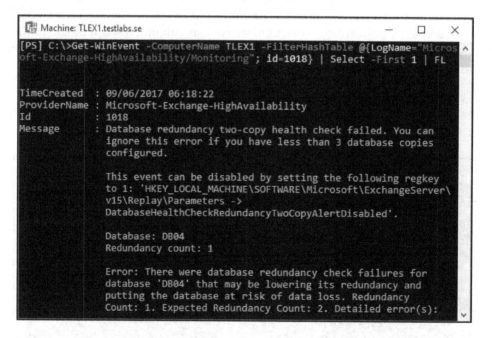

Remember that you can also use the Get-HealthReport to check and monitor database redundancy. In case of any failures, one or more health sets will become unhealthy:

```
Machine: TLEX1.testlabs.se                                        —    □    ×

[PS] C:\>Get-HealthReport -Server TLEX1 | Where {$_.AlertValue -ne "Healthy"}


Server State          HealthSet AlertValue LastTransitionTime  MonitorCount
------ -----          --------- ---------- ------------------  ------------
TLEX1  NotApplicable Store      Unhealthy  04/06/2017 08:27:08 90


[PS] C:\>_
```

See also

- The *Reporting on database status, redundancy, and replication* recipe from Chapter 11, *Exchange Security*
- The *Checking server health and health sets* recipe in this chapter

13
Integration

In this chapter, we will cover the following topics:

- OAuth configuration
- Configuring Exchange archiving for Skype for Business Server
- Configuring and enabling the Unified Contact Store
- Integrating Skype for Business with Outlook on the Web
- Configuring a user with a high-resolution photo
- Office Online Server integration
- Validating an Exchange hybrid

Introduction

In this chapter, we will focus on how Exchange 2016 integrates with Skype for Business, Office Online Server, and Exchange Online.

To give you an idea of the existing infrastructure setup when reading this chapter, the setup is based on one Exchange server, one Skype for Business server and one Office Online server. However, all the recipes also apply if you have a large setup of servers.

Some examples of what you will learn in this chapter include how to use high-resolution photos, archiving, Skype for Business integration in Outlook on the Web, and configuring Unified Contact Store. We will also take a look at how to integrate with Office Online Server and Exchange Online.

When reading this chapter, it's recommended that you start reading the OAuth configuration section and then continue with selecting which recipe you find most interesting.

This chapter also assumes that you are familiar with Skype for Business, Office Online Server, and Exchange Online since we are not looking into these for specific details. They are included to illustrate the integration that can be done.

Performing some basic steps

To work with the code samples in this chapter, follow these steps to launch the Exchange Management Shell:

1. Log on to a workstation or server with the Exchange Management Tools installed.

2. You can connect using remote PowerShell if you don't have Exchange Management Tools installed for some reason. Use the following command:

    ```
    $Session = New-PSSession -ConfigurationName Microsoft.Exchange `
     -ConnectionUri http://servername/PowerShell/ `
     -Authentication Kerberos
    Import-PSSession $Session
    ```

3. Alternatively, open the Exchange Management Shell by clicking on the Windows button and go to **Microsoft Exchange Server 2016 | Exchange Management Shell**.

If any additional steps are required, they will be listed at the beginning of the recipe in the *Getting ready* section.

Using **Run As Administrator** to avoid permission problems.
In this chapter, note that in the examples of cmdlets, I have used the back tick (`` ` ``) character to break up long commands into multiple lines. The purpose for this is to make it easier to read. The back ticks are not required and should be used only if needed.

OAuth configuration

This recipe should be treated as a prerequisite for the upcoming recipes that are based on Exchange 2016 and Skype for Business 2015 integration. OAuth is used for all types of integration between Exchange 2016 and Skype for Business, which we will cover in this recipe. The only recipe that doesn't require OAuth for its integration is the High-Resolution photos.

How to do it...

Let's quickly start collecting the information we will need later in this chapter and configure OAuth in our Exchange and Skype for Business solution. Beware; in the following cmdlet examples, we will be looking at a mix of cmdlets running in both **Exchange Management Shell (EMS)** and **Skype for Business Server Management Shell (SFBMS)**:

1. To start, we have to retrieve the Autodiscover URI since this is needed further down the road. This is done from the EMS and the following example:

```
Get-ClientAccessService | fl Name,` AutoDiscoverServiceInternalUri
```

2. The output would look similar to the what is shown in the following screenshot:

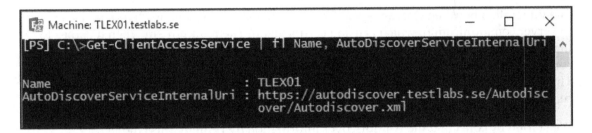

3. Before we start configuring the OAuth, we want to make sure it's not already configured with any value. If the value of ExchangeAutodiscoverUrl is blank, it means that it's not currently configured. This is done by running the cmdlet from SFBMS:

```
Get-CsOAuthConfiguration
```

4. Our next step is to configure OAuth in our Skype for Business 2015 solution. This is done using the output (AutoDiscoverServiceInternalUri) from the first step and replacing XML with svc. This should be done in the SFBMS, and the cmdlet should look similar to the following example:

```
Set-CsOAuthConfiguration -Identity Global -ExchangeAutodiscoverUrl
"https://autodiscover.testlabs.se/autodiscover/autodiscover.svc"
```

5. The final step in the OAuth configuration is to validate that the certificate is in place; it is a requirement to have the server-to-server communication to work. This is simply done by running one of the following cmdlets:

```
Get-CsCertificate
```

6. If you want to be even more specific, you can look for the OAuth certificate by running this:

```
Get-CsCertificate -Type OAuthTokenIssuer
```

How it works...

The integration between Exchange and Skype for Business is based on OAuth and server-to-server communication, which is using certificate(s). The requirement when it comes to the certificate on the Skype for Business server is that the same OAuth certificate needs to be configured on all of your frontend servers, and the certificate needs to be at least 2048 bits. This will be taken care of by the Skype for Business Central Management Store; the certificate will get replicated to all frontend servers in the organization.

We started by collecting the Autodiscover information by running this cmdlet:

```
Get-ClientAccessService | fl Name, AutoDiscoverServiceInternalUri.
```

The outcome is shown in the preceding figure; in the environment we are using, it gave us the URI https://autodiscover.testlabs.se/autodiscover/autodiscover.xml, replacing the .xml with .svc and using that as input when configuring OAuth.

Before we configure OAuth, we want to make sure that we are not overwriting it by mistake. This is as simple as running the Get-CsOAuthConfiguration cmdlet and then looking for the attribute and value of ExchangeAutodiscoverUrl. If it doesn't contain any value, it means that it's not currently configured. Then, we can continue to configure OAuth by running the following one-liner:

```
Set-CsOAuthConfiguration -Identity Global -ExchangeAutodiscoverUrl `
"https://autodiscover.testlabs.se/autodiscover/autodiscover.svc"
```

With the OAuth configuration in place, it should look similar to what is shown in the following screenshot:

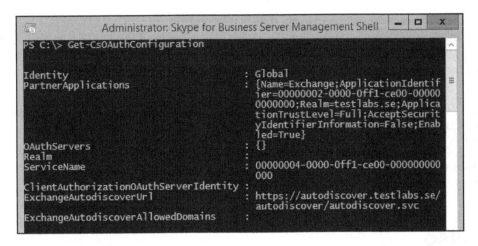

A prerequisite for a fully working server-to-server connection is to have an OAuth certificate installed and assigned on our Skype for Business server together with a working certificate (preferably a bought third-party certificate) on the Exchange server.

We need to validate that the OAuth certificate is in place by running the following cmdlet:

```
Get-CsCertificate -Type OAuthTokenIssuer
```

If the certificate is in place, the result from this cmdlet should look similar to what is shown in the following screenshot:

When running the preceding cmdlet, if it wouldn't give any result, it would prompt with a warning stating that a certificate of the type `OAuthTokenIssuer` is missing.

If we are missing the OAuth certificate, we should request a certificate from our Internal PKI running on the domain controller. This can, of course, be done using PowerShell as well by running two sets of cmdlets: one for requesting a certificate directly from the Internal PKI and the second one for assigning the certificate we just requested:

```
    Request-CsCertificate -New -Type OAuthTokenIssuer -CA
"testlabs.se\testlabs-TLDC01-CA" -FriendlyName "Skype for Business Oauth
certificate" -KeySize 2048 -PrivateKeyExportable $True -Country "SE" -State
"Skane" -City "Malmo" -Organization "Testlabs" -OU "Testlabs"
    Set-CsCertificate -Identity Global -Thumbprint
205E093F4CF20FA57874F98B09F9B12EBDDF8D98 -Type OAuthTokenIssuer -
EffectiveDate "2017-05-11 22:15:02"
```

See also

- The *Configuring Exchange archiving for Skype for Business Server* recipe in this chapter
- The *Integrating Skype for Business with Outlook on the web* recipe in this chapter
- The *Configuring and enabling Unified Contact Store* recipe in this chapter

Configuring Exchange archiving for Skype for Business Server

In this recipe, we are going to configure and look into the integration of archiving for Skype for Business and Exchange 2016. If you didn't read the previous recipe, I would like to recommend that you do. Just like all integration between Exchange server and Skype for Business, OAuth is used for communication.

It's a great way of combining Exchange and Skype for Business to get additional value from both of them and also to simplify and have all information located in the mailbox instead of spreading it out between different systems. This would be a driver when it comes to the in-place hold functionality in Exchange, which is covered in chapter 10.

We will cover how to configure archiving for Skype for Business, for example, the conversation history from instant messaging and conferences. These will be logged and saved into the user's mailbox.

How to do it...

The cmdlets in this recipe are all executed from the Skype for Business Server Management Shell (SFBMS):

1. We'll start by enabling and configuring the archiving for both instant messaging and conferences. This is done by running the cmdlet (SFBMS):

```
Set-CsArchivingConfiguration -EnableArchiving ImAndWebConf `
  -EnableExchangeArchiving $True
```

2. Create a new archiving policy and grant it to one of our users (SFBMS):

```
New-CsArchivingPolicy -Identity "TestlabsArchivingPolicy" `
  -ArchiveInternal $True -ArchiveExternal $TrueGrant-CsArchivingPolicy
-Identity "pdickson" `
  -PolicyName "TestlabsArchivingPolicy"
```

3. This is an optional step; configure the global archiving policy for both internal and external archiving if you want to have this setting applied to the Global policy (SFBMS):

```
Set-CsArchivingPolicy -Identity "Global" -ArchiveInternal $True `
  -ArchiveExternal $True
```

4. Configuring the ExchangeArchivingPolicy property is needed if the Exchange server(s) and Skype for Business server(s) are located in different forests. By configuring this option, we make sure that the instant messages and conference transcripts are saved into the mailbox. Run the following cmdlet (SFBMS):

```
Set-CsUser -Identity pdickson `
  -ExchangeArchivingPolicy ArchivingToExchange
```

5. Create a new client policy and grant it to one of our users (SFBMS):

```
New-CsClientPolicy -Identity "TestlabsClientPolicy" `
  -EnableExchangeDelegateSync $True -EnableIMAutoArchiving $True
  Grant-CsClientPolicy -PolicyName "TestlabsClientPolicy" `
-Identity pdickson
```

6. This is an optional step; if we want to apply the same settings to the Global client policy, this is done by running the cmdlet (SFBMS):

```
Set-CsClientPolicy -Identity "Global" `
    -EnableExchangeDelegateSync $True -EnableIMAutoArchiving $True
```

How it works...

Just like the previous recipe, all integrations between Exchange and Skype for Business are based on OAuth. If you didn't read the first recipe, I would recommend that you take a look at it before continuing to read this recipe.

We started this recipe by configuring archiving for both instant messaging and conferences. In this configuration, we also made sure that the archiving functionality was enabled. This was done by running this cmdlet:

```
Set-CsArchivingConfiguration -EnableArchiving ImAndWebConf `
    -EnableExchangeArchiving $True
```

The options for what kind of transcript should be archived can be set to None, ImOnly, or ImAndWebConf. None means that nothing gets archived, ImOnly means that only instant messaging will be archived, while ImAndWebConf will archive both instant messaging and conferences.

As our next step, we created a new archiving policy and granted it to one of our users. We created a new policy to make sure we don't impact the Global archiving policy that can impact our users. This was completed by running this:

```
New-CsArchivingPolicy -Identity "TestlabsArchivingPolicy" `
    -ArchiveInternal $True -ArchiveExternal $True
Grant-CsArchivingPolicy -Identity "pdickson" `
    -PolicyName "TestlabsArchivingPolicy"
```

Our user named Pete Dickson was granted this newly created policy, which means that both internal and external instant messaging and conferences are enabled for archiving.

When we have validated that all settings work the way we want them to, if we want to apply these settings to the Global archiving policy, that can be done as follows:

```
Set-CsArchivingPolicy -Identity "Global" -ArchiveInternal $True `
    -ArchiveExternal $True
```

When the configuration has been updated for the Global policy, we continue with the next step that is required only if the Exchange server(s) and Skype for Business server(s) are located in different forests:

```
Set-CsUser -Identity pdickson -ExchangeArchivingPolicy `
  ArchivingToExchange
```

The valid options for the `ExchangeArchivingPolicy` are Uninitialized, `UseLyncArchivingPolicy`, `NoArchiving`, or `ArchivingToExchange`. All of them have a user-friendly name, which most likely is self-describing to you. The Uninitialized option might need a bit of description; it means that if the user has not been enabled for in-place hold, it will be archived to the Skype for Business server.

With these settings in place, we are almost done; the final step is to create and grant a client policy to one of our users. This is simply done by running this:

```
New-CsClientPolicy -Identity "TestlabsClientPolicy" `
  -EnableExchangeDelegateSync $True -EnableIMAutoArchiving $True
Grant-CsClientPolicy -PolicyName "TestlabsClientPolicy" -Identity pdickson
```

Our first cmdlet is creating a new client policy and allowing the option of having delegates being able to schedule meetings on behalf of users. The second parameter is to make sure that the archiving is enabled and saved into the conversations folders in the mailbox. As a final step, we are granting this policy to our user.

If we want to have the same settings configured for the Global client policy, this can be easily done by running this:

```
Set-CsClientPolicy -Identity "Global" -EnableExchangeDelegateSync `
  $True -EnableIMAutoArchiving $True
```

Let's take a look at our user that now has these settings in place:

```
Administrator: Skype for Business Server Management Shell

PS C:\> Get-CsUser pdickson | fl Identity,ClientPolicy,ArchivingPolicy,Exch
angeArchivingPolicy,RegistrarPool,SipAddress


Identity                 : CN=Pete Dickson,OU=Sales,DC=testlabs,DC=se
ClientPolicy             : TestlabsClientPolicy
ArchivingPolicy          : TestlabsArchivingPolicy
ExchangeArchivingPolicy  : ArchivingToExchange
RegistrarPool            : tlfe01.testlabs.se
SipAddress               : sip:pdickson@testlabs.se
```

See also

- *OAuth configuration* recipe in this chapter
- *Configuring and enabling Unified Contact Store* recipe in this chapter
- *Placing mailboxes on in-place hold* recipe from `Chapter 11`, *Exchange Security*

Configuring and enabling the Unified Contact Store

The **Unified Contact Store (UCS)** enables the functionality of having all contacts from the Skype for Business client stored in the Exchange mailbox instead of Skype for Business (SQL database). This recipe has the same requirement for the integration to work: OAuth communication should be in place so that it works as expected. Implement this recipe if you want to have both Exchange and Skype for Business contacts collected in one place.

By default, in Skype for Business 2015, the Unified Contact Store is enabled when OAuth is configured and working. This recipe will be completed using both **Exchange Management Shell** (**EMS**) and the Skype for Business Management Shell (SFBMS).

How to do it...

1. This is an optional step, but personally, I like to configure a new policy and then grant it to a specific user instead of changing the Global policy, which would impact all users by default, at least before rolling it to production. Creating a new policy and granting it to the user is accomplished by running this cmdlet:

   ```
   New-CsUserServicesPolicy -Identity `
   "TestlabsAllowUnifiedContactStore" -UcsAllowed $TrueGrant-
   CsUserServicesPolicy -Identity "pdickson" `
        -PolicyName "TestlabsAllowUnifiedContactStore"
   ```

2. Configuring Enterprise partner application from Exchange is done using the EMS and running the following cmdlets:

   ```
   cd $exscripts

   .\Configure-EnterprisePartnerApplication.ps1 `
   -AuthMetadataUrl "https://tlfe01.testlabs.se/metadata/json/1"`
        -ApplicationType Lync
   ```

3. Create a partner application from Skype for Business by running the cmdlet (SFBMS):

```
New-CsPartnerApplication -Identity Exchange `
    -ApplicationTrustLevel Full -MetadataUrl `
"https://autodiscover.testlabs.se/autodiscover/metadata/json/1"
```

4. Validate the configuration and make sure that Exchange trusts Skype for Business and vice versa. It's easily completed by running the cmdlet (SFBMS):

```
Test-CsExStorageConnectivity -SipUri ` "sip:pdickson@testlabs.se"
    $credential = Get-Credential "testlabs\pdickson"
Test-CsUnifiedContactStore -UserSipAddress ` "sip:pdickson@testlabs.se" -
TargetFqdn "tlfe01.testlabs.se" `
    -UserCredential $credential
```

The result from the preceding cmdlet should look similar to the following screenshot:

5. Debugging is possible when it comes to UCS. This is as easy as running the following cmdlet (SFBMS):

```
Debug-CsUnifiedContactStore -Identity pdickson@testlabs.se `
| fl
```

The result should look similar to what is shown in the following screenshot:

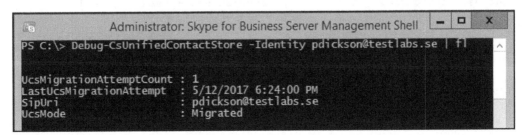

How it works...

In this recipe, we started by creating a new user services policy and making sure that we enable UCS using the `New-CsUserServicesPolicy -Identity ` `"TestlabsAllowUnifiedContactStore" -UcsAllowed $True` cmdlet, and then we granted it to one of our users with `Grant-CsUserServicesPolicy -Identity "pdickson" -PolicyName "TestlabsAllowUnifiedContactStore"`.

These two steps are also pending in that the systems (Exchange and Skype for Business) trust each other; in addition to the already created OAuth connection, we need to configure a new partner application from both Exchange toward Skype for Business and vice versa. We started by going to the built-in scripts folder in Exchange, cd $exscripts, running the script named "Configure-EnterprisePartnerApplication.ps1", and for the AuthMetadataUrl parameters, we type in the frontend server/registrar for our users. The full cmdlet looks like this:

```
.\Configure-EnterprisePartnerApplication.ps1 -AuthMetadataUrl
"https://t1fe01.testlabs.se/metadata/json/1" -ApplicationType Lync
```

 Just to confirm, the parameter for -ApplicationType is named Lync; it's not a typo. I have been researching for a new updated value, but at the time this publication this, this value should be Lync.

The partner application can be retrieved from the Exchange server by running the cmdlet:

```
Get-PartnerApplication -Identity Lync*.
```

On the other hand, we have to configure a partner application from Skype for Business toward Exchange and point the `MetadataUrl` parameter to Autodiscover. This is done by running this:

```
New-CsPartnerApplication -Identity Exchange `
-ApplicationTrustLevel Full -MetadataUrl `
"https://autodiscover.testlabs.se/autodiscover/metadata/json/1".
```

When we have created both applications, let's also retrieve the recently created partner application on the Skype for Business server by running `Get-CsPartnerApplication`; the result would look similar to what is shown in the following screenshot:

```
PS C:\> Get-CsPartnerApplication


Identity                             : Exchange
AuthToken                            : Value=https://autodiscover.testlabs.
                                       se/autodiscover/metadata/json/1
Name                                 : Exchange
ApplicationIdentifier                : 00000002-0000-0ff1-ce00-000000000000
Realm                                : testlabs.se
ApplicationTrustLevel                : Full
AcceptSecurityIdentifierInformation  : False
Enabled                              : True
```

With both partner applications in place, we want to validate the UCS functionality using: `Test-CsExStorageConnectivity -SipUri "sip:pdickson@testlabs.se"`, the attribute `-SipUri` is used to identify one particular user mailbox where the test item should be created. If we get a successful result, we want to go ahead and continue validating the Unified Contact Store with a user account so see that it works. This is done by inserting the user credentials and then validating using these. This is done by running the `$credential = Get-Credential "testlabs\pdickson"` cmdlets followed by this:

```
Test-CsUnifiedContactStore -UserSipAddress "sip:pdickson@testlabs.se" -
TargetFqdn "tlfe01.testlabs.se" -UserCredential $credential.
```

When the connection between the two systems is established, the Skype for Business contacts should be moved from the SQL database to the mailbox folder. For this to work, the user, of course, needs to have logged on and have at least one contact in the contact list.

In addition to these cmdlets, there is an additional cmdlet for extensive debugging of the UCS functionality, and it can be used by running this:

```
Debug-CsUnifiedContactStore -Identity pdickson@testlabs.se | fl.
```

We can validate that the UCS is in place from the Skype for Business client by checking the configuration information and seeing whether **Contact List Provider** is set to UCS or Lync Server. **UCS Connectivity State** should also be set to Exchange connection Active when UCS is working. With UCS configured, it will look similar to what is shown in the following screenshot:

Skype for Business Configuration Information		
Controlled Phones	TRUE	--
GAL or Server Based Search	GAL search	--
PC to PC AV Encryption	AV Encryption Enforced	--
Telephony Mode	Telephony Mode Disabled	--
Line Configured From	Auto Line Configuration	--
Configuration Mode	Auto Configuration	--
EWS Internal URL	https://mail.testlabs.se/EWS/Exchange.asmx	--
EWS External URL	https://mail.testlabs.se/EWS/Exchange.asmx	--
SharePoint Search Center UF		--
Skill Search URL		--
Skype for Business Server	tlfe01.testlabs.se	--
Local Log Folder	C:\Users\pdickson\AppData\Local\Microsoft\Office\16.0\Lync\Tracing	--
Inside User Status	TRUE	--
Contact List Provider	UCS	--
Pairing State	Skype for Business cannot connect to your desk phone because the US	Enabled
UCS Connectivity State	Exchange connection Active	--
MAPI Information	MAPI Status OK	MAPI Status OK
EWS Information		EWS Status OK
License State	Skype for Business ProPlus	--

See also

- *OAuth configuration* recipe in this chapter
- *Configuring Exchange archiving for Skype for Business Server* recipe in this chapter
- *Integrating Skype for Business with Outlook on the web* recipe in this chapter

Integrating Skype for Business with Outlook on the web

If you are using Outlook.com as your private e-mail provider, you've probably noticed that the consumer version of Skype is integrated in the mail functionality nowadays. A similar functionality can also be achieved with Exchange 2016 and Skype for Business 2015 instead of the consumer version of Skype we use Skype for Business.

A scenario when this is ideal would be if there are users that might not have the rich Skype for Business client installed or available for some reason; they can then simply go to the webmail and utilize the instant messaging functionality there.

In this recipe, we will take a look at how this can be configured and validated.

How to do it...

1. To be able to integrate, the Unified Communications Managed API 4.0 Runtime needs to be installed on the Exchange server(s). We can validate that this has been installed by running the cmdlet:

```
Get-ItemProperty "HKLM:\SYSTEM\CurrentControlSet\Services\MSExchange
OWA\InstantMessaging" -Name ImplementationDLLPath
```

2. Retrieve the certificate thumbprint that is used in the Exchange server for web services:

```
Get-ExchangeCertificate
```

3. The output will look similar to what is shown in the following screenshot. Save the thumbprint from the certificate assigned for the web service from the output.

4. Create an override setting for Outlook on the Web by specifying the IM server and the IM certificate thumbprint. This is accomplished by running the cmdlet:

```
New-SettingOverride -Name "IM Override" -Component
OwaServer -Section IMSettings -Parameters
@("IMServerName=tlfe01.testlabs.se",
"IMCertificateThumbprint=
BA4E150BBA6F7D7324A7F694AFC1F46E4FADC98A") -Reason "Configure IM"
```

5. Refresh the IM settings on the Exchange server by running the cmdlet:

```
Get-ExchangeDiagnosticInfo -Process
Microsoft.Exchange.Directory.TopologyService
-Component VariantConfiguration -Argument Refresh
```

6. Retrieve the Skype for Business Site IDs:

```
Get-CsSite | fl DisplayName, SiteID
```

7. Create a new, trusted application pool and a trusted application for Outlook on the web usage; this is done by executing the cmdlet:

```
New-CsTrustedApplicationPool -Identity "mail.testlabs.se" -Registrar
t1fe01.testlabs.se -Site "Default Site" -RequiresReplication $false
New-CsTrustedApplication -ApplicationId OutlookWebApp -
TrustedApplicationPoolFqdn mail.testlabs.se -Port 5199
```

8. Enable the changes that were just done for Skype for Business:

```
Enable-CsTopology
```

9. Once the configurations are set, restart the application pool for Outlook on the Web by running the cmdlet:

```
Restart-WebAppPool MSExchangeOWAAppPool
```

10. Configure Outlook on the Web to be enabled for instant messaging of the instant messaging type OCS:

```
Get-OwaVirtualDirectory | Set-OwaVirtualDirectory -
InstantMessagingEnabled $True -InstantMessagingType OCS
```

11. This is an optional step. If you want to enable the Outlook on the Web integration for the default OwaMailboxPolicy, this is done by running the following:

```
Set-OwaMailboxPolicy -Identity "Default" `
 -InstantMessagingEnabled $True -InstantMessagingType "OCS"
```

12. Validate that the instant messaging integration works as expected, note that the cmdlet is different based on which cumulative update level your environment is currently on.

CU3 and earlier:

```
[xml]$diag = Get-ExchangeDiagnosticInfo -Server tlex01 -Process
Microsoft.Exchange.Directory.TopologyService -Component
VariantConfiguration -Argument Config;
$diag.Diagnostics.Components.VariantConfiguration.Configuration.OwaServer.I
MSettings
```

CU4 and higher:

```
[xml]$diag = Get-ExchangeDiagnosticInfo -Server tlex01 -Process
MSExchangeMailboxAssistants -Component VariantConfiguration -Argument
"Config,Component=OwaServer";
$diag.Diagnostics.Components.VariantConfiguration.Configuration.OwaServer.I
MSettings
```

How it works...

In this recipe, we start by validating that the Unified Communications Managed API 4.0 Runtime has been installed by validating that the ImplementationDLLPath has a valid value set.

Before creating the instant messaging override settings, we need to retrieve the thumbprint of the Exchange certificate assigned for web services. This is done by running Get-ExchangeCertificate and saving the thumbprint for the next step.

The next step is to create a new override setting for Outlook on the Web, defining the thumbprint that is going to be used for this. We are also specifying the Skype for Business server. The full cmdlet will be as follows:

```
New-SettingOverride -Name "IM Override" `
-Component OwaServer -Section IMSettings -Parameters `
@("IMServerName=tlfe01.testlabs.se","IMCertificateThumbprint=7800000`0040BC
7C72721CE1FAD000000000004") -Reason "Configure IM"
```

With this setting in place, it's time to refresh the configuration by running this:

```
Get-ExchangeDiagnosticInfo -Process `
Microsoft.Exchange.Directory.TopologyService -Component `
VariantConfiguration -Argument Refresh
```

Now we need to collect the Site ID from Skype for Business; this is done from the Skype for Business Management Shell by running `Get-CsSite | fl DisplayName, SiteID`. The Site ID will be used in our next step when creating the trusted application pool:

```
New-CsTrustedApplicationPool -Identity "mail.testlabs.se" `
-Registrar tlfe01.testlabs.se -Site "Default Site" `
-RequiresReplication $false.
```

As you can see in the preceding example, the Site ID in my Skype for Business setup is `Default Site`. With the application pool in place, we can continue and create the trusted application too:

```
New-CsTrustedApplication -ApplicationId OutlookWebApp `
-TrustedApplicationPoolFqdn mail.testlabs.se -Port 5199
```

Our Skype for Business server has been configured now, and the final step is to enable the configuration we did earlier by running `Enable-CsTopology`.

Let's finish this configuration by changing the configuring for Outlook on the Web virtual directory, enabling instant messaging for it and specifying OCS as the type. This is done using this:

```
Get-OwaVirtualDirectory | Set-OwaVirtualDirectory `
-InstantMessagingEnabled $True -InstantMessagingType OCS
```

If it's correct, the parameter InstantMessagingType value should be configured to OCS. This has, for some reason, not been updated by Microsoft yet, so it's still named OCS. However, the important part is to make the integration work.

If you want to implement these settings for the `OwaMailboxPolicy` as well, that can simply be done by running:

```
Set-OwaMailboxPolicy -Identity "Default" `
-InstantMessagingEnabled $True - InstantMessagingType "OCS".
```

Our final configuration step is to restart the application pool for Outlook on the Web, which is done by running `Restart-WebAppPool MSExchangeOWAAppPool`. It may take a couple of seconds for the restart, but it's rather quick. Keep in mind to plan for these integration changes since they require restart of services that impact the end users.

The configuration is in place and we want to validate that everything works as we expect it to, pending on what cumulative update level your current environment is on. The cmdlets differ a bit, note the slight difference between them below.

If you are running CU3 or earlier, you can validate the configuration by running this:

```
[xml]$diag=Get-ExchangeDiagnosticInfo -Server tlex01 -Process `
Microsoft.Exchange.Directory.TopologyService -Component `
VariantConfiguration -Argument Config; `
$diag.Diagnostics.Components.VariantConfiguration.Configuration.`
 OwaServer.IMSettings
```

If you are you on CU4 or higher, the following cmdlet should be used:

```
[xml]$diag=Get-ExchangeDiagnosticInfo -Server tlex01 -Process `
MSExchangeMailboxAssistants -Component VariantConfiguration `
 -Argument "Config,Component=OwaServer"; `
$diag.Diagnostics.Components.VariantConfiguration.Configuration.`
 OwaServer.IMSettings
```

After all these steps, it's time to perform a live test and see whether the Outlook on the Web integration works as we want it to. I have signed in with one user on the rich Skype for Business application and with another one to Outlook on the Web. The instant messaging seems to work great between the two; take a look at the following screenshot:

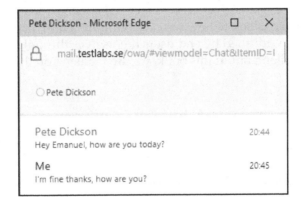

See also

- *OAuth configuration* recipe in this chapter
- *Configuring Exchange archiving for Skype for Business Server* recipe in this chapter
- *Configuring a user with high-resolution photo* recipe in this chapter

Configuring a user with a high-resolution photo

We have had photos in the Global Address List for some time now; they used to be saved in an Active Directory attribute. With Exchange 2013 and higher, we now have the option of using high-resolution photos instead of the traditional 48 x 48 pixels photo that were saved in the thumbnailPhoto attribute in Active Directory.

With Exchange 2013 and higher, Outlook on the Web, Outlook and Skype for Business Web App, and the Skype for Business client support the usage of larger photos: 96 x 96 pixels.

We also have the option of having even larger photos that are sized 648 x 648 pixels; they will work with both the Skype for Business client and the web app client.

 Keep in mind that since these photos are saved in the mailbox and not in the Active Directory attribute, the mailbox size will increase a bit.

In this recipe, we will take a look at how we can configure a user with a high-resolution photo, which can be accomplished by end users themselves through Outlook on the Web or the Skype for Business client, but in this book, we are focusing on the PowerShell piece.

How to do it...

1. Load the photo into a byte variable by running this:

```
$photo = ([Byte[]] $(Get-Content -Path ` "C:\Photos\pdickson.jpg" -Encoding Byte -ReadCount 0))
```

2. Set the photo for a specific user:

```
Set-UserPhoto -Identity pdickson -PictureData $photo -Confirm:$False
```

3. The end result of this recipe should look similar what is shown in the following figure:

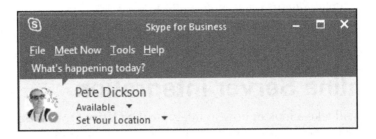

4. This is an optional step; if we want to validate how the photo looks for this specific update, we simply follow the following link and update the email value with a matching one:

> **https://mail.testlabs.se/ews/Exchange.asmx
> /s/GetUserPhoto?email=pdickson@testlabs.se&size=HR648x648**

How it works...

We are now focusing on configuring the end user with a high definition photo instead of saving the photo into the Active Directory attribute, thumbnailPhoto.

We started this recipe by reading the jpg file into a byte variable that was saved as `$photo` and then we used that variable to set it as the photo for a specific user. All this was done by running the following two cmdlets:

```
$photo = ([Byte[]] $(Get-Content -Path "C:\Photos\pdickson.jpg" `
-Encoding Byte -ReadCount 0))
Set-UserPhoto -Identity pdickson -PictureData $photo -Confirm:$False
```

To validate that the photo got saved and that it was saved as the 648 * 648 pixel that it should have been saved as, we can easily use a link to look it up.

> **https://mail.testlabs.se/ews/Exchange.asmx/s/GetUserPhoto?email=pdickson@te
> stlabs.se&size=HR648x648.**

See also

- *OAuth configuration* recipe in this chapter
- *Integrating Skype for Business with Outlook on the web* recipe in this chapter

Office Online Server integration

In this recipe, we will take a look at how to integrate the **Office Online Server (OOS)** with Exchange 2016. In Exchange Online in Office 365, we already have this functionality/workload with Office Online, where you receive an email with an attachment and it gives our end users the option of opening the attachment in a feature-rich browser-based application without having to download it first.

A requirement for this integration is to be on Exchange 2016, Cumulative Update 1 level or higher. If you want your users to be able to view the attachments even outside of your network, the OOS server needs to be reachable from the Internet through TCP port 443.

With this short introduction, let's go through the steps we have to perform in order to have this integration.

Getting ready

Before jumping into the following steps, make sure that you have the name configured in DNS for the OOS. If you are about to publish this server, you also need to have the DNS record in your public DNS zone. Your chosen OOS name needs to be included in the certificate on the OOS server(s). In my example, I have only one OOS server, I've added oos.testlabs.se to the web server certificate on the OOS server and into the internal DNS zone.

How to do it...

1. Validate whether any existing configuration is already done; if not, then create a new Office Web Apps Farm by running this:

```
Get-OfficeWebAppsFarm
New-OfficeWebAppsFarm -InternalURL "https://oos.testlabs.se" ` -
ExternalURL "https://oos.testlabs.se" -CertificateName `
  "OOS certificate"
```

2. Start any Internet browser and go to the URL listed here; validate that there are no certificate errors and that the XML file including the content is being shown:

```
https://oos.testlabs.se/hosting/discovery
```

3. Before configuring, let's validate that the OOS isn't already configured for Exchange. If not, then continue to configure OOS at the organizational level for Exchange 2016 by running this:

```
Get-OrganizationConfig | fl WacDiscoveryEndpoint
Set-OrganizationConfig -WacDiscoveryEndpoint `
    "https://oos.testlabs.se/hosting/discovery"
```

4. Restart the web application pool for Outlook on the Web:

```
Restart-WebAppPool MsExchangeOwaAppPool
```

 If you have Exchange 2013 servers in your organization, remember to configure OOS at the mailbox server level instead of the organizational level because it's not supported to use OOS together with Exchange 2013.

How it works...

In this recipe, the prerequisite is to have Microsoft .NET Framework 4.5.2, Visual C++ Redistributable for Visual Studio 2015 plus a full stack of roles and features. All of them can be installed by running the following one-liner:

```
Install-WindowsFeature Web-Server, Web-Mgmt-Tools, Web-Mgmt-Console,
Web-WebServer, Web-Common-Http, Web-Default-Doc, Web-Static-Content, Web-
Performance, Web-Stat-Compression, Web-Dyn-Compression, Web-Security, Web-
Filtering, Web-Windows-Auth, Web-App-Dev, Web-Net-Ext45, Web-Asp-Net45,
Web-ISAPI-Ext, Web-ISAPI-Filter, Web-Includes, InkandHandwritingServices,
Windows-Identity-Foundation.
```

With the mentioned prerequisites in place, we also need to have the DNS record in place, both internal and external (if you are going to publish the server(s) externally) and include the DNS name in the web certificate on each server (if you have more than one).

Publishing for the OOS servers is easy; it uses only TCP/443 port, and there is no requirement for any pre-authentication so you can simply publish HTTPS for the OOS server(s), and you are good to go.

Regarding the steps, we started by validating that there are no existing Office Web Apps Farm by running the following:

```
Get-OfficeWebAppsFarm.
```

In our example, we did not have any current configuration for the Office Web Apps Farm, so we continued to create a new farm by running this:

```
New-OfficeWebAppsFarm -InternalURL "https://oos.testlabs.se" `
-ExternalURL "https://oos.testlabs.se" -CertificateName `
"OOS certificate"
```

The cmdlet is specifying the parameters `-InternalURL` and `-ExternalURL`; these can differ from each other and should, of course, match the internal and external DNS record. Also, keep in mind that you include both names if you don't use the same for both of them.

The `-CertificateName` parameter specifies the friendly name of the OOS certificate installed on the OOS server; in our example, it was `OOS certificate`.

With the farm in place, we want to validate that it responds to requests. We tested this by starting an Internet browser and navigating to `https://oos.testlabs.se/hosting/discovery`.

Before taking the next step in our configuration, we want to make sure that there is not already a configuration in place that we might overwrite. We are checking the organization configuration and looking for the `-WacDiscoveryEndpoint` parameter by running this:

```
Get-OrganizationConfig | fl WacDiscoveryEndpoint.
```

The parameters value was empty, which means there is no current configuration, so we can continue by running this:

```
Set-OrganizationConfig -WacDiscoveryEndpoint
"https://oos.testlabs.se/hosting/discovery".
```

The only step left is to restart the application pool for OWA by running this:

```
Restart-WebAppPool MsExchangeOwaAppPool.
```

With the integration in place, the instant messing functionality should look similar to what is shown in the following screenshot when opening an attachment directly in a received e-mail:

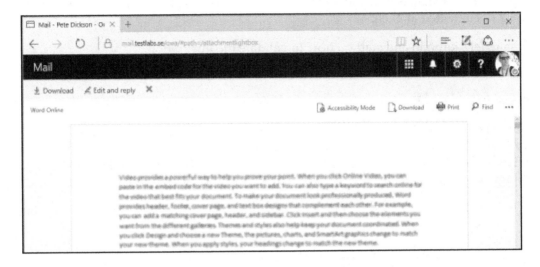

See also

- The *OAuth configuration* recipe in this chapter
- The *Configuring Exchange archiving for Skype for Business Server* recipe in this chapter
- The *Integrating Skype for Business with Outlook on the web* recipe in this chapter

Validating Exchange hybrid

It's very common to find articles, blog posts, and other similar information on how to configure and set up the Exchange hybrid, but it's not very common to find similar information about validating that the functionality is working as expected. We are trying to fill that gap with this recipe.

Therefore, we won't go into details on how to configure and set up the hybrid; instead, we will focus on getting the functionality validated.

Getting ready

In this recipe, we will assume that you have an existing Exchange 2016 hybrid solution configured for Exchange 2016 and Exchange Online that have fulfilled the requirements that are well documented at TechNet.

That said, let's jump in and start on how to validate the integration.

How to do it...

Before the following steps are performed, we assume that the Exchange Hybrid is successfully configured and fulfils all prerequisites. For reference, for this recipe, we have one Exchange 2016 server, configured successfully by running the hybrid wizard configuration using a third-party certificate by a trusted issuer (DigiCert).

1. Validate that the federation trust certificate is in place; this is done by running this:

   ```
   Test-FederationTrustCertificate
   ```

2. With the federation trust certificate in place, let's retrieve the federation trust and test by running the cmdlet:

   ```
   Get-FederationTrust
   Test-FederationTrust
   ```

3. Retrieve the organization relationship information and save the Name attribute into the $name variable and then test it using the cmdlet:

   ```
   $name = (Get-OrganizationRelationship).Name

   Test-OrganizationRelationship -UserIdentity ` pdickson@testlabs.se -Identity $name

   Get-OrganizationRelationship | Test-OrganizationRelationship `
    -UserIdentity pdickson@testlabs.se
   ```

4. The final step is to validate OAuth since it's being used when having a Hybrid solution; we can validate the Hybrid by running three different setups of cmdlets:

```
Test-OAuthConnectivity
Test-OAuthConnectivity -Service EWS -TargetUri `
https://mail.testlabs.se/ews/ -Mailbox "pdickson"
Test-OAuthConnectivity -Service AutoD -TargetUri `
https://mail.testlabs.se/autodiscover/autodiscover.xml `
-Mailbox "pdickson"
Test-OAuthConnectivity -Service Generic -TargetUri `
`https://mail.testlabs.se/ -Mailbox "pdickson"
```

How it works...

In this recipe, the prerequisite is to have a third-party certificate that is issued by a trusted issuer; in my example, I'm using a certificate from DigiCert. The certificate is required in order to have a fully working hybrid solution, since Office 365 (Exchange Online) won't trust a certificate issued by an internal issuer (Internal PKI).

The certificate should be assigned to at least the IIS and SMTP service, since it's going to be used for these services for Autodiscover, Web services, and for the mail flow between the on-premises solution and the cloud solution.

We started to validate that there is an existing federation trust certificate; this is issued during the hybrid configuration and it's important to have an in-place in a hybrid scenario. This is done by running `Test-FederationTrustCertificate`.

With the certificate in place, we want to continue and see whether the federation trust was created successfully, and we also would like to execute one of the Test- cmdlets.

The `Get-FederationTrust` cmdlet is being used to retrieve the federation trust (if any). Normally, we should get a result back with the federation trust information. Now we want to test the federation trust to see whether it actually works or not. This is done by running the following:

```
Test-FederationTrust
```

One thing to note here is that this Test- cmdlet might fail if New-`TestCasConnectivityUser.ps1` hasn't been executed prior to the Test- cmdlet.

If required, the creation of the extest mailbox can be done by running the following:

```
& $env:ExchangeInstallPath\Scripts\New-TestCasConnectivityUser.ps1
```

The outcome from the Test- cmdlet should look similar to what is shown in the following screenshot:

```
Machine: TLEX01.testlabs.se                               —   □   ×

[PS] C:\>Test-FederationTrust

Begin process.

STEP 1 of 6: Getting ADUser information for extest_f55866cfee824...
RESULT: Success.

STEP 2 of 6: Getting FederationTrust object for extest_f55866cfee824...
RESULT: Success.

STEP 3 of 6: Validating that the FederationTrust has the same STS certifica
tes as the actual certificates published by the STS in the federation metad
ata.
RESULT: Success.

STEP 4 of 6: Getting STS and Organization certificates from the federation
trust object...
RESULT: Success.


Validating current configuration for FYDIBOHF25SPDLT.testlabs.se...


Validation successful.

STEP 5 of 6: Requesting delegation token...
RESULT: Success. Token retrieved.

STEP 6 of 6: Validating delegation token...
RESULT: Success.

Closing Test-FederationTrust...
```

If the federation trust was successful, then we continue to our next step and validate the organization relationship. This is also created and configured by the hybrid wizard configuration. There are two ways of validating this; select which method you prefer since both of them work great.

- Method 1:

```
$name = (Get-OrganizationRelationship).Name
Test-OrganizationRelationship -UserIdentity pdickson@testlabs.se `
-Identity $name
```

- The name of the organizational relationship is saved into a variable called $name, which is then used as an input variable to the Test- cmdlet instead of specifying a long name, similar to this example: On-premises to O365 - 279245a5-d3df-4d16-afb2-14e3fbb018a7.

- Method 2:

```
Get-OrganizationRelationship | Test-OrganizationRelationship `
-UserIdentity pdickson@testlabs.se
```

- This method is my personal preferred method since it both retrieves and then pipelines the organization relationship information into the Test- cmdlet just using the -UserIdentity parameter to test with.
- The outcome and result of these two methods of the Test- cmdlets should look similar to what is shown in the following screenshot:

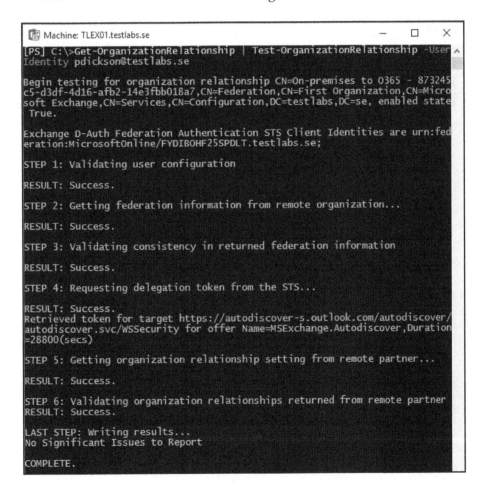

The fourth and final validation is to check whether OAuth is working as expected, and this can easily be done by running the `Test-OAuthConnectivity` cmdlet, an example to validate the EWS service:

```
Test-OAuthConnectivity -Service EWS -TargetUri `
https://mail.testlabs.se/ews/ -Mailbox "pdickson"
```

In addition to EWS, Autodiscover and Generic can also be used as an input to the service parameter. Refer to the examples in the how to do it section.

See also

- The *OAuth configuration* recipe in this chapter
- The *Office Online Server integration* recipe in this chapter
- The *Integrate Skype for Business with Outlook on the web* recipe in this chapter

14

Scripting with the Exchange Web Services Managed API

In this chapter, we will cover the following:

- Getting connected to EWS
- Sending email messages with EWS
- Working with impersonation
- Searching mailboxes
- Retrieving the headers of an email message
- Deleting email items from a mailbox
- Creating calendar items
- Exporting attachments from a mailbox

Introduction

Exchange Web Services (EWS) is available for Exchange 2016 (also for Exchange Online). During the writing of the book, we've used EWS Managed API version 2.2, since that was the latest available release. The API gives developers the ability to write applications that previously used legacy APIs.

Today, developers can call Exchange Management Shell cmdlets from .NET-managed applications to perform administrative tasks programmatically. When it comes to manipulating the contents of a mailbox, such as creating or modifying calendar items, email messages, contacts, or tasks, developers now use EWS.

Working with EWS requires formatting and sending an XML request over HTTP and parsing the XML response from an Exchange server. Initially, developers used either raw XML or auto-generated proxy classes in Visual Studio to do this, and it required some very verbose code that was difficult to read and debug. Fortunately, the Exchange Web Services team developed and released the EWS Managed API in April of 2009. The EWS Managed API is a fully object-oriented .NET wrapper for the EWS XML protocol that makes life much easier for application developers.

Applications written using the Managed API require a fraction of the code that developers had to write previously when working with raw XML or auto-generated proxy classes. This makes for a huge increase in productivity because the code is easier to read and troubleshoot, and the learning curve for new developers is much lower. The good news is that this is also true for Exchange administrators who want to write advanced PowerShell scripts that utilize EWS. The EWS Managed API can be used to do things in PowerShell that are not possible with Exchange Management Shell cmdlets. The EWS Managed API assembly can be loaded into the shell, and, with the right permissions, you can immediately start building scripts that can access and manipulate the data within any mailbox inside the organization.

In this chapter, we will cover some of the key concepts of using EWS in your PowerShell scripts, such as connecting to EWS, sending email messages, and working with items in one or more mailboxes. The end goal is to give you a basic understanding of the EWS Managed API so that you can start building some basic scripts or deciphering the code samples you come across on the internet or within the TechNet documentation.

Performing some basic steps

To work with the code samples in this chapter, follow these steps to download the EWS Managed API:

1. Download the EWS Managed API from the following URL: `http://www.microso ft.com/en-us/download/details.aspx?id=42951`.

2. Download and run `EwsManagedApi.msi`.

3. During the installation and select a destination folder such as `C:\EWS` or choose the default directory `C:\Program Files\Microsoft\Exchange\WebServices\2.2`. You will need to note the location so you can import the `Microsoft.Exchange.WebServices.dll` assembly into the shell.

You can use either a standard PowerShell console or the Exchange Management Shell to run the code for each recipe in this chapter.

Getting connected to EWS

When working with EWS, you first need to create an instance of the `ExchangeService` class that can be used to send SOAP messages to an Exchange server. This class has several properties and methods that can be used to specify explicit credentials, set the web service's endpoint URL, or make a connection using the built-in AutoDiscover client. In this recipe, you'll learn how to make a connection to EWS that can be used to run custom scripts against the web service.

How to do it...

1. The first thing we need to do is load the EWS Managed API assembly into the shell:

   ```
   Add-Type -Path C:\EWS\Microsoft.Exchange.WebServices.dll
   ```

2. Now we can create an instance of the `ExchangeService` class:

   ```
   $svc = New-Object
   Microsoft.Exchange.WebServices.Data.ExchangeService
   ```

3. At this point, we can use the `AutoDiscoverUrl` method to determine the EWS endpoint on the closest Client Access Server for the mailbox with a particular SMTP address:

   ```
   $svc.AutoDiscoverUrl("lsanders@testlabs.se")
   ```

Now that we have an Exchange service connection created, we can send email messages, create and modify items within a mailbox, and perform other tasks. The outcome will look similar to the following screenshot:

How it works...

Before we can start working with the classes in the EWS Managed API, the assembly must be loaded so that the .NET Framework types are available when running scripts that utilize the API. This is only valid for the current shell session, and, if you will be creating scripts, you'll want to make sure that this is always the first thing that is done before invoking any code. We used the `Add-Type` cmdlet in the previous example to load the assembly, but this is also valid:

```
[System.Reflection.Assembly]::LoadFile(
  "C:\ews\Microsoft.Exchange.WebServices.dll"
)
```

This is basically the longhand method of doing the same thing we did before: loading an unreferenced assembly into the shell environment. Notice that in both examples, we are using the path `C:\EWS`. This is not the default path where the assembly is installed, but you can copy it to any folder of your choice. See the following screenshot for an example:

When creating an instance of the `ExchangeService` class, we have the option of versioning the connection. For example:

```
$svc=New-Object
Microsoft.Exchange.WebServices.Data.ExchangeService `
-ArgumentList "Exchange2013_SP1"
```

Here we are passing the Exchange version to the `ExchangeService` class constructor. When you do not provide a value, the most recent version of Exchange will be used, which in this case would be Exchange 2013 SP1, since were using the 2.2 version of the API. The values that can be used for Exchange are `Exchange2007_SP1`, `Exchange2010`, `Exchange2010_SP1`, `Exchange2010_SP2`, `Exchange2013`, and `Exchange2013_SP1`.

Since we didn't specify credentials when creating the `ExchangeService` object, we need to provide the SMTP address associated with the mailbox of the currently logged on user when calling the `AutoDiscoverUrl` method.

There's more...

If you want to use explicit credentials when creating your `ExchangeService` object rather than using the credentials of the currently logged on user, you need to do a couple of things differently. The following code will create an instance of the `ExchangeService` class using an alternate set of credentials:

```
[System.Reflection.Assembly]::LoadFile(
  "C:\ews\Microsoft.Exchange.WebServices.dll"
)
$svc = New-Object Microsoft.Exchange.WebServices.Data.ExchangeService
$svc.Credentials = New-Object `
Microsoft.Exchange.WebServices.Data.WebCredentials `
-ArgumentList "jonand","P@ssw0rd01","testlabs.se"
```

In addition, you also have the option of setting the EWS URL manually:

```
$url =
"https://autodiscover.testlabs.se/EWS/Exchange.asmx"
$svc.Url = New-Object System.Uri -ArgumentList $url
```

Although it is possible to set the URL manually, developers use AutoDiscover as a best practice because it allows the API to determine the best Client Access Server that should be used as the web service's URL. A hardcoded URL value could potentially mean a broken script if things change later on in your environment. The outcome of the preceding cmdlets will look similar to the following screenshot:

```
Machine: TLEX01.testlabs.se                                    —    □    ×
[PS] C:\>$url = "https://autodiscover.testlabs.se/EWS/Exchange.asmx"
[PS] C:\>$svc.Url = New-Object System.Uri -ArgumentList $url
[PS] C:\>
[PS] C:\>$svc.Url

AbsolutePath  : /EWS/Exchange.asmx
AbsoluteUri   : https://autodiscover.testlabs.se/EWS/Exchange.asmx
```

Certificates matter

Just like Outlook Web App, the EWS virtual directory is secured with an SSL certificate. If you are still using the self-signed certificates that are installed by default on Client Access Servers, you'll need to override a security check done by the API to validate the certificate; otherwise, you will be unable to connect.

To do this, we can use the `ServicePointManager` class in the `System.Net` namespace. This class can be used to hook up a certificate validation callback method, and, as long as that method returns `$true`, the API will consider the self-signed certificate to be trusted:

```
$svc = New-Object
Microsoft.Exchange.WebServices.Data.ExchangeService
$spm = [System.Net.ServicePointManager]
$spm::ServerCertificateValidationCallback = {$true}
$svc.AutoDiscoverUrl("lsanders@testlabs.se")
```

Certificate validation callback methods are written to perform additional checks on a certificate. These callback methods return a `Boolean` value that indicates whether or not a certificate can be trusted. Instead of writing a callback method, we're assigning a script block that returns `$true` to the `ServerCertificateValidationCallback` property. This forces the API to consider any EWS endpoint to be secure, regardless of the status of the certificate used to secure it. Keep in mind that self-signed certificates are considered to be a bootstrap security configuration so connections to Exchange can be secured out of the box. The best practice is to replace these certificates with trusted commercial or enterprise PKI certificates. For example, see the following screenshot regarding the URL override:

Sending email messages with EWS

As we saw back in Chapter 2, *Exchange Management Shell Common Tasks*, we can use the built-in PowerShell cmdlet Send-MailMessage to send email messages. This can be a useful tool when writing scripts that need to send notifications, but the EWS Managed API has several distinct advantages over this approach. In this recipe, we'll take a look at how to send email messages through EWS and why this might be a better option for organizations that have an Exchange infrastructure in place.

How to do it...

1. First, we'll import the EWS Managed API assembly, create an instance of the ExchangeService class, and set the EWS endpoint using AutoDiscover:

```
Add-Type -Path
C:\EWS\Microsoft.Exchange.WebServices.dll
$svc = New-Object `
-TypeName
 Microsoft.Exchange.WebServices.Data.ExchangeService
 $svc.AutoDiscoverUrl("administrator@contoso.com")
```

2. Next, we'll create an instance of the EmailMessage class:

```
$msg = New-Object `
-TypeName
Microsoft.Exchange.WebServices.Data.EmailMessage `
-ArgumentList $svc
```

3. At this point, we can set specific properties on the $msg object such as the subject, body, and one or more recipients:

```
$msg.Subject = "Test Email"
$msg.Body = "This is a test"
$msg.From = "administrator@contoso.com"
$msg.ToRecipients.Add("sysadmin@contoso.com")
$msg.SendAndSaveCopy()
```

Once this code has been executed, the message is sent to sysadmin@contoso.com.

How it works...

When we send email messages through EWS, we don't have to worry about specifying an SMTP server since the message is transmitted through the web service. This allows our code to run on any machine that has PowerShell installed, and we don't need to modify the receive connectors on the client access servers to allow a specific host to relay mail. Additionally, EWS will allow us to use AutoDiscover to automatically find the correct endpoint, which prevents the need to hardcode server names into our scripts.

Setting the Subject, Body, and From properties of an EmailMessage object is pretty straightforward. We simply need to assign a value as we would with any other object. Adding recipients requires that we use the Add method of the ToRecipients property. If you have multiple recipients that must be addressed, you can call this method for each one, or you can loop through a collection using the ForEach-Object cmdlet:

```
$to =
"sysadmin@contoso.com","IT@contoso.com",
"help@contoso.com"
$to | ForEach-Object {$msg.ToRecipients.Add($_)}
```

When you call the Add method, you'll notice that the ToRecipients property will be returned for each address added to the message. For example, in the following screenshot, you may notice that I have used the command Out-Null; it is used for having a proper screenshot size.

```
Machine: TLEX01.testlabs.se                                    —    □    ×
[PS] C:\>Add-Type -Path C:\EWS\Microsoft.Exchange.WebServices.dll
[PS] C:\>$svc = New-Object -TypeName Microsoft.Exchange.WebServices.Data.Ex
changeService
[PS] C:\>$svc.AutoDiscoverUrl("lsanders@testlabs.se")
[PS] C:\>$msg = New-Object -TypeName Microsoft.Exchange.WebServices.Data.Em
ailMessage -ArgumentList $svc
[PS] C:\>$msg.Subject = "Test E-Mail"
[PS] C:\>$msg.Body = "This is a test"
[PS] C:\>$msg.From = "lsanders@testlabs.se"
[PS] C:\>$to = "administrator@testlabs.se","pdickson@testlabs.se","emoss@te
stlabs.se"
[PS] C:\>$to | ForEach-Object {$msg.ToRecipients.Add($_) | Out-Null}
[PS] C:\>$msg.SendAndSaveCopy()
[PS] C:\>
```

If you want to simply call this method without having anything returned to the screen, pipe the command to Out-Null (as in the preceding screenshot):

```
$msg.ToRecipients.Add("sales@contoso.com") | Out-Null
```

In addition, we can also carbon copy and blind copy recipients on the message:

```
$msg.CcRecipients.Add("sales@contoso.com") | Out-Null
$msg.BccRecipients.Add("dmsith@contoso.com") | Out-
Null
```

Finally, if you do not want to save a copy of the message in the Sent Items folder, you can simply use the Send method:

```
$msg.Send()
```

Keep in mind that since we did not provide credentials when connecting to EWS, the user running this code will need to have a mailbox on the server which corresponds to the From address being used. Since we are connecting with our currently logged on credentials, the message must be sent from the mailbox of the user running the code.

There's more...

Instead of typing all of the commands required to instantiate the Exchange service object, it makes much more sense to put this code into a reusable function. Call AutoDiscover, create the email message object, and set all of the required properties. Consider the following example:

```
function Send-EWSMailMessage {
  param(
  [Parameter(
    Position=0,
    Mandatory=$true,
    ValueFromPipelineByPropertyName=$true
  )]
  [String[]]
  $PrimarySmtpAddress,

  [Parameter(
    Position=1, Mandatory=$true
  )]
  [String]
  $From,

  [Parameter(
    Position=2, Mandatory=$true
  )]
  [String]
  $Subject,
```

```
[Parameter(
  Position=3, Mandatory=$true
)]
[String]
$Body,

[Parameter(
  Position=4, Mandatory=$false
)]
[String[]]
$Cc,

[Parameter(
  Position=5, Mandatory=$false
)]
[String[]]
$Bcc

)

begin {
  Add-Type -Path C:\EWS\Microsoft.Exchange.WebServices.dll
}

process {
  $svc = New-Object `
  -TypeName Microsoft.Exchange.WebServices.Data.ExchangeService
  $svc.AutodiscoverUrl($From)

  $msg = New-Object `
  -TypeName Microsoft.Exchange.WebServices.Data.EmailMessage `
  -ArgumentList $svc
  $msg.Subject = $Subject
  $msg.Body = $Body

  $PrimarySmtpAddress | %{
    $msg.ToRecipients.Add($_) | Out-Null
  }

if ($Cc -ne $null)
{
    $msg.CcRecipients.Add($Cc) | Out-Null
}

if ($Bcc -ne $null)
{
    $msg.BccRecipients.Add($Bcc) | Out-Null
}
```

```
    $msg.SendAndSaveCopy()
  }
}
```

This is an advanced function that can be run in a couple of different ways. Notice that the first parameter is called `PrimarySmtpAddress` and it accepts a value from the pipeline by property name. This will allow us to add the function to the Exchange Management Shell and take advantage of the pipeline to send email messages. For example, once this function has been loaded into EMS, we can do something like this:

```
Get-Mailbox -OrganizationalUnit contoso.com/sales |
   Send-EWSMailMessage -From administrator@contoso.com `
   -Subject 'Sales Meeting' `
   -Body 'Tomorrows sales meeting has been cancelled' `
-Cc administrator@contoso.com `
-Bcc manager@contoso.com
```

Here, you can see that we're retrieving all the users from the `Sales` OU and piping those objects to our `Send-EWSMailMessage` function. One message will be addressed and sent to each recipient because the `PrimarySmtpAddress` parameter receives its value from each object that comes across the pipeline. Notice that a carbon copy email will be sent to the specified mailbox when using the `Cc` parameter and a blind carbon copy email will be sent to the specified mailbox using the `Bcc` parameter.

Since the `PrimarySmtpAddress` parameter also accepts an array of string objects, we can run the function and specify a list of recipients, as shown in the following example:

```
Send-EWSMailMessage -From administrator@testlabs.se `
-PrimarySmtpAddress helpdesk@testlabs.se,lsanders@testlabs.se `
-Subject 'Critical alert on TLEX01' `
-Body 'TLEX01 Server is low on disk space' `
-Cc itmanager@testlabs.se
```

Also notice that the email will be sent as a carbon copy to the specified mailbox using the `Cc` parameter. This could be helpful if the function is used for sending out important emails that might be of interest to the manager too. Both the `Cc` and `Bcc` parameters can be used and accepts an array of string objects. The following screenshot shows an example of how the PowerShell function can be used:

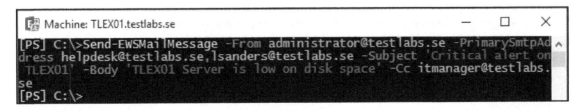

See also

- *Sending SMTP emails through PowerShell* recipe from `Chapter 2`, *Exchange Management Shell Common Tasks*

Working with impersonation

When building PowerShell scripts that leverage the EWS Managed API, we can use impersonation to access a user's mailbox on their behalf without having to provide their credentials. In order to utilize impersonation, we need permissions inside the Exchange organization, and then we need to configure the `ExchangeService` connection object with the impersonated user ID. In this recipe, you'll learn how to assign the permissions and write a script that uses EWS impersonation.

Getting ready

You will need to use the Exchange Management Shell in this recipe in order to assign permissions for application impersonation.

How to do it...

The first thing you need to do is assign your account the `ApplicationImpersonation` RBAC role from the Exchange Management Shell:

```
New-ManagementRoleAssignment -Role ApplicationImpersonation `
-User administrator
```

After we've been granted the permissions, we need to import the EWS Managed API assembly and configure the `ExchangeService` connection object:

```
Add-Type -Path C:\EWS\Microsoft.Exchange.WebServices.dll
$svc = New-Object -TypeName `
Microsoft.Exchange.WebServices.Data.ExchangeService
$id = New-Object -TypeName `
Microsoft.Exchange.WebServices.Data.ImpersonatedUserId `
-ArgumentList "SmtpAddress","dsmith@contoso.com"
$svc.ImpersonatedUserId = $id
$svc.AutoDiscoverUrl("dsmith@contoso.com")
```

We now have an `ExchangeService` connection to EWS as the impersonated user `dsmith`.

How it works...

In order to access a mailbox using the permissions of an impersonated user, we use RBAC to create a management role assignment for the user that will be calling the code. Like any other management role assignment, this can be done directly for one user or to a group. Keep in mind that you can also associate scopes when assigning the `ApplicationImpersonation` role. The command shown in our example would give the administrator account impersonation rights to any mailbox in the organization.

Once we have impersonation rights, we load the EWS Managed API assembly and create an instance of the `ExchangeService` class to bind to the EWS endpoint.

Notice that, when we create the `$id` object, we're creating an instance of the `ImpersonatedUserId` class and passing two values to the constructor. First, we specify that we want to identify the user to impersonate, using a data type of `SmtpAddress`. The next value passed to the constructor is the actual email address for the impersonated user. The final step is to assign this object to the `$svc.ImpersonatedUserId` property.

Now that our `ExchangeService` connection is configured for impersonation, we can do things like send emails, modify calendar items, or search the mailbox of the impersonated user.

There's more...

Let's take a look at how we could use impersonation using a modified version of the `Send-EwsMailMessage` function, included in the *Sending email messages with EWS* recipe earlier in this chapter. Add the following function to your shell session:

```
function Send-EWSMailMessage {
  param(
  [Parameter(
    Position=0,
    Mandatory=$true,
    ValueFromPipelineByPropertyName=$true
  )]
  [String[]]
  $PrimarySmtpAddress,

  [Parameter(
    Position=1, Mandatory=$true
  )]
  [String]
  $From,
```

```
[Parameter(
  Position=2, Mandatory=$true
)]
[String]
$Subject,

[Parameter(
  Position=3, Mandatory=$true
)]
[String]
$Body,

[Parameter(
  Position=4, Mandatory=$false
)]
[String[]]
$Cc,

[Parameter(
  Position=5, Mandatory=$false
)]
[String[]]
$Bcc

)

begin {
  Add-Type -Path C:\EWS\Microsoft.Exchange.WebServices.dll
}

process {
  $svc = New-Object `
  -TypeName Microsoft.Exchange.WebServices.Data.ExchangeService
  $id = New-Object -TypeName `
  Microsoft.Exchange.WebServices.Data.ImpersonatedUserId `
  -ArgumentList "SmtpAddress",$From
  $svc.ImpersonatedUserId = $id
  $svc.AutodiscoverUrl($From)

  $msg = New-Object `
  -TypeName Microsoft.Exchange.WebServices.Data.EmailMessage `
  -ArgumentList $svc
  $msg.Subject = $Subject
  $msg.Body = $Body

  $PrimarySmtpAddress | %{
    $msg.ToRecipients.Add($_) | Out-Null
  }
```

```
    if ($Cc -ne $null)
{
        $msg.CcRecipients.Add($Cc) | Out-Null
}

    if ($Bcc -ne $null)
{
        $msg.BccRecipients.Add($Bcc) | Out-Null
}

    $msg.SendAndSaveCopy()
  }
}
```

As you can see, we've modified this version of the function so that the SMTP address specified using the -From parameter is used as the impersonated user ID. Let's say that you are logged into Windows using the domain administrator account, which has been assigned the ApplicationImpersonation RBAC role. Once the function has been loaded into the shell you could execute the following command:

```
Send-EWSMailMessage -From sysadmin@testlabs.se `
-PrimarySmtpAddress helpdesk@testlabs.se `
-Subject 'Critical alert on TLEX04' `
-Body 'TLEX04 Server is low on disk space' `
-Cc administrator@testlabs.se `
-Bcc itmanager@testlabs.se
```

Using this command, the email message is sent through EWS from the sysadmin mailbox. The message appears to the recipient as if the sysadmin account had sent it. The following screenshot shows an illustrative example on how it could be used:

Searching mailboxes

The EWS Managed API can be used to search one or more folders within an Exchange mailbox. The latest version of the API supports searches using Advanced Query Syntax, allowing us to search folders using the indexes created by the Exchange Search service.

This makes searching a mailbox folder very fast and less resource intensive than methods that were used with first versions of the API. In this recipe, you'll learn how to search the contents of a mailbox through PowerShell and the EWS Managed API.

How to do it...

1. First, load the assembly, create the ExchangeService object, and connect to EWS:

```
Add-Type -Path C:\EWS\Microsoft.Exchange.WebServices.dll
$svc = New-Object Microsoft.Exchange.WebServices.Data.ExchangeService
$svc.AutoDiscoverUrl("lsanders@testlabs.se")
```

2. Next, create a view for the total number of items that should be returned from the search:

```
$view = New-Object -TypeName `
Microsoft.Exchange.WebServices.
Data.ItemView `
-ArgumentList 100
```

3. The next step is to create a property set containing all the properties of each message we want returned, and then associate that property set with the $view object created in the last step:

```
$propertyset = New-Object Microsoft.Exchange.WebServices.Data.PropertySet
(
[Microsoft.Exchange.WebServices.Data.BasePropertySet]::IdOnly,
[Microsoft.Exchange.WebServices.Data.ItemSchema]::Subject,
[Microsoft.Exchange.WebServices.Data.ItemSchema]::HasAttachments,
[Microsoft.Exchange.WebServices.Data.ItemSchema]::DisplayTo,
[Microsoft.Exchange.WebServices.Data.ItemSchema]::DisplayCc,
[Microsoft.Exchange.WebServices.Data.ItemSchema]::DateTimeSent,
[Microsoft.Exchange.WebServices.Data.ItemSchema]::DateTimeReceived
)

$view.PropertySet = $propertyset
```

4. Next, define a search query using AQS syntax:

```
$query = "Subject:'Critical alert on TLEX01'"
```

5. We can then perform the search using the `FindItems` method of our Exchange Service object:

```
$items = $svc.FindItems("Inbox",$query,$view)
```

6. Finally, loop through each item and return a custom object that contains the properties for each message:

```
$items | Foreach-Object{
New-Object PSObject -Property @{
  Id = $_.Id.ToString()
  Subject = $_.Subject
  To = $_.DisplayTo
  Cc = $_.DisplayCc
  HasAttachments = [bool]$_.HasAttachments
  Sent = $_.DateTimeSent
  Received = $_.DateTimeReceived
  }
}
```

When executing this code, any of the last 100 items in the administrator inbox that have the word "sales" in the subject line will be returned.

How it works...

Since we are not supplying credentials when creating the `ExchangeService` object and we're not using impersonation, the search will be performed in the administrator mailbox, as this is the logged-on user. You probably noticed that the property set only contains a few key properties of each message. Although there are many more available properties that can be returned, as a best practice we should only retrieve the properties that interest us. That way, if we are executing the code over and over, perhaps even against multiple mailboxes, we are not burdening the Exchange servers by requesting unnecessary data.

The key to a successful search is constructing the appropriate AQS query. You can use an AQS query for specific properties of a message using word phrase restriction, date range restriction, or message type restriction. For example, instead of querying using the `Subject` property, we can search for messages retrieved within a certain time frame:

```
$svc.FindItems(
  "Inbox",
  "Sent:05/01/2017..05/30/2017",
  $view
)
```

Notice that the first value passed in the call to `FindItems` is the folder that we want to search, next is the AQS query that specifies that we only want to retrieve items that were sent between specific dates in May, and finally we pass in the `$view` object that specifies the total items to return with a defined property set.

There are a number of well-known mailbox folders that can be searched using the `FindItems` method:

- `ArchiveDeletedItems`: The Deleted Items folder in the archive mailbox
- `ArchiveMsgFolderRoot`: The root of the message folder hierarchy in the archive mailbox
- `ArchiveRecoverableItemsDeletions`: The root of the folder hierarchy of recoverable items that have been soft-deleted from the Deleted Items folder of the archive mailbox
- `ArchiveRecoverableItemsPurges`: The root of the hierarchy of recoverable items that have been hard-deleted from the Deleted Items folder of the archive mailbox
- `ArchiveRecoverableItemsRoot`: The root of the Recoverable Items folder hierarchy in the archive mailbox
- `ArchiveRecoverableItemsVersions`: The root of the Recoverable Items versions folder hierarchy in the archive mailbox
- `ArchiveRoot`: The root of the folder hierarchy in the archive mailbox
- `Calendar`: The Calendar folder
- `Contacts`: The Contacts folder
- `DeletedItems`: The Deleted Items folder
- `Drafts`: The Drafts folder
- `Inbox`: The Inbox folder
- `JunkEmail`: The Junk Email folder
- `RecoverableItemsDeletions`: The root of the folder hierarchy of recoverable items that have been soft-deleted from the Deleted Items folder
- `RecoverableItemsPurges`: The root of the folder hierarchy of recoverable items that have been hard-deleted from the Deleted Items folder
- `RecoverableItemsRoot`: The root of the Recoverable Items folder hierarchy
- `RecoverableItemsVersions`: The root of the Recoverable Items versions folder hierarchy in the archive mailbox
- `SearchFolders`: The Search Folders folder, also known as the Finder folder
- `SentItems`: The Sent Items folder

For details, see the full list of members for the `WellKnownFolderName` enumeration in the Exchange Web Services Managed API SDK documentation on MSDN (even though this is for 2.0, it still applies to version 2.2):

`http://msdn.microsoft.com/en-us/library/microsoft.exchange.web`
`services.data.wellknownfoldername(v=exchg.80).aspx`
`http://msdn.microsoft.com/en-us/library/jj536567(v=exchg.150).as`
`px`

There's more...

One piece of interesting information not returned by the code in the previous example is the body of the message. This is because there are a number of properties that the `FindItems` method will not return, one of which is the message body. In order to retrieve the message body, we can bind it to the message after the search has been performed using the ID of the message.

Let's extend the previous code so that we can retrieve the body of the message and add the ability to impersonate the target mailbox. Add the following code to a file called `MailboxSearch.ps1`:

```
Param($query,$mailbox)

Add-Type -Path C:\EWS\Microsoft.Exchange.WebServices.dll
$svc = New-Object Microsoft.Exchange.WebServices.Data.ExchangeService

$id = New-Object -TypeName `
Microsoft.Exchange.WebServices.Data.ImpersonatedUserId `
-ArgumentList "SmtpAddress",$mailbox

$svc.ImpersonatedUserId = $id
$svc.AutoDiscoverUrl($mailbox)

$view = New-Object -TypeName `
Microsoft.Exchange.WebServices.Data.ItemView `
-ArgumentList 100

$propertyset = New-Object Microsoft.Exchange.WebServices.Data.PropertySet (
   [Microsoft.Exchange.WebServices.Data.BasePropertySet]::IdOnly,
   [Microsoft.Exchange.WebServices.Data.ItemSchema]::Subject,
   [Microsoft.Exchange.WebServices.Data.ItemSchema]::HasAttachments,
   [Microsoft.Exchange.WebServices.Data.ItemSchema]::DisplayTo,
   [Microsoft.Exchange.WebServices.Data.ItemSchema]::DisplayCc,
   [Microsoft.Exchange.WebServices.Data.ItemSchema]::DateTimeSent,
   [Microsoft.Exchange.WebServices.Data.ItemSchema]::DateTimeReceived
```

```
)

$view.PropertySet = $propertyset

$items = $svc.FindItems("Inbox",$query,$view)

$items | Foreach-Object{
  $emailProps = New-Object -TypeName `
  Microsoft.Exchange.WebServices.Data.PropertySet(
    [Microsoft.Exchange.WebServices.Data.BasePropertySet]::IdOnly,
    [Microsoft.Exchange.WebServices.Data.ItemSchema]::Body
  )

  $emailProps.RequestedBodyType = "Text"
  $email = [Microsoft.Exchange.WebServices.Data.EmailMessage]::Bind(
    $svc, $_.Id, $emailProps
  )
  New-Object PSObject -Property @{
    Id = $_.Id.ToString()
    Subject = $_.Subject
    To = $_.DisplayTo
    Cc = $_.DisplayCc
    HasAttachments = [bool]$_.HasAttachments
    Sent = $_.DateTimeSent
    Received = $_.DateTimeReceived
    Body = $email.Body
  }
}
```

When running the script, provide values for the -Query and -Mailbox parameters:

```
c:\MailboxSearch.ps1 -query "Sent:05/01/2017..05/30/2017" `
-mailbox lsanders@testlabs.se
```

When the script executes, the first 100 items in the Lee Sanders mailbox that were sent between May 1 and May 30 will be returned. The script will output a custom object for each item that contains the Id, Subject, To, Cc, HasAttachments, Sent, Received, and Body properties. Notice that, even though the body might be composed as HTML, we've only requested the text type for the body in the property set used when binding to the message. See the following screenshot for a similar example of the preceding cmdlet:

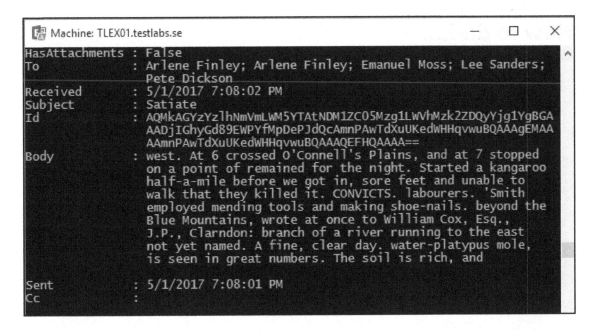

```
Machine: TLEX01.testlabs.se                          —    □    ×
HasAttachments : False
To             : Arlene Finley; Arlene Finley; Emanuel Moss; Lee Sanders;
                 Pete Dickson
Received       : 5/1/2017 7:08:02 PM
Subject        : Satiate
Id             : AQMkAGYzYzlhNmVmLWM5YTAtNDM1ZC05Mzg1LWVhMzk2ZDQyYjg1YgBGA
                 AADjIGhyGd89EWPYfMpDePJdQcAmnPAwTdXuUKedWHHqvwuBQAAAgEMAA
                 AAmnPAwTdXuUKedWHHqvwuBQAAAQEFHQAAAA==
Body           : west. At 6 crossed O'Connell's Plains, and at 7 stopped
                 on a point of remained for the night. Started a kangaroo
                 half-a-mile before we got in, sore feet and unable to
                 walk that they killed it. CONVICTS. labourers. 'Smith
                 employed mending tools and making shoe-nails. beyond the
                 Blue Mountains, wrote at once to William Cox, Esq.,
                 J.P., Clarndon: branch of a river running to the east
                 not yet named. A fine, clear day. water-platypus mole,
                 is seen in great numbers. The soil is rich, and

Sent           : 5/1/2017 7:08:01 PM
Cc             :
```

Notice that the date format is changed due to the regional settings in my lab environment. Use the date format that applies to your environment.

See also

- *Exporting attachments from a mailbox* recipe in this chapter

Retrieving the headers of an email message

When troubleshooting mail flow issues, you may need to take a look at the headers of an email message. This is easy to do through Outlook for items in your own mailbox, but if you want to do this on behalf of another user, it requires you to have permissions to their mailbox, and then you need to open their mailbox in Outlook to view the headers. In this recipe, we'll take a look at how you can retrieve the headers of a message in your own mailbox, as well as another user's mailbox, using the EWS Managed API and PowerShell.

How to do it...

1. First, load the assembly, create the `ExchangeService` object, and connect to EWS:

```
Add-Type -Path C:\EWS\Microsoft.Exchange.WebServices.dll
$svc = New-Object Microsoft.Exchange.WebServices.Data.ExchangeService
$svc.AutoDiscoverUrl("lsanders@testlabs.se")
```

2. Next, create a view for the total number of items that should be returned from the search:

```
$view = New-Object -TypeName `
   Microsoft.Exchange.WebServices
.Data.ItemView `
   -ArgumentList 100
```

3. The next step is to create a property set that will include the message ID. We then need to associate that property set with the `$view` object created in the last step:

```
$schema = [Microsoft.Exchange.WebServices.Data.ItemSchema]

$propertyset = New-Object -TypeName `
Microsoft.Exchange.WebServices.Data.PropertySet (
  $schema::IdOnly
  )

$view.PropertySet = $propertyset
```

4. Next, define a search query using AQS syntax:

```
$query = "Subject:'Sales'"
```

5. We can then perform the search, using the `FindItems` method of our Exchange Service object:

```
$items = $svc.FindItems("Inbox",$query,$view)
```

6. Loop through each item returned by the search and retrieve the message header information:

```
$items | Foreach-Object{

$headerview = New-Object -TypeName `
Microsoft.Exchange.WebServices.Data.ItemView `
-ArgumentList 1
```

```
$headerprops = New-Object -TypeName `
  Microsoft.Exchange.WebServices.Data.PropertySet (
  $schema::InternetMessageHeaders
)

$headerview.PropertySet = $headerprops

$message = [Microsoft.Exchange.WebServices.Data.Item]::Bind(
  $svc, $_.Id, $headerview.PropertySet
)

$message.InternetMessageHeaders
  }
```

How it works...

The code in this example is very similar to what we used in the recipe for *Searching mailboxes*. Again, since we are not supplying credentials when creating the ExchangeService object, and we're not using impersonation, the search will be performed in the administrator mailbox. When calling the FindItems method, we're specifying the folder to search, the AQS search query to be used, and the item view.

For each item returned by the search, we need to create a new view and property set for the single instance of the message that returns only the message headers. We then bind to the message and return the header information.

The header information returned will provide details of which server received the message, the content type of the message, the subject and date, and all of the X-Headers included with the message.

There are a number of well-known mailbox folders that can be searched using the FindItems method. For details, see the recipe earlier in this chapter titled *Searching mailboxes*.

There's more...

Of course, we'll primarily need to retrieve the message headers for an item in another user's mailbox. Here is an extended version of our previous code that implements EWS impersonation and provides parameters for the mailbox and folder to be searched.

Add the following code to a script called `GetMessageHeaders.ps1`:

```
Param($query, $mailbox, $folder)

Add-Type -Path C:\EWS\Microsoft.Exchange.WebServices.dll
$svc = New-Object Microsoft.Exchange.WebServices.Data.ExchangeService

$id = New-Object -TypeName `
Microsoft.Exchange.WebServices.Data.ImpersonatedUserId `
-ArgumentList "SmtpAddress",$mailbox

$svc.ImpersonatedUserId = $id
$svc.AutoDiscoverUrl($mailbox)

$view = New-Object -TypeName `
Microsoft.Exchange.WebServices.Data.ItemView `
-ArgumentList 100

$schema = [Microsoft.Exchange.WebServices.Data.ItemSchema]

$propertyset = New-Object -TypeName `
Microsoft.Exchange.WebServices.Data.PropertySet (
  $schema::IdOnly
)

$view.PropertySet = $propertyset

$query = $query

$items = $svc.FindItems($folder,$query,$view)

$items | Foreach-Object{

  $headerview = New-Object -TypeName `
  Microsoft.Exchange.WebServices.Data.ItemView `
  -ArgumentList 1

  $headerprops = New-Object -TypeName `
    Microsoft.Exchange.WebServices.Data.PropertySet (
    $schema::InternetMessageHeaders
  )

  $headerview.PropertySet = $headerprops

  $message = [Microsoft.Exchange.WebServices.Data.Item]::Bind(
    $svc, $_.Id, $headerview.PropertySet
  )
```

```
$message.InternetMessageHeaders
}
```

To run the script against an alternate mailbox, provide the query and the SMTP address associated with the mailbox:

```
c:\GetMessageHeaders.ps1 -query "Subject:'Financial report FY17'"`
-mailbox lsanders@testlabs.se `
-folder Inbox
```

When the script executes, the headers for each message matching the AQS query will be returned and the output will look similar to the following screenshot:

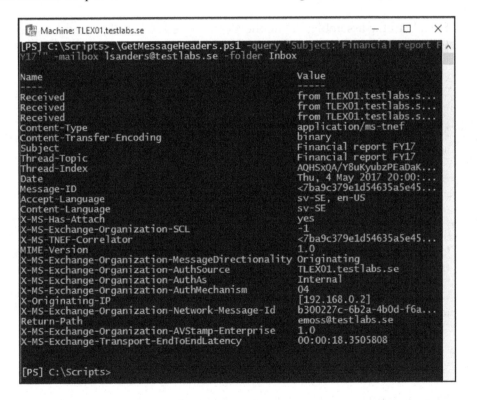

See also

- *Working with impersonation* recipe in this chapter

Deleting email items from a mailbox

The Exchange Management Shell provides cmdlets that allow you to delete items from one or more mailboxes. This can also be done with the EWS Managed API, and you can get a little more control over how the items are deleted compared to what the built-in cmdlets provide. In this recipe, you'll learn how to use the EWS Managed API to delete items from one or more mailboxes using PowerShell.

How to do it...

1. First, load the assembly, create the `ExchangeService` object, and connect to EWS:

```
Add-Type -Path C:\EWS\Microsoft.Exchange.WebServices.dll
$svc = New-Object Microsoft.Exchange.WebServices.Data.ExchangeService
$svc.AutoDiscoverUrl("administrator@testlabs.se")
```

2. Next, create a view for the total number of items that should be returned from the search:

```
$view = New-Object -TypeName `
   Microsoft.Exchange.WebServices
.Data.ItemView `
   -ArgumentList 100
```

3. Create a property set that will include the message id. We then need to associate that property set with the `$view` object created in the last step:

```
$propertyset = New-Object
Microsoft.Exchange.WebServices.Data.PropertySet (
   [Microsoft.Exchange.WebServices.Data.BasePropertySet]::IdOnly
)

$view.PropertySet = $propertyset
```

4. Next, define a search query using AQS syntax:

```
z$query = "body:'Inappropriate content'"
```

5. We can then perform the search using the `FindItems` method of our Exchange Service object:

```
$items = $svc.FindItems("Inbox",$query,$view)
```

6. For each item returned by the search, bind to the message and call the `Delete` method, specifying the delete mode that should be used:

```
$items | Foreach-Object{
$message =       [Microsoft.Exchange.WebServices.Data.Item]::Bind(
$svc, $_.Id
)

$message.Delete("SoftDelete")
    }
```

How it works...

The code in this example is very similar to what we used in the recipe for *Searching mailboxes*. Again, since we are not supplying credentials when creating the `ExchangeService` object and we're not using impersonation, the search will be performed in the administrator mailbox. When calling the `FindItems` method, we're specifying the folder to search, the AQS search query to be used, and the item view.

Notice that this time we only need to specify the ID of the message in the property set. This is because we only want to call the `Delete` method on the item class and we don't need to retrieve any other data from the message. In this example, we've defined a string of inappropriate content that should be found in the message body.

We loop through each item returned by the search and create an instance of the message using the item class `Bind` method. At that point, we call the `Delete` method, which accepts one of three values from the `DeleteMode` enumeration. The valid values for this method are defined as follows:

- `HardDelete`: Permanently deletes the item
- `MoveToDeletedItems`: Moves the item to the Deleted Items folder of the target mailbox
- `SoftDelete`: The item is moved to the dumpster and can be recovered by the mailbox owner using the Recoverable Items feature of Outlook and OWA

Having the ability to specify the delete mode gives you a little more control when deleting items in a mailbox than the built-in Exchange Management Shell cmdlets.

There are a number of well-known mailbox folders that can be searched for using the FindItems method. For details, see the recipe earlier in this chapter titled *Searching mailboxes*.

There's more...

Whenever you are executing code that can perform a destructive operation, it makes sense to implement the ShouldProcess method introduced with PowerShell v2 advanced functions. Implementing ShouldProcess in an advanced function gives you the ability to add the common risk mitigation parameters such as -Whatif and -Confirm. The following function takes our previous code up a notch, written as an advanced function that implements ShouldProcess. Add the following function to your Exchange Management Shell session:

```
function RemovemailboxItem {
  [CmdletBinding(
    SupportsShouldProcess = $true, ConfirmImpact = "High"
  )]
  param(
    [Parameter(
      Position=0,
      Mandatory=$true,
      ValueFromPipelineByPropertyName=$true
    )]
    [String]
    $PrimarySmtpAddress,
    [Parameter(
      Position = 1, Mandatory = $true
    )]
    [String]
    $SearchQuery,
    [Parameter(
      Position = 2, Mandatory = $false
    )]
    [int]
    $ResultSize = 100,
    [Parameter(
      Position = 3, Mandatory = $false
    )]
    [string]
    $Folder = "Inbox",
    [Parameter(
```

```
      Position = 4, Mandatory = $false
    )]
    [ValidateSet(
     'HardDelete',
     'SoftDelete',
     'MoveToDeletedItems'
    )]
    $DeleteMode = "MoveToDeletedItems"
  )
  begin {
    Add-Type -Path C:\EWS\Microsoft.Exchange.WebServices.dll
  }
  process {
    $svc = New-Object -TypeName `
    Microsoft.Exchange.WebServices.Data.ExchangeService
    $id = New-Object -TypeName `
    Microsoft.Exchange.WebServices.Data.ImpersonatedUserId `
    -ArgumentList "SmtpAddress",$PrimarySmtpAddress

    $svc.ImpersonatedUserId = $id
    $svc.AutoDiscoverUrl($PrimarySmtpAddress)

    $view = New-Object -TypeName `
    Microsoft.Exchange.WebServices.Data.ItemView `
    -ArgumentList 100

    $propertyset = New-Object -TypeName `
    Microsoft.Exchange.WebServices.Data.PropertySet (
       [Microsoft.Exchange.WebServices.Data.BasePropertySet]::IdOnly
    )

    $view.PropertySet = $propertyset
    $items = $svc.FindItems($Folder,$SearchQuery,$view)

    $items | %{
      $message = [Microsoft.Exchange.WebServices.Data.Item]::Bind(
        $svc, $_.Id
      )

      if ($pscmdlet.ShouldProcess($message.Subject)) {
       $message.Delete($DeleteMode)
      }
    }
  }
}
```

We now have a `RemovemailboxItem` function that supports impersonation, allowing the code to execute against one or more mailboxes. In addition, it supports pipeline input by property name, so you can utilize the `Get-Mailbox` cmdlet to delete items from multiple mailboxes using a simple one-liner. Consider the following example:

```
Get-Mailbox -ResultSize Unlimited |
  RemovemailboxItem -SearchQuery "Body:'Free Surface Book'" `
  -DeleteMode HardDelete
```

In this example, we pipe every mailbox in the organization down to the `RemovemailboxItem` function , which will perform a hard delete on each message that matches the AQS query. Since the `ConfirmImpact` property is set to `High`, you'll be prompted for confirmation before each message is deleted.

To force a delete operation without confirmation, you can set the `-Confirm` parameter to `$false`. To do this on a single mailbox, you could use the following syntax:

```
RemovemailboxItem -PrimarySmtpAddress sysadmin@contoso.com `
-SearchQuery "Body:'Buy cheap drugs'" `
-DeleteMode HardDelete `
-Confirm:$false
```

You can also use the `-Whatif` parameter here to test the command to ensure that the correct messages will be deleted:

```
RemovemailboxItem -PrimarySmtpAddress sysadmin@contoso.com `
-SearchQuery "Body:'Buy cheap drugs'" `
-DeleteMode HardDelete `
-Whatif
```

To illustrate an example, we use the cmdlet `Get-Mailbox` and pipe the result into the created function together with a search query that searches for all mails with a subject that has `Free Surface Book` included. The function will soft delete the mails that are returned, which means they will end up in the dumpster.

See the following screenshot for a similar output using the created function:

```
Machine: TLEX01.testlabs.se                                    —    □    ×
[PS] C:\>Remove-MailboxItem -PrimarySmtpAddress emoss@testlabs.se -SearchQu
ery "Subject:'Free Surface Book'" -DeleteMode SoftDelete

Confirm
Are you sure you want to perform this action?
Performing the operation "Remove-MailboxItem" on target "Free Surface
Book".
[Y] Yes  [A] Yes to All  [N] No  [L] No to All  [S] Suspend  [?] Help
(default is "Y"):
```

See also

- *Searching mailboxes* recipe in this chapter

Creating calendar items

Imagine that you have a monitoring script written in PowerShell that checks memory, CPU, or disk utilization on all of your Exchange servers. In addition to alerting your team of any critical problems via email, it might also be nice to schedule a reminder in the future for non-critical issues by creating a calendar item in one or more mailboxes. The EWS Managed API makes it easy to create a calendar item through PowerShell with just a few commands.

How to do it...

1. First, load the assembly, create the `ExchangeService` object, and connect to EWS:

```
Add-Type -Path C:\EWS\Microsoft.Exchange.WebServices.dll
$svc = New-Object
Microsoft.Exchange.WebServices.Data.ExchangeService
$svc.AutoDiscoverUrl("administrator@testlabs.se")
```

2. Next, create a new `Appointment` object:

```
$appt = New-Object -TypeName `
Microsoft.Exchange.WebServices
.Data.Appointment `
-ArgumentList $svc
```

3. Fill out the subject and body for the appointment:

```
$appt.Subject = "Review Disk Space Utilization on Server(s)"
$appt.Body = "TLEX01 has only 40% free disk space on drive C:"
```

4. Set the start and end times for the appointment:

```
$start = (Get-Date).AddDays(1)
$appt.Start = $start
$appt.End = $start.AddHours(1)
```

5. Add one or more required attendees to the appointment:

```
$appt.RequiredAttendees.Add("helpdesk@testlabs.se")
$appt.RequiredAttendees.Add("sysadmin@testlabs.se")
```

6. Finally, save the appointment and send a copy to all attendees:

```
$mode = [Microsoft.Exchange.WebServices.Data.SendInvitationsMode]
$appt.Save($mode::SendToAllAndSaveCopy)
```

How it works...

Using the code in this example, we are creating the calendar item in the mailbox of the user calling the code. The `Appointment` class is used to create the item and, after we've created an instance of this class, we set the details of the appointment using the `Subject` and `Body` properties.

The `Start` and `End` properties need to be assigned a `DateTime` object. In our example, we're using the `AddDays` method of the current date and time to set the start time for the meeting in exactly 24 hours in the future. We then use the same object to increment the time by one hour and assign that to the `End` property for the appointment.

When adding attendees to the appointment, we use the `RequiredAttendees.Add` method. When you call the `Add` method, you'll notice that the `RequiredAttendees` property will be returned for each required attendee added to the appointment. If you want to simply call this method without having anything returned to the screen, there's a few ways you can accomplish this. First, you can pipe the command to `Out-Null`:

```
$appt.RequiredAttendees.Add("helpdesk@testlabs.se") | Out-Null
$appt.RequiredAttendees.Add("sysadmin@testlabs.se") | Out-Null
```

Another way you'll see this written is by casting the commands to `[void]`:

```
[void]$appt.RequiredAttendees.Add("helpdesk@testlabs.se")
[void]$appt.RequiredAttendees.Add("sysadmin@testlabs.se")
```

Finally, you can assign the commands to `$null`, which is said to be the fastest method:

```
$null = $appt.RequiredAttendees.Add("helpdesk@testlabs.se")
$null = $appt.RequiredAttendees.Add("sysadmin@testlabs.se")
```

In addition to adding required attendees, we can also add one or more optional attendees to the item:

```
$null = $appt.OptionalAttendees.Add("IT@testlabs.se")
```

Finally, when calling the `Save` method for the appointment, you need to pass in a value from the `SendInvitationsMode` enumeration. The valid values that can be used are `SendOnlyToAll`, `SendToAllAndSaveCopy`, and `SendToNone`.

There's more...

Let's make this easier by wrapping all of the code up into a reusable function. Add the following code to your PowerShell session:

```
function New-CalendarItem {
  [CmdletBinding()]
  param(
  [Parameter(
    Position=1, Mandatory=$true
  )]
  [String]
  $Subject,
  [Parameter(
    Position=2, Mandatory=$true
  )]
  [String]
```

```
    $Body,
    [Parameter(
      Position=3, Mandatory=$true
    )]
    [String]
    $Start,
    [Parameter(
      Position=4, Mandatory=$true
    )]
    [String]
    $End,
    [Parameter(
      Position=5
    )]
    [String[]]
    $RequiredAttendees,
    [Parameter(
      Position=8
    )]
    [String]
    $Mailbox
    )

    begin{
      Add-Type -Path C:\EWS\Microsoft.Exchange.WebServices.dll
    }
    process {
      $svc = New-Object -TypeName `
    Microsoft.Exchange.WebServices.Data.ExchangeService
      $id = New-Object -TypeName `
      Microsoft.Exchange.WebServices.Data.ImpersonatedUserId `
      -ArgumentList "SmtpAddress",$Mailbox
      $svc.ImpersonatedUserId = $id
      $svc.AutodiscoverUrl($Mailbox)
      $appt = New-Object -TypeName `
      Microsoft.Exchange.WebServices.Data.Appointment `
      -ArgumentList $svc

      $appt.Subject = $Subject
      $appt.Body = $Body
      $appt.Start = $Start
      $appt.End = $End
      if($RequiredAttendees) {
        $RequiredAttendees | Foreach-Object{
          $null = $appt.RequiredAttendees.Add($_)
        }
      }
      $mode = [Microsoft.Exchange.WebServices.Data.SendInvitationsMode]
```

```
    $appt.Save($mode::SendToAllAndSaveCopy)
  }
}
```

This function can be used to create a calendar item in the mailbox of another user. For this to work, you'll need to be assigned the `ApplicationImpersonation` RBAC role. To run the function, you might do something like this:

```
New-CalendarItem -Subject "Reboot Server" `
-Body "Reboot EXCH-SRV01 server after 5PM today" `
-Start (Get-Date).AddHours(6) `
-End (Get-Date).AddHours(7) `
-Mailbox sysadmin@testlabs.se `
-RequiredAttendees helpdesk@testlabs.se,admins@testlabs.se
```

In this example, the calendar item is created in the sysadmin mailbox. Multiple attendees will be added to the item and will receive an invitation for the meeting when it is saved. Notice that the meeting is scheduled for six hours in the future, with a total duration of one hour. For example, see the following screenshot:

If you want to create calendar items in multiple mailboxes, loop through a collection with the `Foreach-Object` cmdlet and run the function for each user:

```
$start = Get-Date "Friday, May 26, 2017 5:00:00 PM"
$end = $start.AddHours(2)
Get-DistributionGroupMember ITSupport | Foreach-Object{
  New-CalendarItem -Subject "Install Hotfixes" `
  -Body "Start patching servers after 5PM today" `
  -Start $start `
  -End $end `
  -Mailbox $_.PrimarySMTPAddress
}
```

In this example, each member of the IT Support distribution group will have a calendar item created in their mailbox that will serve as a reminder; no attendees will be added to the item.

See also

- *Sending email messages with EWS* recipe in this chapter

Exporting attachments from a mailbox

The Exchange Management Shell provides cmdlets that allow you to export email messages from one mailbox to another mailbox. These emails can then be exported to a PST file, or you can open an alternate mailbox and access the data. The only limitation is that this provides no option to export only the message attachments. The EWS Managed API has this functionality built in. In this recipe, you'll learn how to export email attachments from an Exchange mailbox using PowerShell.

How to do it...

1. First, load the assembly, create the ExchangeService object, and connect to EWS:

```
Add-Type -Path C:\EWS\Microsoft.Exchange.WebServices.dll
$svc = New-Object Microsoft.Exchange.WebServices.Data.ExchangeService
$svc.AutoDiscoverUrl("administrator@testlabs.se")
```

2. Next, create a view for the total number of items that should be returned from the search:

```
$view = New-Object -TypeName `
Microsoft.Exchange.WebServices
.Data.ItemView `
    -ArgumentList 100
```

3. Next, create a property set and then associate that property set with the $view object:

```
$base = [Microsoft.Exchange.WebServices.Data.BasePropertySet]

$propertyset = New-Object -TypeName `
Microsoft.Exchange.WebServices.Data.PropertySet (
$base::FirstClassProperties
)

$view.PropertySet = $propertyset
```

4. Define a query for the type of attachments you are looking for. For example, if you are looking for attachments in Microsoft Word format, use the following:

```
$query = "Attachment:docx"
```

5. We can then perform the search using the FindItems method of our Exchange Service object:

```
$items = $svc.FindItems("Inbox",$query,$view)
```

6. Finally, we loop through each item returned and export the attachments to the specified folder on the filesystem, such as c:\export:

```
$items | ForEach-Object{
   if($_.HasAttachments  ) {
$_.Load()
$_.Attachments | ForEach-Object {
   $_.Load()
   $filename = $_.Name
   Set-Content -Path c:\export\$filename `
   -Value $_.Content `
   -Encoding Byte `
   -Force
   }
  }
 }
```

How it works...

The code in this example is very similar to what we used in the recipe for *Searching mailboxes*. Again, since we are not supplying credentials when creating the ExchangeService object and we're not using impersonation, the search will be performed in the administrator mailbox. When calling the FindItems method, we're specifying the folder to search, the AQS search query to be used, and the item view.

As you can see, we're using the Attachment property in the AQS query. This allows us to search for a string within the filename or inside the file itself. When the results are returned, we loop through each message, and use the Load method to load the attachment, which allows us to then access the Content property of each attachment. The Content property stores the message attachment as a byte array, which can easily be used to recreate the file using the Set-Content cmdlet by specifying the encoding as Byte.

There are a number of well-known mailbox folders that can be searched using the FindItems method. For details, see the recipe earlier in this chapter titled *Searching mailboxes*.

There's more...

Like many of our previous examples, reusability is key. Let's take this code and add a few enhancements so it can be run via a PowerShell script. Add the following code to a file called AttachmentExport.ps1:

```
Param($folder, $query, $path, $mailbox)

Add-Type -Path C:\EWS\Microsoft.Exchange.WebServices.dll
$svc = New-Object Microsoft.Exchange.WebServices.Data.ExchangeService

$id = New-Object -TypeName `
Microsoft.Exchange.WebServices.Data.ImpersonatedUserId `
-ArgumentList "SmtpAddress",$mailbox

$svc.ImpersonatedUserId = $id
$svc.AutoDiscoverUrl($mailbox)

$view = New-Object -TypeName `
Microsoft.Exchange.WebServices.Data.ItemView `
-ArgumentList 100

$base = [Microsoft.Exchange.WebServices.Data.BasePropertySet]

$propertyset = New-Object -TypeName `
Microsoft.Exchange.WebServices.Data.PropertySet (
  $base::FirstClassProperties
)

$view.PropertySet = $propertyset

$items = $svc.FindItems($folder,$query,$view)

$items | Foreach-Object{
  if($_.HasAttachments) {
    $_.Load()
    $_.Attachments | ForEach-Object {
      $_.Load()
      $filename = $_.Name

      Set-Content -Path $path\$filename `
      -Value $_.Content `
```

```
    -Encoding Byte `
    -Force
}
}
}
```

Using this script, we can export the attachments from one or more mailboxes since we've included the code to support impersonation. Just make sure your account has been assigned the `ApplicationImpersonation` RBAC role when running this script against another mailbox. Let's say we wanted to export all of the Excel files that are attached to messages in the `sysadmin` mailbox. Run this script with the following syntax:

```
c:\AttachmentExport.ps1 -folder Inbox `
-mailbox emoss@testlabs.se `
-query "attachment:docx" `
-path c:\Export
```

You can also export all attachments simply by using a wildcard in the search query:

```
c:\AttachmentExport.ps1 -folder Inbox `
-mailbox emoss@testlabs.se `
-query "attachment:xlsx" `
-path c:\Export
```

Keep in mind that since our item view is set to `100`, we may need to increase the number if we want to search through mailbox folders with a higher item count.

See the following screenshot for an example usage of the script and the result:

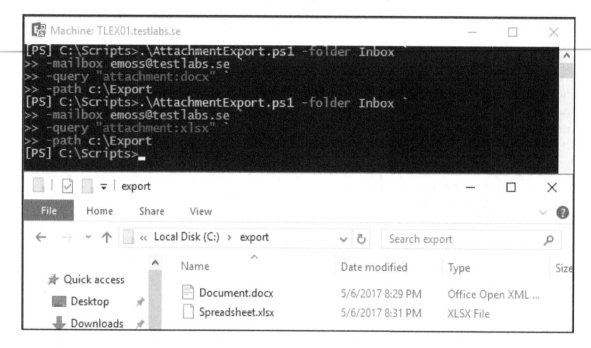

See also

- *Searching mailboxes* recipe in this chapter

Common Shell Information

Exchange Management Shell reference

This appendix provides additional information related to the **Exchange Management Shell (EMS)**. You can use this section as a reference to find commonly-used automatic shell variables and type accelerators, along with a list of commonly-used EMS scripts that are installed with Exchange 2016. Additionally, common filterable properties supported by EMS cmdlets that include filter parameters are outlined in detail.

Commonly-used shell variables

PowerShell and the Exchange Management Shell provide several automatic variables. The following table provides a list of commonly-used automatic variables with a description for each one:

Variable Name	Description
$$	This contains the last token in the last command received.
$?	This contains the execution status of the last command.
$^	This contains the first token in the last command received.
$_	This contains the current object being processed within a pipeline.
$Args	This contains an array of undeclared arguments received by a function, script, or script block.

Variable Name	Description
$Error	This contains an array of error objects recorded in the current shell session. The latest error can be accessed using the zero index of the array, that is, $error[0].
$ExBin	This references the full path to the Exchange Server\Bin directory. This variable is only present when starting the shell using the Exchange Management Shell shortcut on a machine with the Exchange tools installed.
$ExScripts	This references the full path to the Exchange scripts directory. This variable is only present when starting the shell using the Exchange Management Shell shortcut on a machine with the Exchange tools installed.
$False	This provides a Boolean false value when used in commands and scripts.
$ForEach	This contains the enumerator inside a ForEach-Object loop.
$Home	This contains the full path to the user's home directory.
$Host	This contains an object that represents the current PowerShell host application.
$Input	This contains the enumerator for items passed to a function. The $Input variable can access the current object being processed within a pipeline.
$MaximumHistoryCount	This specifies the maximum number of entries that can be saved in the command history in the current shell session.
$Null	This provides a null or empty value when used in commands and scripts.
$Profile	This contains the full path to the PowerShell profile for the current user and the current host application.
$PSHome	This contains the full path to the installation directory of Windows PowerShell.
$Pwd	This contains the path to the current location.
$True	This provides a Boolean true value.

To view the variables currently defined in your shell session, run `Get-Variable`. You can also read more about PowerShell variables by running the `Get-Help <TopicName>` cmdlet on the following topics:

- `about_Automatic_Variables`
- `about_Environment_Variables`
- `about_Preference_Variables`

 `Get-Variable` only references PowerShell-specific variables, and not the shell variables that are specific to the Exchange Management Shell.

Commonly-used type accelerators

Type accelerators, also referred to as type shortcuts, allows you to create an object of a specific .NET Framework type, without having to enter the entire type name. This is a feature that is supported by both PowerShell and the Exchange Management Shell, and allows you to reduce the amount of typing required when creating an object or explicitly typing a variable. The following table lists some of the most commonly-used type shortcuts:

Type shortcut	.NET framework type
[int]	System.Int32
[long]	System.Int64
[string]	System.String
[bool]	System.Boolean
[byte]	System.Byte
[double]	System.Double
[decimal]	System.Decimal
[datetime]	System.DateTime
[array]	System.Array
[hashtable]	System.Collections.HashTable
[switch]	System.Management.Automation.SwitchParameter
[adsi]	System.DirectoryServices.DirectoryEntry

Scripts available in the $Exscripts directory

The following table lists some of the most commonly-used EMS PowerShell scripts that are installed with Exchange 2016:

Name	Description
AddUsersToPFRecursive.ps1	Adds a user and their permissions to the client permissions list for a public folder and all the folders beneath it in the hierarchy.
AntispamCommon.ps1	This script is referenced by other anti-spam scripts in Exchange 2007 and is not intended to be used directly.
CheckDatabaseRedundancy.ps1	This script was used in Exchange 2010 to monitor the redundancy of replicated mailbox databases. With the introduction of Managed Availability, this script was replaced with integrated, native functionality that alerts administrators through event log notifications.
CITSConstants.ps1	This file contains global constants used by the CI Troubleshooter library.
CITSLibrary.ps1	This file contains the Content Index Troubleshooter functions.
CITSTypes.ps1	This file contains additional types used by the CI Troubleshooter library.
CollectOverMetrics.ps1	Reports on the database availability group, switchover, and failover metrics.
CollectReplicationMetrics.ps1	Reports on the replication status and statistics for databases.
ConfigureAdam.ps1	This is used to modify the default configuration of the **Active Directory Application Mode** (**ADAM**) directory service on the Edge Transport server.
Configure-EnterprisePartnerApplication.ps1	This script configures a Partner Application that uses the OAuth protocol to authenticate to Exchange.
Configure-SMBIPsec.ps1	This script is to be used to help you add the necessary IPsec configuration to protect SMB (File Share) communication.
ConvertOABVDir.ps1	Converts the OAB virtual directory to an IIS web application/application pool.
ConvertTo-MessageLatency.ps1	This script provides end-to-end latency information gathered from message tracking logs.

Name	Description
Create-PublicFolderMailboxesForMigration.ps1	This script creates the target public folder mailboxes for the migration. In addition, it calculates the number of mailboxes necessary to handle the estimated user load.
DagCommonLibrary.ps1	This contains a collection of DAG-related functions for use by other scripts.
DatabaseMaintSchedule.ps1	Generates the maintenance and quota notification schedule time based on a set of input values.
DiagnosticScriptCommonLibrary.ps1	This script is a library of functions for common diagnostic script executions.
Disable-AntimalwareScanning.ps1	This script disables anti-malware scanning.
Disable-InMemoryTracing.ps1	This script is used to undo the changes made by the Enable-InMemoryTracing.ps1 script.
Enable-AntimalwareScanning.ps1	This script enables anti-malware scanning.
Enable-CrossForestConnector.ps1	Configures a send connector for cross-forest trust for anonymous users.
Enable-InMemoryTracing.ps1	Enables in-memory Tracing.
Enable-OutlookCertificateAuthentication.ps1	This script configures virtual directories to allow Outlook for smart card authentication.
ExchUCUtil.ps1	This script configures Exchange Unified Messaging for the use of Office Communications Server.
Export-MailPublicFoldersForMigration.ps1	Exports the properties of all the mail- enabled public folders to a CSV file.
Export-ModernPublicFolderStatistics.ps1	This script creates the folder name-to-folder size and deleted item size mapping file used to migrate public folders to Exchange 2016.
Export-OutlookClassification.ps1	Generates the Classifications.xml file for Outlook.
Export-PublicFolderStatistics.ps1	Generates a CSV file with lists of public folders and the individual sizes.
Export-RetentionTags.ps1	This script exports retention tags to an external file.
get-AntispamFilteringReport.ps1	This generates a report on anti-spam filtering.
get-AntispamSCLHistogram.ps1	Reports on all the entries for the Content Filter and groups by SCL values.
get-AntispamTopBlockedSenderDomains.ps1	Reports on the top 10 (unless specified otherwise) sender domains blocked by anti-spam agents.

Name	Description
`get-AntispamTopBlockedSenderIPs.ps1`	Reports on the top 10 (unless specified otherwise) sender IPs blocked by anti-spam agents.
`get-AntispamTopBlockedSenders.ps1`	Reports on the top 10 (unless specified otherwise) senders blocked by anti-spam agents.
`get-AntispamTopRBLProviders.ps1`	Reports on the top 10 (unless specified otherwise) reasons for rejection by blocklist providers.
`get-AntispamTopRecipients.ps1`	Reports on the top 10 (unless specified otherwise) recipients rejected by anti-spam agents.
`Get-DlEligibilityList.ps1`	This script goes through all the distribution lists in the organization, outputs a detailed eligibility file (`DlEligibilityList.txt`), and lists which distribution lists are eligible to be upgraded to Office 365 Groups.
`Get-PublicFolderMailboxSize.ps1`	Retrieves the size of the public folder mailbox, excluding the size of deleted folders.
`Get-UCPool.ps1`	This script reports on the UC Pools created by OCS/Lync/Skype.
`Import-MailPublicFoldersForMigration.ps1`	This script imports the mail-enabled public folders from a CSV file and calls the `Enable-MailPublicFolder` cmdlet.
`Import-RetentionTags.ps1`	Imports retention tags from an external file.
`Install-AntispamAgents.ps1`	This script installs the anti-spam agents on a mailbox server.
`MailboxDatabaseReseedUsingSpares.ps1`	This script validates the safety of the environment, before swapping fails to copy database to a spare disk and reseeding.
`Merge-PublicFolderMailbox.ps1`	This script merges the contents of the given public folder mailbox with the target public folder mailbox.
`MigrateUMCustomPrompts.ps1`	Migrates a copy of all Unified Messaging custom prompts.
`MoveMailbox.ps1`	This script works like the `Move-Mailbox` cmdlet in Exchange 2007 and performs synchronous mailbox moves.
`Move-PublicFolderBranch.ps1`	This script moves the contents of folders that reside along with the given folder to the target public folder mailbox.
`Move-TransportDatabase.ps1`	Moves the queue database to an alternate location.

Name	Description
new-TestCasConnectivityUser.ps1	This script creates a test user that can be used when testing client connectivity.
Prepare-MoveRequest.ps1	Prepares mailboxes for cross-forest mailbox moves.
PublicFolderToMailboxMapGenerator.ps1	This script creates the public folder-to-mailbox mapping file by using the output from the Export-ModernPublicFolderStatistics.ps1 script.
RedistributeActiveDatabases.ps1	This script attempts to redistribute active databases evenly across a number of mailbox servers within a DAG.
ReinstallDefaultTransportAgents.ps1	Reinstalls default transport agents on servers.
RemoveUserFromPFRecursive.ps1	This script removes a user from the client permissions list for a public folder and all the folders beneath it in the hierarchy.
ReplaceUserPermissionOnPFRecursive.ps1	Replaces the permissions of a user for a public folder with a new set of permissions and applies it to all the folders beneath it in the hierarchy.
ReplaceUserWithUserOnPFRecursive.ps1	This script replaces a user for a new user on the client permissions list for a public folder and applies it to all the folders beneath it in the hierarchy.
Reset-AntispamUpdates.ps1	Removes the anti-spam agents from the server.
ResetAttachmentFilterEntry.ps1	This script is used to reset the list of attachment-types that are blocked by the attachment-filtering feature to the factory set defaults.
ResumeMailboxDatabaseCopy.ps1	This script resumes activation and log file replication for specified mailbox databases.
RollAlternateServiceAccountPassword.ps1	This script performs a first-time or periodic maintenance on the alternate service account (ASA) credential used to enable Kerberos authentication on CAS services.
Split-PublicFolderMailbox.ps1	This script splits the given public folder mailbox based on the size of the folders.
StartDagServerMaintenance.ps1	This script initiates the DAG server maintenance.
StopDagServerMaintenance.ps1	This script stops the DAG server maintenance and resumes mailbox database copies.
Sync-MailPublicFolders.ps1	Syncs mail-enabled public folder objects from the local Exchange deployment into Office 365.

Name	Description
Troubleshoot-CI.ps1	This script performs troubleshooting on Content Index catalogs.
Troubleshoot-DatabaseLatency.ps1	This script diagnoses disk subsystem issues (used by SCOM).
Troubleshoot-DatabaseSpace.ps1	This script troubleshoots log growth (used by SCOM).
Uninstall-AntispamAgents.ps1	Uninstalls the anti-spam agents.
Update-AppPoolManagedFrameworkVersion.ps1	This script is used during the installation and updates the procedure for updating the Application Pool.
Update-MalwareFilteringServer.ps1	This script updates the malware filter definitions.

Please note that scripts may be added to this directory as you install cumulative updates. To view all the scripts in the `$ExScripts` folder, run `Get-ChildItem $exscripts -Filter *.ps1`.

Properties that can be used with the -Filter parameter

There are a number of EMS cmdlets that provide a `-Filter` parameter that can be used to narrow searches based on the value of an OPATH property. These properties can also map to a particular LDAP attribute.

The following table lists some of the commonly used properties and the cmdlets that can be used to query their values using the `-Filter` parameter:

Property Name	Attribute	Cmdlets Supported	Input Value
Alias	mailNickname	Get-DistributionGroup Get-DynamicDistributionGroup Get-Mailbox Get-MailContact Get-MailPublicFolder Get-MailUser Get-Recipient Get-RemoteMailbox	String/Wildcard
City	L	Get-Contact Get-Recipient Get-User	String/Wildcard
Company	Company	Get-Contact Get-Recipient Get-User	String/Wildcard

Property Name	Attribute	Cmdlets Supported	Input Value
Database	homeMDB	Get-Mailbox Get-Recipient	DN
Department	department	Get-Contact Get-Recipient Get-User	String/Wildcard
DisplayName	displayName	Get-CASMailbox Get-Contact Get-DistributionGroup Get-DynamicDistributionGroup Get-Group Get-Mailbox Get-MailboxStatistics Get-MailContact Get-MailPublicFolder Get-MailUser Get-Recipient Get-RemoteMailbox Get-UMMailbox Get-User	String/Wildcard
DistinguishedName	distinguishedName	Get-CASMailbox Get-Contact Get-DistributionGroup Get-DynamicDistributionGroup Get-Group Get-Mailbox Get-MailContact Get-MailPublicFolder Get-MailUser Get-Recipient Get-RemoteMailbox Get-UMMailbox Get-User	DN
EmailAddresses	proxyAddresses	Get-CASMailbox Get-DistributionGroup Get-DynamicDistributionGroup Get-Mailbox Get-MailContact Get-MailPublicFolder Get-MailUser Get-Recipient Get-RemoteMailbox Get-UMMailbox	Email address (wildcard)
FirstName	givenName	Get-Contact Get-Recipient Get-User	String/Wildcard
HiddenFromAddressListsEnabled	msExchHideFromAddressLists	Get-DistributionGroup Get-DynamicDistribution Group Get-Mailbox Get-MailContact Get-MailPublicFolder Get-MailUser Get-Recipient Get-RemoteMailbox	$true $false

Property Name	Attribute	Cmdlets Supported	Input Value
HomePhone	homePhone	Get-Contact Get-User	String/Wildcard
LastName	sn	Get-Contact Get-Recipient Get-User	String/Wildcard
Manager	manager	Get-Contact Get-Recipient Get-User	String/Wildcard
Name	name	Get-CASMailbox Get-Contact Get-DistributionGroup Get-DynamicDistributionGroup Get-Group Get-Mailbox Get-MailContact Get-MailPublicFolder Get-MailUser Get-Recipient Get-RemoteMailbox Get-UMMailbox Get-User	String
Phone	telephoneNumber	Get-Contact Get-Recipient Get-User	String/Wildcard
PrimarySmtpAddress	N/A	Get-CASMailbox Get-DistributionGroup Get-DynamicDistributionGroup Get-Mailbox Get-MailContact Get-MailPublicFolder Get-MailUser Get-Recipient Get-RemoteMailbox Get-UMMailbox	SMTP Address
SamAccountName	SamAccountName	Get-CASMailbox Get-DistributionGroup Get-Group Get-Mailbox Get-MailUser Get-Recipient Get-RemoteMailbox Get-UMMailbox Get-User	String
StateOrProvince	st	Get-Contact Get-Recipient Get-User	String/Wildcard
StreetAddress	streetAddress	Get-Contact Get-User	String
Title	title	Get-Contact Get-Recipient Get-User	String

Property Name	Attribute	Cmdlets Supported	Input Value
UserPrincipalName	userPrincipalName	Get-Mailbox Get-MailUser Get-Recipient Get-RemoteMailbox Get-User	User logon name User principal name/Wildcard

The preceding table only includes a list of commonly used filterable properties that can be used with the -Filter parameter. In addition to this list, there are several other properties that can be filtered. Refer to the following TechNet article for a complete list: http://techn et.microsoft.com/en-us/library/bb738155(v=exchg.150).aspx.

Properties that can be used with the -RecipientFilter parameter

Similarly to the -Filter parameter, there are a number of EMS cmdlets that provide a -RecipientFilter parameter which can be used to define the criteria used for dynamic distribution groups, email address policies, and address lists. The following cmdlets support this parameter:

- New-AddressList
- New-DynamicDistributionGroup
- New-EmailAddressPolicy
- New-GlobalAddressList
- Set-AddressList
- Set-DynamicDistributionGroup
- Set-EmailAddressPolicy
- Set-GlobalAddressList

The following table lists some of the common properties used when creating a recipient filter using the -RecipientFilter parameter:

Property Name	LDAP Attribute	Input Value
AcceptMessagesOnlyFrom	authOrig	String/Wildcard
ActiveSyncEnabled	n/a	$true or $false
Alias	mailNickname	String/Wildcard
City	L	String/Wildcard

Company	Company	String/Wildcard
Database	homeMDB	Mailbox database identity DN
DisplayName	displayName	String/Wildcard
EmailAddresses	proxyAddresses	Email address (wildcard)
ExternalEmailAddress	targetAddress	Email address (wildcard)
FirstName	givenName	String/Wildcard
HiddenFromAddressListsEnabled	msExchHideFromAddressLists	$true $false
LastName	Sn	String/Wildcard
ManagedBy	managedBy	String/Wildcard
Manager	Manager	String/Wildcard
Name	Name	String
Office	physicalDeliveryOfficeName	String
SamAccountName	SamAccountName	String/Wildcard
StateOrProvince	St	String/Wildcard
StreetAddress	streetAddress	String
Title	Title	String
UserPrincipalName	userPrincipalName	User logon name User principal name/Wildcard

The preceding table only includes a list of commonly used filterable properties that can be used with the `-RecipientFilter` parameter. In addition to this list, there are many other properties that can be filtered. Refer to the following TechNet article for a complete list: `https://technet.microsoft.com/en-gb/library/bb738157(v=exchg.160).aspx`.

B
Query Syntaxes

Exchange 2010 used a subset of **Advanced Query Syntax (AQS)** in discovery searches such as those performed by the `Search-Mailbox cmdlet` for example. AQS was also shared with other Windows search components such as Windows Desktop Search.

Since Exchange 2013, that AQS has been replaced by **Keyword Query Language**, or KQL for short. KQL is shared with other Office 2013 and 2016 applications, with the most important one being SharePoint 2013/2016. Exchange and SharePoint can, together, form a single discovery domain across emails stored in Exchange and documents in SharePoint, making it crucial for a single and unified query syntax that can be used across both platforms.

This appendix provides additional information related to working with KQL when performing queries with Exchange Search.

The following Exchange Management Shell cmdlets provide a `-SearchQuery` parameter that can be used to define a KQL query:

- `New-MailboxSearch`
- `Set-MailboxSearch`
- `Search-Mailbox`

Additionally, `New-ComplianceSearch` has a `-ContentMatchQuery` parameter that also uses KQL.

The tables in this appendix outline some KQL keywords that can be used with these cmdlets to perform Exchange searches.

Using the word phrase search

The following table outlines some of the properties that can be used to define a KQL query using a word phrase restriction:

Property	Examples	Description

Attachments	`attachment:report.xlsx`
	`attachment:salesreport.docx`
	`attachment:pptx`
	`attachment:*`
	`hasattachment=yes`
	`hasattachment:true`
		This searches for items that have an attachment with a specific name, such as `report.xlsx`, or `salesreport.docx`. You can include partial filenames, as shown in the third example, to find all attachments with a certain extension. The last three examples find all messages that have an attachment.

Bcc	`Bcc:Bob` `Bcc:Bob Smith`	This searches for items where `Bob` was included in the blind carbon copy line.
Body	`Body:financial` `Content:financial`	This searches for items where the word `financial` appears in the message body.
Category	`Category:'Red*'`	Returns messages that have been assigned the red category.
Cc	`Cc:administrator` `Cc:sales@contoso.com`	This searches for items where `administrator` or `sales@contoso.com` are included in the carbon copy line.

Property	Examples	Description
From	From:Bob From:"Bob Smith" From:"bob@contoso.com" From:contoso.com	This searches for items sent from Bob, Bob Smith, or bob@contoso.com. The last example matches messages sent from a specified domain.
Importance	Importance:High	Returns messages that are marked as high importance.
IsRead	IsRead:no IsRead:false	Returns messages that have not yet been read (or have been marked as unread).
Not Defined	Financial Report	This searches for items that contain both Financial and Report in all word phrase properties.
Participants	Participants:bob@contoso.comBob Smith	This searches for items sent or received with Bob Smith in the To, Cc, or Bcc fields.
RetentionPolicy	Retentionpolicy:critical	This searches for items that have the critical retention tag applied.
Size	Size>1048576	Returns messages larger than 1,048,576 bytes (1 MB) in size.

Property	Examples	Description
Subject	Subject:sales Subject:(sales meeting) Subject:(sales OR meeting)	The first example searches for items with the word sales in the subject line. The second one, searches for items with the words sales and meeting in the subject line. In the third example, we are searching for items with the words sales or meeting in the subject line.
To	To:Bob To:"bob@contoso.com" To:Bob Smith	This searches for items sent to Bob or Bob Smith.

When performing a word phrase search, the property names and search terms are case insensitive. If you want an exact match, enclose the search query in double quotes; otherwise, the search will default to a prefix match. For example, searching for the term report would match the word reporting unless enclosed in double quotes, indicating an exact search.

Examples

If you want to delete all the messages in the administrator mailbox where the sender's email address is sales@contoso.com, use one of the following cmdlets:

```
Search-Mailbox administrator '
-SearchQuery "from:sales@contoso.com" '
-DeleteContent '
-Force

New-ComplianceSearch -Name "Delete Sales Emails"`
-ExchangeLocation administrator `
-ContentMatchQuery "from:sales@contoso.com"
Start-ComplianceSearch " Delete Sales Emails "
New-ComplianceSearchAction -SearchName "Delete Sales Emails"`
-Purge -PurgeType SoftDelete
```

If you want to create a discovery search based on messages that contain the phrase `Employee Salary` in every mailbox, use the following code:

```
New-MailboxSearch -Name MySearch '
-TargetMailbox "Discovery Search Mailbox" '
-SearchQuery 'Body:"Employee Salary"' '
-MessageTypes Email '
-IncludeUnsearchableItems '
-LogLevel Full
```

For more examples on how to delete emails from mailboxes, please refer to `Chapter 4`, *Managing Mailboxes*, as well as `Chapter 10`, *Compliance and Audit Logging*.

Using a date range search

The following table outlines the properties that can be used to define a KQL query using a date range restriction:

Property	Example	Description
Received	Received:today	This searches for items received today.
	Received:05/15/2017	This searches for items received on May 15.
	Received>=01/01/2017 AND received<=03/31/2017	This searches for items received between January 1st and March 31st.
Sent	Sent:today	This searches for items sent today.
	Sent:05/15/2017	This searches for items sent on May 15th.

You can use relative dates when performing a date range restricted search. For example, today, tomorrow, or yesterday can be used with the Received or Sent keywords.

You can use a specific day of the week: (Sunday, Monday, Tuesday, Wednesday, Thursday, Friday, or Saturday) with the Received or Sent keywords.

You can also use a specific month: (January, February, March, April, May, June, July, August, September, October, November, or December) with the Received or Sent keywords.

Examples

If you want to delete all messages in the administrator mailbox that were received today, use the following command:

```
Search-Mailbox administrator '
-SearchQuery "Received:today" '
-DeleteContent -Force
```

If you want to delete all messages in the administrator mailbox that have been received between March and July, use the following command:

```
Search-Mailbox administrator '
-SearchQuery "Received:03/01/2017..07/01/2017" '
-DeleteContent -Force
```

Using the message type search

The following table outlines the properties that can be used to define a KQL query using a message type restriction:

Property	Example	Description
Kind	Kind:email	This searches all email items
	Kind:meetings	This searches all meeting items
	Kind:tasks	This searches all task items
	Kind:notes	This searches all note items
	Kind:docs	This searches all doc items
	Kind:journals	This searches all journal items
	Kind:contacts	This searches all contact items
	Kind:im	This searches all instant messaging items
	Kind:voicemail	This searches all voicemail items

Examples

If you want to delete all contacts from a mailbox, use the following command:

```
Search-Mailbox administrator '
-SearchQuery "Kind:Contacts" '
-DeleteContent -Force
```

If you want to delete all the notes from a mailbox, use the following code:

```
Search-Mailbox administrator '
-SearchQuery "Kind:Notes" '
-DeleteContent -Force
```

Using search operators

The following table outlines the Boolean search operators that can be used to define a KQL query using a logical connector between two keywords:

Connector	Example	Description

AND	`Subject:sales AND`
	`Subject:report`
	`Subject:(sales AND`
	`report)`
		These examples search for items with both `sales` and `report` in the subject line

OR	`Subject:sales OR`
	`Subject:report`
	`Subject:(sales OR report)`
		These examples search for items with the word `sales` or `report` in the subject line

NOT	`NOT Body:sales` `Body:(NOT sales)`	These examples search for items without the word `sales` in the body

Examples

If you want to delete meeting items that have specific content in the body, such as the phrase `Social Security Number`, use the following commands:

```
Search-Mailbox administrator '
-SearchQuery 'Body:"Social Security Number" AND Kind:Meeting' '
-DeleteContent -Force
```

If you want to perform a discovery search based on keywords used in either the body or subject of the message in a particular mailbox, use the following commands:

```
New-MailboxSearch -Name MyTestSearch '
-SourceMailboxes administrator '
-TargetMailbox "Discovery Search Mailbox" '
-SearchQuery 'Body:"Social Security Number" OR Subject:"SSN"' '
-MessageTypes Email '
-IncludeUnsearchableItems -LogLevel Full
```

You can also use property operators (such as >=, or .. for properties that have date or numeric values), quotation marks, parentheses, and wildcards, to help refine search queries. We have already seen examples of these throughout this appendix, with the exception of wildcards. Prefix wildcard searches (where the asterisk is placed at the end of a word) match for zero or more characters in keywords or `property:value` queries. For example, `Subject:cat*` returns messages that contain the word `cat`, `catalogue`, `category`, and so on, in the subject line.

Index

Made in the
USA
Columbia, SC